The Open University

MST224

Mathematical methods

Book 2

Linear algebra

Cover image: This shows a simulation of the patterns formed by smoke particles moving in air, which is itself in turbulent motion. The positions of the particles are described by relatively simple differential equations, yet the patterns that they form are complex and intriguing. Similar patterns are also relevant to understanding how clouds produce rain, and are a subject of ongoing research at The Open University.

This publication forms part of an Open University module. Details of this and other Open University modules can be obtained from the Student Registration and Enquiry Service, The Open University, PO Box 197, Milton Keynes MK7 6BJ, United Kingdom (tel. +44 (0)845 300 6090; email general-enquiries@open.ac.uk).

Alternatively, you may visit the Open University website at www.open.ac.uk where you can learn more about the wide range of modules and packs offered at all levels by The Open University.

To purchase a selection of Open University materials visit www.ouw.co.uk, or contact Open University Worldwide, Walton Hall, Milton Keynes MK7 6AA, United Kingdom for a brochure (tel. +44 (0)1908 858779; fax +44 (0)1908 858787; email ouw-customer-services@open.ac.uk).

The Open University has had Woodland Carbon Code Pending Issuance Units assigned from Doddington North forest creation project (IHS ID103/26819) that will, as the trees grow, compensate for the greenhouse gas emissions from the manufacture of the paper in MST224 *Block 2*. More information can be found at https://www.woodlandcarboncode.org.uk/

The Open University, Walton Hall, Milton Keynes, MK7 6AA.

First published 2013.

Edited, designed and typeset by The Open University, using the Open University TeX System.

Printed in the United Kingdom by Halstan & Co. Ltd, Amersham, Bucks.

ISBN 978 1 7800 7480 1

1.1

Contents

Contents

Vectors and matrices

Introduction

This book is largely concerned with *matrices*, i.e. rectangular arrays of numbers or other elements. Such arrays have many applications and are an essential tool in many fields of study, including physics, engineering and of course mathematics itself.

The book consists of three units. The first, Unit 4, concerns *vectors* and *matrices*. It starts with a review of vectors – a mainly geometric concept that you should have already encountered in your earlier studies. It then introduces matrices and shows how matrices that take the form of a single row or column can be used to represent a vector. Having formed this link between its two main subjects, the unit goes on to show how square matrices can be used to represent geometric *transformations*, such as stretching (dilation) or turning (rotation). From this it develops the general rules for adding and multiplying matrices, and hence provides the foundations of *matrix algebra*.

The remaining two units, Units 5 and 6, continue the discussion of matrices. Unit 5 concentrates particularly on the use of matrices in the treatment of *systems of simultaneous linear equations*, and thus leads to the subject known as *linear algebra*. Unit 6 extends this work by focusing on the treatment of *systems of linear differential equations*.

Studying these three units in sequence will teach you a great deal about matrices, and will especially emphasise the significance of *eigenvalues* and *eigenvectors*, two concepts that will be mentioned several times and which play an important part in many different applications.

Study guide

Section 1 reviews simple features of *scalar* and *vector* quantities in two and three dimensions. Much of this should be familiar to you from previous study. If so, feel free to skim the text, but make sure that you do the exercises.

Section 2 explains two important ways of forming a product from two vectors **a** and **b**. The *scalar product* **a · b** produces a scalar quantity. The *vector product* **a × b** produces a vector, perpendicular to the plane containing **a** and **b**. Each kind of product is of great utility in the physical sciences.

Section 3 introduces *matrices*. It relates vectors and matrices, and considers the use of square matrices to represent geometric *transformations* of a plane. This leads to a discussion of the *multiplication of matrices* and hence to some simple examples of *matrix algebra*.

Section 4 provides more practice in matrix multiplication and gives the general rules of matrix algebra, applicable to matrices of any size. In addition, it provides methods for calculating entities known as *determinants* and *inverses* of matrices. It also revisits the scalar and vector products of Section 2, using matrix notation, thereby emphasising the ability of matrix methods to encapsulate and simplify important results.

1 Vectors

1.1 Indicating and representing vectors

One way to distinguish *vector* quantities from *scalar* quantities is as follows.

> A **scalar** quantity is one that can be specified by a single number or by the combination of a number and a unit of measurement.
>
> A **vector** quantity is one that requires both a **magnitude** *and* a **direction** for its complete specification.

Examples of scalar quantities include the *number* $\pi = 3.1415\ldots$, a *mass* of $5\,\text{kg}$, a *distance* of $2.5\,\text{m}$, a *speed* of $3.0 \times 10^{-6}\,\text{m s}^{-1}$, and a *temperature* of $-30°\text{C}$. Those scalars that can be described by numbers alone, such as the number of peas in a pod, are called **numerical quantities**.

A common example of a vector quantity is **displacement**. The displacement from London to Brighton is (approximately) $74\,\text{km}$ due South, and the (approximate) displacement from Milton Keynes to Oxford is $47\,\text{km}$ South-West. Note that the specification of a displacement involves a magnitude (in this case given by a distance in km) and a direction (in this case given as a compass bearing). The magnitude of a vector quantity is not allowed to be negative. It is correct to say that the displacement from Brighton to London is $74\,\text{km}$ North, but it is not correct to describe that displacement as $-74\,\text{km}$ South.

Figure 1 represents part of a plane that includes the points A, B, C and D. The displacement from A to B is indicated by an arrow. That is appropriate since an arrow has a magnitude (its length expressed in appropriate units) and a direction (its orientation).

A symbol that is conventionally used to represent the displacement from A to B is $\overrightarrow{AB}$. However, an even more common convention is the use of a bold letter, traditionally $\mathbf{s}$, to represent a displacement. This too can be seen in Figure 1, where the displacement $\overrightarrow{AB}$ is represented by the symbol $\mathbf{s}_1$, and the displacement $\overrightarrow{CD}$ is represented by $\mathbf{s}_2$.

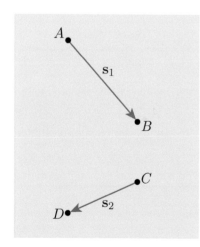

Figure 1 Displacement vectors represented by arrows may be indicated by symbols such as $\overrightarrow{AB}$ or $\mathbf{s}_1$

Displacement, specified by a direction and a distance, is not the only vector quantity. Other examples include *velocity*, which is specified by a direction and a speed, and *force*, which is specified by a direction and a force strength. Note that distance, speed and force strength are each non-negative quantities.

Throughout this module, symbols representing vectors will generally be printed in bold. So, for example, we may indicate a force by $\mathbf{F}$ and a velocity by $\mathbf{v}$. When writing by hand, the same indication is given by underlining the symbol, e.g. $\underline{v}$.

Underlining symbols that represent vectors

It is very important to underline handwritten symbols that denote vectors. If you fail to do so, those reading your work may not be able to tell that you are referring to a vector, and you may be penalised.

The magnitude of a vector, $\mathbf{s}$ say, is best handwritten as $|\mathbf{s}|$. Sometimes in the text, when there is no possibility of ambiguity, we will simply display it as s. The magnitude of a vector is sometimes referred to as its **modulus**.

Exercise 1

The displacement from Brighton to Oxford is (approximately) 133 km North-West. Use this, together with the displacements given in the text above, to sketch a rough map showing the relative locations of London, Brighton, Oxford and Milton Keynes. According to your map, what is the approximate distance between Milton Keynes and London? How should this distance be described in terms of the displacement vector from London to Milton Keynes?

1.2   Equating vectors

Having reviewed the definition and representation of vectors, we can now begin to develop the *algebra* of vectors. This will occupy several subsections and will lead us into detailed considerations of the addition and multiplication of vectors. We begin, however, with the fundamental idea of what it means to say that two vectors are *equal*.

Recalling that a vector quantity is completely specified by its direction and magnitude, we have the following definition.

> Two vectors are **equal** if they have the same direction and the same magnitude.

Figure 2 is similar to Figure 1 apart from an extra point E and a new displacement vector, $\mathbf{s}_3$, that stretches from B to E. The direction and distance from B to E is the same as that from C to D, so the displacement $\mathbf{s}_3$ is equal to the displacement $\mathbf{s}_2$, and we can write $\mathbf{s}_2 = \mathbf{s}_3$.

Note that the different starting points of $\mathbf{s}_2$ and $\mathbf{s}_3$ in Figure 2 do not prevent the displacements from being equal. We may use points such as B and E when we specify a displacement, but the relevant displacement, $\mathbf{s}_3$ in this case, is completely specified by its direction and magnitude; it is not in any sense 'tied' to the particular points B and E.

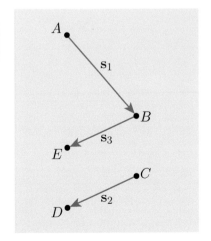

Figure 2   The displacement $\mathbf{s}_2$ is equal to the displacement $\mathbf{s}_3$

More generally, when we use arrows to represent any kind of vector quantity, the point at which we choose to draw the tail of the arrow is of no intrinsic significance. (Of course, the *effect* that a vector has when applied at one point may be quite different from the effect of applying the same vector at a different point, but that is irrelevant to the specification of the vector.) Thus, when considering vectors in their own right (rather than their effects), we are free to move the arrows that represent the vectors from one place to another, provided that we do not change their direction or magnitude. This is a principle that we will use in the next section, when we consider the scaling and addition of vectors.

1.3 Scaling and adding vectors

Scaling vectors

The two arrows in Figure 3(a) represent vectors $\mathbf{g}$ and $\mathbf{h}$. Both vectors point in the same direction and are therefore said to be **parallel**. The arrow representing $\mathbf{h}$ is twice as long as the arrow representing $\mathbf{g}$, so we write $\mathbf{h} = 2\mathbf{g}$ and say that the vector $\mathbf{h}$ is equal to $\mathbf{g}$ *scaled* by 2. More generally, if $\mathbf{v}$ is a vector and m is a positive scalar, then the scaled vector $\mathbf{p} = m\mathbf{v}$ is a vector in the same direction as $\mathbf{v}$ but with magnitude $m|\mathbf{v}|$.

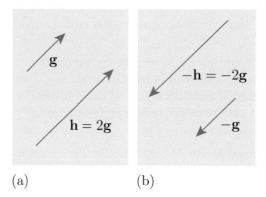

(a)   (b)

Figure 3 Multiplying a vector by a scalar

We can also scale a vector by a negative value. If m is a negative scalar, the vector $m\mathbf{v}$ will still have a positive magnitude $|m|\,|\mathbf{v}|$ (magnitudes are never negative), but $m\mathbf{v}$ will point in the *opposite* direction to $\mathbf{v}$. Vectors that point in opposite directions are often said to be **antiparallel**.

A special case of scaling occurs when $m = -1$. The negatively scaled vector $(-1)\mathbf{v}$ is normally written as $-\mathbf{v}$. The two arrows in Figure 3(b) therefore represent the scaled vectors $-\mathbf{g}$ and $-\mathbf{h} = -2\mathbf{g}$.

What happens when we scale a vector by zero (i.e. when $m = 0$)? The above definitions imply that the result is a vector of zero magnitude: this is called the **zero vector**, and is represented by the bold symbol $\mathbf{0}$.

We do not usually associate a direction with the zero vector, as all zero vectors are equal.

Collecting together the results of this subsection, we have the following.

Scaling a vector

For any vector $\mathbf{v}$ and any scalar m, the result of **scaling** $\mathbf{v}$ by m is represented by the product $m\mathbf{v}$ and is the vector with magnitude $|m|\,|\mathbf{v}|$ that is:

- parallel to $\mathbf{v}$ if $m > 0$
- antiparallel to $\mathbf{v}$ if $m < 0$
- the zero vector $\mathbf{0}$ if $m = 0$.

Adding vectors

Consider two successive displacements indicated in Figure 4. The first, $\mathbf{s}_1$, takes us from P to Q. The second, $\mathbf{s}_2$, takes us from Q to R. The net result is described by the single displacement $\mathbf{s}$, which takes us directly from P to R. In this sort of situation we interpret $\mathbf{s}$ as the result of *adding* the displacements $\mathbf{s}_1$ and $\mathbf{s}_2$, so we write

$$\mathbf{s} = \mathbf{s}_1 + \mathbf{s}_2 \quad \text{or} \quad \overrightarrow{PR} = \overrightarrow{PQ} + \overrightarrow{QR}.$$

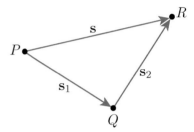

Figure 4   Two successive displacements $\mathbf{s}_1$ and $\mathbf{s}_2$, and their net result, $\mathbf{s}$

Note that in adding the displacements we have had to take the directions of $\mathbf{s}_1$ and $\mathbf{s}_2$ into account; we were not able simply to add their magnitudes. To emphasise this we refer to the general process of adding vectors as **vector addition**, and we call the outcome the **resultant**.

In the simple case of vector addition considered above, we could determine the resultant by using a triangular diagram. This graphical approach provides the basis of a more general *triangle rule* that we can use to add any two vectors of the same physical type – two displacements say, or two velocities. The triangle rule takes into account our freedom to locate the tail of a vector arrow wherever we want; it can be stated as follows.

The triangle rule

To add a vector $\mathbf{a}$ to a vector $\mathbf{b}$ of the same physical type, first draw an arrow to represent $\mathbf{a}$, then draw an arrow to represent $\mathbf{b}$ so that its tail is coincident with the head of the arrow representing $\mathbf{a}$. An arrow drawn from the tail of $\mathbf{a}$ to the head of $\mathbf{b}$ then represents the *resultant* of the *vector addition* $\mathbf{a} + \mathbf{b}$ (see Figure 5).

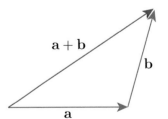

Figure 5   The triangle rule for vector addition

Combining this interpretation of vector addition with what has already been said about scaling a vector allows us to make sense of **vector subtraction**, since we can write

$$\mathbf{a} - \mathbf{b} = \mathbf{a} + (-1)\mathbf{b}.$$

As you can see, the expression on the right is just the vector sum of $\mathbf{a}$ and the negatively scaled vector $-\mathbf{b}$ (which is antiparallel to $\mathbf{b}$). A trivial case occurs when $\mathbf{a} = \mathbf{b}$, which gives the very natural-looking vector equation

$$\mathbf{a} - \mathbf{a} = \mathbf{0}.$$

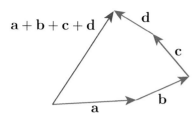

Figure 6 Extending the triangle rule to more than two vectors

The definition of the sum of two vectors is readily extended to give the sum of many vectors, $\mathbf{a} + \mathbf{b} + \mathbf{c} + \cdots$. We simply use the triangle rule to find the sum $\mathbf{s} = \mathbf{a} + \mathbf{b}$, and then use it again to add $\mathbf{c}$ to $\mathbf{s}$, and we keep on going in this way until all the vectors in the sum have been added. Figure 6 illustrates the process. In effect, the arrows are strung together in a chain, head to tail, with the head of one arrow coincident with the tail of the next. The arrow representing the final resultant vector is then obtained by joining the tail of the first arrow to the head of the last.

It is clear from the triangle rule that $\mathbf{a} + \mathbf{b} = \mathbf{b} + \mathbf{a}$, and it follows that when adding (and subtracting) several vectors, the order in which we carry out the various additions and subtractions has no influence on the final result. We describe this by saying that vector addition is **commutative**.

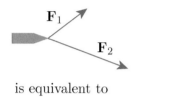

is equivalent to

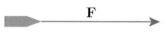

provided that

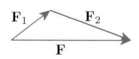

Figure 7 Forces $\mathbf{F}_1$ and $\mathbf{F}_2$ are equivalent to the resultant $\mathbf{F}$

Vector addition: a real-world perspective

The ability to add vectors together using the triangle rule is of great practical use. For example, suppose that two different forces, $\mathbf{F}_1$ and $\mathbf{F}_2$, act at a single point on an object, as shown in Figure 7. The net effect of those forces is the same as that of the single force given by the vector sum

$$\mathbf{F} = \mathbf{F}_1 + \mathbf{F}_2,$$

which can be determined using the triangle rule.

Velocities may be added in the same way. Suppose that an aeroplane is travelling with velocity $\mathbf{u}$ relative to the surrounding air. Further suppose that the air is moving with velocity $\mathbf{w}$ relative to the ground. The velocity of the aeroplane relative to the ground will then be given by the vector sum

$$\mathbf{v} = \mathbf{u} + \mathbf{w},$$

which can be determined using the triangle rule.

Example 1

The vector $\mathbf{a}$ points to the East and has magnitude 3. The vector $\mathbf{b}$ points to the North and has magnitude 2.

(a) Draw a diagram (with North at the top and East to the right) showing arrows representing $\mathbf{a}$, $2\mathbf{b}$ and $\mathbf{c} = \mathbf{a} + 2\mathbf{b}$.

(b) What is the magnitude of the vector $\mathbf{c}$?

(c) What is the angle between the direction of $\mathbf{c}$ and the direction of $\mathbf{a}$? Specify your answer as an angle between 0 and $\pi/2$ radians.

Solution

(a) An appropriate diagram is shown in Figure 8.

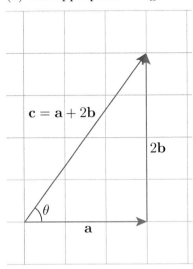

Figure 8

The arrow for **a** is 3 units long. The arrow for **b** is 2 units long, so the arrow for **2b** is 4 units long. The arrows for **a** and **2b** are mutually perpendicular. The arrow for **c** is then as shown in the diagram.

(b) The arrow for **c** forms the hypotenuse of a right-angled triangle. Using Pythagoras's theorem, the magnitude of **c** is

$$|\mathbf{c}| = \sqrt{3^2 + 4^2} = 5.$$

(c) Let θ be the angle between the directions of **c** and **a**. Then the diagram shows that $\tan\theta = 4/3$, so $\theta = \arctan(4/3) = 0.927$ radians.

Exercise 2

(a) Find the magnitude of the vector $\mathbf{h} = 2\mathbf{a} - 3\mathbf{b}$, where **a** and **b** are as defined in Example 1.

(b) What is the angle between the direction of **h** and the direction of **2a**? Specify your answer as an angle between 0 and $\pi/2$ radians.

1.4   Cartesian components and basic vector algebra

Despite the usefulness of the triangle rule, graphical methods are not generally very accurate and are difficult to apply in three dimensions. For these reasons, this subsection will introduce methods based on the use of *Cartesian components of vectors* that will enable us to define the equality, scaling and addition of vectors in algebraic terms. We start with a review of Cartesian coordinates.

Cartesian coordinate systems

Cartesian coordinates are named in honour of philosopher and mathematician René Descartes (1596–1650), who pioneered the geometric use of coordinates in his 1637 book *La Géométrie*.

Figure 9(a) shows a three-dimensional system of **Cartesian coordinates**. Such a system consists of three mutually perpendicular **axes** that meet at a point O called the **origin**. The axes are conventionally labelled x, y and z, with the z-axis oriented vertically. Each axis is given a positive sense, as indicated by the single arrowhead drawn on that axis. This gives a unique meaning to terms such as *positive x-direction* (i.e. parallel to the arrowed direction on the x-axis), and *negative z-direction* (i.e. antiparallel to the arrowed direction on the z-axis).

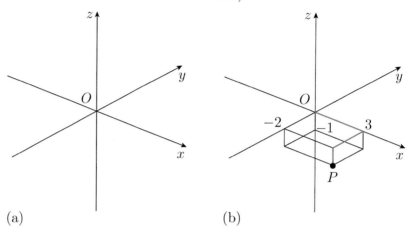

(a)   (b)

Figure 9 (a) A three-dimensional Cartesian coordinate system with origin at the point O. (b) The coordinates of any point P may be read from the axes, and described by an ordered triple (x, y, z).

If number lines are drawn along each axis, with 0 at the origin and the numbers increasing in the positive direction, it becomes possible to associate a numerical value called a **coordinate** with every point on each axis. As indicated in Figure 9(b), any three values of the x-, y- and z-coordinates, such as $x = 3$, $y = -2$ and $z = -1$, will then determine a unique point in space, such as P. Moreover, every point in three-dimensional space will correspond to a unique set of the three coordinate values. (That's what we mean by saying that space has *three* dimensions.) We can now agree to indicate any specified point by presenting its three coordinate values $x = x_1$, $y = y_1$ and $z = z_1$ as an **ordered triple** of values (x_1, y_1, z_1), always giving the three coordinates in the same conventional order, separated by commas and enclosed in round brackets. Using that convention, we can represent the point P by $(3, -2, -1)$ and say that the origin O is at the point $(0, 0, 0)$. A similar system may be applied to two dimensions by simply omitting the third coordinate and representing a point by an *ordered pair* of values such as (x_1, y_1).

In many physical situations it is necessary to associate coordinates with measured distances in specified directions. This can be done by multiplying each coordinate by an appropriate unit of measurement, such as the metre (m).

Right-handed systems of coordinates

When working in three dimensions there are two fundamentally different ways of arranging three mutually perpendicular axes. The resulting systems of Cartesian coordinates are described as *right-handed systems* and *left-handed systems*; it is important to know how to tell them apart since, by convention, we use only right-handed systems unless there is a very good reason to do otherwise. Figure 10 shows a **right-handed system** of coordinates, and its caption describes the *right-hand rule* that can be used to distinguish such a system from its left-handed counterpart.

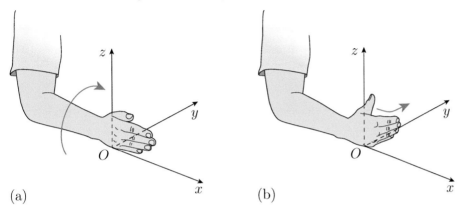

(a)   (b)

Figure 10   The handedness of a given Cartesian system can be checked using the **right-hand rule**. (a) Point the straightened fingers of your right hand in the direction of the positive x-axis, and rotate your wrist until you find that you can bend your fingers in the direction of the positive y-axis. (b) Extend the thumb of your right hand. If it points in the direction of the positive z-axis, the frame is right-handed. (If your thumb points in the negative z-direction, the system is left-handed.)

Using right-handed systems of Cartesian coordinates

When using Cartesian coordinates in three dimensions, it is conventional to work with right-handed systems.

Conventionally oriented two-dimensional axes are also described as right-handed.

Exercise 3

Imagine that you are standing with your feet at the origin of a three-dimensional system of Cartesian coordinates. Your head is at some point on the positive z-axis, and you are looking into the region between the positive x-axis and the positive y-axis. Suppose that the system is right-handed and the positive x-axis is on your right. What will be on your left – the positive y-axis or the negative y-axis?

Exercise 4

Which of the sets of perpendicular axes in the figure below define right-handed coordinate systems?

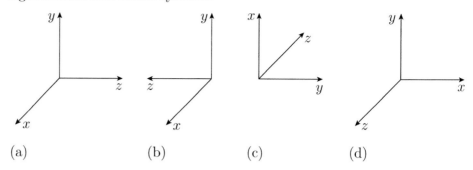

(a)   (b)   (c)   (d)

The x-axis points out of the plane of the page in (a) and (b). The z-axis points respectively into and out of the plane of the page in (c) and (d).

Cartesian unit vectors

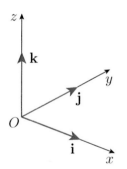

Figure 11   The unit vectors **i**, **j** and **k** each have magnitude 1 and respectively point in the positive x-, y- and z-directions

When working with vectors in a region described by a right-handed system of Cartesian coordinates, it is often helpful to introduce a set of three special vectors, one directed parallel to each positive coordinate axis, and each having magnitude 1. These three vectors are called **Cartesian unit vectors** and are illustrated in Figure 11; they are conventionally labelled **i** in the positive x-direction, **j** in the positive y-direction, and **k** in the positive z-direction. For neatness, **i**, **j** and **k** have been drawn along the axes, with their tails at the origin but, as you know, that is not essential: the tails can be placed anywhere because the vectors are completely specified by their direction and magnitude. Note that the magnitude of a unit vector really is the numerical quantity 1; there are no units.

The great merit of unit vectors is that they can be easily scaled to produce vectors of any desired magnitude in any of the positive or negative coordinate directions. For example, $6\mathbf{i}$ is a vector in the positive x-direction with magnitude $|6|\,|\mathbf{i}| = 6 \times 1 = 6$. Similarly, $-3\mathbf{k}$ is a vector in the negative z-direction with magnitude $|-3|\,|\mathbf{k}| = 3 \times 1 = 3$. More generally, if λ is a non-zero scalar, the direction of $\lambda\mathbf{j}$ will depend on whether λ is greater than zero or less than zero; in either case, the magnitude of $\lambda\mathbf{j}$ will be just $|\lambda|$.

Even in those cases where we associate coordinates with physical lengths by multiplying them by units such as the metre, it is still the case that unit vectors have magnitude 1, *not* 1 metre. So, for example, for the displacement vector $\mathbf{s} = (2.5\,\text{m})\,\mathbf{i}$, we say that its magnitude is $|\mathbf{s}| = |(2.5\,\text{m})\,\mathbf{i}| = |2.5\,\text{m}|\,|\mathbf{i}| = 2.5\,\text{m} \times 1 = 2.5\,\text{m}$.

Cartesian components

Now, the crucial observation is that in three dimensions any vector can be represented by a *linear combination* of the unit vectors $\mathbf{i}$, $\mathbf{j}$ and $\mathbf{k}$. This is indicated in Figure 12 for a vector $\mathbf{a}$, which is depicted as the vector sum of the three mutually perpendicular vectors $a_x\mathbf{i}$, $a_y\mathbf{j}$ and $a_z\mathbf{k}$. Algebraically, we can write this sum as

$$\mathbf{a} = a_x\mathbf{i} + a_y\mathbf{j} + a_z\mathbf{k}.$$

This is called the **Cartesian component form** of $\mathbf{a}$. The three vectors $a_x\mathbf{i}$, $a_y\mathbf{j}$ and $a_z\mathbf{k}$ are called the **Cartesian component vectors** of $\mathbf{a}$. However, each of those component vectors is itself the result of multiplying a Cartesian unit vector by a scalar. The three scalars involved, a_x, a_y and a_z, are called the **Cartesian scalar components** or simply **Cartesian components** of $\mathbf{a}$. In Figure 12 each Cartesian scalar component is positive, but in the general case each may be positive, zero or negative. Scalar components are referred to more frequently than component vectors, so any general references to 'components' or even 'Cartesian components' should always be interpreted as 'Cartesian scalar components' unless there is a clear indication to the contrary. With this in mind we will usually refer to a_x as the x-component of $\mathbf{a}$, a_y as the y-component, and a_z as the z-component.

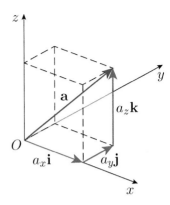

Figure 12 The vector $\mathbf{a}$ is the vector sum of the three mutually perpendicular component vectors $a_x\mathbf{i}$, $a_y\mathbf{j}$ and $a_z\mathbf{k}$

In three dimensions, a vector can often be most conveniently specified in terms of its components. For a vector $\mathbf{a}$ this might be done using the linear combination $a_x\mathbf{i} + a_y\mathbf{j} + a_z\mathbf{k}$ or an ordered triple (a_x, a_y, a_z). In either case, the vector is said to be in **component form**. We thus have two equivalent ways of writing a vector in component form.

Note that the ordered triple notation for a vector is identical to that for the coordinates of a point.

$$\mathbf{a} = a_x\mathbf{i} + a_y\mathbf{j} + a_z\mathbf{k}, \tag{1}$$

or equivalently,

$$\mathbf{a} = (a_x, a_y, a_z). \tag{2}$$

If a vector $\mathbf{a}$ has a known direction and a known magnitude a, then we can use trigonometry to determine its scalar components. The general procedure is illustrated in Figure 13 for the case of the x-component. It shows that

$$a_x = a\cos\theta_x, \quad \text{where } 0 \le \theta_x \le \pi, \tag{3}$$

where θ_x is the angle between the direction of $\mathbf{a}$ and the positive x-direction. Similar formulas, with the analogous angles θ_y and θ_z, give the y- and z-components a_y and a_z.

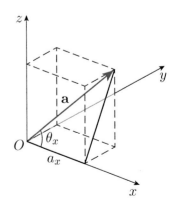

Figure 13 Finding the x-component of a vector

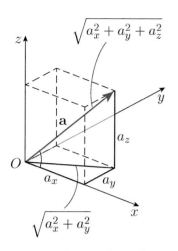

Figure 14　Finding the magnitude of a vector with known components

Conversely, if we know the component form of a vector **a**, so the values of a_x, a_y and a_z are known, then it is easy to determine the magnitude and direction of **a**. Using Pythagoras's theorem twice, as in Figure 14, shows that the magnitude of **a** is given by

$$a = |\mathbf{a}| = \sqrt{a_x^2 + a_y^2 + a_z^2}. \tag{4}$$

Substituting this result into equation (3) and rearranging shows that the angle θ_x between **a** and the x-axis is given by

$$\cos\theta_x = \frac{a_x}{a} = \frac{a_x}{\sqrt{a_x^2 + a_y^2 + a_z^2}}, \quad \text{where } 0 \le \theta_x \le \pi. \tag{5}$$

Again, similar results will apply in the y- and z-directions, giving analogous expressions for $\cos\theta_y$ and $\cos\theta_z$. These three cosines will uniquely determine the direction of any non-zero vector.

Incidentally, you may have noticed that in Figures 12, 13 and 14, the vector **a** has been drawn with its tail at the origin, but this, of course, is not essential. The results that we have quoted depend only on the components of vectors and not on the point that we have chosen to represent the origin of our coordinate system.

We should also note that a common way of specifying a point with coordinates (x, y, z) is in terms of a displacement from the origin of a Cartesian coordinate system to the point. Such a vector is referred to as the **position vector** of the given point and is usually represented by the symbol **r**. The components of the position vector are $r_x = x$, $r_y = y$ and $r_z = z$, so we may write $\mathbf{r} = x\mathbf{i} + y\mathbf{j} + z\mathbf{k}$ or equivalently $\mathbf{r} = (x, y, z)$. As far as addition and scaling are concerned, position vectors may be treated in the same way as any other displacements.

Exercise 5

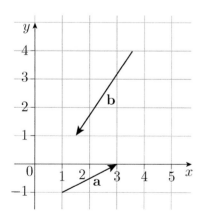

The figure in the margin shows two vectors, **a** and **b**, in a two-dimensional Cartesian coordinate system. In this system the components of **a** and **b** happen to be integers.

(a) Determine the components of **a** and **b** by visual inspection, then express each vector as a linear combination of unit vectors and as an ordered pair of scalar components.

(b) Use the components of **a** and **b** to determine their magnitudes, and for each vector find the angle between the direction of the vector and the positive x-direction.

Unit vectors in other directions

Given a vector **a**, it is often necessary to construct a **unit vector** in the same direction, as indicated in Figure 15. Such a general unit vector is usually denoted by $\widehat{\mathbf{a}}$; it will have magnitude 1, and is obtained by dividing the non-zero vector **a** by its own magnitude. Thus

$$\widehat{\mathbf{a}} = \frac{\mathbf{a}}{|\mathbf{a}|}. \qquad (6)$$

The vector $\widehat{\mathbf{a}}$ is just **a** scaled by $1/|\mathbf{a}|$, so $\widehat{\mathbf{a}}$ lies in the same direction as **a** and has magnitude

$$|\widehat{\mathbf{a}}| = \left| \frac{1}{|\mathbf{a}|} \mathbf{a} \right| = \frac{1}{|\mathbf{a}|} |\mathbf{a}| = 1.$$

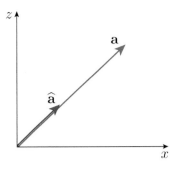

Figure 15 A unit vector $\widehat{\mathbf{a}}$ in the direction of vector **a**

The x-component of the unit vector $\widehat{\mathbf{a}}$ is given by $\cos\theta_x$, the quantity described by equation (5). In fact, using its component form, we can write the unit vector in the direction of **a** as

$$\widehat{\mathbf{a}} = (\widehat{a}_x, \widehat{a}_y, \widehat{a}_z) = (\cos\theta_x, \cos\theta_y, \cos\theta_z) = \left(\frac{a_x}{a}, \frac{a_y}{a}, \frac{a_z}{a} \right). \qquad (7)$$

We see that the information contained in $\widehat{\mathbf{a}}$ is just the *direction* of **a**.

As a simple illustration of this, suppose that $\mathbf{a} = (1, 2, 0)$. It then follows from equation (4) that $a = \sqrt{1^2 + 2^2} = \sqrt{5}$, so the unit vector in the direction of **a** is $\widehat{\mathbf{a}} = (1/\sqrt{5}, 2/\sqrt{5}, 0)$.

Basic vector algebra with Cartesian components

Vectors were introduced earlier as essentially geometric entities, and actions such as equating, scaling and adding vectors were all introduced in geometric terms. Now, however, following the introduction of components, we can give each of these actions an algebraic interpretation in terms of components. So, for example, we already know that two vectors $\mathbf{a} = (a_x, a_y, a_z)$ and $\mathbf{b} = (b_x, b_y, b_z)$ will be equal if they have the same direction and magnitude, but we also know that the direction and magnitude of a vector are determined by the vector's components. Consequently, the two vectors will be equal if their corresponding components are equal, so a necessary and sufficient condition for $\mathbf{a} = \mathbf{b}$ is that

$$a_x = b_x, \quad a_y = b_y, \quad a_z = b_z.$$

Similarly, the scaling of the vector **a** by the scalar λ to produce the vector $\lambda\mathbf{a}$ can be interpreted as the multiplication of each component of **a** by λ. So the operation of scaling is represented algebraically by the relation

$$\lambda\mathbf{a} = \lambda(a_x, a_y, a_z) = (\lambda a_x, \lambda a_y, \lambda a_z).$$

In a similar way, the vector sum $\mathbf{a} + \mathbf{b}$ that was introduced geometrically using the triangle rule can be reinterpreted in terms of the sum of corresponding components. So given $\mathbf{a} = (a_x, a_y, a_z)$ and $\mathbf{b} = (b_x, b_y, b_z)$, we can say that their vector sum is given by

$$\mathbf{a} + \mathbf{b} = (a_x + b_x, a_y + b_y, a_z + b_z).$$

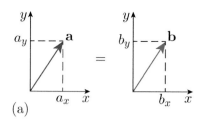

(a)

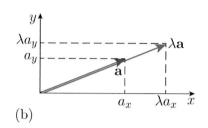

(b)

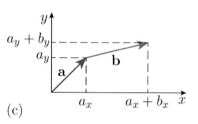

(c)

Figure 16   A component-based reinterpretation (in two dimensions) of the basic operations of vector algebra: (a) the equivalence of two vectors; (b) the scaling of a vector by a scalar; (c) the addition of two vectors

These algebraic reinterpretations are indicated graphically (in two dimensions) in Figure 16, but the transition from geometry to algebra that they constitute is of such significance that we also reproduce their three-dimensional versions in the following summary.

Basic vector algebra in terms of Cartesian components

- Given the component form of a vector $\mathbf{a} = (a_x, a_y, a_z)$, or equivalently, $\mathbf{a} = a_x\mathbf{i} + a_y\mathbf{j} + a_z\mathbf{k}$, the **magnitude** of $\mathbf{a}$ is given by

$$a = |\mathbf{a}| = \sqrt{a_x^2 + a_y^2 + a_z^2}, \tag{8}$$

and the **direction** of $\mathbf{a}$ can be indicated by the **unit vector**

$$\hat{\mathbf{a}} = \frac{\mathbf{a}}{|\mathbf{a}|} = \left(\frac{a_x}{a}, \frac{a_y}{a}, \frac{a_z}{a}\right) = (\cos\theta_x, \cos\theta_y, \cos\theta_z). \tag{9}$$

- Given also a second vector $\mathbf{b} = (b_x, b_y, b_z)$, or equivalently, $\mathbf{b} = b_x\mathbf{i} + b_y\mathbf{j} + b_z\mathbf{k}$, the vectors $\mathbf{a}$ and $\mathbf{b}$ are said to be **equal**, and we write $\mathbf{a} = \mathbf{b}$, when

$$a_x = b_x, \quad a_y = b_y, \quad a_z = b_z. \tag{10}$$

- The **scaling** of vector $\mathbf{a}$ by the scalar λ produces the scaled vector

$$\lambda\mathbf{a} = (\lambda a_x, \lambda a_y, \lambda a_z), \tag{11}$$

or equivalently,

$$\lambda\mathbf{a} = \lambda a_x\mathbf{i} + \lambda a_y\mathbf{j} + \lambda a_z\mathbf{k}. \tag{12}$$

- The vector **addition** of the vectors $\mathbf{a}$ and $\mathbf{b}$ produces the **resultant**

$$\mathbf{a} + \mathbf{b} = (a_x + b_x, a_y + b_y, a_z + b_z), \tag{13}$$

or equivalently,

$$\mathbf{a} + \mathbf{b} = (a_x + b_x)\mathbf{i} + (a_y + b_y)\mathbf{j} + (a_z + b_z)\mathbf{k}. \tag{14}$$

These first steps in vector algebra naturally suggest that we can go further, based on the further exploitation of Cartesian components. We will do this in the next section when we discuss two extremely useful ways of forming products of vectors.

Example 2

Let $\mathbf{a} = \mathbf{i} + \mathbf{j} + \mathbf{k}$, $\mathbf{b} = 2\mathbf{i} - 3\mathbf{j} - \mathbf{k}$ and $\mathbf{c} = 3\mathbf{i} + \mathbf{k}$.

(a) Express $\mathbf{d} = 2\mathbf{a} - 3\mathbf{b}$ and $\mathbf{e} = \mathbf{a} - 2\mathbf{b} + 4\mathbf{c}$ in component form.

(b) Find the magnitudes of the vectors $\mathbf{d}$ and $\mathbf{e}$.

(c) Evaluate $|\mathbf{a}|$, and write down a unit vector in the direction of $\mathbf{a}$.

(d) Find the components of a vector $\mathbf{g}$ such that $\mathbf{a} + \mathbf{g} = \mathbf{b}$.

Solution

(a) $\mathbf{d} = 2(\mathbf{i} + \mathbf{j} + \mathbf{k}) - 3(2\mathbf{i} - 3\mathbf{j} - \mathbf{k}) = -4\mathbf{i} + 11\mathbf{j} + 5\mathbf{k},$

$\mathbf{e} = (\mathbf{i} + \mathbf{j} + \mathbf{k}) - 2(2\mathbf{i} - 3\mathbf{j} - \mathbf{k}) + 4(3\mathbf{i} + \mathbf{k}) = 9\mathbf{i} + 7\mathbf{j} + 7\mathbf{k}.$

(b) Using equation (8),

$$|\mathbf{d}| = \sqrt{(-4)^2 + 11^2 + 5^2} = \sqrt{162} = 9\sqrt{2},$$
$$|\mathbf{e}| = \sqrt{9^2 + 7^2 + 7^2} = \sqrt{179}.$$

(c) $|\mathbf{a}| = \sqrt{1^2 + 1^2 + 1^2} = \sqrt{3}.$

Using equation (9), a unit vector in the direction of $\mathbf{a}$ is

$$\widehat{\mathbf{a}} = \frac{\mathbf{a}}{|\mathbf{a}|} = \frac{1}{\sqrt{3}}(\mathbf{i} + \mathbf{j} + \mathbf{k}).$$

(d) If $\mathbf{a} + \mathbf{g} = \mathbf{b}$, then

$$\mathbf{g} = \mathbf{b} - \mathbf{a} = (2\mathbf{i} - 3\mathbf{j} - \mathbf{k}) - (\mathbf{i} + \mathbf{j} + \mathbf{k})$$
$$= \mathbf{i} - 4\mathbf{j} - 2\mathbf{k}.$$

Thus the scalar components of $\mathbf{g}$ are $g_x = 1$, $g_y = -4$ and $g_z = -2$.

Exercise 6

Let $\mathbf{a} = 2\mathbf{i} - \mathbf{j}$, $\mathbf{b} = \mathbf{i} + 3\mathbf{j} + 5\mathbf{k}$ and $\mathbf{c} = \mathbf{j} - 2\mathbf{k}$.

(a) Find the magnitudes of $\mathbf{a}$ and $\mathbf{b}$.

(b) Find the values of θ_x, θ_y and θ_z, giving the direction of $\mathbf{a}$.

(c) Find the vectors $\mathbf{a} + \mathbf{b}$, $2\mathbf{a} - \mathbf{b}$ and $\mathbf{c} + 2\mathbf{b} - 3\mathbf{a}$ in component form.

(d) For the displacement vector $\overrightarrow{PQ} = 2\mathbf{a} - \mathbf{b}$, where the point P is $(0, 2, 3)$, find the endpoint Q.

(e) For the displacement vector $\overrightarrow{RS} = \mathbf{a} + 2\mathbf{b}$, where the point R is $(1, 1, 0)$, find the endpoint S.

Exercise 7

Confirm that the unit vector

$$\widehat{\mathbf{a}} = \left(\frac{a_x}{a}, \frac{a_y}{a}, \frac{a_z}{a} \right)$$

does indeed have magnitude 1.

Vector equation of a straight line

One useful application of position vectors (in two or three dimensions) is in obtaining a vector equation of a straight line.

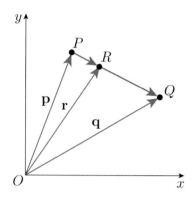

Figure 17

Example 3

Find the position vector of a point R lying on the straight-line segment PQ (see Figure 17) in terms of the position vectors of P and Q.

Solution

Using the triangle rule, the position vector $\overrightarrow{OR}$ can be written as

$$\overrightarrow{OR} = \overrightarrow{OP} + \overrightarrow{PR}.$$

Now $\overrightarrow{PR} = t\,\overrightarrow{PQ}$ for some number t, and the point R traces out the line segment PQ as t varies from 0 to 1. Thus the straight-line segment PQ is described by the vector equation

$$\overrightarrow{OR} = \overrightarrow{OP} + t\,\overrightarrow{PQ} \quad (0 \leq t \leq 1).$$

Writing $\mathbf{p} = \overrightarrow{OP}$, $\mathbf{q} = \overrightarrow{OQ}$, $\mathbf{r} = \overrightarrow{OR}$, and noting (using the triangle rule) that $\overrightarrow{PQ} = \overrightarrow{OQ} - \overrightarrow{OP} = \mathbf{q} - \mathbf{p}$, this equation can also be written as

$$\mathbf{r} = \mathbf{p} + t(\mathbf{q} - \mathbf{p}) = (1 - t)\mathbf{p} + t\mathbf{q} \quad (0 \leq t \leq 1).$$

Note that if the parameter t in Example 3 is allowed to range over all the real numbers $(-\infty < t < \infty)$, then the point R traces out the entire straight line of which PQ is a segment. Also note that the ideas in Example 3 are easily extended to three dimensions.

If $0 \leq t \leq 1$, then the equation represents only the line segment PQ.

> **Vector equation of a straight line**
>
> If P and Q are any two distinct points on a straight line in space, with position vectors $\mathbf{p}$ and $\mathbf{q}$, respectively, then the **vector equation of the straight line** is
>
> $$\mathbf{r}(t) = \mathbf{p} + t(\mathbf{q} - \mathbf{p}) = (1 - t)\mathbf{p} + t\mathbf{q} \quad (-\infty < t < \infty), \qquad (15)$$
>
> where $\mathbf{r}(t)$ represents the position vector of any point on the line.

Exercise 8

Write down, in component form, the vector equation of the straight line on which lie the points with Cartesian coordinates $(1, 1, 2)$ and $(2, 3, 1)$.

Vector-valued functions

Recall that a *real-valued function* $f(t)$ is an entity that gives a real value for each value of the variable t. The vector equation of a straight line introduced above, equation (15), is an example of something called a **vector-valued function**, i.e. an entity $\mathbf{r}(t)$ that gives a vector for each value of the variable t. The components of the straight line $\mathbf{r}(t)$ in the solution to Exercise 8 were linear functions of t: $\mathbf{r}(t) = (1 + t, 1 + 2t, 2 - t)$. More generally, the components of some *curve* in space will be $\mathbf{r}(t) = (x(t), y(t), z(t))$, where $x(t)$, $y(t)$ and $z(t)$ are some general real-valued functions of t (Figure 18).

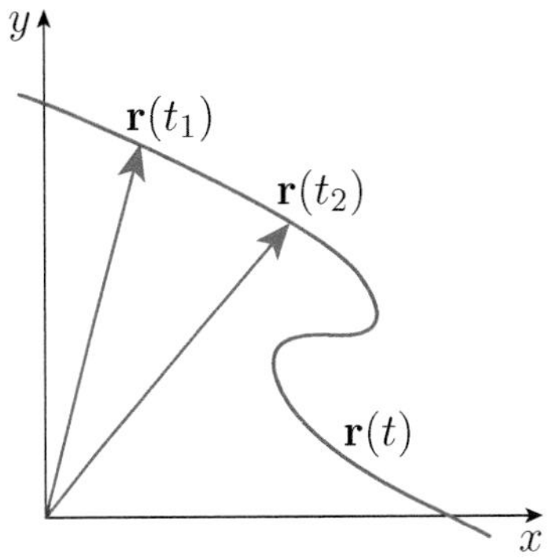

Suppose that the position of a particle moving along some curved path is given by $\mathbf{r}(t) = (x(t), y(t), z(t))$ at time t. We want to find the velocity and acceleration of the particle, given by the derivatives of $\mathbf{r}(t)$ with respect to t. These are obtained by differentiating the components.

Figure 18 A curve $\mathbf{r}(t)$ in two-dimensional space. The vectors $\mathbf{r}(t_1)$ and $\mathbf{r}(t_2)$ indicate the values of $\mathbf{r}(t)$ at two values of the independent variable t.

Example 4

A particle has position $\mathbf{r}(t) = (3t^2 - 2, t^4, -t + 1)$ at time t. Find its velocity.

Solution

The velocity of the particle is given by the derivative of $\mathbf{r}(t)$ with respect to t:

$$\mathbf{v}(t) = \dot{\mathbf{r}}(t) = \frac{d}{dt}(3t^2 - 2, t^4, -t + 1) = (6t, 4t^3, -1).$$

Exercise 9

Find the acceleration $\mathbf{a} = \dot{\mathbf{v}}$ of the particle of Example 4.

---

2 Products of vectors

There are two very useful ways of forming the product of two vectors $\mathbf{a}$ and $\mathbf{b}$. The first method produces a scalar quantity, represented by $\mathbf{a} \cdot \mathbf{b}$, and is called the *scalar product* or the *dot product* of the two vectors. The second method produces a vector quantity, represented by $\mathbf{a} \times \mathbf{b}$, and is called the *vector product* or the *cross product* of the two vectors.

We discuss the two products in turn, starting with the scalar product. In each case we start with a geometric view that emphasises directions and magnitudes, just as we did when defining the scaling and addition of vectors. However, we very quickly go on to express each product algebraically, in terms of components, and to examine its characteristic properties and applications.

Figure 19   The angle θ $(0 \leq \theta \leq \pi)$ between two vectors

2.1 The scalar product

Consider two (non-zero) vectors **a** and **b**. No matter how **a** and **b** are specified (they might be given as displacements between particular points, or the velocities of particular objects), we can always use our freedom to move the arrows that represent vectors parallel to themselves to ensure that their tails meet at a point. This makes it easy to visualise the angle θ between the directions of **a** and **b**, as indicated in Figure 19, and we can always take that angle to be in the range $0 \leq \theta \leq \pi$. Using θ we can define the scalar product geometrically, as follows.

> The **scalar product** of two vectors **a** and **b** is the scalar quantity
>
> $$\mathbf{a} \cdot \mathbf{b} = |\mathbf{a}|\,|\mathbf{b}| \cos \theta, \tag{16}$$
>
> where θ $(0 \leq \theta \leq \pi)$ is the angle between the directions of **a** and **b**.

The product $\mathbf{a} \cdot \mathbf{b}$ is read as 'a dot b', and for this reason is often referred to as the **dot product**.

The angle θ always lies in the range $0 \leq \theta \leq \pi$, so the value of $\mathbf{a} \cdot \mathbf{b}$ is:

- positive when θ is an acute angle (i.e. in the range $0 \leq \theta < \frac{\pi}{2}$)
- negative when θ is an obtuse angle (i.e. in the range $\frac{\pi}{2} < \theta \leq \pi$)
- zero when θ is a right angle (i.e. when $\theta = \frac{\pi}{2}$).

The last of these conditions tells us that if $\theta = \frac{\pi}{2}$, i.e. when **a** and **b** are perpendicular, then $\mathbf{a} \cdot \mathbf{b} = 0$. The definition also implies that if $\theta = 0$, i.e. when **a** and **b** are parallel, then $\mathbf{a} \cdot \mathbf{b} = |\mathbf{a}|\,|\mathbf{b}| = ab$.

A special case worth remembering is that the scalar product of **a** with itself is just the square of the magnitude of **a**.

> $$\mathbf{a} \cdot \mathbf{a} = |\mathbf{a}|^2 = a^2. \tag{17}$$

Note that the scalar product is a product in the mathematical sense, with a number of mathematically significant properties. For example, it is *commutative* so that

$$\mathbf{a} \cdot \mathbf{b} = \mathbf{b} \cdot \mathbf{a}. \tag{18}$$

It also has the further properties of being *distributive over addition*, meaning that

This property does not obviously follow from equation (16), but will become obvious once we discuss the component form of the scalar product.

$$\mathbf{a} \cdot (\mathbf{b} + \mathbf{c}) = \mathbf{a} \cdot \mathbf{b} + \mathbf{a} \cdot \mathbf{c}, \tag{19}$$

and *linear* with respect to multiplication by a scalar λ, so that

$$(\lambda \mathbf{a}) \cdot \mathbf{b} = \mathbf{a} \cdot (\lambda \mathbf{b}) = \lambda (\mathbf{a} \cdot \mathbf{b}). \tag{20}$$

These properties allow us to make sense of scalar products that involve sums and brackets.

Example 5

Expand the expression $\mathbf{x} \cdot \mathbf{y}$, given that $\mathbf{x} = 2\mathbf{u} + \mathbf{v}$ and $\mathbf{y} = \mathbf{u} - 5\mathbf{v}$. Calculate its value when $\mathbf{u}$ and $\mathbf{v}$ are perpendicular unit vectors.

Solution

Using the mathematical properties of the scalar product, we can see that

$$\begin{aligned}
\mathbf{x} \cdot \mathbf{y} &= (2\mathbf{u} + \mathbf{v}) \cdot (\mathbf{u} - 5\mathbf{v}) \\
&= (2\mathbf{u}) \cdot (\mathbf{u} - 5\mathbf{v}) + \mathbf{v} \cdot (\mathbf{u} - 5\mathbf{v}) \\
&= (2\mathbf{u}) \cdot \mathbf{u} + (2\mathbf{u}) \cdot (-5\mathbf{v}) + \mathbf{v} \cdot \mathbf{u} + \mathbf{v} \cdot (-5\mathbf{v}) \\
&= 2(\mathbf{u} \cdot \mathbf{u}) - 10(\mathbf{u} \cdot \mathbf{v}) + \mathbf{v} \cdot \mathbf{u} - 5(\mathbf{v} \cdot \mathbf{v}) \\
&= 2(\mathbf{u} \cdot \mathbf{u}) - 9(\mathbf{u} \cdot \mathbf{v}) - 5(\mathbf{v} \cdot \mathbf{v}).
\end{aligned}$$

This solution is given in detail to show you there are no unexpected pitfalls when dealing with scalar products. The basic lesson is that the familiar rules of algebra still apply, so with practice you will not need to go through all these intermediate steps.

Now $\mathbf{u} \cdot \mathbf{u} = |\mathbf{u}|^2 = 1$ and $\mathbf{v} \cdot \mathbf{v} = |\mathbf{v}|^2 = 1$ when $\mathbf{u}$ and $\mathbf{v}$ are unit vectors. Furthermore, $\mathbf{u} \cdot \mathbf{v} = 0$ when $\mathbf{u}$ and $\mathbf{v}$ are perpendicular vectors. So when $\mathbf{u}$ and $\mathbf{v}$ are perpendicular unit vectors, we have

$$\mathbf{x} \cdot \mathbf{y} = 2 - 0 - 5 = -3.$$

Exercise 10

Three vectors $\mathbf{a}$, $\mathbf{b}$ and $\mathbf{c}$ of magnitudes 2, 4 and 1, respectively, lying in the same plane, are represented by arrows as shown in the figure below.

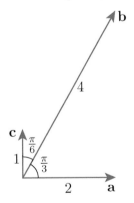

The angle between the vectors $\mathbf{a}$ and $\mathbf{b}$ is $\frac{\pi}{3}$ radians, and that between the vectors $\mathbf{b}$ and $\mathbf{c}$ is $\frac{\pi}{6}$ radians. Use the definition of the scalar product to find the values of $\mathbf{a} \cdot \mathbf{b}$, $\mathbf{b} \cdot \mathbf{c}$, $\mathbf{a} \cdot \mathbf{c}$ and $\mathbf{b} \cdot \mathbf{b}$.

Exercise 11

(a) Expand the expression $(\mathbf{a} + \mathbf{b}) \cdot (\mathbf{a} - \mathbf{b})$.

(b) Expand the expression $|\mathbf{a} + \mathbf{b}|^2$.

Recall that $|\mathbf{a}|^2 = \mathbf{a} \cdot \mathbf{a}$.

(c) Write down the value of $\mathbf{a} \cdot \mathbf{b}$, in terms of $|\mathbf{a}|$ and $|\mathbf{b}|$, when $\mathbf{a}$ and $\mathbf{b}$ are antiparallel.

The scalar product in terms of components

Since $\mathbf{i}$, $\mathbf{j}$ and $\mathbf{k}$ are mutually perpendicular unit vectors, the following useful relations must be true.

$$\mathbf{i}\cdot\mathbf{i} = \mathbf{j}\cdot\mathbf{j} = \mathbf{k}\cdot\mathbf{k} = 1, \tag{21}$$

and all other scalar products of Cartesian unit vectors (such as $\mathbf{i}\cdot\mathbf{j}$) give zero.

Consequently, using the usual rules of algebra, it can be seen that

$$\begin{aligned}
\mathbf{a}\cdot\mathbf{b} &= (a_x\mathbf{i} + a_y\mathbf{j} + a_z\mathbf{k})\cdot(b_x\mathbf{i} + b_y\mathbf{j} + b_z\mathbf{k}) \\
&= a_x\mathbf{i}\cdot(b_x\mathbf{i} + b_y\mathbf{j} + b_z\mathbf{k}) + a_y\mathbf{j}\cdot(b_x\mathbf{i} + b_y\mathbf{j} + b_z\mathbf{k}) \\
&\quad + a_z\mathbf{k}\cdot(b_x\mathbf{i} + b_y\mathbf{j} + b_z\mathbf{k}) \\
&= a_xb_x\mathbf{i}\cdot\mathbf{i} + a_xb_y\mathbf{i}\cdot\mathbf{j} + a_xb_z\mathbf{i}\cdot\mathbf{k} + a_yb_x\mathbf{j}\cdot\mathbf{i} + a_yb_y\mathbf{j}\cdot\mathbf{j} + a_yb_z\mathbf{j}\cdot\mathbf{k} \\
&\quad + a_zb_x\mathbf{k}\cdot\mathbf{i} + a_zb_y\mathbf{k}\cdot\mathbf{j} + a_zb_z\mathbf{k}\cdot\mathbf{k} \\
&= a_xb_x + a_yb_y + a_zb_z.
\end{aligned}$$

This gives us the following very useful expression for the scalar product of two vectors in terms of their components.

Component form of the scalar product

If $\mathbf{a} = a_x\mathbf{i} + a_y\mathbf{j} + a_z\mathbf{k}$ and $\mathbf{b} = b_x\mathbf{i} + b_y\mathbf{j} + b_z\mathbf{k}$, then

$$\mathbf{a}\cdot\mathbf{b} = a_xb_x + a_yb_y + a_zb_z. \tag{22}$$

Many other results follow from this. For example, the relation $\mathbf{a}\cdot(\mathbf{b}+\mathbf{c}) = \mathbf{a}\cdot\mathbf{b} + \mathbf{a}\cdot\mathbf{c}$ that was stated earlier becomes easy to prove. It is also easy to confirm that the Cartesian scalar components of a vector $\mathbf{a}$ are given by

$$a_x = \mathbf{i}\cdot\mathbf{a}, \quad a_y = \mathbf{j}\cdot\mathbf{a}, \quad a_z = \mathbf{k}\cdot\mathbf{a}, \tag{23}$$

and it follows from equations (16) and (22) that the angle between two non-zero vectors is given by

$$\cos\theta = \frac{\mathbf{a}\cdot\mathbf{b}}{|\mathbf{a}|\,|\mathbf{b}|} = \frac{a_xb_x + a_yb_y + a_zb_z}{ab}, \tag{24}$$

where $0 \leq \theta \leq \pi$.

As we are now using the scalar product in a more algebraic way, this is an appropriate point at which to note that the use of algebra has allowed mathematicians to generalise the idea of what constitutes a vector and, consequently, what constitutes a scalar product of vectors. Using components, it is easy to imagine extending the definitions given earlier to more than three dimensions, but the mathematical generalisations go well beyond this. As you will see in Unit 11, even functions may be treated as 'vectors' in an appropriate space. In these generalised approaches, the analogue of the scalar product is often called the *inner product*, and the generalisation of the condition $\mathbf{a} \cdot \mathbf{b} = 0$, the vanishing of the inner product of two (generalised) vectors, is referred to as the *orthogonality condition*. For this reason, even when dealing with 'ordinary' two- or three-dimensional vectors, you will often find that the terms **perpendicular** and **orthogonal** are used interchangeably. You will also find that the scalar product of two- or three-dimensional vectors is sometimes said to provide a **test for orthogonality**, since two non-zero vectors $\mathbf{a}$ and $\mathbf{b}$ are orthogonal (i.e. perpendicular, in this case) if and only if $\mathbf{a} \cdot \mathbf{b} = 0$.

Example 6

Consider the vectors $\mathbf{a} = 2\mathbf{i} - 3\mathbf{j} + \mathbf{k}$ and $\mathbf{b} = -\mathbf{i} + 2\mathbf{j} + 4\mathbf{k}$. Find the magnitudes of $\mathbf{a}$ and $\mathbf{b}$, and the angle between them.

Solution

$$|\mathbf{a}| = \sqrt{2^2 + (-3)^2 + 1^2} = \sqrt{14},$$
$$|\mathbf{b}| = \sqrt{(-1)^2 + 2^2 + 4^2} = \sqrt{21}.$$

However, from equation (22),

$$\mathbf{a} \cdot \mathbf{b} = (2 \times -1) + (-3 \times 2) + (1 \times 4) = -4,$$

so if θ is the angle between $\mathbf{a}$ and $\mathbf{b}$, then

$$\cos \theta = \frac{\mathbf{a} \cdot \mathbf{b}}{|\mathbf{a}|\,|\mathbf{b}|} = \frac{-4}{\sqrt{14} \times \sqrt{21}} = -\frac{4}{7\sqrt{6}}.$$

The negative sign means that θ is obtuse, so $\theta \simeq 1.806$ radians.

Exercise 12

(a) If $\mathbf{a} = 4\mathbf{i} + \mathbf{j} - 5\mathbf{k}$ and $\mathbf{b} = \mathbf{i} - 3\mathbf{j} + \mathbf{k}$, show that $\mathbf{a} \cdot \mathbf{b} = -4$. What does the negative sign tell you?

(b) Are the vectors $\mathbf{c} = (3, 5, -2)$ and $\mathbf{d} = (3, -1, -2)$ orthogonal?

Exercise 13

If $\mathbf{p} = 3\mathbf{i} + 2\mathbf{j} - \mathbf{k}$, $\mathbf{q} = -\mathbf{i} + \mathbf{j} + 2\mathbf{k}$ and $\mathbf{r} = 2\mathbf{i} - \mathbf{j} - \mathbf{k}$, and λ is a scalar, find the value of λ that makes $\mathbf{p} + \lambda\mathbf{q}$ orthogonal to $\mathbf{r}$.

Resolving a vector into perpendicular components

The process of splitting a vector into components in specified perpendicular directions is called **resolution**. So when we write $\mathbf{a}$ in component form as $\mathbf{a} = (a_x, a_y, a_z)$ or $\mathbf{a} = a_x\mathbf{i} + a_y\mathbf{j} + a_z\mathbf{k}$, we are showing how $\mathbf{a}$ may be *resolved* into its Cartesian components.

However, it is often useful to be able to resolve a given vector into components along perpendicular directions that are *not* aligned with the Cartesian unit vectors. This subsection will show you how to do this. First, however, we give a physical perspective on the sort of situation in which the technique is useful.

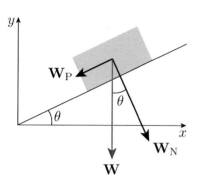

Figure 20 The vectors $\mathbf{W}_P$ and $\mathbf{W}_N$ are respectively parallel and normal to the plane; since they are perpendicular,
$\mathbf{W} = \mathbf{W}_P + \mathbf{W}_N$

Resolving a vector: a physical perspective

Figure 20 shows a box on a rough wooden plane inclined at an angle θ to the horizontal. The owner of the box wants scientific advice on the maximum angle θ that can be tolerated before the box starts to slide down the plane.

The situation is described in a two-dimensional system of Cartesian coordinates with the x-axis pointing to the right and the y-axis pointing vertically upwards. In that system the weight of the box (the force exerted on the box by the Earth's gravity) points vertically downwards and is described by the vector $\mathbf{W} = -W\mathbf{j}$.

We will not go into the details of the analysis, but what is crucial is the ability to express $\mathbf{W}$ as the sum of two *orthogonal vectors*, one pointing parallel to the plane (denoted $\mathbf{W}_P$), the other directed at right angles (i.e. normal) to the plane (denoted $\mathbf{W}_N$). We do this by *resolving* $\mathbf{W}$ in these directions.

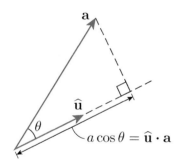

Figure 21 Finding the scalar component of $\mathbf{a}$ in the direction of a unit vector $\widehat{\mathbf{u}}$

As a general case, suppose that an arbitrary vector $\mathbf{a}$ makes an angle θ with a unit vector $\widehat{\mathbf{u}}$ (see Figure 21). Denote the scalar component of $\mathbf{a}$ in the direction of $\widehat{\mathbf{u}}$ by a_u. (Note that generally, a_u may be positive or negative, depending on the size of θ.) Simple trigonometry then shows that

$$a_u = a\cos\theta \quad (0 \le \theta \le \pi),$$

but from the definition of the scalar product, and the fact that $|\widehat{\mathbf{u}}| = 1$, we see that

$$\widehat{\mathbf{u}} \cdot \mathbf{a} = a\cos\theta \quad (0 \le \theta \le \pi).$$

This implies the following result, which is true irrespective of the sign of a_u.

The scalar component of $\mathbf{a}$ in the direction of a unit vector $\widehat{\mathbf{u}}$ is

$$a_u = \widehat{\mathbf{u}} \cdot \mathbf{a}. \tag{25}$$

Of course, this is just a generalisation of equation (23), which showed that in the Cartesian case $a_x = \mathbf{i} \cdot \mathbf{a}$, $a_y = \mathbf{j} \cdot \mathbf{a}$ and $a_z = \mathbf{k} \cdot \mathbf{a}$. Note that equation (25) can be used to find the 'components' (more generally called *projections*) of $\mathbf{a}$ in the direction of any three unit vectors $\widehat{\mathbf{u}}$, $\widehat{\mathbf{v}}$ and $\widehat{\mathbf{w}}$, but only when those unit vectors are mutually perpendicular can we say that $\mathbf{a} = a_u\widehat{\mathbf{u}} + a_v\widehat{\mathbf{v}} + a_w\widehat{\mathbf{w}}$.

Example 7

Consider Figure 22, which shows a two-dimensional vector $\mathbf{a} = (1, 3)$ and two mutually perpendicular unit vectors $\widehat{\mathbf{u}} = (1/\sqrt{2}, 1/\sqrt{2})$ and $\widehat{\mathbf{v}} = (-1/\sqrt{2}, 1/\sqrt{2})$.

(a) Show that $\mathbf{a}$ can be expressed in the form $\mathbf{a} = a_u\widehat{\mathbf{u}} + a_v\widehat{\mathbf{v}}$, with a_u and a_v given by equation (25).

(b) Calculate a_u and a_v, and hence express $\mathbf{a}$ as a linear combination of the unit vectors $\widehat{\mathbf{u}}$ and $\widehat{\mathbf{v}}$.

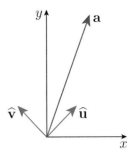

Figure 22   The vector $\mathbf{a} = (1, 3)$ and the unit vectors $\widehat{\mathbf{u}} = \left(\frac{1}{\sqrt{2}}, \frac{1}{\sqrt{2}}\right)$ and $\widehat{\mathbf{v}} = \left(-\frac{1}{\sqrt{2}}, \frac{1}{\sqrt{2}}\right)$

Solution

(a) Since $\widehat{\mathbf{u}}$ and $\widehat{\mathbf{v}}$ are perpendicular unit vectors, we can certainly write $\mathbf{a} = \alpha\widehat{\mathbf{u}} + \beta\widehat{\mathbf{v}}$, for some values of α and β. We can determine α and β as follows.

From equation (25), the components of $\mathbf{a}$ in the $\widehat{\mathbf{u}}$ and $\widehat{\mathbf{v}}$ directions are

$$a_u = \widehat{\mathbf{u}} \cdot \mathbf{a} = \widehat{\mathbf{u}} \cdot (\alpha\widehat{\mathbf{u}} + \beta\widehat{\mathbf{v}}) = \alpha\widehat{\mathbf{u}} \cdot \widehat{\mathbf{u}} + \beta\widehat{\mathbf{u}} \cdot \widehat{\mathbf{v}} = \alpha,$$
$$a_v = \widehat{\mathbf{v}} \cdot \mathbf{a} = \widehat{\mathbf{v}} \cdot (\alpha\widehat{\mathbf{u}} + \beta\widehat{\mathbf{v}}) = \alpha\widehat{\mathbf{v}} \cdot \widehat{\mathbf{u}} + \beta\widehat{\mathbf{v}} \cdot \widehat{\mathbf{v}} = \beta.$$

Hence $\mathbf{a} = a_u\widehat{\mathbf{u}} + a_v\widehat{\mathbf{v}}$, with a_u and a_v the components of $\mathbf{a}$ in the $\widehat{\mathbf{u}}$ and $\widehat{\mathbf{v}}$ directions, respectively.

(b) We have

$$a_u = \widehat{\mathbf{u}} \cdot \mathbf{a} = \left(\tfrac{1}{\sqrt{2}}, \tfrac{1}{\sqrt{2}}\right) \cdot (1, 3) = \tfrac{1}{\sqrt{2}}(4) = 2\sqrt{2},$$
$$a_v = \widehat{\mathbf{v}} \cdot \mathbf{a} = \left(-\tfrac{1}{\sqrt{2}}, \tfrac{1}{\sqrt{2}}\right) \cdot (1, 3) = \tfrac{1}{\sqrt{2}}(2) = \sqrt{2}.$$

The vector $\mathbf{a}$ can therefore be written as the linear combination

$$\mathbf{a} = 2\sqrt{2}\,\widehat{\mathbf{u}} + \sqrt{2}\,\widehat{\mathbf{v}}.$$

Exercise 14

Consider the vectors $\mathbf{a} = 2\mathbf{i} - 3\mathbf{j} + \mathbf{k}$ and $\mathbf{b} = -\mathbf{i} + 2\mathbf{j} + 4\mathbf{k}$.

(a) Which of the following vectors is perpendicular to $\mathbf{a}$?

$$\mathbf{c} = -\mathbf{i} + \mathbf{j} + 3\mathbf{k}, \quad \mathbf{d} = -2\mathbf{i} + \mathbf{k}, \quad \mathbf{e} = -\mathbf{i} - \mathbf{j} - \mathbf{k}.$$

(b) Find the component of the vector $\mathbf{a} + 2\mathbf{b}$ in the direction of the displacement vector from the origin to the point $(1, 1, 1)$.

(c) Find the component of the vector $\mathbf{a} + 2\mathbf{b}$ in the direction of the vector $\mathbf{a} - 2\mathbf{b}$.

Exercise 15

A vector $\mathbf{v}$ has magnitude 4 and makes an angle of $\pi/3$ with the negative x-axis, as shown in the figure in the margin. Find the components of $\mathbf{v}$ in the $\mathbf{i}$- and $\mathbf{j}$-directions, and hence express $\mathbf{v}$ as a linear combination of $\mathbf{i}$ and $\mathbf{j}$.

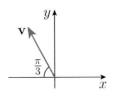

Exercise 16

The three unit vectors

$$\hat{\mathbf{u}} = \frac{1}{\sqrt{2}}(1,0,1), \quad \hat{\mathbf{v}} = \frac{1}{\sqrt{2}}(1,0,-1) \quad \text{and} \quad \hat{\mathbf{w}} = (0,1,0)$$

are mutually perpendicular. Express the vector $\mathbf{a} = (2,1,0)$ as a linear combination of these unit vectors.

2.2 The vector product

The *vector product* of two given vectors is a *vector*, whose direction is perpendicular to both the given vectors. It can be defined in geometric terms as follows.

The product $\mathbf{a} \times \mathbf{b}$ is read as 'a cross b', and for this reason is often referred to as the **cross product**.

> The **vector product** of two vectors $\mathbf{a}$ and $\mathbf{b}$ is the vector quantity
>
> $$\mathbf{a} \times \mathbf{b} = (|\mathbf{a}|\,|\mathbf{b}|\sin\theta)\,\hat{\mathbf{n}}, \tag{26}$$
>
> where θ $(0 \le \theta \le \pi)$ is the angle between the directions of $\mathbf{a}$ and $\mathbf{b}$, and $\hat{\mathbf{n}}$ is a unit vector that is normal (i.e. perpendicular) to both $\mathbf{a}$ and $\mathbf{b}$, and whose sense is given by the right-hand rule shown in Figure 23.

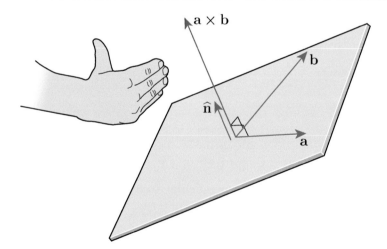

Figure 23   The **right-hand rule** for vector products. To find the sense of the unit vector $\hat{\mathbf{n}}$ that is normal to both $\mathbf{a}$ and $\mathbf{b}$, first point the straightened fingers of your right hand in the direction of $\mathbf{a}$. Then rotate your wrist until you find that you can bend your fingers in the direction of $\mathbf{b}$. The outstretched thumb of your right hand then points in the sense of the unit vector $\hat{\mathbf{n}}$, which has the same direction as $\mathbf{a} \times \mathbf{b}$.

Notice that $\hat{\mathbf{n}}$ is not defined if $\mathbf{a}$ and $\mathbf{b}$ are parallel $(\theta = 0)$ or antiparallel $(\theta = \pi)$, or if $\mathbf{a}$ or $\mathbf{b}$ is the zero vector. In each of these cases, either $\sin\theta = 0$ or $|\mathbf{a}| = 0$ or $|\mathbf{b}| = 0$, so $\mathbf{a} \times \mathbf{b} = \mathbf{0}$, the zero vector.

A special case worth remembering is that the vector product of a vector $\mathbf{a}$ with itself is the zero vector: $\mathbf{a} \times \mathbf{a} = \mathbf{0}$.

More generally, since the quantity $\widehat{\mathbf{n}}$ that determines the direction of $\mathbf{a} \times \mathbf{b}$ is a unit vector, it follows that the magnitude of $\mathbf{a} \times \mathbf{b}$ is simply given by $|\mathbf{a}|\,|\mathbf{b}| \sin \theta$.

The vector product, like the scalar product, is *distributive over vector addition*, so we can say that

$$\mathbf{a} \times (\mathbf{b} + \mathbf{c}) = (\mathbf{a} \times \mathbf{b}) + (\mathbf{a} \times \mathbf{c}). \tag{27}$$

This result is not easily derived from equation (26).

It is also *linear* with respect to multiplication by a scalar λ, so that

$$\mathbf{a} \times (\lambda \mathbf{b}) = \lambda \mathbf{a} \times \mathbf{b}. \tag{28}$$

These properties again allow us to expand expressions that involve sums and brackets in the usual way.

However, unlike the scalar product, the vector product is *not* commutative. This means that for vectors that are non-zero and neither parallel nor antiparallel, $\mathbf{a} \times \mathbf{b} \neq \mathbf{b} \times \mathbf{a}$. The reason for this is the use of the right-hand rule to determine the sense of $\widehat{\mathbf{n}}$. If we make $\mathbf{b}$ the first term in the product, the right-hand rule will tell us to reverse the sense of $\widehat{\mathbf{n}}$, and that means changing the sign of the vector product, so

$$\mathbf{a} \times \mathbf{b} = -\mathbf{b} \times \mathbf{a}. \tag{29}$$

This *non-commutativity* is a very important distinction that should always be kept in mind.

Example 8

Using the definition of the vector product, confirm that $\mathbf{i} \times \mathbf{j} = \mathbf{k}$, $\mathbf{j} \times \mathbf{k} = \mathbf{i}$ and $\mathbf{k} \times \mathbf{i} = \mathbf{j}$.

Solution

Using the definition of the vector product (including the right-hand rule), and recalling that unit vectors have magnitude 1,

$$\mathbf{i} \times \mathbf{j} = \left(|\mathbf{i}|\,|\mathbf{j}| \sin \tfrac{\pi}{2}\right) \mathbf{k} = \mathbf{k}.$$

Similarly,

$$\mathbf{j} \times \mathbf{k} = \mathbf{i} \quad \text{and} \quad \mathbf{k} \times \mathbf{i} = \mathbf{j}.$$

Exercise 17

(a) Confirm that $\mathbf{j} \times \mathbf{i} = -\mathbf{k}$, $\mathbf{k} \times \mathbf{j} = -\mathbf{i}$ and $\mathbf{i} \times \mathbf{k} = -\mathbf{j}$.

(b) State and justify the value of $\mathbf{i} \times \mathbf{i}$, $\mathbf{j} \times \mathbf{j}$ and $\mathbf{k} \times \mathbf{k}$.

(c) Expand and simplify $(\mathbf{i} \times (\mathbf{i} + \mathbf{k})) - ((\mathbf{i} + \mathbf{j}) \times \mathbf{k})$.

(d) Expand and simplify $(\mathbf{i} + \mathbf{k}) \times (\mathbf{i} + \mathbf{j} + \mathbf{k})$.

The vector product in terms of components

The best way to get better insight into the vector product is to express it in terms of components. This will again mark an important transition from an approach that is primarily geometric to one that is more algebraic. Fundamental to this development are the results concerning the vector products of unit vectors that were discussed in the last subsection.

$$\mathbf{i} \times \mathbf{j} = \mathbf{k}, \qquad \mathbf{j} \times \mathbf{k} = \mathbf{i}, \qquad \mathbf{k} \times \mathbf{i} = \mathbf{j}, \tag{30}$$

$$\mathbf{j} \times \mathbf{i} = -\mathbf{k}, \qquad \mathbf{k} \times \mathbf{j} = -\mathbf{i}, \qquad \mathbf{i} \times \mathbf{k} = -\mathbf{j}, \tag{31}$$

and all other vector products of pairs of Cartesian unit vectors give $\mathbf{0}$.

Using these results, together with the familiar rules of algebra but taking care not to change the order of vectors in any vector product, it can be seen that

$$
\begin{aligned}
\mathbf{a} \times \mathbf{b} &= (a_x\mathbf{i} + a_y\mathbf{j} + a_z\mathbf{k}) \times (b_x\mathbf{i} + b_y\mathbf{j} + b_z\mathbf{k}) \\
&= a_xb_x\mathbf{i} \times \mathbf{i} + a_xb_y\mathbf{i} \times \mathbf{j} + a_xb_z\mathbf{i} \times \mathbf{k} + a_yb_x\mathbf{j} \times \mathbf{i} + a_yb_y\mathbf{j} \times \mathbf{j} \\
&\quad + a_yb_z\mathbf{j} \times \mathbf{k} + a_zb_x\mathbf{k} \times \mathbf{i} + a_zb_y\mathbf{k} \times \mathbf{j} + a_zb_z\mathbf{k} \times \mathbf{k} \\
&= (a_yb_z - a_zb_y)\mathbf{i} + (a_zb_x - a_xb_z)\mathbf{j} + (a_xb_y - a_yb_x)\mathbf{k}.
\end{aligned}
$$

This gives us two equivalent ways of expressing the vector product.

Component form of the vector product

If $\mathbf{a} = a_x\mathbf{i} + a_y\mathbf{j} + a_z\mathbf{k}$ and $\mathbf{b} = b_x\mathbf{i} + b_y\mathbf{j} + b_z\mathbf{k}$, then

$$\mathbf{a} \times \mathbf{b} = (a_yb_z - a_zb_y)\mathbf{i} + (a_zb_x - a_xb_z)\mathbf{j} + (a_xb_y - a_yb_x)\mathbf{k}, \tag{32}$$

or equivalently,

$$\mathbf{a} \times \mathbf{b} = (a_yb_z - a_zb_y, \ a_zb_x - a_xb_z, \ a_xb_y - a_yb_x). \tag{33}$$

Note that the correctness of these expressions is crucially dependent on the use of a right-handed system of coordinates.

Note the pattern in equations (32) and (33). The x-component of the product, c_x say, is given by

$$c_x = a_yb_z - a_zb_y,$$

so the first three subscripts are x, y, z in alphabetical order. In both the terms on the right above, the subscripts are y and z, but in the second term $(-a_zb_y)$ their order has reversed and the term has incurred an overall minus sign. Similar comments apply to each of the other components. In each case the first three subscripts are a *cyclic* rearrangement of x, y, z – i.e. either y, z, x or z, x, y (see Figure 24). Also, in each case the final term on the right involves a departure from cyclic reordering and incurs a minus sign as a result. Note that the x-component of $\mathbf{a} \times \mathbf{b}$ is independent of a_x and b_x, the y-component is independent of a_y and b_y, and the z-component is independent of a_z and b_z.

Figure 24   The cyclic basis of the vector product. The arrows indicate a positive sense; products formed in the reverse sense incur a minus sign. This provides an easy way of remembering that $\mathbf{i} \times \mathbf{j} = \mathbf{k}$ but $\mathbf{j} \times \mathbf{i} = -\mathbf{k}$, and so on.

Example 9

Evaluate $\mathbf{a} \times \mathbf{b}$, where $\mathbf{a} = (2, 3, 4)$ and $\mathbf{b} = (1, -1, -3)$.

Solution

Using equation (33), and working in ordered triple notation,

$$\mathbf{a} \times \mathbf{b} = (2, 3, 4) \times (1, -1, -3)$$
$$= (3(-3) - 4(-1), 4(1) - 2(-3), 2(-1) - 3(1))$$
$$= (-5, 10, -5).$$

Since $\mathbf{a} \times \mathbf{b}$ should be perpendicular to both $\mathbf{a}$ and $\mathbf{b}$, a quick check on our calculation is provided by verifying that $(-5, 10, -5) \cdot \mathbf{a}$ and $(-5, 10, -5) \cdot \mathbf{b}$ both vanish.

Despite their symmetry, equations (32) and (33) are not easy to remember and are mainly used in formal arguments and machine calculations. When it comes to calculations performed by hand, it is usual to employ a more memorable expression based on algebraic entities called determinants that will be described in Section 4 of this unit. For that reason we mainly defer exercises that require you to evaluate vector products until Section 4, where you will be able to use the determinant method.

The vector product: a physical perspective

The vector product really opens up the world of three dimensions to physical scientists and engineers. For example, the turning effect of a force is described by a vector quantity called *torque* that is defined by a vector product. Figure 25 shows a rigid rod with one end pivoted at the origin O and the other end at the point P with position vector $\mathbf{r} = (x, y, z)$. If a force $\mathbf{F}$ is applied to the rod at the point P, its turning effect about the origin will be described by the torque $\mathbf{T} = \mathbf{r} \times \mathbf{F}$. This will be true irrespective of the relative orientations of $\mathbf{r}$ and $\mathbf{F}$.

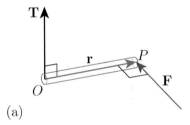

(a)

If $\mathbf{F}$ acts at right angles to $\mathbf{r}$ (see Figure 25(a)), then the torque about the origin will be in the direction $\widehat{\mathbf{T}}$, perpendicular to $\mathbf{r}$ and $\mathbf{F}$, and will have magnitude $T = rF$. If the rod is pivoted in such a way that it cannot rotate about an axis in the direction of $\widehat{\mathbf{T}}$ but must instead rotate about some other axis through the origin, then the turning effect of $\mathbf{F}$ will be described by the *component* of $\mathbf{T}$ along the allowed axis, whatever its direction.

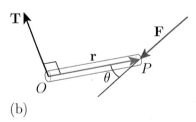

(b)

Figure 25   The torque $\mathbf{T}$ about the origin due to a force $\mathbf{F}$ applied at the point P with position vector $\mathbf{r}$: (a) when the force is at right angles to the rod; (b) when the force is at an angle θ to the rod

Similarly, if the force $\mathbf{F}$ is applied at an angle θ to the rod (see Figure 25(b)), then the magnitude of its turning effect about an axis through the origin in the direction of $\widehat{\mathbf{T}}$ will be reduced to $T = rF \sin \theta$, and will vanish completely if $\mathbf{F}$ is parallel or antiparallel to $\mathbf{r}$ since θ will then be 0 or π.

Figure 26   An open part of the LHC shows the beam tubes and bending magnets for the electrically charged particles that are accelerated by the machine

As another example, consider an electrically charged particle travelling through the powerful magnetic field inside CERN's Large Hadron Collider (LHC) (see Figure 26). Such a particle is subject to an electromagnetic force **F** that acts at right angles to both the particle's velocity vector **v** and the magnetic field vector, which is represented by **B**. As the particle moves through the LHC, the direction of the electromagnetic force continuously changes. Yet no matter what the orientations of the particle's velocity and the magnetic field, the force is at all times described by the equation **F** = q**v** × **B**, where q is the charge on the particle.

Areas and vector products

The vector product has several useful geometric applications. The following example introduces one of them.

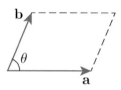

Figure 27   A parallelogram

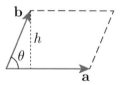

Figure 28   The perpendicular height of a parallelogram

Example 10

Any two non-zero vectors **a** and **b** define a parallelogram, as shown in Figure 27. Find an expression for the area of the parallelogram in terms of **a** × **b**.

Solution

The area A of the parallelogram defined by the two vectors **a** and **b** is equal to the product of its base length |**a**| and its perpendicular height $h = |\mathbf{b}| \sin \theta$ (see Figure 28). Thus $A = |\mathbf{a}|\,|\mathbf{b}| \sin \theta$, and this is the magnitude of **a** × **b**. So the area of the parallelogram is

$$A = |\mathbf{a} \times \mathbf{b}|.$$

The area A of a parallelogram with sides defined by vectors **a** and **b** is given by

$$A = \text{base length} \times \text{perpendicular height} = |\mathbf{a} \times \mathbf{b}|. \tag{34}$$

This result can be used to determine the areas of other figures, such as a *rectangle* (a special kind of parallelogram with **a** perpendicular to **b**) or a *triangle*, which has half the area of the corresponding parallelogram.

Exercise 18

Using position vectors, find the area of a triangle with corners at the points $(0, 0, 0)$, $(2, 1, 1)$ and $(1, -1, -1)$.

Exercise 19

Using the vector product, confirm that the area of a parallelogram with corners at the points $(0,0,0)$, $(a,b,0)$, $(c,d,0)$ and $(a+c, b+d, 0)$ is $|ad - bc|$. Check that the formula gives the right answer in the case that the parallelogram is a rectangle, with $b = c = 0$.

Volumes and triple products

A **parallelepiped** is a solid body like a distorted brick, all of whose faces are parallelograms, as shown in Figure 29.

> The volume V of a parallelepiped with sides defined by vectors $\mathbf{a}$, $\mathbf{b}$ and $\mathbf{c}$ is given by
>
> $$V = \text{base area} \times \text{vertical height} = |(\mathbf{a} \times \mathbf{b}) \cdot \mathbf{c}|. \tag{35}$$

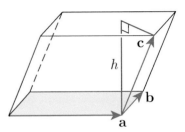

Figure 29 A parallelepiped: in the case shown, the vector **c** leans forward, out of the page, and to the right, so **c** is *not* perpendicular to either **a** or **b**

That this formula is correct can be seen as follows. The base is a parallelogram defined by the vectors $\mathbf{a}$ and $\mathbf{b}$. The area of the base is therefore equal to the magnitude of $\mathbf{a} \times \mathbf{b}$. The vertical height h is the magnitude of the scalar component of the vector $\mathbf{c}$ in the direction perpendicular to the base. That direction is parallel or antiparallel to the direction of $\mathbf{a} \times \mathbf{b}$. So the product $(\mathbf{a} \times \mathbf{b}) \cdot \mathbf{c}$ has a magnitude equal to the base area times the perpendicular height. We may therefore express the volume of the parallelepiped as $|(\mathbf{a} \times \mathbf{b}) \cdot \mathbf{c}|$.

The expression for the volume of the parallelepiped involves the quantity $(\mathbf{a} \times \mathbf{b}) \cdot \mathbf{c}$, which is an example of the **scalar triple product** of vectors. As the name implies, it is a scalar quantity obtained from three vectors. Such products arise in many situations and can be written in a number of equivalent ways. For example, by expressing all the products in terms of components, it is also possible to establish a **cyclic identity** according to which

$$\mathbf{a} \cdot (\mathbf{b} \times \mathbf{c}) = \mathbf{b} \cdot (\mathbf{c} \times \mathbf{a}) = \mathbf{c} \cdot (\mathbf{a} \times \mathbf{b}). \tag{36}$$

Combining this with the freedom to exchange the order of vectors in the scalar product (but not in the vector product) leads to some more equivalent expressions, including the following relationship that will be used in a later unit:

$$\mathbf{a} \cdot (\mathbf{b} \times \mathbf{c}) = (\mathbf{a} \times \mathbf{b}) \cdot \mathbf{c}. \tag{37}$$

Proving the equality of these two expressions involves a lot of algebraic manipulation of their components. This is straightforward but time consuming. However, the equality of their magnitudes is obvious, since either of those magnitudes can be used to describe the volume of the parallelepiped with sides defined by the three vectors $\mathbf{a}$, $\mathbf{b}$ and $\mathbf{c}$.

The scalar triple product (in all its equivalent forms) is not the only way of forming a meaningful product of three vectors. There is also a **vector triple product**, $(\mathbf{a} \times \mathbf{b}) \times \mathbf{c}$. This produces a vector quantity that will be perpendicular to $\mathbf{c}$ and to the vector that results from $\mathbf{a} \times \mathbf{b}$.

Since it involves taking vector products, the vector triple product is naturally not commutative. Moreover, the vector triple product is not *associative* either. That is, $\mathbf{a} \times (\mathbf{b} \times \mathbf{c})$ is generally different from $(\mathbf{a} \times \mathbf{b}) \times \mathbf{c}$. This may seem rather surprising but is easily established as follows. Since $(\mathbf{a} \times \mathbf{b}) \times \mathbf{c}$ is perpendicular to the direction of $\mathbf{a} \times \mathbf{b}$, its only non-zero components must be in the plane that is perpendicular to $\mathbf{a} \times \mathbf{b}$, i.e. the plane containing $\mathbf{a}$ and $\mathbf{b}$. Similarly, the only non-zero components of $\mathbf{a} \times (\mathbf{b} \times \mathbf{c})$ must be in the plane containing $\mathbf{b}$ and $\mathbf{c}$. So, provided that $\mathbf{a}$, $\mathbf{b}$ and $\mathbf{c}$ are not all in the same plane, any non-zero triple products $\mathbf{a} \times (\mathbf{b} \times \mathbf{c})$ and $(\mathbf{a} \times \mathbf{b}) \times \mathbf{c}$ must point in different directions.

Exercise 20

Suppose that $\mathbf{a}$ and $\mathbf{b}$ have a non-zero vector product, and that $\mathbf{c}$ is a non-zero vector such that $(\mathbf{a} \times \mathbf{b}) \times \mathbf{c} = \mathbf{0}$. What can you say about the direction of $\mathbf{c}$?

We end our discussion of vectors with a warning. Although a powerful vector algebra has been developed with operations of scaling, addition and two kinds of multiplication, there is no **vector division**. So do not try to divide by a vector. The absence is caused by a lack of uniqueness in attempts to define vector division. When dealing with non-zero scalar quantities, the equation $ax = b$ has the unique solution $x = b/a$. When dealing with non-zero vectors, however, the corresponding equation $\mathbf{a} \cdot \mathbf{x} = b$, where b is a scalar, has many solutions. If $\mathbf{x} = \mathbf{x}_1$ is one solution (so $\mathbf{a} \cdot \mathbf{x}_1 = b$), then another solution is $\mathbf{x}_2 = \mathbf{x}_1 + \lambda \mathbf{c}$, where λ is any scalar and $\mathbf{c}$ is any vector orthogonal to $\mathbf{a}$ (so $\mathbf{a} \cdot (\lambda \mathbf{c}) = 0$, and hence $\mathbf{a} \cdot \mathbf{x}_2 = \mathbf{a} \cdot \mathbf{x}_1 = b$).

3 Matrices, vectors and linear transformations

In Sections 1 and 2 of this unit you were introduced to the algebra of vectors. Sections 3 and 4 will provide a comparable introduction to the algebra of *matrices*. As you will see, there are many deep links between vectors and matrices, but there are also some important differences. In particular, the treatment of matrices is generally more 'algebraic' and less 'geometric'. This can make matrix algebra appear more abstract and harder to visualise. For that reason, rather than plunging directly into the presentation of algebraic rules for scaling, adding and multiplying matrices, most of Section 3 will be devoted to examining a particular application of matrices that emphasises their use in geometry. This is the subject of *linear transformations of a plane*, which will be introduced below, alongside matrices themselves. This will allow us to introduce some of the basic ideas of matrix algebra in a concrete setting. The more general aspects of matrix algebra will then be introduced in Section 4.

3.1   Matrices and linear transformations

Matrices

Here are four rectangular arrays of numbers enclosed in brackets.

(a) $\begin{bmatrix} 2 & -7 \\ 0 & 3 \end{bmatrix}$ (b) $\begin{bmatrix} -2 & 1 & 4 \\ 3 & 0 & -1 \\ 2 & 3 & 2 \end{bmatrix}$ (c) $\begin{bmatrix} -\pi & \pi \end{bmatrix}$ (d) $\begin{bmatrix} 0.8 \\ 0.3 \\ 0.6 \end{bmatrix}$

We follow the convention of using square brackets to indicate matrices. Some texts use round brackets.

These are all examples of matrices. A matrix can be defined as follows.

> A **matrix** is a rectangular array of elements (usually numbers or physical quantities) arranged in rows and columns, and enclosed in brackets. It obeys several mathematical rules that collectively comprise **matrix algebra**.

A matrix with m rows and n columns is said to be of **order** $m \times n$. We generally represent entire matrices by symbols printed in bold type, so if **A** represents an $m \times n$ matrix, we may write

$m \times n$ is read as 'm by n'; the $\times$ does *not* mean multiplication.

$$\mathbf{A} = \begin{bmatrix} a_{11} & a_{12} & \cdots & a_{1n} \\ a_{21} & a_{22} & \cdots & a_{2n} \\ \vdots & \vdots & \vdots & \vdots \\ a_{m1} & a_{m2} & \cdots & a_{mn} \end{bmatrix}, \tag{38}$$

where a_{ij} represents the element in the ith row and the jth column. (The significance of the symbol a_{ij} is sometimes recalled using the mnemonic 'arc': element $\underline{a}$, $\underline{r}$ow i, $\underline{c}$olumn j.)

There is no universal convention on how to hand-write matrices. Capital letters are often used, except when the matrix represents a vector. Some people underline with a straight line, some with a curly line; some even underline twice. We leave it to you to choose a convention.

A matrix in which all of the elements are zero is called a **zero matrix** and will be denoted **0**, irrespective of its order. Matrices of order $n \times n$ have equal numbers of rows and columns and are called **square matrices**. (Examples (a) and (b) given above are square matrices.) Any matrix of order $1 \times n$ takes the form of a single row of elements and is called a **row matrix**. Similarly, a matrix of order $n \times 1$ is called a **column matrix**. (Examples (c) and (d) given above are row and column matrices, respectively.) If $n = 2$ or 3, a row matrix looks a lot like a vector presented as an ordered pair or an ordered triple, though the matrices do not contain commas. In fact, row and column matrices are often used to represent vectors algebraically. For that reason we often refer to row and column matrices as **row vectors** and **column vectors**.

Two matrices are said to be equal if they have the same order and each of the corresponding elements is equal. So, for example, $\begin{bmatrix} 3 & 8 \end{bmatrix} = \begin{bmatrix} 1+2 & 4 \times 2 \end{bmatrix}$, but $\begin{bmatrix} 3 & 8 \end{bmatrix} \neq \begin{bmatrix} 3 & 8 & 0 \end{bmatrix}$ because the last matrix is not of order 1×2. More formally, we have the following.

> Two matrices $\mathbf{A}$ and $\mathbf{B}$ are **equal** if they have the same order and $a_{ij} = b_{ij}$ for all $i = 1, \ldots, n$ and for all $j = 1, \ldots, m$.

Exercise 21

What is the order of each of the four example matrices (a), (b), (c) and (d) given at the start of this subsection?

Linear transformations

Figure 30 represents a two-dimensional plane overlaid by a two-dimensional Cartesian coordinate system. This subsection concerns 'transformations' that affect the points in the plane but not the coordinate system. That's why the coordinates were described as 'overlaid'. You might like to think of the plane as an elastic sheet that can be rotated or stretched, while the coordinate axes are drawn on an overlying transparent plastic sheet that is not affected by the distortion of the underlying plane.

In Figure 30 we have drawn the ('overlaid') coordinate axes in black. We have also drawn a grid of straight (white) lines and a square of unit area with unit vectors along its edges. The grid lines and the vectors should be thought of as drawn on the plane (which is coloured grey), so they will all be affected by the transformation of the plane.

Using the overlying coordinates, any point in the plane can be described by a position vector (x, y). Such a point can also be represented by a row vector or by a column vector; in the case of a column vector we call it the **position column vector** and denote it by

$$\mathbf{x} = \begin{bmatrix} x \\ y \end{bmatrix}.$$

The usual Cartesian unit vectors on the plane can be described by $(1, 0)$ and $(0, 1)$. These too may be represented by appropriate row or column vectors; in the case of column vectors we call them **unit column vectors**, and denote them by

$$\mathbf{i} = \begin{bmatrix} 1 \\ 0 \end{bmatrix} \quad \text{and} \quad \mathbf{j} = \begin{bmatrix} 0 \\ 1 \end{bmatrix}.$$

(Note that by reusing the symbols $\mathbf{i}$ and $\mathbf{j}$ in this new way we are deliberately blurring the distinction between vectors and column matrices. It should be clear from the context which of them we are referring to, but the point is to demonstrate that matrices provide another way of dealing with vectors.)

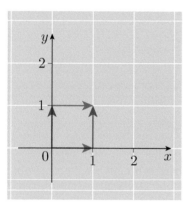

Figure 30   A plane and an overlying coordinate system. A square edged by unit vectors and a grid of straight lines have been drawn on the plane. Distortions of the plane do not affect the coordinate system.

Figure 31 shows the effect of subjecting the whole plane to a transformation that moves any point with position vector (x, y) to a new location with position vector $(ax + by, cx + dy)$, where a, b, c and d are real numbers. The particular transformation shown in Figure 31 was obtained using the values $a = 1.0$, $b = -0.9$, $c = 0.3$ and $d = 1.5$, but it is a typical example of what is generally known as a **linear transformation** of the plane. Note that although the transformation generally tends to move points in the plane, and therefore changes their coordinates, it does not change the coordinates of the point at the origin. That particular point in the plane starts with the coordinates $(x, y) = (0, 0)$, and the effect of the transformation is to make its new coordinates $(ax + by, cx + dy) = (0, 0)$, so the origin does not move at all. This is characteristic of linear transformations.

Our aim now is to show how linear transformations of the plane can be represented in a very natural way using matrices. As a first step towards this goal, we introduce the following *multiplication rule* for determining the product of a 2×2 square matrix and a 2×1 column matrix. You will see later that this is a special case of the general rule for matrix multiplication.

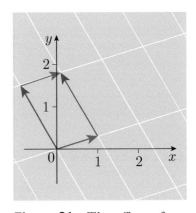

Figure 31 The effect of a linear transformation on the plane. The transformation will generally change the coordinates of points in the plane but has no effect on the coordinate system (shown in black). The origin is unaffected, and straight lines are transformed into straight lines.

The product of a 2×2 matrix $\mathbf{A} = \begin{bmatrix} a & b \\ c & d \end{bmatrix}$ and a 2×1 matrix $\mathbf{x} = \begin{bmatrix} x \\ y \end{bmatrix}$ is a 2×1 matrix given by

$$\mathbf{Ax} = \begin{bmatrix} a & b \\ c & d \end{bmatrix} \begin{bmatrix} x \\ y \end{bmatrix} = \begin{bmatrix} ax + by \\ cx + dy \end{bmatrix}. \tag{39}$$

At first sight this rule may seem rather arbitrary, but there is actually a very sensible pattern behind it. As indicated by the hand symbols in Figure 32(a), the expression $ax + by$ in the first row and first (and only) column of the product, is the result of adding the products of the corresponding elements in the first row of $\mathbf{A}$ and the first (and only) column of $\mathbf{x}$. Similarly, as indicated in Figure 32(b), the expression $cx + dy$ in the second row and first (and only) column of the product, is the result of adding the products of the corresponding elements in the second row of $\mathbf{A}$ and the first (and only) column of $\mathbf{x}$.

$$\begin{bmatrix} a & b \\ c & d \end{bmatrix} \begin{bmatrix} x \\ y \end{bmatrix} = \begin{bmatrix} ax + by \\ cx + dy \end{bmatrix} \qquad\qquad \begin{bmatrix} a & b \\ c & d \end{bmatrix} \begin{bmatrix} x \\ y \end{bmatrix} = \begin{bmatrix} ax + by \\ cx + dy \end{bmatrix}$$

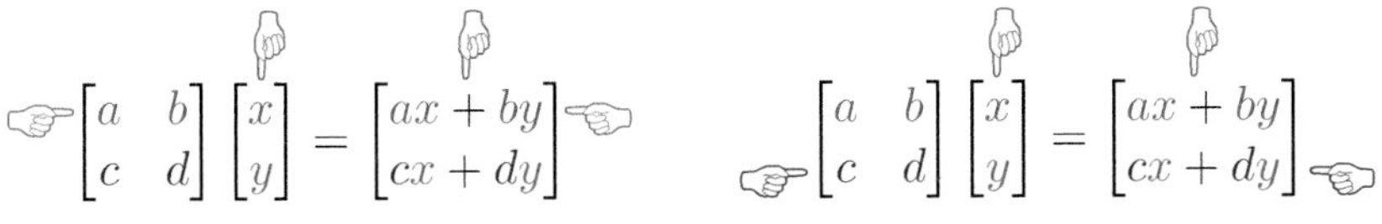

(a)   (b)

Figure 32 (a) Obtaining $ax + by$; (b) obtaining $cx + dy$

If we now substitute into the matrix $\mathbf{A}$ the values $a = 1.0$, $b = -0.9$, $c = 0.3$ and $d = 1.5$ that characterise the transformation shown in Figure 31, we see that

$$\mathbf{A} = \begin{bmatrix} a & b \\ c & d \end{bmatrix} = \begin{bmatrix} 1.0 & -0.9 \\ 0.3 & 1.5 \end{bmatrix}.$$

The multiplication rule given in equation (39) then tells us that the product of $\mathbf{A}$ and the unit column vector $\mathbf{i}$ is

$$\mathbf{Ai} = \begin{bmatrix} 1.0 & -0.9 \\ 0.3 & 1.5 \end{bmatrix} \begin{bmatrix} 1 \\ 0 \end{bmatrix} = \begin{bmatrix} 1.0 \\ 0.3 \end{bmatrix},$$

Note how naturally we can move between the vector notation $(.,.)$ and the column vector notation $\begin{bmatrix} . \\ . \end{bmatrix}$.

and this exactly describes what happens to the unit vector $(1,0)$ when it is affected by the linear transformation of Figure 31; it becomes the vector $(1.0, 0.3)$.

Similarly, according to the multiplication rule, the product of $\mathbf{A}$ and the unit column vector $\mathbf{j}$ is

$$\mathbf{Aj} = \begin{bmatrix} 1.0 & -0.9 \\ 0.3 & 1.5 \end{bmatrix} \begin{bmatrix} 0 \\ 1 \end{bmatrix} = \begin{bmatrix} -0.9 \\ 1.5 \end{bmatrix},$$

which exactly describes what happens to the unit vector $(0,1)$ when it is affected by the linear transformation of Figure 31; it becomes the vector $(-0.9, 1.5)$.

In fact, the multiplication rule tells us that the product of $\mathbf{A}$ and a position column matrix $\mathbf{x}$ (representing a general point in the plane) is just

Note that the quantity on the extreme right is a 2×1 column vector, *not* a 2×2 matrix.

$$\mathbf{Ax} = \begin{bmatrix} 1.0 & -0.9 \\ 0.3 & 1.5 \end{bmatrix} \begin{bmatrix} x \\ y \end{bmatrix} = \begin{bmatrix} 1.0x - 0.9y \\ 0.3x + 1.5y \end{bmatrix},$$

which exactly represents the general effect of the linear transformation on a position vector (x, y); it becomes the position vector $(1.0x - 0.9y, 0.3x + 1.5y)$.

So, thanks to the multiplication rule for matrices, we can say that the effect of the particular linear transformation of the plane that was shown in Figure 31 is to transform any point represented by a 2×1 column vector $\mathbf{x}$ into the point represented by the 2×1 matrix product $\mathbf{Ax}$, where $\mathbf{A} = \begin{bmatrix} 1.0 & -0.9 \\ 0.3 & 1.5 \end{bmatrix}.$

Though this is only one example, you should not be surprised by the following general rule.

> Any **linear transformation** of the plane can be represented by a 2×2 matrix $\mathbf{A}$. The effect of the linear transformation on a position vector represented by the 2×1 column vector $\mathbf{x}$ is to transform it into the position vector represented by the 2×1 matrix product $\mathbf{Ax}$.

Of course, all this is deliberately ponderous for the sake of clarity. Those familiar with such transformations usually just say '$\mathbf{A}$ transforms $\mathbf{x}$ to $\mathbf{Ax}$'. Indeed, mathematicians often prefer to describe the effect of the linear transformation in terms of the 'mapping' of vectors rather than their transformation, and will generally say '$\mathbf{A}$ maps $\mathbf{x}$ to $\mathbf{Ax}$'. The column vector $\mathbf{Ax}$ is then described as the *image* of x under the *mapping* represented by **A**. The implication is the same, whichever form of language is used: 2×2 matrices can be used to represent linear transformations of the plane, and to work out their effects on position vectors.

Example 11

What is the effect of the linear transformation represented by $\mathbf{A} = \begin{bmatrix} 3 & 2 \\ 1 & 4 \end{bmatrix}$ on a point with coordinates $(2, 1)$?

Solution

First, we note that a point with coordinates $(2, 1)$ can be represented by the position column vector $\mathbf{x} = \begin{bmatrix} 2 \\ 1 \end{bmatrix}$.

The effect of the transformation on $\mathbf{x}$ is then given by

$$\mathbf{Ax} = \begin{bmatrix} 3 & 2 \\ 1 & 4 \end{bmatrix} \begin{bmatrix} 2 \\ 1 \end{bmatrix} = \begin{bmatrix} 3 \times 2 + 2 \times 1 \\ 1 \times 2 + 4 \times 1 \end{bmatrix} = \begin{bmatrix} 8 \\ 6 \end{bmatrix}.$$

So the point $(2, 1)$ is transformed to the point $(8, 6)$.

Exercise 22

Consider the linear transformation represented by $\mathbf{A} = \begin{bmatrix} 1 & 2 \\ 3 & 4 \end{bmatrix}$.

Use the matrix **A** to find the effect of the transformation on each of the following position column vectors.

(a) $\begin{bmatrix} 3 \\ 1 \end{bmatrix}$ (b) $\begin{bmatrix} -1 \\ 1 \end{bmatrix}$ (c) $\begin{bmatrix} 0 \\ 0 \end{bmatrix}$

We have now achieved our aim of showing how linear transformations of the plane can be represented using matrices. In the next subsection we consider matrix representations of some specific linear transformations with easily visualised actions.

3.2   Some linear transformations of the plane

In this section we examine some specific transformations of the plane. Identifying the 2×2 matrix

$$\mathbf{A} = \begin{bmatrix} a & b \\ c & d \end{bmatrix}$$

associated with a particular transformation of the plane is most easily accomplished by examining the effect of the matrix on the unit column vectors. To see the reason for this, consider the matrix products

$$\mathbf{Ai} = \begin{bmatrix} a & b \\ c & d \end{bmatrix} \begin{bmatrix} 1 \\ 0 \end{bmatrix} = \begin{bmatrix} a \\ c \end{bmatrix}, \quad \mathbf{Aj} = \begin{bmatrix} a & b \\ c & d \end{bmatrix} \begin{bmatrix} 0 \\ 1 \end{bmatrix} = \begin{bmatrix} b \\ d \end{bmatrix}.$$

These show that the transformation represented by the matrix $\mathbf{A}$ is the one that maps $\mathbf{i} = (1, 0)$ to (a, c), and also maps $\mathbf{j} = (0, 1)$ to (b, d). This leads to the following general principle.

> The square matrix $\mathbf{A}$ describing a given linear transformation has columns that are identical to the column vectors produced by the action of the transformation on the unit column vectors.

So if you know what the transformation does to the unit vectors, then you can write down its matrix. The use of this principle is shown in the following example.

Example 12

The matrix $\mathbf{D} = \begin{bmatrix} 1 & 0 \\ 0 & 2 \end{bmatrix}$ is said to represent a **rescaling** (or **dilation**) of the plane by a factor of 2 in the positive y-direction.

(a) Work out the effect of this transformation on the point with position vector $(1, 2)$, and the point with position vector $(2, 1)$.

(b) Write down the effect of the transformation on the unit vectors $(1, 0)$ and $(0, 1)$, and justify your answer.

(c) Sketch a diagram to show the general effect of the transformation on the plane and the unit square in Figure 30. Comment on the appropriateness of the description of its action.

Solution

(a) The matrix product

$$\mathbf{D} \begin{bmatrix} 1 \\ 2 \end{bmatrix} = \begin{bmatrix} 1 & 0 \\ 0 & 2 \end{bmatrix} \begin{bmatrix} 1 \\ 2 \end{bmatrix} = \begin{bmatrix} 1 \\ 4 \end{bmatrix}$$

shows that the position vector $(1, 2)$ is mapped to $(1, 4)$.

The matrix product

$$\mathbf{D} \begin{bmatrix} 2 \\ 1 \end{bmatrix} = \begin{bmatrix} 1 & 0 \\ 0 & 2 \end{bmatrix} \begin{bmatrix} 2 \\ 1 \end{bmatrix} = \begin{bmatrix} 2 \\ 2 \end{bmatrix}$$

shows that the position vector $(2, 1)$ is mapped to $(2, 2)$.

(b) $(1, 0)$ is mapped to $(1, 0)$, and $(0, 1)$ is mapped to $(0, 2)$. This is in agreement with the comments made above. The unit vectors $(1, 0)$ and $(0, 1)$ are represented in matrix notation by the unit column vectors. The result of multiplying these unit column vectors by $\mathbf{D}$ is to produce the columns of $\mathbf{D}$ itself.

(c) Figure 33 shows the effect of the transformation. It stretches the plane by a factor of 2 in the positive y-direction, making the description of its action appropriate.

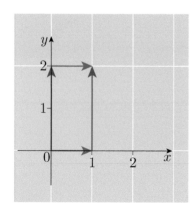

Figure 33   The rescaling of the plane by a factor of 2 in the positive y-direction

The general rescaling of the plane allows the x-coordinate of every point to be multiplied by a real number κ, while the y-coordinate is multiplied by λ. Such a transformation is shown in Figure 34 and is represented by the following matrix.

> **The two-dimensional dilation matrix**
>
> $$\mathbf{D}(\kappa, \lambda) = \begin{bmatrix} \kappa & 0 \\ 0 & \lambda \end{bmatrix}. \qquad (40)$$

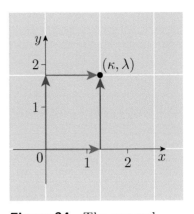

Figure 34 The general rescaling of the plane by κ in the x-direction and λ in the y-direction

Exercise 23

The matrix $\mathbf{D}(3,2) = \begin{bmatrix} 3 & 0 \\ 0 & 2 \end{bmatrix}$ represents a rescaling of the plane.

(a) Write down the effect of the transformation on the unit vectors $(1,0)$ and $(0,1)$.

(b) Work out the effect of this transformation on the point with coordinates $x = 3$ and $y = -2$.

(c) What is the effect of the transformation on the area of a unit square (i.e. a square that may be edged by unit vectors)?

Rotations about the origin constitute an important class of linear transformations, often encountered in science and engineering. The effect of a rotation about the origin by an angle α in the positive (i.e. anticlockwise) sense is shown in Figure 35. Such a transformation of the plane can be represented by the following matrix.

> **The two-dimensional rotation matrix**
>
> $$\mathbf{R}(\alpha) = \begin{bmatrix} \cos\alpha & -\sin\alpha \\ \sin\alpha & \cos\alpha \end{bmatrix}. \qquad (41)$$

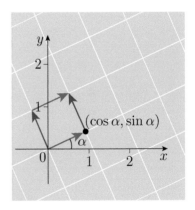

Figure 35 The rotation of the plane represented by $\mathbf{R}(\alpha)$

Exercise 24

(a) Recalling that $\sin\frac{\pi}{4} = \cos\frac{\pi}{4} = \frac{1}{\sqrt{2}}$, write down the matrix that represents a rotation about the origin by $\frac{\pi}{4}$ radians in the anticlockwise sense. (Be explicit, i.e. replace trigonometric functions by arithmetical quantities.)

(b) Write down the effect of this transformation on the unit vectors $(1,0)$ and $(0,1)$.

(c) Work out the effect of this transformation on the point with coordinates $x = -1$ and $y = -1$.

(d) What is the effect of the transformation on the area of a unit square?

We end with one of the simplest transformations of the plane: the **identity** transformation. This is the transformation that leaves everything where it was. It is represented by the following matrix.

The two-dimensional identity matrix

$$\mathbf{I} = \begin{bmatrix} 1 & 0 \\ 0 & 1 \end{bmatrix}. \tag{42}$$

Exercise 25

The identity matrix $\mathbf{I}$ can arise as a special case of the dilation matrix $\mathbf{D}(\kappa, \lambda)$ or the rotation matrix $\mathbf{R}(\alpha)$. For what values of κ, λ and α will this happen?

3.3   Basic matrix algebra and successive transformations

Now that several different matrices have been studied, we can start to develop some of the ideas of basic matrix algebra. For now we restrict the detailed discussion to two dimensions, so that the concrete setting of transformations of the plane can continue to be used. A more general treatment will be provided in Section 4.

Note that throughout this subsection we will be making extensive use of subscripts to distinguish matrix elements; in particular, we will write

$$\mathbf{A} = \begin{bmatrix} a_{11} & a_{12} \\ a_{21} & a_{22} \end{bmatrix} \quad \text{and} \quad \mathbf{B} = \begin{bmatrix} b_{11} & b_{12} \\ b_{21} & b_{22} \end{bmatrix}.$$

Scaling and adding matrices

We start by defining the scaling and adding of matrices, both of which have very natural definitions.

Given a matrix $\mathbf{A}$ of any order, the operation of **scaling** the matrix by a scalar λ produces a matrix $\lambda\mathbf{A}$, of the same order, in which each element is multiplied by λ. Thus, in the case of a 2×2 matrix,

$$\lambda\mathbf{A} = \lambda \begin{bmatrix} a_{11} & a_{12} \\ a_{21} & a_{22} \end{bmatrix} = \begin{bmatrix} \lambda a_{11} & \lambda a_{12} \\ \lambda a_{21} & \lambda a_{22} \end{bmatrix}. \tag{43}$$

Given two matrices $\mathbf{A}$ and $\mathbf{B}$ of the same order, the operation of **adding** the two matrices produces a matrix $\mathbf{A} + \mathbf{B}$, of the same order, in which each element is the sum of the corresponding elements of $\mathbf{A}$ and $\mathbf{B}$.

Thus, in the case of 2×2 matrices,

$$\mathbf{A} + \mathbf{B} = \begin{bmatrix} a_{11} & a_{12} \\ a_{21} & a_{22} \end{bmatrix} + \begin{bmatrix} b_{11} & b_{12} \\ b_{21} & b_{22} \end{bmatrix} = \begin{bmatrix} a_{11} + b_{11} & a_{12} + b_{12} \\ a_{21} + b_{21} & a_{22} + b_{22} \end{bmatrix}. \quad (44)$$

As you saw in Section 1, a position vector $\mathbf{r}$ may be written as a linear combination of unit vectors. We can now use the scaling and adding of matrices, together with the unit column vectors $\mathbf{i}$ and $\mathbf{j}$, to provide a similar way of writing a position column vector $\mathbf{x}$.

Example 13

Write the position column vector $\mathbf{x} = \begin{bmatrix} x \\ y \end{bmatrix}$ as a linear combination of the unit column vectors $\mathbf{i}$ and $\mathbf{j}$.

Solution

$$\mathbf{x} = \begin{bmatrix} x \\ y \end{bmatrix} = x \begin{bmatrix} 1 \\ 0 \end{bmatrix} + y \begin{bmatrix} 0 \\ 1 \end{bmatrix} = x\mathbf{i} + y\mathbf{j}.$$

Exercise 26

Evaluate the result of the following scalings and additions.

(a) $3 \begin{bmatrix} 1 \\ 0 \end{bmatrix} - 2 \begin{bmatrix} 0 \\ 1 \end{bmatrix}$ (b) $4 \left(\begin{bmatrix} 1 \\ 1 \end{bmatrix} - 3 \begin{bmatrix} 1 \\ -1 \end{bmatrix} \right)$ (c) $2 \begin{bmatrix} 1 & 0 \\ -2 & 3 \end{bmatrix}$

(d) $2 \left(\begin{bmatrix} 1 & 0 \\ -2 & 3 \end{bmatrix} + 2 \begin{bmatrix} 0 & 1 \\ -1 & 0 \end{bmatrix} \right)$ (e) $2 \left(\begin{bmatrix} a & b \\ c & d \end{bmatrix} + 2 \begin{bmatrix} a & 2b \\ -2c & d \end{bmatrix} \right)$

Multiplying matrices

You have already had plenty of practice at multiplying 2×2 square matrices and 2×1 column matrices. Now we extend matrix multiplication to the case of multiplying one 2×2 matrix by another 2×2 matrix. The result is always a 2×2 matrix, and the four elements in the product are worked out using a straightforward extension to the method used earlier. Formally, we can define the product of two 2×2 matrices as follows.

The product of a 2×2 matrix $\mathbf{A}$ and a 2×2 matrix $\mathbf{B}$ is another 2×2 matrix given by

$$\mathbf{AB} = \begin{bmatrix} a_{11} & a_{12} \\ a_{21} & a_{22} \end{bmatrix} \begin{bmatrix} b_{11} & b_{12} \\ b_{21} & b_{22} \end{bmatrix}$$

$$= \begin{bmatrix} a_{11}b_{11} + a_{12}b_{21} & a_{11}b_{12} + a_{12}b_{22} \\ a_{21}b_{11} + a_{22}b_{21} & a_{21}b_{12} + a_{22}b_{22} \end{bmatrix}. \quad (45)$$

It is not recommended that you try to remember this equation, but you should try to remember the process by which the four elements in the result are determined from the elements of $\mathbf{A}$ and $\mathbf{B}$. This may be described by saying that the element in the ith row and the jth column of the product is the sum of the element-by-element products of the ith row of the first matrix and the jth column of the second matrix. In Figure 36 this is illustrated by the hand symbols for the case of the element $a_{11}b_{12} + a_{12}b_{22}$ in the first row and the second column of the product. All the other elements may be worked out in a similar way.

$$\begin{bmatrix} a_{11} & a_{12} \\ a_{21} & a_{22} \end{bmatrix} \begin{bmatrix} b_{11} & b_{12} \\ b_{21} & b_{22} \end{bmatrix} = \begin{bmatrix} a_{11}b_{11} + a_{12}b_{21} & a_{11}b_{12} + a_{12}b_{22} \\ a_{21}b_{11} + a_{22}b_{21} & a_{21}b_{12} + a_{22}b_{22} \end{bmatrix}$$

Figure 36   Obtaining the element in the first row and the second column of the product of two matrices

Exercise 27

Work out the following matrix products using the method of Figure 36.

(a) $\begin{bmatrix} 2 & 0 \\ 1 & 1 \end{bmatrix} \begin{bmatrix} 0 & 3 \\ 1 & 1 \end{bmatrix}$ (b) $\begin{bmatrix} 1 & 2 \\ 2 & -3 \end{bmatrix} \begin{bmatrix} 1 & 3 \\ 2 & -1 \end{bmatrix}$ (c) $\begin{bmatrix} 1 & 3 \\ 2 & -1 \end{bmatrix} \begin{bmatrix} 1 & 2 \\ 2 & -3 \end{bmatrix}$

Successive transformations

Now consider what happens when we carry out one transformation of the plane and then perform another transformation on the result – e.g. a rescaling followed by a rotation. Let us represent the first transformation by the dilation matrix $\mathbf{D}(\kappa, \lambda)$ given in equation (40), and the second by the rotation matrix $\mathbf{R}(\alpha)$ given in equation (41). For the sake of definiteness, consider their action on a specific point initially located at the position represented by the column vector $\mathbf{x}_0 = \begin{bmatrix} x_0 \\ y_0 \end{bmatrix}$. This is indicated schematically in Figure 37.

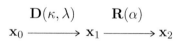

$$\mathbf{D}(\kappa, \lambda) \qquad \mathbf{R}(\alpha)$$
$$\mathbf{x}_0 \longrightarrow \mathbf{x}_1 \longrightarrow \mathbf{x}_2$$

Figure 37   The effect of successive transformations on $\mathbf{x}_0$

Suppose that the first transformation, the rescaling, transforms $\mathbf{x}_0$ into the position column vector $\mathbf{x}_1 = \mathbf{D}(\kappa, \lambda)\,\mathbf{x}_0$, so that

$$\begin{bmatrix} x_1 \\ y_1 \end{bmatrix} = \begin{bmatrix} \kappa & 0 \\ 0 & \lambda \end{bmatrix} \begin{bmatrix} x_0 \\ y_0 \end{bmatrix} = \begin{bmatrix} \kappa x_0 \\ \lambda y_0 \end{bmatrix}. \tag{46}$$

Also suppose that the second transformation, the rotation, then transforms $\mathbf{x}_1$ into the position column vector $\mathbf{x}_2 = \mathbf{R}(\alpha)\,\mathbf{x}_1$, so that

$$\begin{bmatrix} x_2 \\ y_2 \end{bmatrix} = \begin{bmatrix} \cos\alpha & -\sin\alpha \\ \sin\alpha & \cos\alpha \end{bmatrix} \begin{bmatrix} x_1 \\ y_1 \end{bmatrix} = \begin{bmatrix} x_1 \cos\alpha - y_1 \sin\alpha \\ x_1 \sin\alpha + y_1 \cos\alpha \end{bmatrix}.$$

Note that when multiplying factors such as $\cos\alpha$ and x_1, we prefer to write the result as $x_1 \cos\alpha$ since the alternative $\cos\alpha x_1$ could be misinterpreted as $\cos(\alpha x_1)$.

But from equation (46) we have $x_1 = \kappa x_0$ and $y_1 = \lambda y_0$, so we can rewrite this result as

$$\mathbf{x}_2 = \mathbf{R}(\alpha)\,\mathbf{D}(\kappa, \lambda)\,\mathbf{x}_0 = \begin{bmatrix} \kappa x_0 \cos\alpha - \lambda y_0 \sin\alpha \\ \kappa x_0 \sin\alpha + \lambda y_0 \cos\alpha \end{bmatrix}.$$

Now, this is significant because it has the same general form as the result of applying a single 2×2 matrix, $\mathbf{C}$ say, to $\mathbf{x}_0$. The effect of $\mathbf{C}$ is indicated schematically in Figure 38. If our definition of matrix multiplication makes sense, we should expect the matrix $\mathbf{C}$ to be the product $\mathbf{R}(\alpha)\,\mathbf{D}(\kappa, \lambda)$. Let us check to see if this is correct. First, let

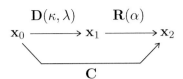

$$\mathbf{C} = \mathbf{R}(\alpha)\,\mathbf{D}(\kappa, \lambda) = \begin{bmatrix} \cos\alpha & -\sin\alpha \\ \sin\alpha & \cos\alpha \end{bmatrix} \begin{bmatrix} \kappa & 0 \\ 0 & \lambda \end{bmatrix} = \begin{bmatrix} \kappa\cos\alpha & -\lambda\sin\alpha \\ \kappa\sin\alpha & \lambda\cos\alpha \end{bmatrix}.$$

Figure 38   The effect of the combined transformation $\mathbf{C}$ on $\mathbf{x}_0$

Then note that

$$\mathbf{C}\mathbf{x}_0 = \begin{bmatrix} \kappa\cos\alpha & -\lambda\sin\alpha \\ \kappa\sin\alpha & \lambda\cos\alpha \end{bmatrix} \begin{bmatrix} x_0 \\ y_0 \end{bmatrix} = \begin{bmatrix} \kappa x_0\cos\alpha - \lambda y_0\sin\alpha \\ \kappa x_0\sin\alpha + \lambda y_0\cos\alpha \end{bmatrix} = \mathbf{x}_2.$$

This confirms our expectations. The conclusion is clear and can be stated in general terms as follows.

> The effect on a column vector $\mathbf{x}$ of a first transformation, represented by $\mathbf{A}$, followed by a second transformation, represented by $\mathbf{B}$, is equivalent to the effect of a single transformation, represented by the matrix product $\mathbf{BA}$.

Pay close attention to the order of the matrices in the above result. The first matrix to act, $\mathbf{A}$, is the one that appears on the *right* in the product $\mathbf{BA}$. This may look a little odd if you are not familiar with matrices, but it has to be so, since we are constructing a product that will act on any column vector that appears even further to the right in the combination $\mathbf{BAx}$.

Exercise 28

Find a matrix $\mathbf{C}$ that can act on a column vector $\mathbf{x}$ to reproduce the effect of a rescaling represented by $\mathbf{D}(2, 1)$ followed by a rotation $\mathbf{R}\!\left(\frac{\pi}{4}\right)$.

In the example above, and in all the work that led up to it, we have been careful to preserve the order of matrices in a matrix product. This is important because matrix multiplication is not generally commutative: $\mathbf{AB}$ may be very different from the product $\mathbf{BA}$.

Exercise 29

Find the matrix $\mathbf{F}$ that represents the product of the transformations in Exercise 28 but in the reverse order, i.e. $\mathbf{F} = \mathbf{D}(2, 1)\,\mathbf{R}\!\left(\frac{\pi}{4}\right)$. Show that, in general, $\mathbf{F}$ is not the same matrix as $\mathbf{C}$, i.e. $\mathbf{D}(2, 1)\,\mathbf{R}\!\left(\frac{\pi}{4}\right) \neq \mathbf{R}\!\left(\frac{\pi}{4}\right)\mathbf{D}(2, 1)$.

It is not really surprising that the result of a rotation $\mathbf{R}\!\left(\frac{\pi}{4}\right)$ followed by a rescaling $\mathbf{D}(2, 1)$ differs from the result of performing those operations in the reverse order. It is symptomatic of the following general rule.

> **Matrix multiplication is non-commutative**
>
> Though there are cases where matrices *do* commute, generally
>
> $$\mathbf{AB} \neq \mathbf{BA}.$$

Despite being non-commutative, matrix multiplication is *associative*, so

$$(\mathbf{AB})\mathbf{C} = \mathbf{A}(\mathbf{BC}). \tag{47}$$

It is also the case that matrix multiplication is *distributive over addition*, so

$$\mathbf{A}(\mathbf{B} + \mathbf{C}) = \mathbf{AB} + \mathbf{AC}, \tag{48}$$

and matrix multiplication is *linear* with respect to scalar multiplication, so

$$\lambda(\mathbf{AB}) = \mathbf{A}(\lambda \mathbf{B}), \quad \text{where } \lambda \text{ is a scalar.} \tag{49}$$

As usual, we can use these properties to make sense of matrix expressions that involve brackets.

Matrices are ideally suited to describing situations where the order of operations really matters, as in much of science and also in everyday life. Do not think of a matrix inequality such as $\mathbf{AB} \neq \mathbf{BA}$ as something frightful. It might just signify that the operations of putting sugar into tea cups and drinking tea from those cups do not commute: the order in which you do things clearly matters in this situation, and many others.

Despite the generally non-commutative nature of matrix multiplication, there are cases where the matrices *do* commute, so their order may be reversed without changing the result. One such case is when one of the transformations is the identity transformation represented by the identity matrix $\mathbf{I}$ (first introduced in equation (42)). Commutation in this case makes good sense, since the identity transformation doesn't change anything, so you would expect it to have the same lack of effect whether it was done first or last. As you can easily confirm for any 2×2 matrix $\mathbf{A}$,

$$\mathbf{IA} = \mathbf{AI} = \mathbf{A}. \tag{50}$$

Exercise 30

Show that products of rotations in two dimensions do commute by establishing that

$$\mathbf{R}(\alpha)\,\mathbf{R}(\beta) = \mathbf{R}(\beta)\,\mathbf{R}(\alpha) = \mathbf{R}(\alpha + \beta).$$

3.4 Undoing transformations and matrix inversion

Often, after performing an operation such as a linear transformation of the plane, we need to reverse the changes that have been made and undo the transformation. In matrix algebra this is achieved by following the action of a matrix, $\mathbf{A}$ say, by the action of the *inverse matrix*, which is denoted $\mathbf{A}^{-1}$. The combination of the two, represented by their matrix product, results in no change, so it must be equal to the identity matrix $\mathbf{I}$. The same must be true if we perform the inverse transformation first, and then follow that with the original transformation. Interestingly, inverse transformations do not always exist. However, when they do exist, they are *unique*, so what we can say in general is the following.

> Given a square matrix $\mathbf{A}$, its **inverse matrix**, if it exists, is denoted $\mathbf{A}^{-1}$, has the same order as $\mathbf{A}$, and satisfies the condition
>
> $$\mathbf{A}\mathbf{A}^{-1} = \mathbf{A}^{-1}\mathbf{A} = \mathbf{I}. \tag{51}$$
>
> Also, if $\mathbf{A}$ and $\mathbf{B}$ are square matrices of the same order, and $\mathbf{AB} = \mathbf{BA} = \mathbf{I}$, then $\mathbf{B} = \mathbf{A}^{-1}$.

The process of finding the inverse of a matrix is called **matrix inversion**. In some cases it is easy, even obvious. In other cases it can be difficult or simply impossible. A matrix that can be inverted is said to be **invertible**. In this subsection we examine some simple cases, describe a general procedure for finding the inverse of a 2×2 matrix, and determine the criterion for deciding whether a given 2×2 matrix is invertible. The inversion of larger matrices will be discussed in Section 4.

Simple matrix inversions

> The inverse of the identity matrix is the identity matrix itself, i.e. $\mathbf{I}^{-1} = \mathbf{I}$. This is clear, since $\mathbf{I}\mathbf{I} = \mathbf{I}$.
>
> The inverse of the dilation matrix $\mathbf{D}(\kappa, \lambda)$ is $\mathbf{D}^{-1}(\kappa, \lambda) = \mathbf{D}(1/\kappa, 1/\lambda)$.
>
> The inverse of the rotation matrix $\mathbf{R}(\alpha)$ is $\mathbf{R}^{-1}(\alpha) = \mathbf{R}(-\alpha)$.

All of the above inverses are guaranteed to exist, apart from the inverse dilation matrix in the special case that $\kappa = 0$ or $\lambda = 0$.

Example 14

Confirm by matrix multiplication that the matrix $\begin{bmatrix} 1/\kappa & 0 \\ 0 & 1/\lambda \end{bmatrix}$ is the inverse of the dilation matrix $\begin{bmatrix} \kappa & 0 \\ 0 & \lambda \end{bmatrix}$, for non-zero κ and λ.

Solution

It is sufficient to note that

$$\begin{bmatrix} 1/\kappa & 0 \\ 0 & 1/\lambda \end{bmatrix}\begin{bmatrix} \kappa & 0 \\ 0 & \lambda \end{bmatrix} = \begin{bmatrix} \kappa & 0 \\ 0 & \lambda \end{bmatrix}\begin{bmatrix} 1/\kappa & 0 \\ 0 & 1/\lambda \end{bmatrix} = \begin{bmatrix} 1 & 0 \\ 0 & 1 \end{bmatrix}.$$

Exercise 31

Confirm by explicit matrix multiplication that the inverse of the rotation matrix $\mathbf{R}(\alpha)$ is $\mathbf{R}(-\alpha)$.

Inversion of a general 2×2 matrix

Consider the matrix product

$$\mathbf{AB} = \begin{bmatrix} 2 & 3 \\ 1 & 4 \end{bmatrix} \begin{bmatrix} 4 & -3 \\ -1 & 2 \end{bmatrix} = \begin{bmatrix} 5 & 0 \\ 0 & 5 \end{bmatrix}.$$

It is obvious that $\mathbf{A}$ is not the inverse of $\mathbf{B}$, but it is also clear that $\frac{1}{5}\mathbf{A}$ will be the inverse of $\mathbf{B}$. This technique, of first identifying a matrix with the right structure and than scaling it by an appropriate factor, is the basis of the following general rule for finding the inverse of a 2×2 matrix.

Inverse of a 2×2 matrix

Given the 2×2 matrix $\mathbf{A} = \begin{bmatrix} a & b \\ c & d \end{bmatrix}$, its inverse matrix, if it exists, is given by

$$\mathbf{A}^{-1} = \frac{1}{ad - bc} \begin{bmatrix} d & -b \\ -c & a \end{bmatrix}. \tag{52}$$

Example 15

Using the general expressions given above for a 2×2 matrix $\mathbf{A}$ and its inverse $\mathbf{A}^{-1}$, verify by matrix multiplication that $\mathbf{A}^{-1}\mathbf{A} = \mathbf{I}$.

Solution

$$\frac{1}{ad - bc} \begin{bmatrix} d & -b \\ -c & a \end{bmatrix} \begin{bmatrix} a & b \\ c & d \end{bmatrix} = \frac{1}{ad - bc} \begin{bmatrix} da - bc & db - bd \\ -ca + ac & -cb + ad \end{bmatrix} = \begin{bmatrix} 1 & 0 \\ 0 & 1 \end{bmatrix}.$$

Exercise 32

Using equation (52) again, verify that $\mathbf{AA}^{-1} = \mathbf{I}$.

Exercise 33

Let $\mathbf{A} = \begin{bmatrix} 1 & 1 \\ 0 & 1 \end{bmatrix}$, $\mathbf{B} = \begin{bmatrix} 1 & 0 \\ 0 & -1 \end{bmatrix}$ and $\mathbf{C} = \begin{bmatrix} 1 & -1 \\ 1 & 1 \end{bmatrix}$.

(a) Find the inverses of $\mathbf{A}$, $\mathbf{B}$, $\mathbf{C}$ and $\mathbf{D} = \mathbf{ABC}$.

(b) Verify that $\mathbf{D}^{-1} = \mathbf{C}^{-1}\mathbf{B}^{-1}\mathbf{A}^{-1}$. (In other words, verify that $(\mathbf{ABC})^{-1} = \mathbf{C}^{-1}\mathbf{B}^{-1}\mathbf{A}^{-1}$.)

Note the interesting pattern revealed by this exercise:

$$(\mathbf{ABC})^{-1} = \mathbf{C}^{-1}\mathbf{B}^{-1}\mathbf{A}^{-1}.$$

As you will see in Section 4, this is actually a general result: the inverse of a product of matrices is equal to the product of the inverses *in reverse order.*

Criterion for the existence of an inverse

In equation (52), the general formula for inverting a 2×2 matrix $\mathbf{A}$, it is necessary to divide every term in a matrix by the quantity $ad - bc$. This is mathematically meaningful only if $ad - bc$ is not equal to zero. That is why it is impossible to invert some 2×2 matrices. As you will see later, the quantity $ad - bc$ for the matrix $\mathbf{A}$ is a particularly simple example of a mathematical entity called a *determinant.* Every square matrix $\mathbf{A}$ has a determinant, usually denoted $\det \mathbf{A}$, but only in the case of 2×2 matrices can it be generally expressed as simply as $ad - bc$. Using the determinant we can say the following.

> ### Criterion for the existence of A^{-1}
>
> Given the 2×2 matrix $\mathbf{A} = \begin{bmatrix} a & b \\ c & d \end{bmatrix}$, its inverse matrix $\mathbf{A}^{-1}$ exists if and only if
>
> $$\det \mathbf{A} = ad - bc \neq 0. \tag{53}$$

From the matrix inversion formula equation (52), it is clear why $ad - bc$ is important, but in the case of 2×2 matrices it is possible to get a deeper and mathematically more interesting insight into the origin of the existence criterion. Viewed as a transformation of the plane, the effect of the matrix $\mathbf{A}$ is to map the unit vectors $(1, 0)$ and $(0, 1)$ into the vectors (a, c) and (b, d), as indicated in Figure 39.

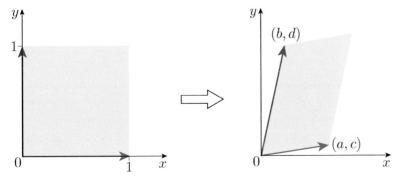

Figure 39   The geometric effect of a general linear transformation of the plane

As a result, a unit square of area 1 is mapped into a parallelogram of area $ad - bc$. (You established that the area of a parallelogram is $|ad - bc|$ in Exercise 19.)

Consequently, if the matrix $\mathbf{A}$ that describes the mapping has $\det \mathbf{A} = 0$, so $ad - bc = 0$, then the area of that parallelogram must also be zero. This means that the corners of the parallelogram must be either on the same line (i.e. collinear), or all at the same point. This is indicated in Figure 40. In this extreme case, the action of $\mathbf{A}$ has been to collapse the unit square to such an extent that there is insufficient information in the resulting 'parallelogram' (actually either a line or a point) to allow the original unit square to be reconstructed by the inverse transformation $\mathbf{A}^{-1}$. That is why the inverse transformation cannot exist.

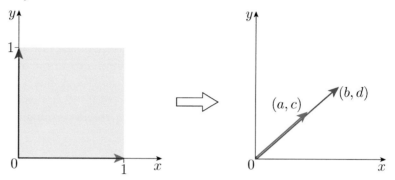

Figure 40   The geometric effect of a linear transformation with zero determinant; the parallelogram is reduced to a line or a point

---

Exercise 34

Which of the following matrices has no inverse?

$$\begin{bmatrix} 1 & -2 \\ 2 & 4 \end{bmatrix}, \quad \begin{bmatrix} -2 & 4 \\ -1 & 2 \end{bmatrix}, \quad \begin{bmatrix} 4 & 1 \\ 2 & -2 \end{bmatrix}, \quad \begin{bmatrix} -2 & 1 \\ 4 & 2 \end{bmatrix}.$$

Exercise 35

Referring to the three matrices $\mathbf{A}$, $\mathbf{B}$ and $\mathbf{C}$ introduced in Exercise 33, calculate the determinants of $\mathbf{A}$, $\mathbf{B}$, $\mathbf{C}$ and $\mathbf{ABC}$. Verify that $\det(\mathbf{ABC}) = \det \mathbf{A} \det \mathbf{B} \det \mathbf{C}$.

Exercise 36

The determinant of

$$\mathbf{A} = \begin{bmatrix} 1 & 2 \\ 3 & 6 \end{bmatrix}$$

vanishes. What is the effect of this transformation on the Cartesian unit vectors? Does $\mathbf{A}$ indeed transform the unit square to a geometric object with no area?

---

4 Matrix algebra

Section 3 was concerned with examples of matrix action that were easy to visualise, so the discussion was mostly confined to 2×2 matrices that could be interpreted geometrically. Such transformations are important, but they are only one indication of the great wealth of applications of matrix algebra in general. There are many applications of matrices that do not involve geometry, and many that involve matrices larger than 2×2.

An example from biology

As a brief example, consider a biologist studying the effects of nutrition on a group of animals. Suppose that two nutrients n_1 and n_2 are being fed to the animals in two different foodstuffs f_1 and f_2. Also suppose that the mass of nutrient n_i per kilogram of foodstuff f_j is a_{ij}. The situation is depicted schematically in Figure 41.

A feeding scheme that supplies each animal with a mass M_j of foodstuff f_j will automatically supply each animal with a mass m_i of nutrient n_i given by $m_i = a_{i1}M_1 + a_{i2}M_2$. You should recognise this as the ith element in the matrix

$$\begin{bmatrix} m_1 \\ m_2 \end{bmatrix} = \begin{bmatrix} a_{11} & a_{12} \\ a_{21} & a_{22} \end{bmatrix} \begin{bmatrix} M_1 \\ M_2 \end{bmatrix}. \tag{54}$$

It would take quite a lot of effort to use matrix mathematics for such a simple problem. Suppose, however, that the biologist is actually interested in 20 nutrients being delivered in different proportions by 20 foodstuffs. The delivery of nutrients by a given combination of foodstuffs would then be described by the product of a 20×20 matrix $\mathbf{A}$ and a 20×1 feeding matrix $\mathbf{M}$. Matrix multiplication would provide a useful tool for keeping track of such a complicated arrangement, which would be described by a system of 20 equations. In addition, the problem of finding the combination of foodstuffs that ensures the delivery of the required amounts of each nutrient might be tackled by determining the inverse of the 20×20 matrix.

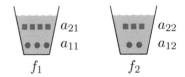

Figure 41 Foodstuff f_1 contains a quantity a_{11} of nutrient n_1 (red circle), and a_{21} of nutrient n_2 (blue square); similarly for foodstuff f_2

Similar (less contrived) problems arise every day in a range of activities. As a result, the study of the **matrix algebra** of general $m \times n$ matrices is an important part of almost every course in higher mathematics, pure or applied. In addition, the algebraic principles that it teaches extend beyond the domain of matrices, rich as that is. In particular, matrix algebra is now recognised as the principal example of a broader subject known as *linear algebra*, which will be introduced in Unit 5.

Many aspects of 2×2 matrix algebra were covered in Section 3. In this section we generalise to the case of $m \times n$ matrices.

4.1 Notation and fundamentals of matrix algebra

As usual, we represent a matrix of order $m \times n$ (i.e. m rows and n columns) by a bold symbol, such as $\mathbf{A}$, with a_{ij} representing the element in its ith row and jth column. In an extension of our earlier notation we henceforth use the notation $[a_{ij}]$ to indicate the whole matrix of elements a_{ij}. So writing $\mathbf{A} = [a_{ij}]$ means exactly the same as equation (38). Similarly, we write $\mathbf{B} = [b_{ij}]$ for a matrix $\mathbf{B}$ of elements b_{ij}, etc.

Concepts such as equating matrices, adding matrices (of the same order) and scaling matrices are all easily generalised to the case of $m \times n$ matrices. We will state the rules describing them later, but there will be no surprises. Slightly more challenging is the generalisation of matrix multiplication, so we deal with that first.

The first thing to remember about the general case of matrix multiplication is that it is possible only when the matrices involved are of the appropriate orders. As indicated by the hand symbols in Figures 32 and 36, matrix multiplication involves summing the products of corresponding elements from a row of the first matrix and a column of the second matrix. This is possible only if the number of columns in the first matrix is equal to the number of rows in the second. This is embodied in the following rule concerning the order of matrix products.

> **Rule for the existence and order of a matrix product**
>
> An $m \times q$ matrix $\mathbf{A}$ may be multiplied by an $r \times n$ matrix $\mathbf{B}$ to form the matrix product $\mathbf{AB}$ if and only if $q = r$, in which case the product $\mathbf{AB}$ will be of order $m \times n$.

Because of this rule, when considering multiplying $\mathbf{A}$ by $\mathbf{B}$, you may find it helpful to picture something like Figure 42, with the order of $\mathbf{A}$ written to the left of the order of $\mathbf{B}$. This will produce a row of four integers. If the two inner integers are equal, the matrices can be multiplied together. In such cases, the order of the matrix product $\mathbf{AB}$ is given by the two outer integers.

Supposing that the matrices $\mathbf{A}$ and $\mathbf{B}$ are suitable for multiplication, how should the result be determined? The answer is based on a straightforward generalisation of the method used for multiplying 2×2 matrices in Section 3. It is embodied in the following rule.

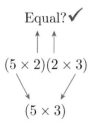

Figure 42   A visual reminder of the rule for the existence and order of a matrix product. Here $\mathbf{A}$ has order 5×2, $\mathbf{B}$ has order 2×3, and $\mathbf{AB}$ has order 5×3.

> **Rule for the evaluation of a matrix product**
>
> The element in the ith row and jth column of the matrix product $\mathbf{AB}$ is the sum of the element-by-element products of the ith row of $\mathbf{A}$ with the jth column of $\mathbf{B}$.

This way of combining rows and columns should already be familiar from earlier examples, but the whole idea is illustrated again, schematically, in Figure 43.

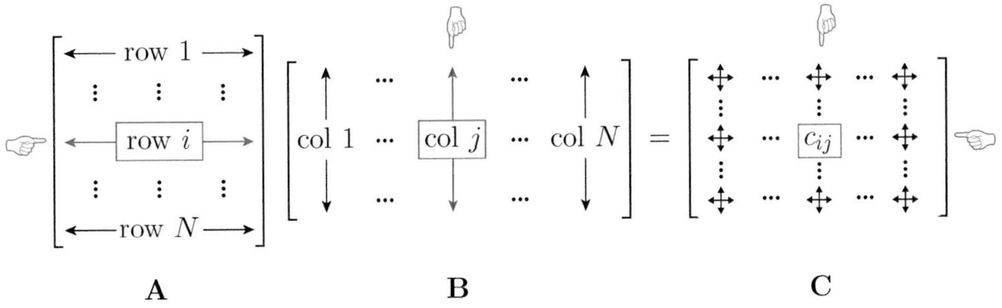

Figure 43   A visual prompt to help you to remember the rule for the evaluation of a matrix product

The consequence of the rule can be represented formally (but less helpfully) by saying that when an $m \times r$ matrix $\mathbf{A}$ multiplies an $r \times n$ matrix $\mathbf{B}$ to form the $m \times n$ matrix product $\mathbf{AB} = \mathbf{C}$, the element c_{ij} in the ith row and jth column of $\mathbf{C}$ is given by

$$c_{ij} = \sum_{k=1}^{r} a_{ik}b_{kj} = a_{i1}b_{1j} + a_{i2}b_{2j} + \cdots + a_{ir}b_{rj}. \tag{55}$$

Don't try to remember this formula. Remember instead the method shown in Figure 43 that underlies it.

Example 16

Consider the matrix product

$$\begin{bmatrix} 2 & -1 & 3 \\ -2 & 1 & 2 \end{bmatrix} \begin{bmatrix} 3 & -1 \\ 2 & 2 \\ -2 & -2 \end{bmatrix}.$$

Write down the order of the resulting matrix, and evaluate the product.

Solution

The product of a 2×3 matrix and a 3×2 matrix is a 2×2 matrix:

$$\begin{bmatrix} 2 & -1 & 3 \\ -2 & 1 & 2 \end{bmatrix} \begin{bmatrix} 3 & -1 \\ 2 & 2 \\ -2 & -2 \end{bmatrix}$$

$$= \begin{bmatrix} 2(3) - 1(2) + 3(-2) & 2(-1) - 1(2) + 3(-2) \\ -2(3) + 1(2) + 2(-2) & -2(-1) + 1(2) + 2(-2) \end{bmatrix}$$

$$= \begin{bmatrix} 6 - 2 - 6 & -2 - 2 - 6 \\ -6 + 2 - 4 & 2 + 2 - 4 \end{bmatrix}$$

$$= \begin{bmatrix} -2 & -10 \\ -8 & 0 \end{bmatrix}.$$

Exercise 37

Evaluate the following matrix products, where they exist.

(a) $\begin{bmatrix} 1 & 2 \\ 2 & -3 \end{bmatrix} \begin{bmatrix} 1 & 3 \\ 2 & -1 \end{bmatrix}$ (b) $\begin{bmatrix} 2 & 1 \end{bmatrix} \begin{bmatrix} 1 & 6 \\ 0 & 2 \end{bmatrix}$ (c) $\begin{bmatrix} 1 \\ 2 \end{bmatrix} \begin{bmatrix} 3 & 0 & -4 \end{bmatrix}$

(d) $\begin{bmatrix} 3 & 1 & 2 \\ 0 & 5 & 1 \end{bmatrix} \begin{bmatrix} -2 & 0 & 1 \\ 1 & 3 & 0 \\ 4 & 1 & -1 \end{bmatrix}$ (e) $\begin{bmatrix} 2 \\ 4 \\ -1 \end{bmatrix} \begin{bmatrix} 3 & 2 \\ 4 & -1 \end{bmatrix}$

As you saw in Section 3, matrix multiplication is *associative* (so $(\mathbf{AB})\mathbf{C} = \mathbf{A}(\mathbf{BC})$) and *distributive over matrix addition* (so $\mathbf{A}(\mathbf{B} + \mathbf{C}) = \mathbf{AB} + \mathbf{AC}$). Matrix multiplication is also *linear* with regard to scalar multiplication (so $\mathbf{A}\lambda\mathbf{B} = \lambda\mathbf{AB}$). However, matrix multiplication is *not* generally commutative. This last point is so important that it deserves its own box, even though you have seen it before.

In general,

$$\mathbf{AB} \neq \mathbf{BA},$$

although there are cases where matrices *do* commute

Exercise 38

Contrast this with rotations in two dimensions, which do commute, as we showed in Exercise 30.

In three-dimensional space, rotations do not, in general, commute. For example, consider the matrices

$$\mathbf{A} = \begin{bmatrix} 0 & -1 & 0 \\ 1 & 0 & 0 \\ 0 & 0 & 1 \end{bmatrix} \quad \text{and} \quad \mathbf{B} = \begin{bmatrix} 1 & 0 & 0 \\ 0 & 0 & -1 \\ 0 & 1 & 0 \end{bmatrix}.$$

The first matrix transforms space by rotation of $\frac{\pi}{2}$ about the z-axis; the second matrix transforms space by rotation of $\frac{\pi}{2}$ about the x-axis.

Let $\mathbf{C}$ be the transformation of performing $\mathbf{A}$ and then $\mathbf{B}$; let $\mathbf{D}$ be the transformation of performing $\mathbf{B}$ and then $\mathbf{A}$. Calculate the matrices $\mathbf{C}$ and $\mathbf{D}$, and hence decide if $\mathbf{A}$ and $\mathbf{B}$ commute.

Transposing a matrix

In another extension to our earlier notation, we introduce the operation of taking the *transpose*, which interchanges the rows and columns of a matrix, so that the first row of a matrix becomes the first column of the transposed matrix, and so on. This operation is indicated by a superscript T, so we can write

$$\begin{bmatrix} a & b \\ c & d \end{bmatrix}^T = \begin{bmatrix} a & c \\ b & d \end{bmatrix} \quad \text{and} \quad \begin{bmatrix} 2 & 7 \\ -6 & 1 \\ 0 & 4 \end{bmatrix}^T = \begin{bmatrix} 2 & -6 & 0 \\ 7 & 1 & 4 \end{bmatrix}.$$

This useful operation has many applications, including allowing us to save space by writing potentially long column matrices as transposed row matrices, as in $\mathbf{L} = \begin{bmatrix} 1 & 0 & 0 & 0 & 0 & 0 \end{bmatrix}^T$.

Using our compact notation for matrices, with $\mathbf{A} = [a_{ij}]$, we can define the transpose as follows.

Given any matrix $\mathbf{A}$, its **transpose** $\mathbf{A}^T$ is defined by $[a_{ij}]^T = [a_{ji}]$.

$\mathbf{A}^T$ is read as 'A transpose'.

Example 17

Show that in the case that $\mathbf{A}$ is a 2×2 matrix and $\mathbf{x}$ is a 2×1 matrix, it will be always be the case that $(\mathbf{Ax})^T = \mathbf{x}^T \mathbf{A}^T$.

Solution

Let $\mathbf{A} = \begin{bmatrix} a & b \\ c & d \end{bmatrix}$ and $\mathbf{x} = \begin{bmatrix} x \\ y \end{bmatrix}$. Then

$$\mathbf{Ax} = \begin{bmatrix} a & b \\ c & d \end{bmatrix} \begin{bmatrix} x \\ y \end{bmatrix} = \begin{bmatrix} ax + by \\ cx + dy \end{bmatrix},$$

so

$$(\mathbf{Ax})^T = \begin{bmatrix} ax + by & cx + dy \end{bmatrix}.$$

But

$$\mathbf{x}^T \mathbf{A}^T = \begin{bmatrix} x & y \end{bmatrix} \begin{bmatrix} a & c \\ b & d \end{bmatrix} = \begin{bmatrix} xa + yb & xc + yd \end{bmatrix}.$$

So it is true that $(\mathbf{Ax})^T = \mathbf{x}^T \mathbf{A}^T$ in this case.

In fact, this example illustrates the following general result concerning the transposition of matrix products.

If the matrix product $\mathbf{AB}$ exists, then its transpose $(\mathbf{AB})^T$ is given by

$$(\mathbf{AB})^T = \mathbf{B}^T \mathbf{A}^T. \tag{56}$$

Notice the reversed sequence of the matrices: the transpose of a product is the product of the transposes *in reverse order*.

General rules of matrix algebra

We are now in a position to summarise the general rules of matrix algebra, including those for scaling and adding that were promised earlier. In summarising the rules, we again use the compact notation in which $\mathbf{A} = [a_{ij}]$ and $\mathbf{B} = [b_{ij}]$.

Basic rules of matrix algebra

- Two matrices $\mathbf{A} = [a_{ij}]$ and $\mathbf{B} = [b_{ij}]$ are **equal** if they have the same order $m \times n$, and

$$a_{ij} = b_{ij} \quad \text{for all } i = 1, 2, \ldots, m \text{ and } j = 1, 2, \ldots, n.$$

- If $\mathbf{A} = [a_{ij}]$ and $\mathbf{B} = [b_{ij}]$ are any two matrices of the same order, then their **matrix sum** is defined by

$$\mathbf{A} + \mathbf{B} = [a_{ij} + b_{ij}] \quad \text{(i.e. element-wise addition)}.$$

- If $\mathbf{A} = [a_{ij}]$ is any matrix, then there exists a **zero matrix 0**, of the same order, such that

$$\mathbf{A} + \mathbf{0} = \mathbf{A} \quad \text{(i.e. the elements are unaltered by adding 0)}.$$

- If $\mathbf{A} = [a_{ij}]$ is any matrix and k is any scalar, then the **scalar multiplication** of $\mathbf{A}$ by k is defined by

$$k\mathbf{A} = [ka_{ij}] \quad \text{(i.e. element-wise multiplication by } k\text{)}.$$

- If $\mathbf{A} = [a_{ij}]$ is a matrix of order $m \times r$ and $\mathbf{B} = [b_{ij}]$ is a matrix of order $r \times n$, then the **matrix product $\mathbf{C} = \mathbf{AB}$** exists and is a matrix of order $m \times n$, where the element c_{ij} is defined by

$$c_{ij} = a_{i1}b_{1j} + a_{i2}b_{2j} + \cdots + a_{ir}b_{rj}.$$

- If $\mathbf{A} = [a_{ij}]$ is any matrix of order $m \times n$, then there exists an **identity matrix I** of order $m \times m$ such that

$$\mathbf{IA} = \mathbf{A},$$

and there also exists an identity matrix of order $n \times n$, also denoted $\mathbf{I}$, such that

$$\mathbf{AI} = \mathbf{A}.$$

- If $\mathbf{A} = [a_{ij}]$ is a matrix of order $m \times n$, then its **transpose $\mathbf{A}^T$** is a matrix of order $n \times m$ defined by

$$[a_{ij}]^T = [a_{ji}] \quad \text{(i.e. the interchange of rows and columns)}.$$

- If the matrix product $\mathbf{AB}$ exists, then the **transposed product** $(\mathbf{AB})^T$ also exists, and is given by

$$(\mathbf{AB})^T = \mathbf{B}^T\mathbf{A}^T \quad \text{(note the reversed order)}.$$

Additionally, note the following.

- The **subtraction** of a matrix should be interpreted as the addition of a matrix that has been multiplied by the scalar -1.

- The **power** of a matrix should be interpreted as repeated multiplication, as in $\mathbf{A}^2 = \mathbf{AA}$, $\mathbf{A}^3 = \mathbf{AAA}$, etc.

- Expressions involving *brackets* should be interpreted in the usual way, though the ordering of products of matrices should not be changed since matrix multiplication is generally **non-commutative**.

Exercise 39

Let $\mathbf{A} = \begin{bmatrix} 1 & 2 \\ 3 & 4 \\ 5 & 6 \end{bmatrix}$, $\mathbf{B} = \begin{bmatrix} 2 & 5 \\ -1 & -4 \\ 3 & 1 \end{bmatrix}$ and $\mathbf{C} = \begin{bmatrix} 1 & 0 \\ 2 & 3 \end{bmatrix}$.

(a) Write down $\mathbf{A}^T$, $\mathbf{B}^T$ and $\mathbf{C}^T$.

(b) Verify that $(\mathbf{A} + \mathbf{B})^T = \mathbf{A}^T + \mathbf{B}^T$.

(c) Verify that $(\mathbf{A}\mathbf{C})^T = \mathbf{C}^T \mathbf{A}^T$.

4.2 Determinants, inverses and matrix algebra

Determinants

The term *determinant* was introduced into mathematics in 1801 by Carl Friedrich Gauss (1777–1855), though the idea can be traced back to the eighteenth century and beyond. (You will learn more about Gauss in Unit 5, when we discuss a technique known as *Gaussian elimination*.) A 'determinant' was originally associated with a general square array of numbers. However, following the introduction of matrices in 1850, by the British mathematician James Sylvester (1814–1897), and the development of matrix theory by Sylvester's friend and colleague Arthur Cayley (1821–1895), the meaning of 'determinant' became strongly associated with square matrices, and we now generally speak of the 'determinant of a (square) matrix'. This is the spirit in which we introduced determinants in Section 3, where we said that the determinant of the 2×2 square matrix $\begin{bmatrix} a & b \\ c & d \end{bmatrix}$ was the quantity $ad - bc$. More generally, according to this modern view, we have the following.

> The **determinant** of any square matrix $\mathbf{A}$ is a single value, denoted $\det \mathbf{A}$, that may be calculated from the elements of $\mathbf{A}$ by following a standard prescription.

The 'standard prescription' for evaluating determinants can be expressed in various ways. The form that we use is called *Laplace's rule*, and will be stated later. First, however, let us look at some examples of determinants, to see what Laplace's rule must achieve.

When using the elements of a square matrix to calculate a determinant, it is conventional to write those elements between vertical lines (a practice introduced by Cayley in 1853). Thus if $\mathbf{A} = \begin{bmatrix} a & b \\ c & d \end{bmatrix}$, we can write

$$\det \mathbf{A} = \begin{vmatrix} a & b \\ c & d \end{vmatrix} = ad - bc. \tag{57}$$

This convention allows us to speak of the 'rows' and 'columns' of a determinant, and to describe a determinant with n rows and n columns as an $n \times n$ determinant, even though, when finally evaluated, the determinant is only a single value.

Determinants may be associated with square matrices of any order. However, in practice a very important case is that of a 3×3 matrix. As you will see later, Laplace's rule tells us that the determinant of such a matrix may be written as follows.

Determinant of a 3×3 matrix

$$\begin{vmatrix} a_1 & a_2 & a_3 \\ b_1 & b_2 & b_3 \\ c_1 & c_2 & c_3 \end{vmatrix} = a_1 \begin{vmatrix} b_2 & b_3 \\ c_2 & c_3 \end{vmatrix} - a_2 \begin{vmatrix} b_1 & b_3 \\ c_1 & c_3 \end{vmatrix} + a_3 \begin{vmatrix} b_1 & b_2 \\ c_1 & c_2 \end{vmatrix}. \tag{58}$$

At present we ask you to simply accept this formula. Shortly, you will learn a simple rule that enables you to construct the determinant of any $n \times n$ matrix.

Having expressed the 3×3 determinant as a linear combination of 2×2 determinants, we can use equation (57) to work out the 2×2 determinants and thus complete the evaluation. You can see this in the following example.

Example 18

If $\mathbf{A} = \begin{bmatrix} 2 & 2 & -1 \\ 3 & 5 & 1 \\ 1 & 2 & 1 \end{bmatrix}$, evaluate $\det \mathbf{A}$.

Solution

Using equation (58),

$$\begin{aligned} \det \mathbf{A} &= 2 \begin{vmatrix} 5 & 1 \\ 2 & 1 \end{vmatrix} - 2 \begin{vmatrix} 3 & 1 \\ 1 & 1 \end{vmatrix} - \begin{vmatrix} 3 & 5 \\ 1 & 2 \end{vmatrix} \\ &= 2 \times (5 - 2) - 2 \times (3 - 1) - (6 - 5) \\ &= 6 - 4 - 1 \\ &= 1. \end{aligned}$$

Exercise 40

Evaluate the determinants of the following.

(a) $\mathbf{A} = \begin{bmatrix} 2 & -1 & 2 \\ 5 & 1 & -1 \\ 2 & 1 & -1 \end{bmatrix}$　　(b) $\mathbf{B} = \begin{bmatrix} 0 & 2 & -1 \\ 3 & 0 & -1 \\ 2 & -1 & 0 \end{bmatrix}$

Examining these examples of 3×3 determinant expansions will help you to make sense of the expansion of determinants in general. The expression on the right-hand side of equation (58) is the sum of three terms. Each of those terms involves a 2×2 determinant. The origin of those 2×2 determinants is shown in Figure 44.

Element
a_{1j}

$$\begin{bmatrix} a_{11} & a_{12} & a_{13} \\ a_{21} & a_{22} & a_{23} \\ a_{31} & a_{32} & a_{33} \end{bmatrix} \quad \begin{bmatrix} a_{11} & a_{12} & a_{13} \\ a_{21} & a_{22} & a_{23} \\ a_{31} & a_{32} & a_{33} \end{bmatrix} \quad \begin{bmatrix} a_{11} & a_{12} & a_{13} \\ a_{21} & a_{22} & a_{23} \\ a_{31} & a_{32} & a_{33} \end{bmatrix}$$

Minor
M_{1j}

$$M_{11} = \begin{vmatrix} a_{22} & a_{23} \\ a_{32} & a_{33} \end{vmatrix} \quad M_{12} = \begin{vmatrix} a_{21} & a_{23} \\ a_{31} & a_{33} \end{vmatrix} \quad M_{13} = \begin{vmatrix} a_{21} & a_{22} \\ a_{31} & a_{32} \end{vmatrix}$$

Cofactor
$C_{1j} = (-1)^{1+j} M_{1j}$

$$C_{11} = +M_{11} \qquad C_{12} = -M_{12} \qquad C_{13} = +M_{13}$$

Figure 44 Expanding a determinant using the first row of elements and their cofactors

As indicated, the first of the 2×2 determinants is obtained from the original 3×3 determinant by deleting all the elements in the same row and column as the element a_{11} and forming the determinant of what remains. This 2×2 determinant is called the *minor* of the element a_{11}, and is denoted M_{11}. In a similar way, the other two 2×2 determinants in Figure 44 are the minors M_{12} and M_{13} of a_{12} and a_{13}, respectively. We can define the **minor** M_{ij} of any element a_{ij} of a determinant in a similar way, by deleting row i and column j, and forming the determinant of what remains.

To obtain the entire expression on the right of equation (58), each of the relevant minors M_{ij} must first be multiplied by the factor $(-1)^{i+j}$ to produce $C_{ij} = (-1)^{i+j} M_{ij}$, which is known as the **cofactor** of a_{ij}. (If $i + j$ is even, then $C_{ij} = M_{ij}$, but if $i + j$ is odd, then $C_{ij} = -M_{ij}$.) Finally, we must multiply each of the relevant cofactors by the corresponding element a_{ij}, and add the resulting products. In the case of equation (58) this gives us $a_{11}C_{11} + a_{12}C_{12} + a_{13}C_{13}$, which reproduces the right-hand side of the equation, including the alternating signs. The whole process is described as 'the expansion of the 3×3 determinant by the cofactors of its first row of elements'.

Laplace's rule for expanding (and hence evaluating) determinants is a simple generalisation of the procedure that has just been described, which you have already seen in Example 18 and carried out in Exercise 40. The main difference is that the rule tells us how to perform the expansion based on *any* row or column, and applies to a determinant of *any* $n \times n$ matrix. The rule may be stated as follows.

Laplace's rule for expanding determinants

Given an $n \times n$ matrix $\mathbf{A} = [a_{ij}]$, its determinant det $\mathbf{A}$ may be expanded in terms of the elements in row i and their cofactors C_{ij} as

$$\det \mathbf{A} = a_{i1}C_{i1} + a_{i2}C_{i2} + \cdots + a_{in}C_{in}, \tag{59}$$

or equivalently, in terms of the elements in column j and their cofactors C_{ij}, as

$$\det \mathbf{A} = a_{1j}C_{1j} + a_{2j}C_{2j} + \cdots + a_{nj}C_{nj}, \tag{60}$$

where $C_{ij} = (-1)^{i+j}M_{ij}$, and M_{ij} is the minor obtained by deleting row i and column j of the original determinant and forming the determinant of what remains.

For obvious reasons, Laplace's rule is sometimes called the **cofactor expansion rule**.

Example 19

Evaluate $\det \mathbf{A} = \begin{vmatrix} 1 & 0 & 0 & 3 \\ 2 & 2 & -1 & 2 \\ 3 & 5 & 1 & -1 \\ 1 & 2 & 1 & -1 \end{vmatrix}$.

Solution

To simplify the evaluation, we should expand using the first row, since that contains two zero elements, so it will minimise the work required. Thus

$$\det \mathbf{A} = a_{11}C_{11} + a_{12}C_{12} + a_{13}C_{13} + a_{14}C_{14}$$
$$= C_{11} + 3C_{14}.$$

Now $C_{11} = (-1)^{1+1}M_{11} = M_{11}$, where M_{11} is the determinant of the matrix obtained by crossing out the first row and first column of $\mathbf{A}$, i.e.

$$C_{11} = M_{11} = \begin{vmatrix} 2 & -1 & 2 \\ 5 & 1 & -1 \\ 2 & 1 & -1 \end{vmatrix}.$$

This determinant was evaluated in Exercise 40, where we obtained the result

$$C_{11} = 3.$$

Further, $C_{14} = (-1)^{1+4}M_{11} = -M_{11}$, where M_{11} is the determinant of the matrix obtained by crossing out the first row and fourth column of $\mathbf{A}$, i.e.

$$C_{14} = -M_{14} = -\begin{vmatrix} 2 & 2 & -1 \\ 3 & 5 & 1 \\ 1 & 2 & 1 \end{vmatrix} = -1,$$

where we have used the result obtained in Example 18. Hence

$$\det \mathbf{A} = 3 - 3 = 0.$$

The evaluation of determinants can be very time consuming, so here are some rules that exploit the intrinsic symmetry of determinants to speed up the process.

> **Rules for the determinant of an $n \times n$ matrix A**
>
> - Interchanging any two rows or any two columns of **A** changes the sign of det **A**.
> - $\det(\mathbf{A}^T) = \det \mathbf{A}$.
> - Multiplying any row or any column of **A** by a scalar k multiplies det **A** by k.
> - For any scalar k, $\det(k\mathbf{A}) = k^n \det \mathbf{A}$.
> - Adding a multiple of one row of **A** to another row does not change det **A**. Nor does the corresponding operation for a pair of columns.
> - If any row or column of **A** consists entirely of zeros, then det **A** $= 0$.

A multiple can be negative or positive, so the last rule covers subtracting a multiple of one row from another row.

Exercise 41

Use the rules given above to show that the following determinant is zero:

$$\begin{vmatrix} 1 & 3 & -2 \\ -3 & 2 & 6 \\ -2 & 4 & 4 \end{vmatrix}.$$

(*Hint*: Try to make a row or column vanish.)

The application of determinants to vector products

The expression for a 3×3 determinant in equation (58) provides a useful mnemonic for the definition of a vector product, given in Subsection 2.2. In fact, the vector product of two vectors can be obtained as follows.

> **Vector product as a determinant**
>
> If $\mathbf{b} = b_x\mathbf{i} + b_y\mathbf{j} + b_z\mathbf{k}$ and $\mathbf{c} = c_x\mathbf{i} + c_y\mathbf{j} + c_z\mathbf{k}$ are two vectors, then their vector product can be obtained by evaluating the determinant
>
> $$\mathbf{b} \times \mathbf{c} = \begin{vmatrix} \mathbf{i} & \mathbf{j} & \mathbf{k} \\ b_x & b_y & b_z \\ c_x & c_y & c_z \end{vmatrix} = \begin{vmatrix} b_y & b_z \\ c_y & c_z \end{vmatrix}\mathbf{i} - \begin{vmatrix} b_x & b_z \\ c_x & c_z \end{vmatrix}\mathbf{j} + \begin{vmatrix} b_x & b_y \\ c_x & c_y \end{vmatrix}\mathbf{k}. \qquad (61)$$

This reproduces the vector product rule that was given in equation (32) (though there we called the vectors **a** and **b**).

In a similar way, the component expression for the scalar triple product of three vectors can be obtained as follows.

Scalar triple product as a determinant

$$\mathbf{a} \cdot (\mathbf{b} \times \mathbf{c}) = \begin{vmatrix} a_x & a_y & a_z \\ b_x & b_y & b_z \\ c_x & c_y & c_z \end{vmatrix}$$

$$= a_x \begin{vmatrix} b_y & b_z \\ c_y & c_z \end{vmatrix} - a_y \begin{vmatrix} b_x & b_z \\ c_x & c_z \end{vmatrix} + a_z \begin{vmatrix} b_x & b_y \\ c_x & c_y \end{vmatrix}. \tag{62}$$

Using these determinant-based expressions, it is easy to find similar formulas for the areas of parallelograms and the volumes of parallelepipeds. Many other geometric results can also be expressed in terms of determinants.

Exercise 42

Use determinant-based methods to do the following.

(a) Evaluate $\mathbf{r} \times \mathbf{s}$, where $\mathbf{r} = (2, 5, 0)$ and $\mathbf{s} = (2, -1, 2)$.

(b) Find the area of the parallelogram with sides defined by the position vectors $\mathbf{r}_1 = (1, 1, 0)$ and $\mathbf{r}_2 = (2, 2, -2)$.

(c) Find the volume of the parallelepiped with sides defined by $\mathbf{a} = (2, 5, 0)$, $\mathbf{b} = (1, -2, 0)$ and $\mathbf{c} = (1, -3, 2)$.

Finding inverse matrices

Determinants are very common in the physical sciences. They are often used as a neat way of summarising important results, as you will see shortly. However, for our immediate purposes, in the context of matrix algebra, determinants are important for the part they play in relation to inverse matrices. Here is a procedure for finding the inverse of any square invertible matrix, based on a generalisation of the method for 2×2 matrices in Section 3. (It is worth noting that for large matrices there are other methods that are computationally more efficient, and more likely to be used in practice.)

Procedure 1 Finding the inverse of an $n \times n$ matrix

Suppose that we are given the $n \times n$ matrix $\mathbf{A} = [a_{ij}]$.

1. Evaluate $\det \mathbf{A}$, and confirm that $\det \mathbf{A} \neq 0$. (If $\det \mathbf{A} = 0$, the matrix $\mathbf{A}$ is **non-invertible**; no inverse exists, and you should abandon the attempt to find it.)

2. Evaluate the cofactor C_{ij} of each element a_{ij}, using the relation $C_{ij} = (-1)^{i+j} M_{ij}$, where M_{ij} is the minor obtained by deleting row i and column j of the original determinant and forming the determinant of what remains.

3. Form the $n \times n$ square matrix $\mathbf{C} = [C_{ij}]$, where the element of $\mathbf{C}$ in row i and column j is the cofactor C_{ij}.

4. Take the transpose of $\mathbf{C}$ to obtain the matrix $\mathbf{C}^T$.

5. Scale the matrix $\mathbf{C}^T$ by $1/\det \mathbf{A}$ to obtain the inverse of $\mathbf{A}$:

$$\mathbf{A}^{-1} = \frac{1}{\det \mathbf{A}} \mathbf{C}^T. \tag{63}$$

Note that given a square matrix $\mathbf{A}$, the matrix $\mathbf{C}^T$ is sometimes called the **adjugate matrix** of $\mathbf{A}$, represented by $\operatorname{adj} \mathbf{A}$. For that reason you will sometimes see the inverse of $\mathbf{A}$ written (elsewhere) as $\mathbf{A}^{-1} = \operatorname{adj} \mathbf{A}/\det \mathbf{A}$.

Example 20

Use Procedure 1 to derive the inverse of a 2×2 matrix, given in equation (52).

Solution

For a general 2×2 matrix $\mathbf{A} = \begin{bmatrix} a & b \\ c & d \end{bmatrix}$, the minors are

$$M_{11} = d, \quad M_{12} = c, \quad M_{21} = b, \quad M_{22} = a.$$

Hence the matrix of the cofactors is

$$\mathbf{C} = \begin{bmatrix} d & -c \\ -b & a \end{bmatrix},$$

and its transpose is

$$\mathbf{C}^T = \begin{bmatrix} d & -b \\ -c & a \end{bmatrix}.$$

The determinant of $\mathbf{A}$ is $\det \mathbf{A} = ad - bc$, so the inverse of $\mathbf{A}$ is

$$\mathbf{A}^{-1} = \frac{1}{\det \mathbf{A}} \mathbf{C}^T = \frac{1}{ad - bc} \begin{bmatrix} d & -b \\ -c & a \end{bmatrix},$$

in agreement with equation (52).

Example 21

In Example 18 we showed that the matrix

$$\mathbf{A} = \begin{bmatrix} 2 & 2 & -1 \\ 3 & 5 & 1 \\ 1 & 2 & 1 \end{bmatrix}$$

has $\det \mathbf{A} = 1$, so it is an invertible matrix. Find $\mathbf{A}^{-1}$.

Solution

The cofactors of $\mathbf{A}$ are

$$C_{11} = + \begin{vmatrix} 5 & 1 \\ 2 & 1 \end{vmatrix} = 3, \qquad C_{12} = - \begin{vmatrix} 3 & 1 \\ 1 & 1 \end{vmatrix} = -2, \qquad C_{13} = + \begin{vmatrix} 3 & 5 \\ 1 & 2 \end{vmatrix} = 1,$$

$$C_{21} = - \begin{vmatrix} 2 & -1 \\ 2 & 1 \end{vmatrix} = -4, \quad C_{22} = + \begin{vmatrix} 2 & -1 \\ 1 & 1 \end{vmatrix} = 3, \qquad C_{23} = - \begin{vmatrix} 2 & 2 \\ 1 & 2 \end{vmatrix} = -2,$$

$$C_{31} = + \begin{vmatrix} 2 & -1 \\ 5 & 1 \end{vmatrix} = 7, \qquad C_{32} = - \begin{vmatrix} 2 & -1 \\ 3 & 1 \end{vmatrix} = -5, \quad C_{33} = + \begin{vmatrix} 2 & 2 \\ 3 & 5 \end{vmatrix} = 4.$$

Thus the matrix of cofactors is

$$\mathbf{C} = [C_{ij}] = \begin{bmatrix} 3 & -2 & 1 \\ -4 & 3 & -2 \\ 7 & -5 & 4 \end{bmatrix}.$$

Since we already know that in this case $\det \mathbf{A} = 1$, it follows from Procedure 1 that

$$\mathbf{A}^{-1} = \mathbf{C}^T = \begin{bmatrix} 3 & -4 & 7 \\ -2 & 3 & -5 \\ 1 & -2 & 4 \end{bmatrix}.$$

Though not required, it is always good practice to confirm the result $\mathbf{A}\mathbf{A}^{-1} = \mathbf{I}$ by explicit matrix multiplication. In this case we get

$$\mathbf{A}\mathbf{A}^{-1} = \begin{bmatrix} 2 & 2 & -1 \\ 3 & 5 & 1 \\ 1 & 2 & 1 \end{bmatrix} \begin{bmatrix} 3 & -4 & 7 \\ -2 & 3 & -5 \\ 1 & -2 & 4 \end{bmatrix} = \begin{bmatrix} 1 & 0 & 0 \\ 0 & 1 & 0 \\ 0 & 0 & 1 \end{bmatrix} = \mathbf{I}.$$

Exercise 43

Find the inverse of the matrix $\mathbf{A}$ of Exercise 40(a), where we showed that $\det \mathbf{A} = 3$.

We should also note the following rules relating to matrices, inverses and determinants.

> **Rules for $n \times n$ matrices, inverses and determinants**
>
> - The matrix $\mathbf{A}$ can be inverted if and only if $\det \mathbf{A} \neq 0$, in which case $\det(\mathbf{A}^{-1}) = 1/\det \mathbf{A}$.
>
> - For two $n \times n$ matrices $\mathbf{A}$ and $\mathbf{B}$, we have $\det(\mathbf{A}\mathbf{B}) = \det \mathbf{A} \det \mathbf{B}$.
>
> - If $\det(\mathbf{A}\mathbf{B}) \neq 0$, so $(\mathbf{A}\mathbf{B})^{-1}$ exists, then $(\mathbf{A}\mathbf{B})^{-1} = \mathbf{B}^{-1}\mathbf{A}^{-1}$.

Note the reversal of order in the last of these rules. This is very similar to the reversal that we saw when expressing the transpose of a product in terms of the product of the transposes.

Learning outcomes

After studying this unit, you should be able to do the following.

- Understand the meaning of the terms scalar, vector, displacement vector, unit vector and position vector, and know what it means to say that two vectors are equal.

- Use vector notation and represent vectors as arrows on diagrams.

- Scale a vector by a scalar, and add two vectors geometrically using the triangle rule.

- Resolve a vector into its Cartesian components, and scale and add vectors given in Cartesian component form.

- Write down the vector equation of a straight line through two given points.

- Calculate the scalar product and vector product of two given vectors.

- Determine whether or not two given vectors are perpendicular or parallel to one another.

- Determine the magnitude of a vector and the angle between the directions of two vectors.

- Resolve a vector in a given direction.

- Use the vector product to determine the area of a parallelogram and the volume of a parallelepiped.

- Understand that a matrix can be used to represent a linear transformation, and know what this means geometrically for a 2×2 matrix.

- Add, subtract and multiply matrices of suitable sizes, and multiply a matrix by a scalar.

- Understand the terms transpose of a matrix, zero matrix, identity matrix, inverse matrix, invertible matrix and non-invertible matrix.

- Evaluate the determinants and inverses of 2×2 and 3×3 matrices, and know how to perform such calculations for $n \times n$ matrices.

- Use the determinant of a matrix to evaluate vector products, areas and volumes.

Solutions to exercises

Solution to Exercise 1

A sketch map is shown below.

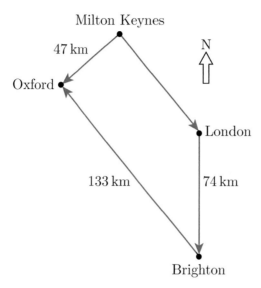

From the map, the approximate distance between Milton Keynes and London is 80 km, and the displacement from Milton Keynes to London is about 80 km South-East. The distance between Milton Keynes and London can be described as the *magnitude* of the displacement from Milton Keynes to London.

Solution to Exercise 2

(a) The equation $\mathbf{h} = 2\mathbf{a} - 3\mathbf{b}$ is interpreted as $\mathbf{h} = 2\mathbf{a} + 3(-\mathbf{b})$, so $\mathbf{h}$ can be represented by the red arrow shown in the figure below.

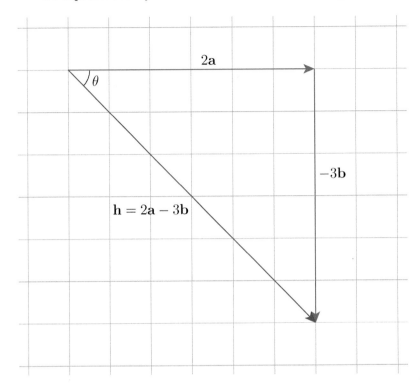

The arrow for $\mathbf{a}$ is 3 units long, and the arrow for $\mathbf{b}$ is 2 units long. So the arrow for $2\mathbf{a}$ is 6 units long, and the arrow for $-3\mathbf{b}$ is 6 units long. These two arrows are perpendicular. The arrow for $\mathbf{h}$ forms the hypotenuse of a right-angled triangle, so we have

$$|\mathbf{h}| = \sqrt{6^2 + 6^2} = 6\sqrt{2}.$$

(b) Let θ be the angle between the directions of $\mathbf{h}$ and $2\mathbf{a}$. Then the diagram shows that $\tan\theta = 6/6 = 1$, so $\theta = \pi/4$ radians.

Solution to Exercise 3

The positive y-axis will be on your left.

Solution to Exercise 4

Systems (b), (c) and (d) are right-handed. System (a) is left-handed.

Solution to Exercise 5

(a) By visual inspection, the vectors are
$$\mathbf{a} = 2\mathbf{i} + \mathbf{j} = (2,1) \quad \text{and} \quad \mathbf{b} = -2\mathbf{i} - 3\mathbf{j} = (-2,-3).$$

(b) Using equation (4), the magnitudes are
$$a = \sqrt{2^2 + 1^2} = \sqrt{5} \quad \text{and} \quad b = \sqrt{(-2)^2 + (-3)^2} = \sqrt{13}.$$

Using equation (5), the angle between $\mathbf{a}$ and the positive x-direction is given by
$$\cos\theta_x = a_x/a = 2/\sqrt{5} = 0.8944 \quad \text{(to 4 d.p.)},$$
so
$$\theta_x = \arccos(0.8944) = 0.464 \text{ radians.}$$

For $\mathbf{b}$, equation (5) gives
$$\cos\theta_x = b_x/b = -2/\sqrt{13} = -0.5547 \quad \text{(to 4 d.p.)},$$
so
$$\theta_x = \arccos(-0.5547) = 2.159 \text{ radians.}$$

Solution to Exercise 6

(a) $|\mathbf{a}| = \sqrt{2^2 + (-1)^2} = \sqrt{5}$,

$|\mathbf{b}| = \sqrt{1^2 + 3^2 + 5^2} = \sqrt{35}$.

(b) We have
$$\theta_x = \arccos\left(\frac{a_x}{a}\right) = \arccos\left(\frac{2}{\sqrt{5}}\right) = 0.4636 \text{ radians,}$$
$$\theta_y = \arccos\left(\frac{a_y}{a}\right) = \arccos\left(\frac{-1}{\sqrt{5}}\right) = 2.0344 \text{ radians,}$$
$$\theta_z = \arccos\left(\frac{a_z}{a}\right) = \arccos\left(\frac{0}{\sqrt{5}}\right) = \pi/2 \text{ radians.}$$

So $\mathbf{a}$ lies in the xy-plane, between the positive x-axis and the negative y-axis.

(c) $\mathbf{a} + \mathbf{b} = 3\mathbf{i} + 2\mathbf{j} + 5\mathbf{k}$,

$2\mathbf{a} - \mathbf{b} = 3\mathbf{i} - 5\mathbf{j} - 5\mathbf{k}$,

$\mathbf{c} + 2\mathbf{b} - 3\mathbf{a} = -4\mathbf{i} + 10\mathbf{j} + 8\mathbf{k}$.

(d) We have $\overrightarrow{PQ} = 2\mathbf{a} - \mathbf{b} = 3\mathbf{i} - 5\mathbf{j} - 5\mathbf{k}$. The point Q has the position vector $\overrightarrow{OQ}$, which is given by
$$\begin{aligned} \overrightarrow{OQ} &= \overrightarrow{OP} + \overrightarrow{PQ} \\ &= (2\mathbf{j} + 3\mathbf{k}) + (3\mathbf{i} - 5\mathbf{j} - 5\mathbf{k}) \\ &= 3\mathbf{i} - 3\mathbf{j} - 2\mathbf{k}, \end{aligned}$$
so Q is the point $(3, -3, -2)$.

(e) We have $\vec{RS} = \mathbf{a} + 2\mathbf{b} = 4\mathbf{i} + 5\mathbf{j} + 10\mathbf{k}$. The point S has the position vector $\vec{OS}$, which is given by

$$\vec{OS} = \vec{OR} + \vec{RS}$$
$$= (\mathbf{i} + \mathbf{j}) + (4\mathbf{i} + 5\mathbf{j} + 10\mathbf{k})$$
$$= 5\mathbf{i} + 6\mathbf{j} + 10\mathbf{k},$$

so S is the point $(5, 6, 10)$.

Solution to Exercise 7

The magnitude of any vector is given by the positive square root of the sum of the squares of its components. In the case of the unit vector $\widehat{\mathbf{a}}$, it follows that the magnitude is

$$\widehat{a} = \sqrt{\left(\frac{a_x}{a}\right)^2 + \left(\frac{a_y}{a}\right)^2 + \left(\frac{a_z}{a}\right)^2},$$

that is,

$$\widehat{a} = \frac{\sqrt{a_x^2 + a_y^2 + a_z^2}}{a} = \frac{a}{a} = 1,$$

as required.

Solution to Exercise 8

Relative to the origin of the Cartesian coordinate system, the two points have position vectors $\mathbf{i} + \mathbf{j} + 2\mathbf{k}$ and $2\mathbf{i} + 3\mathbf{j} + \mathbf{k}$. Thus the vector equation of the line is

$$\mathbf{r}(t) = (1 - t)(\mathbf{i} + \mathbf{j} + 2\mathbf{k}) + t(2\mathbf{i} + 3\mathbf{j} + \mathbf{k})$$
$$= (1 + t)\mathbf{i} + (1 + 2t)\mathbf{j} + (2 - t)\mathbf{k},$$

where $-\infty < t < \infty$.

Solution to Exercise 9

The acceleration is given by

$$\mathbf{a}(t) = \dot{\mathbf{v}}(t) = \frac{d}{dt}(6t, 4t^3, -1) = (6, 12t^2, 0).$$

Solution to Exercise 10

$\mathbf{a} \cdot \mathbf{b} = |\mathbf{a}|\,|\mathbf{b}|\cos\theta = 2 \times 4 \times \cos\frac{\pi}{3} = 4,$

$\mathbf{b} \cdot \mathbf{c} = |\mathbf{b}|\,|\mathbf{c}|\cos\theta = 4 \times 1 \times \cos\frac{\pi}{6} = 2\sqrt{3},$

$\mathbf{a} \cdot \mathbf{c} = |\mathbf{a}|\,|\mathbf{c}|\cos\theta = 2 \times 1 \times \cos\left(\frac{\pi}{3} + \frac{\pi}{6}\right) = 2\cos\frac{\pi}{2} = 0,$

$\mathbf{b} \cdot \mathbf{b} = |\mathbf{b}|\,|\mathbf{b}|\cos\theta = 4 \times 4 \times \cos 0 = 16.$

Solution to Exercise 11

(a) $(\mathbf{a}+\mathbf{b})\cdot(\mathbf{a}-\mathbf{b}) = \mathbf{a}\cdot(\mathbf{a}-\mathbf{b})+\mathbf{b}\cdot(\mathbf{a}-\mathbf{b})$
$$= \mathbf{a}\cdot\mathbf{a}-\mathbf{a}\cdot\mathbf{b}+\mathbf{b}\cdot\mathbf{a}-\mathbf{b}\cdot\mathbf{b}$$
$$= \mathbf{a}\cdot\mathbf{a}-\mathbf{a}\cdot\mathbf{b}+\mathbf{a}\cdot\mathbf{b}-\mathbf{b}\cdot\mathbf{b}$$
$$= \mathbf{a}\cdot\mathbf{a}-\mathbf{b}\cdot\mathbf{b}.$$

(b) From equation (17),
$$|\mathbf{a}+\mathbf{b}|^2 = (\mathbf{a}+\mathbf{b})\cdot(\mathbf{a}+\mathbf{b})$$
$$= \mathbf{a}\cdot(\mathbf{a}+\mathbf{b})+\mathbf{b}\cdot(\mathbf{a}+\mathbf{b})$$
$$= \mathbf{a}\cdot\mathbf{a}+\mathbf{a}\cdot\mathbf{b}+\mathbf{b}\cdot\mathbf{a}+\mathbf{b}\cdot\mathbf{b}$$
$$= \mathbf{a}\cdot\mathbf{a}+\mathbf{a}\cdot\mathbf{b}+\mathbf{a}\cdot\mathbf{b}+\mathbf{b}\cdot\mathbf{b}$$
$$= \mathbf{a}\cdot\mathbf{a}+2\mathbf{a}\cdot\mathbf{b}+\mathbf{b}\cdot\mathbf{b}.$$

(c) When $\mathbf{a}$ and $\mathbf{b}$ are antiparallel, the angle between them is $\theta=\pi$, consequently $\cos\theta=-1$ and $\mathbf{a}\cdot\mathbf{b}=-|\mathbf{a}|\,|\mathbf{b}|=-ab$.

Solution to Exercise 12

(a) $\mathbf{a}\cdot\mathbf{b} = (4\times 1)+(1\times -3)+(-5\times 1)=-4.$

The negative sign tells us that the angle between $\mathbf{a}$ and $\mathbf{b}$ is between $\frac{\pi}{2}$ and π radians, i.e. it is an obtuse angle.

(b) No, the scalar product is $\mathbf{c}\cdot\mathbf{d}=9-5+4=8$. Since this is not equal to zero, the pair of vectors fails the test for orthogonality.

Solution to Exercise 13

For orthogonality, we require $(\mathbf{p}+\lambda\mathbf{q})\cdot\mathbf{r}=0$. This condition gives
$$(\mathbf{p}+\lambda\mathbf{q})\cdot\mathbf{r}=(\mathbf{p}\cdot\mathbf{r})+\lambda(\mathbf{q}\cdot\mathbf{r})=0.$$
We have
$$\mathbf{p}\cdot\mathbf{r}=(3\mathbf{i}+2\mathbf{j}-\mathbf{k})\cdot(2\mathbf{i}-\mathbf{j}-\mathbf{k})=6-2+1=5$$
and
$$\mathbf{q}\cdot\mathbf{r}=(-\mathbf{i}+\mathbf{j}+2\mathbf{k})\cdot(2\mathbf{i}-\mathbf{j}-\mathbf{k})=-2-1-2=-5,$$
so $(\mathbf{p}+\lambda\mathbf{q})\cdot\mathbf{r}=5-5\lambda=0$, hence $\lambda=1$.

Solution to Exercise 14

(a) $\mathbf{a}\cdot\mathbf{c}=-2-3+3=-2$, $\mathbf{a}\cdot\mathbf{d}=-4+0+1=-3$ and $\mathbf{a}\cdot\mathbf{e}=-2+3-1=0$. Thus only $\mathbf{e}$ is perpendicular to $\mathbf{a}$.

(b) We have
$$\mathbf{a}+2\mathbf{b}=\mathbf{j}+9\mathbf{k}.$$

The displacement from the origin to the point $(1,1,1)$ is represented by the position vector $\mathbf{r}=\mathbf{i}+\mathbf{j}+\mathbf{k}$. The corresponding unit vector is $\widehat{\mathbf{r}}=\frac{1}{\sqrt{3}}(\mathbf{i}+\mathbf{j}+\mathbf{k})$. The component of $\mathbf{a}+2\mathbf{b}$ in the direction of the specified displacement is therefore
$$\widehat{\mathbf{r}}\cdot(\mathbf{a}+2\mathbf{b})=\frac{1}{\sqrt{3}}(\mathbf{i}+\mathbf{j}+\mathbf{k})\cdot(\mathbf{j}+9\mathbf{k})=\frac{10}{\sqrt{3}}.$$

(c) First we need to find a unit vector in the direction of the vector $\mathbf{a} - 2\mathbf{b}$. Working in ordered triple notation, $\mathbf{a} - 2\mathbf{b} = (4, -7, -7)$ and its magnitude is $|\mathbf{a} - 2\mathbf{b}| = \sqrt{16 + 49 + 49} = \sqrt{114}$. Consequently, a unit vector in the direction of $\mathbf{a} - 2\mathbf{b}$ is given by $(\mathbf{a} - 2\mathbf{b})/\sqrt{114} = (4, -7, -7)/\sqrt{114}$. So the required component is

$$
\begin{aligned}
(\mathbf{a} + 2\mathbf{b}) \cdot \tfrac{1}{\sqrt{114}}(\mathbf{a} - 2\mathbf{b}) &= (0, 1, 9) \cdot \tfrac{1}{\sqrt{114}}(4, -7, -7) \\
&= \tfrac{-70}{\sqrt{114}} \\
&= -6.56 \quad \text{(to 2 d.p.)}.
\end{aligned}
$$

Solution to Exercise 15

Since $\mathbf{v}$ has magnitude 4, and makes an angle of $2\pi/3$ with the *positive* x-axis, its component along the $\mathbf{i}$-direction is

$$
\mathbf{v} \cdot \mathbf{i} = |\mathbf{v}|\,|\mathbf{i}| \cos(2\pi/3) = -\frac{4}{2} = -2.
$$

Since $\mathbf{v}$ makes an angle of $\pi/6$ with the *positive* y-axis, its component along the $\mathbf{j}$-direction is

$$
\mathbf{v} \cdot \mathbf{j} = |\mathbf{v}|\,|\mathbf{j}| \cos(\pi/6) = 4\frac{\sqrt{3}}{2} = 2\sqrt{3}.
$$

Hence we can write $\mathbf{v}$ as

$$
\mathbf{v} = -2\mathbf{i} + 2\sqrt{3}\,\mathbf{j}.
$$

Solution to Exercise 16

Since $\widehat{\mathbf{u}}$, $\widehat{\mathbf{v}}$ and $\widehat{\mathbf{w}}$ are mutually perpendicular unit vectors, we can write

$$
\mathbf{a} = a_u\widehat{\mathbf{u}} + a_v\widehat{\mathbf{v}} + a_w\widehat{\mathbf{w}},
$$

where a_u, a_v and a_w are the components of $\mathbf{a}$ along the $\widehat{\mathbf{u}}$, $\widehat{\mathbf{v}}$ and $\widehat{\mathbf{w}}$ directions, respectively. Hence

$$
\begin{aligned}
a_u = \mathbf{a} \cdot \widehat{\mathbf{u}} &= \frac{1}{\sqrt{2}}(2, 1, 0) \cdot (1, 0, 1) = \frac{2}{\sqrt{2}} = \sqrt{2}, \\
a_v = \mathbf{a} \cdot \widehat{\mathbf{v}} &= \frac{1}{\sqrt{2}}(2, 1, 0) \cdot (1, 0, -1) = \frac{2}{\sqrt{2}} = \sqrt{2}, \\
a_w = \mathbf{a} \cdot \widehat{\mathbf{w}} &= (2, 1, 0) \cdot (0, 1, 0) = 1.
\end{aligned}
$$

So

$$
\mathbf{a} = \sqrt{2}\,\widehat{\mathbf{u}} + \sqrt{2}\,\widehat{\mathbf{v}} + \widehat{\mathbf{w}}.
$$

We can check that this solution is correct by substituting in the numerical values for $\widehat{\mathbf{u}}$, $\widehat{\mathbf{v}}$ and $\widehat{\mathbf{w}}$:

$$
\mathbf{a} = \sqrt{2}\frac{1}{\sqrt{2}}(1, 0, 1) + \sqrt{2}\frac{1}{\sqrt{2}}(1, 0, -1) + (0, 1, 0) = (2, 1, 0),
$$

as required.

Solution to Exercise 17

(a) Since $\mathbf{a} \times \mathbf{b} = -\mathbf{b} \times \mathbf{a}$ for any vectors $\mathbf{a}$ and $\mathbf{b}$, we have
$$\mathbf{j} \times \mathbf{i} = -\mathbf{k}, \quad \mathbf{k} \times \mathbf{j} = -\mathbf{i} \quad \text{and} \quad \mathbf{i} \times \mathbf{k} = -\mathbf{j}.$$

(b) By definition, $\mathbf{a} \times \mathbf{a} = \mathbf{0}$ for any vector $\mathbf{a}$, so we have
$$\mathbf{i} \times \mathbf{i} = \mathbf{j} \times \mathbf{j} = \mathbf{k} \times \mathbf{k} = \mathbf{0}.$$

(c) $\quad (\mathbf{i} \times (\mathbf{i} + \mathbf{k})) - ((\mathbf{i} + \mathbf{j}) \times \mathbf{k})$
$$= ((\mathbf{i} \times \mathbf{i}) + (\mathbf{i} \times \mathbf{k})) - ((\mathbf{i} \times \mathbf{k}) + (\mathbf{j} \times \mathbf{k}))$$
$$= (\mathbf{0} + (-\mathbf{j})) - (-\mathbf{j} + \mathbf{i})$$
$$= -\mathbf{i}.$$

(d) $\quad (\mathbf{i} + \mathbf{k}) \times (\mathbf{i} + \mathbf{j} + \mathbf{k})$
$$= (\mathbf{i} \times (\mathbf{i} + \mathbf{j} + \mathbf{k})) + (\mathbf{k} \times (\mathbf{i} + \mathbf{j} + \mathbf{k}))$$
$$= (\mathbf{0} + \mathbf{k} + (-\mathbf{j})) + (\mathbf{j} + (-\mathbf{i}) + \mathbf{0})$$
$$= -\mathbf{i} + \mathbf{k}.$$

Solution to Exercise 18

Since the origin is one of the three points, the sides of the triangle will be defined by the position vectors of the other two points, that is, by the vectors $\mathbf{r}_1 = (2, 1, 1)$ and $\mathbf{r}_2 = (1, -1, -1)$. The area of the triangle will be half the area of the parallelogram with sides defined by the vectors $\mathbf{r}_1$ and $\mathbf{r}_2$. It therefore follows from the expression for the area of a parallelogram that the area of the triangle is

$$\tfrac{1}{2}|\mathbf{r}_1 \times \mathbf{r}_2| = \tfrac{1}{2}|(2,1,1) \times (1,-1,-1)|$$
$$= \tfrac{1}{2}|(1(-1) - 1(-1), 1(1) - 2(-1), 2(-1) - 1(1))|$$
$$= \tfrac{1}{2}|(0, 3, -3)|$$
$$= \tfrac{1}{2}\sqrt{3^2 + (-3)^2} = \tfrac{1}{2}\sqrt{18} = \frac{3}{\sqrt{2}}.$$

Solution to Exercise 19

Since the origin is one of the corners, two adjoining sides of the parallelogram will be defined by the position vectors $\mathbf{r}_1 = (a, b, 0)$ and $\mathbf{r}_2 = (c, d, 0)$. Using the vector product method, the area of this parallelogram is

$$|\mathbf{r}_1 \times \mathbf{r}_2| = |(a, b, 0) \times (c, d, 0)|$$
$$= |(b(0) - 0(d), 0(c) - a(0), a(d) - b(c))|$$
$$= |(0, 0, ad - bc)|$$
$$= |ad - bc|.$$

If $b = c = 0$, then the corners are $(0, 0, 0)$, $(a, 0, 0)$, $(0, d, 0)$ and $(a, d, 0)$, so the parallelogram is a rectangle. The above formula for the area becomes $|ad|$, which is as expected.

Solution to Exercise 20

Given that both $\mathbf{a} \times \mathbf{b}$ and $\mathbf{c}$ are non-zero, $(\mathbf{a} \times \mathbf{b}) \times \mathbf{c} = \mathbf{0}$ implies that the angle between the direction of $\mathbf{a} \times \mathbf{b}$ and the direction of $\mathbf{c}$ must be 0 or π radians (so that its sine is zero). However, $\mathbf{a} \times \mathbf{b}$ is always perpendicular to the plane containing $\mathbf{a}$ and $\mathbf{b}$, so we can say that $\mathbf{c}$, which is parallel or antiparallel to $\mathbf{a} \times \mathbf{b}$, must also be perpendicular to the plane containing $\mathbf{a}$ and $\mathbf{b}$.

Solution to Exercise 21

(a) is 2×2 – a square matrix.

(b) is 3×3 – a square matrix.

(c) is 1×2 – a row matrix.

(d) is 3×1 – a column matrix.

Solution to Exercise 22

(a) $\mathbf{A} \begin{bmatrix} 3 \\ 1 \end{bmatrix} = \begin{bmatrix} 1 & 2 \\ 3 & 4 \end{bmatrix} \begin{bmatrix} 3 \\ 1 \end{bmatrix} = \begin{bmatrix} 5 \\ 13 \end{bmatrix}.$

(b) $\mathbf{A} \begin{bmatrix} -1 \\ 1 \end{bmatrix} = \begin{bmatrix} 1 & 2 \\ 3 & 4 \end{bmatrix} \begin{bmatrix} -1 \\ 1 \end{bmatrix} = \begin{bmatrix} 1 \\ 1 \end{bmatrix}.$

(c) $\mathbf{A} \begin{bmatrix} 0 \\ 0 \end{bmatrix} = \begin{bmatrix} 1 & 2 \\ 3 & 4 \end{bmatrix} \begin{bmatrix} 0 \\ 0 \end{bmatrix} = \begin{bmatrix} 0 \\ 0 \end{bmatrix}.$

Solution to Exercise 23

(a) Either by examining the columns of $\mathbf{D}$, or by multiplying $\begin{bmatrix} 1 \\ 0 \end{bmatrix}$ and $\begin{bmatrix} 0 \\ 1 \end{bmatrix}$ by $\mathbf{D}$, we see that $(1, 0)$ is mapped to $(3, 0)$, and $(0, 1)$ is mapped to $(0, 2)$.

(b) $\mathbf{D} \begin{bmatrix} 3 \\ -2 \end{bmatrix} = \begin{bmatrix} 3 & 0 \\ 0 & 2 \end{bmatrix} \begin{bmatrix} 3 \\ -2 \end{bmatrix} = \begin{bmatrix} 9 \\ -4 \end{bmatrix},$

so $(3, -2)$ is mapped to $(9, -4)$.

(c) The transformation rescales the sides of a unit square in proportion to the rescaling of the unit vectors. Since $(1, 0)$ is mapped to $(3, 0)$, and $(0, 1)$ is mapped to $(0, 2)$, the area of the unit square will be enlarged from $1 \times 1 = 1$ to $3 \times 2 = 6$.

Solution to Exercise 24

(a) With $\alpha = \frac{\pi}{4}$, the required rotation matrix is

$$\mathbf{R}(\tfrac{\pi}{4}) = \begin{bmatrix} \frac{1}{\sqrt{2}} & -\frac{1}{\sqrt{2}} \\ \frac{1}{\sqrt{2}} & \frac{1}{\sqrt{2}} \end{bmatrix}.$$

(b) From the columns of $\mathbf{R}(\frac{\pi}{4})$ (or by using matrix multiplication) it can be seen that $(1, 0)$ is mapped to $\left(\frac{1}{\sqrt{2}}, \frac{1}{\sqrt{2}} \right)$, and $(0, 1)$ is mapped to $\left(-\frac{1}{\sqrt{2}}, \frac{1}{\sqrt{2}} \right)$.

(c) $\mathbf{R}(\frac{\pi}{4})\begin{bmatrix} -1 \\ -1 \end{bmatrix} = \begin{bmatrix} \frac{1}{\sqrt{2}} & -\frac{1}{\sqrt{2}} \\ \frac{1}{\sqrt{2}} & \frac{1}{\sqrt{2}} \end{bmatrix}\begin{bmatrix} -1 \\ -1 \end{bmatrix} = \begin{bmatrix} 0 \\ -\frac{2}{\sqrt{2}} \end{bmatrix} = \begin{bmatrix} 0 \\ -\sqrt{2} \end{bmatrix},$

so $(-1, -1)$ is mapped to $(0, -\sqrt{2})$.

(d) $(1, 0)$ is mapped to $\left(\frac{1}{\sqrt{2}}, \frac{1}{\sqrt{2}}\right)$, and $(0, 1)$ is mapped to $\left(-\frac{1}{\sqrt{2}}, \frac{1}{\sqrt{2}}\right)$.

However, $\left(\frac{1}{\sqrt{2}}, \frac{1}{\sqrt{2}}\right)$ and $\left(-\frac{1}{\sqrt{2}}, \frac{1}{\sqrt{2}}\right)$ are also unit vectors. So the unit vectors are mapped to unit vectors, and a unit square remains a unit square. So the area of a unit square is not changed by the transformation. (This is actually a general feature of rotations, not restricted to the case $\alpha = \frac{\pi}{4}$.)

Solution to Exercise 25

$\mathbf{D}(\kappa, \lambda) = \mathbf{I}$ when $\kappa = 1$ and $\lambda = 1$.

$\mathbf{R}(\alpha) = \mathbf{I}$ when α is zero or any even multiple of π, i.e. $\alpha = 2n\pi$, where n is any integer.

Solution to Exercise 26

(a) $3\begin{bmatrix} 1 \\ 0 \end{bmatrix} - 2\begin{bmatrix} 0 \\ 1 \end{bmatrix} = \begin{bmatrix} 3 \\ -2 \end{bmatrix}.$

(b) $4\left(\begin{bmatrix} 1 \\ 1 \end{bmatrix} - 3\begin{bmatrix} 1 \\ -1 \end{bmatrix}\right) = \begin{bmatrix} -8 \\ 16 \end{bmatrix}.$

(c) $2\begin{bmatrix} 1 & 0 \\ -2 & 3 \end{bmatrix} = \begin{bmatrix} 2 & 0 \\ -4 & 6 \end{bmatrix}.$

(d) $2\left(\begin{bmatrix} 1 & 0 \\ -2 & 3 \end{bmatrix} + 2\begin{bmatrix} 0 & 1 \\ -1 & 0 \end{bmatrix}\right) = \begin{bmatrix} 2 & 4 \\ -8 & 6 \end{bmatrix}.$

(e) $2\left(\begin{bmatrix} a & b \\ c & d \end{bmatrix} + 2\begin{bmatrix} a & 2b \\ -2c & d \end{bmatrix}\right) = \begin{bmatrix} 6a & 10b \\ -6c & 6d \end{bmatrix}.$

Solution to Exercise 27

(a) $\begin{bmatrix} 2 & 0 \\ 1 & 1 \end{bmatrix}\begin{bmatrix} 0 & 3 \\ 1 & 1 \end{bmatrix} = \begin{bmatrix} 2(0) + 0(1) & 2(3) + 0(1) \\ 1(0) + 1(1) & 1(3) + 1(1) \end{bmatrix} = \begin{bmatrix} 0 & 6 \\ 1 & 4 \end{bmatrix}.$

(b) $\begin{bmatrix} 1 & 2 \\ 2 & -3 \end{bmatrix}\begin{bmatrix} 1 & 3 \\ 2 & -1 \end{bmatrix} = \begin{bmatrix} 1(1) + 2(2) & 1(3) + 2(-1) \\ 2(1) - 3(2) & 2(3) - 3(-1) \end{bmatrix} = \begin{bmatrix} 5 & 1 \\ -4 & 9 \end{bmatrix}.$

(c) $\begin{bmatrix} 1 & 3 \\ 2 & -1 \end{bmatrix}\begin{bmatrix} 1 & 2 \\ 2 & -3 \end{bmatrix} = \begin{bmatrix} 1(1) + 3(2) & 1(2) + 3(-3) \\ 2(1) - 1(2) & 2(2) - 1(-3) \end{bmatrix} = \begin{bmatrix} 7 & -7 \\ 0 & 7 \end{bmatrix}.$

The solutions to parts (b) and (c) show that the two matrices do not commute.

Solution to Exercise 28

The required matrix is given by the matrix product $\mathbf{C} = \mathbf{R}\left(\frac{\pi}{4}\right)\mathbf{D}(2,1)$.
Recalling that $\sin\frac{\pi}{4} = \cos\frac{\pi}{4} = \frac{1}{\sqrt{2}}$, we have

$$\mathbf{C} = \begin{bmatrix} \frac{1}{\sqrt{2}} & -\frac{1}{\sqrt{2}} \\ \frac{1}{\sqrt{2}} & \frac{1}{\sqrt{2}} \end{bmatrix}\begin{bmatrix} 2 & 0 \\ 0 & 1 \end{bmatrix} = \begin{bmatrix} \frac{1}{\sqrt{2}}(2) - \frac{1}{\sqrt{2}}(0) & \frac{1}{\sqrt{2}}(0) - \frac{1}{\sqrt{2}}(1) \\ \frac{1}{\sqrt{2}}(2) + \frac{1}{\sqrt{2}}(0) & \frac{1}{\sqrt{2}}(0) + \frac{1}{\sqrt{2}}(1) \end{bmatrix}$$

$$= \begin{bmatrix} 2\frac{1}{\sqrt{2}} & -\frac{1}{\sqrt{2}} \\ 2\frac{1}{\sqrt{2}} & \frac{1}{\sqrt{2}} \end{bmatrix}.$$

Solution to Exercise 29

$$\mathbf{F} = \begin{bmatrix} 2 & 0 \\ 0 & 1 \end{bmatrix}\begin{bmatrix} \frac{1}{\sqrt{2}} & -\frac{1}{\sqrt{2}} \\ \frac{1}{\sqrt{2}} & \frac{1}{\sqrt{2}} \end{bmatrix} = \begin{bmatrix} 2\left(\frac{1}{\sqrt{2}}\right) + 0\left(\frac{1}{\sqrt{2}}\right) & 2\left(-\frac{1}{\sqrt{2}}\right) + 0\left(\frac{1}{\sqrt{2}}\right) \\ 0\left(\frac{1}{\sqrt{2}}\right) + 1\left(\frac{1}{\sqrt{2}}\right) & 0\left(-\frac{1}{\sqrt{2}}\right) + 1\left(\frac{1}{\sqrt{2}}\right) \end{bmatrix}$$

$$= \begin{bmatrix} 2\frac{1}{\sqrt{2}} & -2\frac{1}{\sqrt{2}} \\ \frac{1}{\sqrt{2}} & \frac{1}{\sqrt{2}} \end{bmatrix}.$$

$\mathbf{F}$ clearly differs from $\mathbf{C}$.

Solution to Exercise 30

We have

$$\mathbf{R}(\alpha)\,\mathbf{R}(\beta) = \begin{bmatrix} \cos\alpha & -\sin\alpha \\ \sin\alpha & \cos\alpha \end{bmatrix}\begin{bmatrix} \cos\beta & -\sin\beta \\ \sin\beta & \cos\beta \end{bmatrix}$$

$$= \begin{bmatrix} \cos\alpha\cos\beta - \sin\alpha\sin\beta & -\cos\alpha\sin\beta - \sin\alpha\cos\beta \\ \sin\alpha\cos\beta + \cos\alpha\sin\beta & -\sin\alpha\sin\beta + \cos\alpha\cos\beta \end{bmatrix}.$$

Now use the trigonometric identities

$$\cos\alpha\cos\beta \pm \sin\alpha\sin\beta = \cos(\alpha \mp \beta),$$
$$\sin\alpha\cos\beta \pm \cos\alpha\sin\beta = \sin(\alpha \pm \beta)$$

to get

$$\mathbf{R}(\alpha)\,\mathbf{R}(\beta) = \begin{bmatrix} \cos(\alpha+\beta) & -\sin(\alpha+\beta) \\ \sin(\alpha+\beta) & \cos(\alpha+\beta) \end{bmatrix}.$$

But the right-hand side of this equation is just the matrix $\mathbf{R}(\alpha+\beta)$.

Hence we have shown that

$$\mathbf{R}(\alpha)\,\mathbf{R}(\beta) = \mathbf{R}(\alpha+\beta).$$

Now we can either calculate $\mathbf{R}(\beta)\,\mathbf{R}(\alpha)$, and show explicitly that $\mathbf{R}(\alpha)\,\mathbf{R}(\beta) = \mathbf{R}(\beta)\,\mathbf{R}(\alpha)$, or we can save ourselves some work by noticing that

$$\mathbf{R}(\alpha)\,\mathbf{R}(\beta) = \mathbf{R}(\alpha+\beta) = \mathbf{R}(\beta+\alpha) = \mathbf{R}(\beta)\,\mathbf{R}(\alpha).$$

So $\mathbf{R}(\alpha)$ and $\mathbf{R}(\beta)$ commute, as expected on geometric grounds.

Solution to Exercise 31

Remembering that $\cos(-\alpha) = \cos(\alpha)$ and $\sin(-\alpha) = -\sin(\alpha)$, we have

$$\mathbf{R}(\alpha)\,\mathbf{R}(-\alpha) = \begin{bmatrix} \cos\alpha & -\sin\alpha \\ \sin\alpha & \cos\alpha \end{bmatrix} \begin{bmatrix} \cos(-\alpha) & -\sin(-\alpha) \\ \sin(-\alpha) & \cos(-\alpha) \end{bmatrix}$$

$$= \begin{bmatrix} \cos\alpha & -\sin\alpha \\ \sin\alpha & \cos\alpha \end{bmatrix} \begin{bmatrix} \cos\alpha & \sin\alpha \\ -\sin\alpha & \cos\alpha \end{bmatrix}$$

$$= \begin{bmatrix} \cos^2\alpha + \sin^2\alpha & 0 \\ 0 & \cos^2\alpha + \sin^2\alpha \end{bmatrix}$$

$$= \begin{bmatrix} 1 & 0 \\ 0 & 1 \end{bmatrix} = \mathbf{I}.$$

Similarly,

$$\mathbf{R}(-\alpha)\,\mathbf{R}(\alpha) = \begin{bmatrix} \cos(-\alpha) & -\sin(-\alpha) \\ \sin(-\alpha) & \cos(-\alpha) \end{bmatrix} \begin{bmatrix} \cos\alpha & -\sin\alpha \\ \sin\alpha & \cos\alpha \end{bmatrix}$$

$$= \begin{bmatrix} \cos\alpha & \sin\alpha \\ -\sin\alpha & \cos\alpha \end{bmatrix} \begin{bmatrix} \cos\alpha & -\sin\alpha \\ \sin\alpha & \cos\alpha \end{bmatrix}$$

$$= \begin{bmatrix} \cos^2\alpha + \sin^2\alpha & 0 \\ 0 & \cos^2\alpha + \sin^2\alpha \end{bmatrix}$$

$$= \begin{bmatrix} 1 & 0 \\ 0 & 1 \end{bmatrix} = \mathbf{I}.$$

So $\mathbf{R}(\alpha)$ is indeed the inverse of $\mathbf{R}(-\alpha)$, as claimed.

In fact, there was an easier way to prove this. From Exercise 30, we know that $\mathbf{R}(\alpha)\,\mathbf{R}(\beta) = \mathbf{R}(\beta)\,\mathbf{R}(\alpha) = \mathbf{R}(\alpha + \beta)$. Furthermore from Exercise 25, we know that $\mathbf{R}(0) = \mathbf{I}$. Hence

$$\mathbf{R}(\alpha)\,\mathbf{R}(-\alpha) = \mathbf{R}(-\alpha)\,\mathbf{R}(\alpha) = \mathbf{R}(\alpha - \alpha) = \mathbf{R}(0) = \mathbf{I}.$$

Solution to Exercise 32

$$\frac{1}{ad-bc} \begin{bmatrix} d & -b \\ -c & a \end{bmatrix} \begin{bmatrix} a & b \\ c & d \end{bmatrix} = \frac{1}{ad-bc} \begin{bmatrix} ad-bc & -ab+ba \\ cd-dc & -cb+da \end{bmatrix}$$

$$= \begin{bmatrix} 1 & 0 \\ 0 & 1 \end{bmatrix}.$$

Solution to Exercise 33

(a) Using the general inversion formula,

$$\mathbf{A}^{-1} = \begin{bmatrix} 1 & -1 \\ 0 & 1 \end{bmatrix},$$

$$\mathbf{B}^{-1} = \begin{bmatrix} 1 & 0 \\ 0 & -1 \end{bmatrix},$$

$$\mathbf{C}^{-1} = \tfrac{1}{2}\begin{bmatrix} 1 & 1 \\ -1 & 1 \end{bmatrix} = \begin{bmatrix} \tfrac{1}{2} & \tfrac{1}{2} \\ -\tfrac{1}{2} & \tfrac{1}{2} \end{bmatrix}.$$

For the matrix $\mathbf{D} = \mathbf{ABC}$, the product of three matrices can be interpreted as $(\mathbf{AB})\mathbf{C}$ or $\mathbf{A}(\mathbf{BC})$ since matrix multiplication is associative. Adopting the first option,

$$\mathbf{D} = \mathbf{ABC} = (\mathbf{AB})\mathbf{C} = \left(\begin{bmatrix} 1 & 1 \\ 0 & 1 \end{bmatrix} \begin{bmatrix} 1 & 0 \\ 0 & -1 \end{bmatrix} \right) \begin{bmatrix} 1 & -1 \\ 1 & 1 \end{bmatrix}$$
$$= \begin{bmatrix} 1 & -1 \\ 0 & -1 \end{bmatrix} \begin{bmatrix} 1 & -1 \\ 1 & 1 \end{bmatrix}$$
$$= \begin{bmatrix} 0 & -2 \\ -1 & -1 \end{bmatrix}.$$

Applying the matrix inversion formula,

$$\mathbf{D}^{-1} = (\mathbf{ABC})^{-1} = -\tfrac{1}{2} \begin{bmatrix} -1 & 2 \\ 1 & 0 \end{bmatrix} = \tfrac{1}{2} \begin{bmatrix} 1 & -2 \\ -1 & 0 \end{bmatrix}.$$

(b) We have

$$\mathbf{B}^{-1}\mathbf{A}^{-1} = \begin{bmatrix} 1 & 0 \\ 0 & -1 \end{bmatrix} \begin{bmatrix} 1 & -1 \\ 0 & 1 \end{bmatrix} = \begin{bmatrix} 1 & -1 \\ 0 & -1 \end{bmatrix},$$

hence

$$\mathbf{C}^{-1}\mathbf{B}^{-1}\mathbf{A}^{-1} = \tfrac{1}{2} \begin{bmatrix} 1 & 1 \\ -1 & 1 \end{bmatrix} \begin{bmatrix} 1 & -1 \\ 0 & -1 \end{bmatrix} = \tfrac{1}{2} \begin{bmatrix} 1 & -2 \\ -1 & 0 \end{bmatrix},$$

which is indeed equal to $\mathbf{D}^{-1} = (\mathbf{ABC})^{-1}$.

Solution to Exercise 34

$\begin{bmatrix} -2 & 4 \\ -1 & 2 \end{bmatrix}$ has no inverse, because its determinant is $-2 \times 2 - (-1 \times 4) = 0$.

In the other three cases, the determinant is not zero, so inverses will exist.

Solution to Exercise 35

$\det \mathbf{A} = 1$, $\det \mathbf{B} = -1$ and $\det \mathbf{C} = 2$.

It was shown in Exercise 33 that

$$\mathbf{ABC} = \begin{bmatrix} 0 & -2 \\ -1 & -1 \end{bmatrix}.$$

Consequently, $\det(\mathbf{ABC}) = -2$.

Thus $\det(\mathbf{ABC}) = \det \mathbf{A} \det \mathbf{B} \det \mathbf{C}$.

You will see later that this is more generally true: the determinant of a product of matrices is always equal to the product of the individual determinants.

Solution to Exercise 36

The columns of $\mathbf{A}$ show the effect that it will have on the Cartesian unit (column) vectors $\mathbf{i}$ and $\mathbf{j}$: they will become the vectors $(1, 3)$ and $(2, 6)$, respectively. These vectors are parallel. Hence $\mathbf{A}$ does indeed transform the unit square to a geometric object with no area, namely to a finite portion of a straight line.

(b) $(\mathbf{A} + \mathbf{B})^T = \left(\begin{bmatrix} 1 & 2 \\ 3 & 4 \\ 5 & 6 \end{bmatrix} + \begin{bmatrix} 2 & 5 \\ -1 & -4 \\ 3 & 1 \end{bmatrix} \right)^T = \begin{bmatrix} 3 & 7 \\ 2 & 0 \\ 8 & 7 \end{bmatrix}^T = \begin{bmatrix} 3 & 2 & 8 \\ 7 & 0 & 7 \end{bmatrix}$

and

$\mathbf{A}^T + \mathbf{B}^T = \begin{bmatrix} 1 & 3 & 5 \\ 2 & 4 & 6 \end{bmatrix} + \begin{bmatrix} 2 & -1 & 3 \\ 5 & -4 & 1 \end{bmatrix} = \begin{bmatrix} 3 & 2 & 8 \\ 7 & 0 & 7 \end{bmatrix}.$

Thus $(\mathbf{A} + \mathbf{B})^T = \mathbf{A}^T + \mathbf{B}^T$.

(c) $(\mathbf{A}\mathbf{C})^T = \left(\begin{bmatrix} 1 & 2 \\ 3 & 4 \\ 5 & 6 \end{bmatrix} \begin{bmatrix} 1 & 0 \\ 2 & 3 \end{bmatrix} \right)^T = \begin{bmatrix} 5 & 6 \\ 11 & 12 \\ 17 & 18 \end{bmatrix}^T = \begin{bmatrix} 5 & 11 & 17 \\ 6 & 12 & 18 \end{bmatrix}$

and

$\mathbf{C}^T \mathbf{A}^T = \begin{bmatrix} 1 & 2 \\ 0 & 3 \end{bmatrix} \begin{bmatrix} 1 & 3 & 5 \\ 2 & 4 & 6 \end{bmatrix} = \begin{bmatrix} 5 & 11 & 17 \\ 6 & 12 & 18 \end{bmatrix}.$

Thus $(\mathbf{A}\mathbf{C})^T = \mathbf{C}^T \mathbf{A}^T$.

Solution to Exercise 40

(a) The determinant of $\mathbf{A} = \begin{bmatrix} 2 & -1 & 2 \\ 5 & 1 & -1 \\ 2 & 1 & -1 \end{bmatrix}$ is

$\det \mathbf{A} = 2 \begin{vmatrix} 1 & -1 \\ 1 & -1 \end{vmatrix} + \begin{vmatrix} 5 & -1 \\ 2 & -1 \end{vmatrix} + 2 \begin{vmatrix} 5 & 1 \\ 2 & 1 \end{vmatrix}$

$= 2 \times (-1 + 1) + (-5 + 2) + 2 \times (5 - 2) = 0 - 3 + 6 = 3.$

(b) The determinant of $\mathbf{B} = \begin{bmatrix} 0 & 2 & -1 \\ 3 & 0 & -1 \\ 2 & -1 & 0 \end{bmatrix}$ is

$\det \mathbf{B} = 0 - 2 \begin{vmatrix} 3 & -1 \\ 2 & 0 \end{vmatrix} - 1 \begin{vmatrix} 3 & 0 \\ 2 & -1 \end{vmatrix}$

$= -2 \times (0 + 2) - 1 \times (-3 - 0) = -4 + 3 = -1.$

Solution to Exercise 41

If we follow the last rule by adding twice the first column to the third, we do not change the determinant but we do obtain a column of zeros. Hence the determinant is zero.

Solution to Exercise 42

(a) We have

$\mathbf{r} \times \mathbf{s} = \begin{vmatrix} \mathbf{i} & \mathbf{j} & \mathbf{k} \\ 2 & 5 & 0 \\ 2 & -1 & 2 \end{vmatrix} = \begin{vmatrix} 5 & 0 \\ -1 & 2 \end{vmatrix} \mathbf{i} - \begin{vmatrix} 2 & 0 \\ 2 & 2 \end{vmatrix} \mathbf{j} + \begin{vmatrix} 2 & 5 \\ 2 & -1 \end{vmatrix} \mathbf{k}$

$= 10\mathbf{i} - 4\mathbf{j} - 12\mathbf{k} = (10, -4, -12).$

(b) The area is given by $|\mathbf{r}_1 \times \mathbf{r}_2|$, where

$$\mathbf{r}_1 \times \mathbf{r}_2 = \begin{vmatrix} \mathbf{i} & \mathbf{j} & \mathbf{k} \\ 1 & 1 & 0 \\ 2 & 2 & -2 \end{vmatrix} = \begin{vmatrix} 1 & 0 \\ 2 & -2 \end{vmatrix} \mathbf{i} - \begin{vmatrix} 1 & 0 \\ 2 & -2 \end{vmatrix} \mathbf{j} + \begin{vmatrix} 1 & 1 \\ 2 & 2 \end{vmatrix} \mathbf{k}$$

$$= -2\mathbf{i} + 2\mathbf{j} = (-2, 2, 0).$$

So, taking the magnitude, the area is

$$|\mathbf{r}_1 \times \mathbf{r}_2| = \sqrt{(-2)^2 + (-2)^2} = \sqrt{8} = 2\sqrt{2}.$$

(c) The volume is given by $|\mathbf{a} \cdot (\mathbf{b} \times \mathbf{c})|$, where the sides may be taken in any order. We have

$$\mathbf{a} \cdot (\mathbf{b} \times \mathbf{c}) = \begin{vmatrix} 2 & 5 & 0 \\ 1 & -2 & 0 \\ 1 & -3 & 2 \end{vmatrix} = 2 \begin{vmatrix} -2 & 0 \\ -3 & 2 \end{vmatrix} - 5 \begin{vmatrix} 1 & 0 \\ 1 & 2 \end{vmatrix} + 0 \begin{vmatrix} 1 & -2 \\ 1 & -3 \end{vmatrix}$$

$$= 2(-4) - 5(2) = -18.$$

So, taking the magnitude, the volume is

$$|\mathbf{a} \cdot (\mathbf{b} \times \mathbf{c})| = 18.$$

Note that the determinant may be obtained more quickly by expanding on the third column rather than the first row, in which case we would get

$$\mathbf{a} \cdot (\mathbf{b} \times \mathbf{c}) = 0 - 0 + 2 \begin{vmatrix} 2 & 5 \\ 1 & -2 \end{vmatrix} = 2(-4 - 5) = -18,$$

as before.

Solution to Exercise 43

The cofactors of $\mathbf{A} = \begin{bmatrix} 2 & -1 & 2 \\ 5 & 1 & -1 \\ 2 & 1 & -1 \end{bmatrix}$ are

$$C_{11} = + \begin{vmatrix} 1 & -1 \\ 1 & -1 \end{vmatrix} = 0, \qquad C_{12} = - \begin{vmatrix} 5 & -1 \\ 2 & -1 \end{vmatrix} = 3, \qquad C_{13} = + \begin{vmatrix} 5 & 1 \\ 2 & 1 \end{vmatrix} = 3,$$

$$C_{21} = - \begin{vmatrix} -1 & 2 \\ 1 & -1 \end{vmatrix} = 1, \qquad C_{22} = + \begin{vmatrix} 2 & 2 \\ 2 & -1 \end{vmatrix} = -6, \qquad C_{23} = - \begin{vmatrix} 2 & -1 \\ 2 & 1 \end{vmatrix} = -4,$$

$$C_{31} = + \begin{vmatrix} -1 & 2 \\ 1 & -1 \end{vmatrix} = -1, \qquad C_{32} = - \begin{vmatrix} 2 & 2 \\ 5 & -1 \end{vmatrix} = 12, \qquad C_{33} = + \begin{vmatrix} 2 & -1 \\ 5 & 1 \end{vmatrix} = 7.$$

Thus

$$\mathbf{C} = \begin{bmatrix} 0 & 3 & 3 \\ 1 & -6 & -4 \\ -1 & 12 & 7 \end{bmatrix} \quad \text{and} \quad \mathbf{C}^T = \begin{bmatrix} 0 & 1 & -1 \\ 3 & -6 & 12 \\ 3 & -4 & 7 \end{bmatrix}.$$

So

$$\mathbf{A}^{-1} = \frac{1}{\det \mathbf{A}} \mathbf{C}^T = \frac{1}{3} \begin{bmatrix} 0 & 1 & -1 \\ 3 & -6 & 12 \\ 3 & -4 & 7 \end{bmatrix}.$$

As usual, you should check that $\mathbf{A}\mathbf{A}^{-1} = \mathbf{I}$ by explicit multiplication.

Acknowledgements

Grateful acknowledgement is made to the following source:

Figure 26: Taken from
https://lhc-div-mms-web.cern.ch/lhc-div-mms/Interconnect.

Every effort has been made to contact copyright holders. If any have been inadvertently overlooked, the publishers will be pleased to make the necessary arrangements at the first opportunity.

Unit 5

Linear algebra

Introduction

Figure 1 shows the network of water pipes connecting the pump and five taps that control the heating system in a (fictional) greenhouse. The engineer who maintains the pump can determine the pressure P at which hot water is supplied to the system, and the tightness T_i ($i = 1, \ldots, 5$) of each tap. He knows from experience that making the system perform as required throughout the day is no easy matter. The effect of each part of the system depends on the rate at which hot water flows through it. Because the system is closed, all the water that flows into any junction must flow out again. As a result, there are only three key rates of flow, namely f_1, f_2 and f_3, that together determine the rate of flow in every part of the system (see Figure 1). However, the equations that relate these flow rates to the supply pressure and tap settings are not simple.

The engineer knows that the system is described by the following simultaneous equations (which you are not expected to derive):

$$T_1 f_1 + T_4 f_1 - T_4 f_2 = P,$$
$$T_2 f_2 + T_5 f_2 - T_5 f_3 - T_4 f_1 + T_4 f_2 = 0,$$
$$T_3 f_3 - T_5 f_2 + T_5 f_3 = 0.$$

These equations can be expressed in terms of matrices as

$$\begin{bmatrix} T_1 + T_4 & -T_4 & 0 \\ -T_4 & T_2 + T_4 + T_5 & -T_5 \\ 0 & -T_5 & T_3 + T_5 \end{bmatrix} \begin{bmatrix} f_1 \\ f_2 \\ f_3 \end{bmatrix} = \begin{bmatrix} P \\ 0 \\ 0 \end{bmatrix}.$$

Solving this matrix equation is typical of the kind of problem that is best treated using the methods of linear algebra.

Linear algebra is a branch of mathematics that grew out of the solution of systems of equations like that given above. The equations are said to be *linear* because the variables of interest, in this case the flow rates f_1, f_2 and f_3, appear only to the first degree in each term; there are no powers of flow rates, such as f_1^2 or f_2^3, nor are there any products of flow rates, such as $f_1 f_2$ or $f_2 f_3$. Although there are several variables, the equations are a generalisation of the kind of *linear* equation that describes a straight line in two-dimensional Cartesian coordinates, $y = mx + c$. This 'linearity' makes the equations well suited to representation by matrices, and once they are in matrix form, solving them is assisted by everything that mathematicians have learned from their studies of matrix algebra and determinants. Linear algebra is the subject that gathers together those insights and methods, and generalises them to create a coherent body of mathematical knowledge rather than an assortment of calculational tricks.

Linear algebra is an important topic in modern mathematics. It can be approached in many different ways, ranging from the very abstract, in which there is little or no mention of linear equations, matrices or determinants, to the very practical, in which there is a concentration on matrix methods and the practicalities of computer-based calculations.

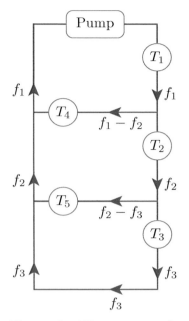

Figure 1 The pump and network of taps that control a hot water heating system

The prefix *eigen* comes from German and indicates 'inherent', as these things are inherent to a matrix.

In this unit we aim to steer a middle course, emphasising the language of matrices and determinants while providing an introduction to those parts of the subject that are most relevant to applications without getting bogged down in calculational details. With this aim in mind, we will concentrate on two important approaches to problem solving that are characteristic of linear algebra. The first is the use of 'row operations', which form the basis of a range of methods for solving systems of linear equations. The second is the subject of 'eigenvalues' and 'eigenvectors', which are numbers and vectors associated with a matrix. As you will see, knowing the eigenvalues and eigenvectors of a matrix can greatly assist the solution of problems involving that matrix.

Study guide

Section 1 shows how to use row operations to solve a system of n simultaneous equations of the form $\mathbf{Ax} = \mathbf{b}$, where $\mathbf{A}$ is a given $n \times n$ matrix, $\mathbf{b}$ is a given column vector with n elements, and we are required to find $\mathbf{x}$, the n-element column vector that represents the solution. The method that we will use is called *Gaussian elimination*.

Section 2 addresses the question of determining the result $\mathbf{x}_k = \mathbf{A}^k\mathbf{x}_0$ of k applications of a square matrix $\mathbf{A}$ to an initial column vector $\mathbf{x}_0$. This leads us to study the equation $\mathbf{Ax} = \lambda\mathbf{x}$, where the scalar λ is called an *eigenvalue* of the matrix $\mathbf{A}$, with $\mathbf{x}$ being the corresponding *eigenvector*.

Section 3 gives the general method for finding eigenvalues and eigenvectors. (This will be of particular use in the next unit.)

In each of Sections 1 and 3, there are procedures for solving problems in linear algebra. Take care that you understand the examples given for these procedures and can do the corresponding exercises; these give a good idea of the assessable learning outcomes of this unit.

Section 4, which is optional, contains some further results concerning the eigenvalues and eigenvectors of *symmetric* matrices.

1 Linear algebra, row operations and Gaussian elimination

1.1 Linear equations and their manipulation

You should already be familiar with the notion of a linear equation as a generalisation of $y = mx + c$, but let us start with a definition so that there can be no doubt.

Linear equation

An equation involving n variables $x_1, x_2, \ldots, x_n$ is said to be **linear** in each of those variables if it can be written in the form

$$a_1 x_1 + a_2 x_2 + a_3 x_3 + \cdots + a_n x_n = d,$$

where $a_1, a_2, \ldots, a_n$ and d are constants.

Example 1

Show that the Cartesian equation of a straight line, $y = mx + c$, is a linear equation by identifying each of the variables and constants.

Solution

The equation can be rewritten in the form $y - mx = c$. If we compare this with the general form of a linear equation of $n = 2$ variables, we can see that the rewritten Cartesian equation is linear if we make the identifications $a_1 = 1$, $x_1 = y$, $a_2 = -m$, $x_2 = x$ and $d = c$.

Exercise 1

The Cartesian equation of a plane that passes through the origin of a three-dimensional system of coordinates is $ax + by + cz = 0$, where a, b and c are constants. Is this equation linear in the variables x, y and z? Justify your answer.

A very simple system of linear equations to solve would consist of the two equations

$$3x + 2y = 8,$$
$$x - y = 1.$$

In order to solve them, we should try to isolate one of the variables, x or y. In this case that can easily be done by adding twice the second equation to the first. This eliminates y and produces the equation

$$5x = 10,$$

implying that $x = 2$. Substituting this back into either of the original equations immediately shows that $y = 1$.

What follows will not always be so easy, but much of this first section will essentially be a systematic elaboration of the manipulation that has just been carried out.

Consider first a system of three simultaneous linear equations, (E_1), (E_2) and (E_3):

$$x_1 - 4x_2 + 2x_3 = -9, \qquad (E_1)$$
$$3x_1 - 2x_2 + 3x_3 = 7, \qquad (E_2)$$
$$8x_1 - 2x_2 + 9x_3 = 34, \qquad (E_3)$$

with three unknowns, x_1, x_2 and x_3.

We may obtain a system of two simultaneous equations, for x_2 and x_3, by subtracting suitable multiples of (E_1) from (E_2) and (E_3). In this example, we may subtract 3 times (E_1) from (E_2), to obtain

$$10x_2 - 3x_3 = 34. \qquad (E_{2a}) = (E_2) - 3(E_1)$$

(Note that we have shown on the right the manipulations required to obtain the equation on the left.) We may also subtract 8 times (E_1) from (E_3), to obtain

$$30x_2 - 7x_3 = 106. \qquad (E_{3a}) = (E_3) - 8(E_1)$$

So now we have two simultaneous equations, neither of which involves x_1.

Next we may subtract 3 times (E_{2a}) from (E_{3a}), to obtain

$$2x_3 = 4, \qquad (E_{3b}) = (E_{3a}) - 3(E_{2a})$$

which tells us that $x_3 = 4/2 = 2$. Substituting this result back into (E_{2a}) tells us that $x_2 = (3x_3 + 34)/10 = 4$, and substituting the values for x_3 and x_2 back into (E_1) tells us that $x_1 = 4x_2 - 2x_3 - 9 = 3$. So the complete solution of the system is $x_1 = 3$, $x_2 = 4$, $x_3 = 2$.

Next we examine a convenient way to represent this process, using matrix notation.

1.2   The augmented matrix and row operations

Given a set of linear equations, the first thing to do is write them in a standard way, with the constants on the right and the three variable terms on the left. Equations (E_1), (E_2) and (E_3) above are written in this way. Notice how the variable terms in x_1, x_2 and x_3 are lined up in separate vertical columns. If there are any missing terms (where the coefficient is zero), leave a gap in the column. The form of equations (E_1), (E_2) and (E_3) immediately suggests that they can be expressed as a single matrix equation

$$\begin{bmatrix} 1 & -4 & 2 \\ 3 & -2 & 3 \\ 8 & -2 & 9 \end{bmatrix} \begin{bmatrix} x_1 \\ x_2 \\ x_3 \end{bmatrix} = \begin{bmatrix} -9 \\ 7 \\ 34 \end{bmatrix}. \tag{1}$$

The correctness of this suggestion can be confirmed by working out the matrix multiplication on the left-hand side. This gives

$$\begin{bmatrix} x_1 - 4x_2 + 2x_3 \\ 3x_1 - 2x_2 + 3x_3 \\ 8x_1 - 2x_2 + 9x_3 \end{bmatrix} = \begin{bmatrix} -9 \\ 7 \\ 34 \end{bmatrix}.$$

The matrix on the left can equal the matrix on the right only if corresponding elements are equal, which gives the three equations (E_1), (E_2) and (E_3).

We can represent the matrix equation (1) symbolically by

$$\mathbf{Ax} = \mathbf{b}, \quad \text{where } \mathbf{A} = \begin{bmatrix} 1 & -4 & 2 \\ 3 & -2 & 3 \\ 8 & -2 & 9 \end{bmatrix}, \quad \mathbf{x} = \begin{bmatrix} x_1 \\ x_2 \\ x_3 \end{bmatrix} \text{ and } \mathbf{b} = \begin{bmatrix} -9 \\ 7 \\ 34 \end{bmatrix}.$$

Remember that the emboldening of printed symbols, such as $\mathbf{A}$, $\mathbf{x}$, $\mathbf{b}$, can be indicated in handwritten work by using an underline, as in $\underline{A}$, $\underline{x}$, $\underline{b}$. It is particularly important to remember this when using a symbol to represent a vector quantity.

Any system of linear equations may be represented in a similar way, even if some initial rearrangement is needed to achieve the required layout. Once the equations have been expressed in matrix form it is conventional to call $\mathbf{A}$ the **coefficient matrix**, $\mathbf{x}$ the **unknown vector**, and $\mathbf{b}$ the **right-hand-side vector** or sometimes the **constant vector** since it represents the terms that are independent of the variables.

Exercise 2

Write each of the following systems in the matrix form $\mathbf{Ax} = \mathbf{b}$.

(a) $x_1 + x_2 - x_3 = 2,$
$5x_1 + 2x_2 + 2x_3 = 20,$
$4x_1 - 2x_2 - 3x_3 = 15.$

(b) $-2 + x_2 - x_3 = -x_1,$
$-2x_3 - 2x_2 = 5x_1 - 20,$
$-2x_2 - 3x_3 = 15 - 4x_1.$

(c) $2x + 3y - 4z = 0,$
$2x \qquad + 3z = 3,$
$6y - 2z = 0.$

Using matrix notation, we could represent each of the intermediate stages of the calculation in Subsection 1.1 as a matrix equation. All we would have to do is to change the coefficient matrix and the right-hand-side vector in an appropriate way at each stage. You are welcome to check this for yourself, but doing so is really something of a waste of time since it would involve a lot of repetitive writing that would not achieve anything new. A better approach is to introduce a new 'shorthand' that captures just the essential information and the steps in the calculation. To do this, we introduce a notational device called the **augmented matrix** that combines the elements of the coefficient matrix and the right-hand-side vector. For the matrix equation (1) given above, the augmented matrix is written as

$$\mathbf{A}|\mathbf{b} = \left[\begin{array}{ccc|c} 1 & -4 & 2 & -9 \\ 3 & -2 & 3 & 7 \\ 8 & -2 & 9 & 34 \end{array} \right]$$

Don't look for any deep significance in the augmented matrix. It's not a new 'kind' of matrix, just a useful means of efficiently displaying the crucial information in a system of linear equations. To show how that information changes as the equations are manipulated, it is helpful to label each row. We do this with a bold $\mathbf{R}$ (for row) and a subscript as follows:

$$\mathbf{A}|\mathbf{b} = \begin{bmatrix} 1 & -4 & 2 & | & -9 \\ 3 & -2 & 3 & | & 7 \\ 8 & -2 & 9 & | & 34 \end{bmatrix} \begin{matrix} \mathbf{R}_1 \\ \mathbf{R}_2 \\ \mathbf{R}_3 \end{matrix} .$$

Using these notational devices, we can compactly indicate any step in the manipulation of the simultaneous equations. For instance, suppose that we want to change the second equation by subtracting three times the first equation from it. We can show this using the augmented matrix by doing the following steps.

1. Write down row $\mathbf{R}_1$ unchanged.

2. Indicate the planned change as $\mathbf{R}_2 - 3\mathbf{R}_1$, and write that to the left of the second row.

3. Write the values resulting from the change in the second row.

4. Relabel the second row as $\mathbf{R}_{2a}$.

5. Write down row $\mathbf{R}_3$ unchanged.

So in this particular case we get

$$\mathbf{R}_2 - 3\mathbf{R}_1 \quad \begin{bmatrix} 1 & -4 & 2 & | & -9 \\ 0 & 10 & -3 & | & 34 \\ 8 & -2 & 9 & | & 34 \end{bmatrix} \begin{matrix} \mathbf{R}_1 \\ \mathbf{R}_{2a} \\ \mathbf{R}_3 \end{matrix} .$$

Having just reduced the coefficient of x_1 to 0 in the second row, the next step in solving the simultaneous equations is to make a similar reduction in the third row. This is again achieved by subtracting (or adding) an appropriate multiple of another entire row. In this case we subtract 8 times $\mathbf{R}_1$ from $\mathbf{R}_3$, indicating this as follows:

$$\begin{matrix} \\ \\ \mathbf{R}_3 - 8\mathbf{R}_1 \end{matrix} \begin{bmatrix} 1 & -4 & 2 & | & -9 \\ 0 & 10 & -3 & | & 34 \\ 0 & 30 & -7 & | & 106 \end{bmatrix} \begin{matrix} \mathbf{R}_1 \\ \mathbf{R}_{2a} \\ \mathbf{R}_{3a} \end{matrix} .$$

Here we are again showing the steps that must be taken on the left, the resulting augmented matrix in the middle, and the updated row labels on the right. Our next step is to reduce to zero the coefficient of x_2 in the third row without upsetting the pattern of zeros in the first column. This

Note that we had to subtract a multiple of $\mathbf{R}_{2a}$ here. Had we tried to subtract a multiple of $\mathbf{R}_1$ from $\mathbf{R}_{3a}$, we would have gained an unwanted non-zero entry in the first column of the third row.

is achieved as follows:

$$\mathbf{R}_{3a} - 3\mathbf{R}_{2a} \quad \begin{bmatrix} 1 & -4 & 2 & | & -9 \\ 0 & 10 & -3 & | & 34 \\ 0 & 0 & 2 & | & 4 \end{bmatrix} .$$

Since we have completed all the row operations involved in our particular problem, we have deliberately omitted an updated set of row labels to the right of the final augmented matrix, though we could easily have included them if they were needed.

Note that all the operations that we have recorded on the left have involved subtracting multiples of one row from another row. These are all examples of what are generally referred to as **row operations** on the augmented matrix. The full range of allowable row operations mimics those steps that we might have taken in solving the original system of equations. They can all be built from successive combinations of the following three *elementary row operations*.

Elementary row operations

- Interchange any two complete rows ($\mathbf{R}_i \leftrightarrow \mathbf{R}_j$).

- Multiply each element in a row by the same constant ($\mathbf{R}_i \to \lambda\mathbf{R}_i$).

- Add (or subtract) a constant multiple of one row to (or from) another row ($\mathbf{R}_i \to \mathbf{R}_i \pm \lambda\mathbf{R}_j$).

Note that row operations always involve *entire* rows of the augmented matrix, thus including the entries from the right-hand-side vector as well as those from the coefficient matrix.

The overall effect of the row operations involved in our example has been to produce a triangle of zeros in the bottom left-hand corner of the augmented matrix. If we use that augmented matrix to write down the final set of linear equations in matrix form, we obtain

$$\begin{bmatrix} 1 & -4 & 2 \\ 0 & 10 & -3 \\ 0 & 0 & 2 \end{bmatrix} \begin{bmatrix} x_1 \\ x_2 \\ x_3 \end{bmatrix} = \begin{bmatrix} -9 \\ 34 \\ 4 \end{bmatrix}.$$

The coefficient matrix is now said to be an **upper triangular matrix**, since the only non-zero elements that it contains are on or above the **leading diagonal**, i.e. the diagonal from top left to bottom right, here containing the numbers 1, 10 and 2.

The leading diagonal is sometimes called the *main diagonal*.

Performing the matrix multiplication on the left-hand side gives the linear equations

$$\begin{aligned} x_1 - 4x_2 + 2x_3 &= -9, \\ 10x_2 - 3x_3 &= 34, \\ 2x_3 &= 4. \end{aligned}$$

Note that the upper triangular structure of the coefficient matrix means that each successive equation has one fewer unknown than its predecessor. Thanks to our successive elimination of unknown variables, we can see from the last equation that $x_3 = 2$, and we can substitute that into the equation immediately above it to find that $x_2 = 4$. This procedure is called **back substitution**. Having found the values of x_2 and x_3, we can perform another back substitution to find $x_1 = 3$.

So we have determined our solution $x_1 = 3$, $x_2 = 4$, $x_3 = 2$. However, it is always good practice to check it by writing down the solution in matrix form, and then using matrix multiplication to confirm that it solves the original matrix equation.

In this case $\mathbf{x} = \begin{bmatrix} 3 & 4 & 2 \end{bmatrix}^T$, and we can check its correctness as follows:

$$\begin{bmatrix} 1 & -4 & 2 \\ 3 & -2 & 3 \\ 8 & -2 & 9 \end{bmatrix} \begin{bmatrix} 3 \\ 4 \\ 2 \end{bmatrix} = \begin{bmatrix} 1 \times 3 - 4 \times 4 + 2 \times 2 \\ 3 \times 3 - 2 \times 4 + 3 \times 2 \\ 8 \times 3 - 2 \times 4 + 9 \times 2 \end{bmatrix} = \begin{bmatrix} -9 \\ 7 \\ 34 \end{bmatrix}.$$

So our solution is correct. Even more pleasingly, it has been arrived at in a systematic way that can provide the basis of a general method for solving systems of simultaneous linear equations. This is the subject of the next subsection.

1.3 Gaussian elimination: non-singular cases

The technique that we have just been using is an example of *Gaussian elimination* – a general method for finding the unique solution of a system of linear equations, when such a solution exists. This subsection provides a more formal introduction to that method. As you will soon see, there are cases where no solution exists, other cases where an infinite number of solutions exist, and some cases where the solution is unique but the system of equations must be reformulated before Gaussian elimination can be used to find it. In this subsection and the one that follows, we will use examples and exercises to explore each of these exceptional cases, but first we set out a general procedure that is enough by itself to solve most cases of practical interest.

Procedure 1   Gaussian elimination

To solve a system of n linear equations in n unknowns, with coefficient matrix $\mathbf{A}$ and right-hand-side vector $\mathbf{b}$, it is often sufficient to carry out the following three steps.

1. **Formulation**: Write down the augmented matrix $\mathbf{A}|\mathbf{b}$ with rows $\mathbf{R}_1, \ldots, \mathbf{R}_n$.

2. **Elimination**: Adapt the following row operations as necessary.

    (a) Subtract a multiple of $\mathbf{R}_1$ from $\mathbf{R}_2$, to reduce to zero the first element in the first column below the leading diagonal.

    (b) Similarly, subtract a multiple of $\mathbf{R}_1$ from $\mathbf{R}_3, \ldots, \mathbf{R}_n$ to reduce to zero all the other elements in the first column below the leading diagonal.

    (c) In the new matrix obtained, subtract multiples of $\mathbf{R}_2$ from $\mathbf{R}_3, \ldots, \mathbf{R}_n$ to reduce to zero all the elements in the second column below the leading diagonal.

    (d) Continue this process until $\mathbf{A}|\mathbf{b}$ is reduced to $\mathbf{U}|\mathbf{c}$, where $\mathbf{U}$ is an upper triangular matrix.

3. **Solution**: Solve the system of equations with coefficient matrix $\mathbf{U}$ and right-hand-side vector $\mathbf{c}$ by back substitution.

Remember that performing a row operation really involves three sub-steps:
- write down the plan
- implement the plan
- relabel the rows.

Though not part of the procedure, it is generally good practice to write the solution as a column matrix, and then confirm by matrix multiplication that it is indeed a solution of the original system of equations.

Example 2

Solve the simultaneous equations

$$3x_1 + x_2 - x_3 = 1,$$
$$5x_1 + x_2 + 2x_3 = 6,$$
$$4x_1 - 2x_2 - 3x_3 = 3,$$

and check the solution by matrix multiplication.

Solution

Following Procedure 1, starting with the formulation, the augmented matrix representing these equations is

$$\begin{bmatrix} 3 & 1 & -1 & | & 1 \\ 5 & 1 & 2 & | & 6 \\ 4 & -2 & -3 & | & 3 \end{bmatrix} \begin{matrix} \mathbf{R}_1 \\ \mathbf{R}_2 \\ \mathbf{R}_3 \end{matrix} .$$

Moving on to the elimination stage, to reduce the elements below the leading diagonal in column 1 to zero, replace $\mathbf{R}_2$ by $\mathbf{R}_2 - \frac{5}{3}\mathbf{R}_1$ and call the result $\mathbf{R}_{2a}$, then replace $\mathbf{R}_3$ by $\mathbf{R}_3 - \frac{4}{3}\mathbf{R}_1$ and call the result $\mathbf{R}_{3a}$:

$$\begin{matrix} \\ \mathbf{R}_2 - \frac{5}{3}\mathbf{R}_1 \\ \mathbf{R}_3 - \frac{4}{3}\mathbf{R}_1 \end{matrix} \begin{bmatrix} 3 & 1 & -1 & | & 1 \\ 0 & -\frac{2}{3} & \frac{11}{3} & | & \frac{13}{3} \\ 0 & -\frac{10}{3} & -\frac{5}{3} & | & \frac{5}{3} \end{bmatrix} \begin{matrix} \mathbf{R}_1 \\ \mathbf{R}_{2a} \\ \mathbf{R}_{3a} \end{matrix} .$$

To reduce the element below the leading diagonal in column 2 to zero, replace $\mathbf{R}_{3a}$ by $\mathbf{R}_{3a} - 5\mathbf{R}_{2a}$:

$$\begin{matrix} \\ \\ \mathbf{R}_{3a} - 5\mathbf{R}_{2a} \end{matrix} \begin{bmatrix} 3 & 1 & -1 & | & 1 \\ 0 & -\frac{2}{3} & \frac{11}{3} & | & \frac{13}{3} \\ 0 & 0 & -20 & | & -20 \end{bmatrix} .$$

It would be neater to replace $\mathbf{R}_2$ by $3\mathbf{R}_2 - 5\mathbf{R}_1$, and $\mathbf{R}_3$ by $3\mathbf{R}_3 - 4\mathbf{R}_1$, since this would avoid the use of fractions. We do not do this because it would involve combining elementary row operations where we prefer to use them individually at this stage. Nonetheless, such shortcuts are common, and we will use them later in the unit. You will probably use them yourself as your confidence grows.

This completes the elimination stage. We now have to solve the equations represented by the new matrix, i.e.

$$3x_1 + x_2 - x_3 = 1,$$
$$-\frac{2}{3}x_2 + \frac{11}{3}x_3 = \frac{13}{3},$$
$$-20x_3 = -20.$$

It is clear from the last equation that $x_3 = 1$. So by back substitution, $x_2 = \frac{1}{2}(11x_3 - 13) = -1$ and $x_1 = \frac{1}{3}(1 - x_2 + x_3) = 1$.

We may verify that $\mathbf{x} = [1 \quad -1 \quad 1]^T$ is a solution of the matrix version of the equations as follows:

$$\begin{bmatrix} 3 & 1 & -1 \\ 5 & 1 & 2 \\ 4 & -2 & -3 \end{bmatrix} \begin{bmatrix} 1 \\ -1 \\ 1 \end{bmatrix} = \begin{bmatrix} 3 - 1 - 1 \\ 5 - 1 + 2 \\ 4 + 2 - 3 \end{bmatrix} = \begin{bmatrix} 1 \\ 6 \\ 3 \end{bmatrix} .$$

Exercise 3

Solve the simultaneous equations

$$x_1 + x_2 - x_3 = 2,$$
$$5x_1 + 2x_2 + 2x_3 = 20,$$
$$4x_1 - 2x_2 - 3x_3 = 15,$$

and check the solution by matrix multiplication.

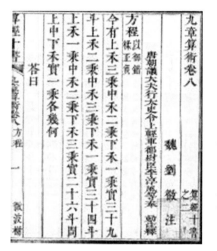

Figure 2   An ancient problem in linear algebra

All the examples of Gaussian elimination considered so far have started with a non-zero coefficient on the first variable in the first equation. One problem with Procedure 1 is that it will not work if that first entry in $\mathbf{R}_1$ is zero, since we would then have to divide by zero, which is not allowed. Fortunately, this is easy to overcome. All we have to do is reorder the equations in an appropriate way before formulating the augmented matrix. However, there is a deeper lesson to be learned from this. Reordering the equations is equivalent to interchanging complete rows in the augmented matrix, which is one of the allowed elementary row operations. Cases often arise in which it is advantageous to make such an interchange either before or even during the elimination stage. The following example illustrates this. (It is based on a problem set and solved in the Chinese text *Nine Chapters on the Mathematical Art* (Figure 2) written between 200 BC and 100 BC.)

Example 3

There are three types of corn, of which three bundles of the first, two of the second, and one of the third make 39 measures. Two of the first, three of the second and one of the third make 34 measures. And one of the first, two of the second and three of the third make 26 measures. How many measures of corn are contained in one bundle of each type?

Solution

Let x_i represent the number of measures in one bundle of type i, with $i = 1, 2, 3$. The problem is then specified by the simultaneous equations

$$3x_1 + 2x_2 + x_3 = 39,$$
$$2x_1 + 3x_2 + x_3 = 34,$$
$$x_1 + 2x_2 + 3x_3 = 26.$$

If we just press ahead and solve this problem as given, we will have to introduce fractions as soon as we try to eliminate x_1 from the second row. We can avoid the immediate use of fractions if we first interchange the first and third equations, so that the coefficient of x_1 in the first equation is 1. The augmented matrix of the reordered set of equations is then

$$\begin{bmatrix} 1 & 2 & 3 & | & 26 \\ 2 & 3 & 1 & | & 34 \\ 3 & 2 & 1 & | & 39 \end{bmatrix} \begin{matrix} \mathbf{R}_1 \\ \mathbf{R}_2 \\ \mathbf{R}_3 \end{matrix} .$$

Reducing the coefficients below the leading diagonal in the first column to zero gives

$$\begin{array}{c} \\ \mathbf{R}_2 - 2\mathbf{R}_1 \\ \mathbf{R}_3 - 3\mathbf{R}_1 \end{array} \left[\begin{array}{ccc|c} 1 & 2 & 3 & 26 \\ 0 & -1 & -5 & -18 \\ 0 & -4 & -8 & -39 \end{array}\right] \begin{array}{c} \mathbf{R}_1 \\ \mathbf{R}_{2a} \\ \mathbf{R}_{3a} \end{array} .$$

Reducing the coefficient below the leading diagonal in the second column to zero produces

$$\begin{array}{c} \\ \\ \mathbf{R}_{3a} - 4\mathbf{R}_{2a} \end{array} \left[\begin{array}{ccc|c} 1 & 2 & 3 & 26 \\ 0 & -1 & -5 & -18 \\ 0 & 0 & 12 & 33 \end{array}\right] .$$

This completes the elimination. Back substitution then gives $x_3 = \frac{33}{12} = \frac{11}{4}$, $x_2 = 18 - 5x_3 = \frac{17}{4}$ and $x_1 = 26 - 2x_2 - 3x_3 = \frac{37}{4}$.

Now check that the solution $\mathbf{x} = \frac{1}{4}[37 \quad 17 \quad 11]^T$ satisfies the original matrix equation:

$$\frac{1}{4}\begin{bmatrix} 1 & 2 & 3 \\ 2 & 3 & 1 \\ 3 & 2 & 1 \end{bmatrix}\begin{bmatrix} 37 \\ 17 \\ 11 \end{bmatrix} = \frac{1}{4}\begin{bmatrix} 37 + 34 + 33 \\ 74 + 51 + 11 \\ 111 + 34 + 11 \end{bmatrix} = \begin{bmatrix} 26 \\ 34 \\ 39 \end{bmatrix} .$$

You may find it convenient to rearrange the data in the following exercise.

Exercise 4

The economy of Ruritania has collapsed, and each of its three banks has been nationalised. Under state ownership, all bank employees are divided into three grades: managers, software engineers and clerks, with members of a given grade paid identically, without bonuses. Bank A employs three managers, two software engineers and 24 clerks. Bank B employs one manager, one software engineer and 26 clerks. Bank C employs no managers, three software engineers and 25 clerks. Under this radically new dispensation, the monthly salary bill of each bank is 137 thousand rurs, where the rur is the name for the unit of the (recently devalued) currency. How many thousand rurs per month are received by a manager, by a software engineer and by a clerk?

In some cases it may be necessary to interchange a pair of rows later in the process, in order to achieve an upper triangular matrix at the end of the elimination stage. Here is an example where this happens.

Example 4

Solve the following system of equations:

$$x_1 + 10x_2 - 3x_3 = 8,$$
$$x_1 + 10x_2 + 2x_3 = 13,$$
$$x_1 + 4x_2 + 2x_3 = 7.$$

Solution

The corresponding augmented matrix is

$$\left[\begin{array}{ccc|c} 1 & 10 & -3 & 8 \\ 1 & 10 & 2 & 13 \\ 1 & 4 & 2 & 7 \end{array}\right]\begin{array}{l} \mathbf{R}_1 \\ \mathbf{R}_2 \\ \mathbf{R}_3 \end{array}.$$

To reduce the elements below the leading diagonal in column 1 to zero, replace $\mathbf{R}_2$ by $\mathbf{R}_2 - \mathbf{R}_1$ and call the result $\mathbf{R}_{2a}$, then replace $\mathbf{R}_3$ by $\mathbf{R}_3 - \mathbf{R}_1$ and call the result $\mathbf{R}_{3a}$:

$$\begin{array}{l} \\ \mathbf{R}_2 - \mathbf{R}_1 \\ \mathbf{R}_3 - \mathbf{R}_1 \end{array}\left[\begin{array}{ccc|c} 1 & 10 & -3 & 8 \\ 0 & 0 & 5 & 5 \\ 0 & -6 & 5 & -1 \end{array}\right]\begin{array}{l} \mathbf{R}_1 \\ \mathbf{R}_{2a} \\ \mathbf{R}_{3a} \end{array}.$$

In this case there is no need to perform another subtraction because a zero has fortuitously appeared in $\mathbf{R}_{2a}$. All that is needed is an interchange of the last two rows:

$$\begin{array}{l} \\ \mathbf{R}_{3a} \\ \mathbf{R}_{2a} \end{array}\left[\begin{array}{ccc|c} 1 & 10 & -3 & 8 \\ 0 & -6 & 5 & -1 \\ 0 & 0 & 5 & 5 \end{array}\right].$$

It follows that $x_3 = 1$, and by back substitution $x_2 = -\frac{1}{6}(-1 - 5x_3) = 1$ and $x_1 = 8 - 10x_2 + 3x_3 = 1$. (As usual, the matrix solution $\mathbf{x} = \begin{bmatrix} 1 & 1 & 1 \end{bmatrix}^T$ should be confirmed as correct, as a check.)

In the previous example, the final exchange of rows was made to achieve an upper triangular matrix. However, it would have been possible to have solved the system of equations as soon as the unexpected zero appeared in $\mathbf{R}_{2a}$. In each of the following exercises, a solution becomes possible as soon as x_1 is eliminated from all but one of the equations, even though an upper triangular matrix is not apparent. It is left to you to decide whether to make use of this potential shortcut or to follow the systematic approach adopted earlier.

Exercise 5

Solve the system of equations whose augmented matrix is

$$\left[\begin{array}{ccc|c} 0 & 0 & 1 & 2 \\ 2 & 1 & 0 & 5 \\ 1 & 2 & 0 & 7 \end{array}\right].$$

Exercise 6

Solve the system of equations whose augmented matrix is

$$\left[\begin{array}{cccc|c} 1 & 1 & 1 & 1 & 10 \\ 1 & 1 & 2 & 1 & 12 \\ 1 & 3 & 1 & 1 & 16 \\ 4 & 1 & 1 & 1 & 22 \end{array}\right].$$

A comment on the efficiency of Gaussian elimination

All of the examples and exercises in this subsection have involved a square coefficient matrix $\mathbf{A}$ with $\det \mathbf{A} \neq 0$. Such matrices are described as **non-singular** and, as explained in Unit 4, are invertible, meaning that it is possible to construct an inverse matrix, denoted $\mathbf{A}^{-1}$, such that $\mathbf{A}\mathbf{A}^{-1} = \mathbf{I}$. Such matrices may be contrasted with *singular* matrices that have $\det \mathbf{A} = 0$ and are non-invertible. The non-singular case is important because of the following general result.

> The system of linear equations represented by the matrix equation $\mathbf{A}\mathbf{x} = \mathbf{b}$, where $\mathbf{A}$ is a square matrix, has a unique solution if and only if $\mathbf{A}$ is non-singular (i.e. $\det \mathbf{A} \neq 0$).
>
> Such a system of equations is said to be a **non-singular system**.

In the non-singular case, the unique solution of the system of equations $\mathbf{A}\mathbf{x} = \mathbf{b}$ is given by $\mathbf{x} = \mathbf{A}^{-1}\mathbf{b}$, where $\mathbf{A}^{-1}$ is the *inverse* of $\mathbf{A}$, as defined in Unit 4.

It can be shown that the method of Gaussian elimination will always produce this solution, provided that we include any necessary interchanges of rows. Nonetheless, you may wonder why we have chosen to introduce Gaussian elimination when we could have used the methods of Unit 4 to construct the inverse of the coefficient matrix, and then used matrix multiplication to find the solution $\mathbf{x} = \mathbf{A}^{-1}\mathbf{b}$. The reason concerns the *efficiency* of the calculation, which becomes an increasingly important consideration as the number of equations grows and the order of the coefficient matrix increases.

The method for finding a matrix inverse that was described in the previous unit involved a lot of manipulation. Using this method to find the inverse of the $n \times n$ coefficient matrix $\mathbf{A}$ might be sensible if n is small, e.g. $n = 3$ or $n = 4$, but is a bad idea when n is large, for at least two reasons.

- The method given in Unit 4 takes of order $n!$ multiplications to compute $\mathbf{A}^{-1}$. Other methods, based on row operations, take roughly n^3 arithmetic operations. Since n^3 increases far more slowly than $n!$, as n gets large, the methods based on row operations are much more efficient.

  $5! = 120$ and $6! = 720$, while $5^3 = 125$ and $6^3 = 216$.

- Even if we use a faster method to compute $\mathbf{A}^{-1}$, we may find that we require high-precision multiplication to achieve only modest accuracy in our result, since there may be large cancellations between the many terms summed over in our calculations.

For these (and other) reasons, the methods of Unit 4 are not those that are implemented by software packages that solve linear systems of equations. Gaussian elimination is widely regarded as a more efficient method for solving medium to large systems of linear equations – but there are exceptions to this, as the following box indicates.

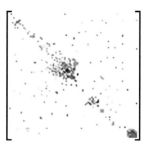

Figure 3   A sparse matrix of order 100×100. The value of each element is indicated by the colour of the corresponding pixel (i.e. picture element). By far the most common value is zero, which is indicated by white.

Gaussian elimination and sparse matrices

A large matrix $\mathbf{A}$ in which many of the elements are zero is said to be a *sparse matrix*. Such matrices arise in various applications, ranging from the modelling of engineering structures and electrical networks, to pure mathematical studies in the field known as number theory. An example of a sparse matrix is shown in Figure 3. In such cases, Gaussian elimination may be an inefficient method for solving $\mathbf{Ax} = \mathbf{b}$, since the development of an upper triangular matrix may well create many more non-zero elements than were initially present. Special methods have been devised for dealing with sparse matrices, which can handle millions of linear equations.

To end this discussion of Gaussian elimination in non-singular cases, we note that, despite its general efficiency, Gaussian elimination should not be thoughtlessly applied to every system of linear equations. In particular, you should not apply it to a system consisting of just two equations, since such a small system is more easily analysed without the formal apparatus of Gaussian elimination.

1.4   Gaussian elimination: singular cases

If $\det \mathbf{A} = 0$, then we say that $\mathbf{A}$ is *singular*, and we also use that term to describe the corresponding system of linear equations $\mathbf{Ax} = \mathbf{b}$. In some singular cases there may be no solution; in others there may be an infinity of solutions. Some 2×2 examples will help us to see why.

Example 5

By this stage it is assumed that you can envisage the relevant 2×2 coefficient matrix without needing to write it down. If this is not the case, treat this example as a further exercise.

For each of the following pairs of simultaneous equations, write down the determinant of the corresponding coefficient matrix and determine whether there is no solution, a unique solution, or an infinity of solutions.

(a) $\quad x + \ y = 4,$ (b) $\quad x + \ y = 4,$ (c) $\quad x + \ y = 4,$
$\quad\ 2x - 3y = 8.$ $2x + 2y = 5.$ $2x + 2y = 8.$

Solution

(a) In this case the determinant of the coefficient matrix is $-3 - 2 = -5$, so the system is non-singular and there is a unique solution.

(b) The determinant of the coefficient matrix is $2 - 2 = 0$, so the system is singular. Subtracting twice the first equation from the second, we obtain $0 = -3$, which is impossible. Hence there is no solution. (The equations are said to be **inconsistent**.)

(c) The determinant of the coefficient matrix is again $2 - 2 = 0$, so the system is singular. Subtracting twice the first equation from the second, we now obtain $0 = 0$, which is indeed true. The equations are consistent in this case. In fact, the second equation is simply the first equation multiplied throughout by 2. Consequently, any pair of values that satisfies the first equation will also satisfy the second equation. There are infinitely many such pairs (choose any value for x and then let $y = 4 - x$). Hence there is an infinity of solutions.

Note that in the example above, the evaluation of the determinant was sufficient to tell us whether a unique solution existed. However, in the singular cases, where there was no unique solution, the value of the determinant did not tell us whether there was no solution or an infinity of solutions. Further investigation is always needed to resolve such cases. This is true irrespective of the order of $\mathbf{A}$. We can gain some geometrical insight into these different behaviours by recalling that a linear equation in two variables can be represented graphically by a straight line. We generally write the equation of such a line as $y = mx + c$, where m represents the *gradient* of the line, and c represents the *intersection* with the y-axis.

The lines corresponding to the equations of Example 5(a) are depicted in Figure 4(a), and are seen to intersect at a unique point. The values of x and y at the intersection represent the unique solution to the linear equations. The lines represented by the equations of Example 5(b) are parallel (see Figure 4(b)), so they never meet and there is no pair of values that simultaneously satisfies the two equations. Finally, in Figure 4(c), the two lines, though superficially different, are actually the same, so any of the infinity of points on one line will also be on the other. Hence there is an infinity of solutions.

A linear equation in three variables (e.g. $ax + by + cz = d$) represents a plane in a three-dimensional system of Cartesian coordinates. The constants (a, b, c and d) will determine the orientation of the plane and its perpendicular distance from the origin (the plane passes through the origin if $d = 0$). A system of three linear equations with a non-singular coefficient matrix of order 3×3 describes three planes that intersect at a unique point. The coordinates of this point represent the unique solution of the non-singular system of equations. This is illustrated in Figure 5(a).

Figures 5(b) and 5(c) show cases in which the planes meet in two or three parallel lines. These are some of the cases where the determinant of the coefficient matrix will be zero, and the singular system of equations will have no solution. Another singular case in which there is no solution is illustrated in Figure 5(d), where the three planes are parallel and do not intersect at all.

In Figure 5(e) we see a case where there are infinitely many solutions since all three planes share a common line. (The case of all three planes coinciding would also represent an infinity of solutions.) In these cases the coefficient matrix is again singular.

This geometrical interpretation can be extended to higher dimensions using the idea of a *hyperplane*, but visualisation is increasingly difficult so we will not pursue that approach here. In any case, the basic point has already been well established and can be summarised as follows.

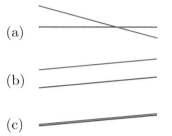

Figure 4 In two dimensions, a pair of simultaneous equations in two variables represents a pair of straight lines. Such lines may (a) intersect at a unique point, (b) be parallel and not intersect at all, or (c) be identical and intersect at an infinity of points.

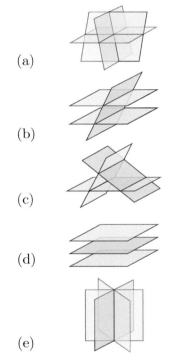

Figure 5 In three dimensions, the planes that represent three linear equations may (a) intersect at a unique point, (b) intersect in two parallel lines, (c) intersect in three parallel lines, (d) not intersect at all, or (e) intersect in the same line or plane

> The system of linear equations represented by the matrix equation $\mathbf{Ax} = \mathbf{b}$ is said to be **singular** when the square matrix $\mathbf{A}$ is singular (i.e. when $\det \mathbf{A} = 0$). Such a system does not possess a unique solution; it may have no solution or an infinity of solutions.

The following exercise is important. It should help you to recognise the possible cases, particularly those in which there is an infinity of solutions.

Exercise 7

In the case of singular systems, this exercise requires you to go no further than considering the *number* of solutions that a system will have. Examples and exercises that involve determining such solutions will be given in Section 3.

For each of the following systems of simultaneous equations, determine whether there is no solution, a unique solution, or an infinity of solutions. (*Hint*: Examining determinants will not be sufficient; you are advised to consider the augmented matrices.)

(a) $\begin{aligned} x_1 - 2x_2 + 5x_3 &= 7, \\ x_1 + 3x_2 - 4x_3 &= 20, \\ x_1 + 18x_2 - 31x_3 &= 40. \end{aligned}$

(b) $\begin{aligned} x_1 - 2x_2 + 5x_3 &= 6, \\ x_1 + 3x_2 - 4x_3 &= 7, \\ 2x_1 + 6x_2 - 12x_3 &= 12. \end{aligned}$

(c) $\begin{aligned} x_1 - 4x_2 + x_3 &= 14, \\ 5x_1 - x_2 - x_3 &= 2, \\ 6x_1 + 14x_2 - 6x_3 &= -52. \end{aligned}$

Figure 6 Carl Friedrich Gauss (1777–1855)

Gaussian elimination – a historical perspective

Carl Friedrich Gauss (Figure 6) is widely regarded as one of the greatest mathematicians of all time, comparable with Archimedes and Newton. He spent most of his career as Professor of Astronomy and Director of the Observatory at the University of Göttingen, in Lower Saxony, now part of Germany. One of his many celebrated achievements was the determination of the orbit of the asteroid Pallas from a small number of observations in 1802. In 1810 he published an important paper about orbit determinations in which he used repeated observations of Pallas to make the best possible determination of its orbit. During this work he took a systematic approach to finding the six unknowns in the system of equations that represented the observations. In doing so, he devised a notation that became widely adopted. It is from this that the method of Gaussian elimination gets its name.

Interestingly, the current – rather broad – use of the term 'Gaussian elimination' may not be entirely justified, even if we ignore the evidence that priority belongs to the Chinese. It appears that the name of Gauss became attached to the general method of systematic elimination only in the 1950s, mainly as a result of confusion among mathematicians who were unaware of the method's detailed history. The original inventor (at least as far as Europe is concerned) seems to have been Isaac Newton (Figure 7), who pointed out in 1670 that algebra textbooks lacked a procedure for solving systems of simultaneous linear equations, and proceeded to supply one.

Figure 7 Isaac Newton (1642–1727)

2 Introducing eigenvalues and eigenvectors

As mentioned in the Introduction, eigenvalues and eigenvectors are scalars (often numbers) and vectors associated with a matrix (the German word 'eigen' may be translated as 'inherent'). They are widely used in the mathematical sciences, particularly physics. Rather than going directly to the definitions, we will first examine some examples of how they arise. We start with what is essentially an algebraic example, based on a mathematical model of population growth. This should help to establish a clear view of an eigenvector. Then, in a second example that is more geometrically based, we give particular emphasis to the idea of an eigenvalue.

'Eigen' is pronounced as 'eye-ghen'.

2.1   Eigenvectors in a model of population growth

Consider the (fictional) towns of Exton and Wyeville, which have a regular interchange of population: each year, one-tenth of Exton's population migrates to Wyeville, while one-fifth of Wyeville's population migrates to Exton (see Figure 8). Other changes in population, such as births, deaths and other migrations, cancel each other and so can be ignored. If x_n represents the population of Exton at the *beginning* of year n, and y_n is the corresponding population of Wyeville, then the populations of the two towns at the beginning of year $n + 1$ are given by

$$x_{n+1} = 0.9x_n + 0.2y_n,$$
$$y_{n+1} = 0.1x_n + 0.8y_n,$$

which may be expressed in matrix form as

$$\begin{bmatrix} x_{n+1} \\ y_{n+1} \end{bmatrix} = \begin{bmatrix} 0.9 & 0.2 \\ 0.1 & 0.8 \end{bmatrix} \begin{bmatrix} x_n \\ y_n \end{bmatrix}.$$

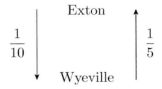

Figure 8 Exton and Wyeville annually exchange fixed fractions of their respective populations

This matrix equation can be represented symbolically by

$$\mathbf{x}_{n+1} = \mathbf{T}\mathbf{x}_n,$$

where the column vectors $\mathbf{x}_n$ and $\mathbf{x}_{n+1}$ represent the populations in Exton and Wyeville at the beginning of years n and $n+1$, respectively, and the square matrix $\mathbf{T}$ is known as the **transition matrix** for the problem. (The entries in such a matrix are all non-negative, and the entries in each column sum to 1.)

This annual exchange of populations is an example of an *iterative process*, in which the values associated with the $(n+1)$th iterate can be determined from the values associated with the nth iterate.

Suppose that initially the population of Exton is 10 000 and that of Wyeville is 8000, i.e. $\mathbf{x}_0 = [x_0 \quad y_0]^T = [10\,000 \quad 8000]^T$. Then after one year (i.e. at the beginning of year $n = 1$), the populations will be given by $\mathbf{x}_1 = \mathbf{T}\mathbf{x}_0$, so

$$\begin{bmatrix} x_1 \\ y_1 \end{bmatrix} = \begin{bmatrix} 0.9 & 0.2 \\ 0.1 & 0.8 \end{bmatrix} \begin{bmatrix} 10\,000 \\ 8000 \end{bmatrix} = \begin{bmatrix} 10\,600 \\ 7400 \end{bmatrix},$$

and after two years they are given by $\mathbf{x}_2 = \mathbf{T}\mathbf{x}_1$, so

$$\begin{bmatrix} x_2 \\ y_2 \end{bmatrix} = \begin{bmatrix} 0.9 & 0.2 \\ 0.1 & 0.8 \end{bmatrix} \begin{bmatrix} 10\,600 \\ 7400 \end{bmatrix} = \begin{bmatrix} 11\,020 \\ 6980 \end{bmatrix}.$$

Note that we might also have written this last result as

$$\mathbf{x}_2 = \mathbf{T}\mathbf{x}_1 = \mathbf{T}\mathbf{T}\mathbf{x}_0 = \mathbf{T}^2\mathbf{x}_0,$$

where we have introduced the power notation $\mathbf{T}^2$ to indicate repeated (matrix) multiplication, just as we use powers such as a^2, a^3 and a^4 to indicate the repeated multiplication of a scalar a. Using the idea of the **power of a matrix** to represent repeated matrix multiplication, we can describe the populations of Exton and Wyeville after n years as

$$\mathbf{x}_n = \mathbf{T}^n\mathbf{x}_0. \tag{2}$$

Given this relation, how do the populations of Exton and Wyeville change over time? The answers can be worked out using equation (2), though the repeated matrix multiplications are tedious to do by hand. To save you the labour, the results are indicated graphically in Figure 9.

As you can see, the populations show a very interesting kind of behaviour. Initially they diverge, changing significantly from year to year, with Exton growing while Wyeville shrinks. However, those changes diminish with time, and after about 15 years the populations change very little, approaching ever more closely 12 000 in Exton and 6000 in Wyeville.

Explicit calculations (with results displayed to only the nearest integer) show that $\mathbf{x}_{29} = \mathbf{x}_{30} = \mathbf{x}_{31} = [12\,000 \quad 6000]^T$. So after about 30 years, the two populations are very stable, despite continuing annual migrations.

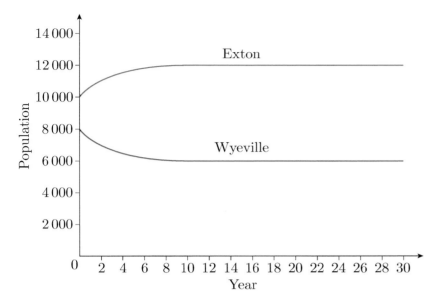

Figure 9   The evolving populations of Exton and Wyeville

Clearly there is something special about the relationship between the 'steady-state' population vector $\mathbf{x} = [x \quad y]^T = [12\,000 \quad 6000]^T$ and the transition matrix $\mathbf{T}$ for this particular problem. It is easy to see the nature of that special relationship by simply working out the matrix product of $\mathbf{T}$ and $\mathbf{x}$:

$$\begin{bmatrix} 0.9 & 0.2 \\ 0.1 & 0.8 \end{bmatrix} \begin{bmatrix} 12\,000 \\ 6000 \end{bmatrix} = \begin{bmatrix} 0.9 \times 12\,000 + 0.2 \times 6000 \\ 0.1 \times 12\,000 + 0.8 \times 6000 \end{bmatrix} = \begin{bmatrix} 12\,000 \\ 6000 \end{bmatrix}.$$

Expressed in symbolic terms,

$$\mathbf{T}\mathbf{x} = \mathbf{x},$$

showing that the action of $\mathbf{T}$ on $\mathbf{x}$ leaves $\mathbf{x}$ unchanged. This obviously explains the stability of the steady-state populations, since repeated applications of the transition matrix will continue to produce the same outcome. This special relationship between $\mathbf{x}$ and $\mathbf{T}$ is described by saying that $\mathbf{x}$ is an *eigenvector* of $\mathbf{T}$.

In fact, this particular example of an eigenvector is very special indeed. Rather more common are cases where $\mathbf{A}$ is a square matrix (not necessarily a transition matrix) and $\mathbf{y}$ is a column vector such that

$$\mathbf{A}\mathbf{y} = \lambda\mathbf{y},$$

where λ is a constant scalar. In these cases we would still describe $\mathbf{y}$ as an *eigenvector* of $\mathbf{A}$, but we would now say that λ is the corresponding *eigenvalue*. In the case of the population model considered above, the eigenvalue λ is 1, because $\mathbf{T}\mathbf{x} = 1\mathbf{x}$. In the next subsection we will consider another example of an eigenvector, but this time we will be specifically concerned with situations in which the corresponding eigenvalue is not 1.

Exercise 8

Use matrix multiplication to determine which, if any, of the following column vectors is an eigenvector of the transition matrix

$$\mathbf{T} = \begin{bmatrix} 0.9 & 0.2 \\ 0.1 & 0.8 \end{bmatrix}.$$

(a) $\begin{bmatrix} 1000 \\ 1000 \end{bmatrix}$ (b) $\begin{bmatrix} 120 \\ 60 \end{bmatrix}$ (c) $\begin{bmatrix} 500 \\ 300 \end{bmatrix}$ (d) $\begin{bmatrix} 20 \\ 10 \end{bmatrix}$

It is clear from this exercise that an eigenvector of a square matrix is not unique. In fact, given any eigenvector $\mathbf{x}$ of a square matrix, any scaled column vector $\mathbf{y} = k\mathbf{x}$, where k is a non-zero scalar constant, will also be an eigenvector of that square matrix. Moreover, $\mathbf{x}$ and $\mathbf{y}$ will correspond to the same eigenvalue λ. (It is important not to confuse the scalar multiple k discussed here with the eigenvalue λ that we will discuss in the next subsection.)

2.2   Eigenvalues in a transformation of the plane

In Unit 4 we saw that a 2×2 matrix $\mathbf{A} = [a_{ij}]$ can be interpreted geometrically as representing a linear transformation of the Cartesian plane. Such transformations map a point with the Cartesian coordinates (x_0, y_0) to a point with the Cartesian coordinates (x_1, y_1), where $x_1 = a_{11}x_0 + a_{12}y_0$ and $y_1 = a_{21}x_0 + a_{22}y_0$. In terms of matrices we can write this as

$$\begin{bmatrix} x_1 \\ y_1 \end{bmatrix} = \begin{bmatrix} a_{11} & a_{12} \\ a_{21} & a_{22} \end{bmatrix} \begin{bmatrix} x_0 \\ y_0 \end{bmatrix}.$$

Geometrically, we may regard the coordinates that appear in the column vector on the right as the components of a position vector, $\mathbf{r}_0 = (x_0, y_0) = x_0\mathbf{i} + y_0\mathbf{j}$, where $\mathbf{i}$ and $\mathbf{j}$ are the unit vectors in the x- and y-directions, respectively. Thus, in geometric terms, the action of the matrix $\mathbf{A}$ is to transform or 'map' one vector $\mathbf{r}_0$ into another vector $\mathbf{r}_1$.

With this geometric view in mind, consider the linear transformation specified by the matrix

$$\mathbf{A} = \begin{bmatrix} 3 & 2 \\ 1 & 4 \end{bmatrix}.$$

Using matrix multiplication, it is easy to see that this particular transformation will map the unit vector $\mathbf{i} = (1, 0)$ to the vector $(3, 1)$, and the unit vector $\mathbf{j} = (0, 1)$ to the vector $(2, 4)$. (If this is not clear, you should explicitly work out the matrix products $\mathbf{A}\mathbf{i}$ and $\mathbf{A}\mathbf{j}$, with $\mathbf{i}$ and $\mathbf{j}$ interpreted as column vectors.) These transformations are illustrated in Figure 10, along with the effect of the transformation on a general vector $\mathbf{r} = (x, y)$ that is mapped to the vector $(3x + 2y, x + 4y)$.

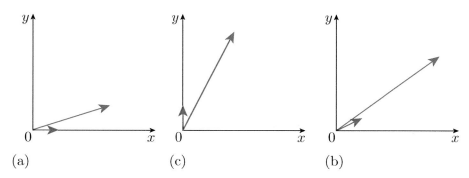

Figure 10   The action of the linear transformation represented by **A** on (a) the unit vector **i**, (b) the unit vector **j**, and (c) the general vector **r** $= (x, y)$. In each case the initial vector is red and the transformed vector is blue.

Note that the action of the linear transformation on a general vector is to change its direction and its magnitude.

Now consider the action of **A** on the column vector $\mathbf{w} = [1 \quad 1]^T$:

$$\mathbf{Aw} = \begin{bmatrix} 3 & 2 \\ 1 & 4 \end{bmatrix} \begin{bmatrix} 1 \\ 1 \end{bmatrix} = \begin{bmatrix} 5 \\ 5 \end{bmatrix}.$$

According to the rules of matrix algebra, we can write this last result as

$$\mathbf{Aw} = \begin{bmatrix} 5 \\ 5 \end{bmatrix} = 5 \begin{bmatrix} 1 \\ 1 \end{bmatrix} = 5\mathbf{w}.$$

This shows that **w** is an *eigenvector* of **A**, and that it corresponds to an *eigenvalue* of 5. The geometric interpretation of this result is shown in Figure 11; the transformation maps an eigenvector **w** into the scaled vector 5**w**, preserving its direction but altering its magnitude.

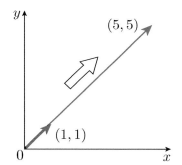

Figure 11   **A** maps its eigenvector **w** into the scaled vector 5**w**

Exercise 9

Use matrix multiplication to confirm that the linear transformation represented by **A** maps the scaled vector $k\mathbf{w}$, where k is any non-zero scalar, into the vector $5k\mathbf{w}$, and comment on the significance of this result.

The vector **w** and its scaled versions $k\mathbf{w}$ are not the only eigenvectors of **A**, nor is 5 the only eigenvalue. Using matrix multiplication, it is also easy to show that $\mathbf{z} = [-2 \quad 1]^T$ is an eigenvector, and that in this case the corresponding eigenvalue is 2:

$$\mathbf{Az} = \begin{bmatrix} 3 & 2 \\ 1 & 4 \end{bmatrix} \begin{bmatrix} -2 \\ 1 \end{bmatrix} = \begin{bmatrix} -4 \\ 2 \end{bmatrix} = 2\mathbf{z}.$$

This means, of course, that any non-zero scaled vector of the form $k\mathbf{z}$ will also be an eigenvector of **A**, corresponding to the eigenvalue 2. This is why we describe $\mathbf{z} = [-2 \quad 1]^T$ as *an* eigenvector corresponding to eigenvalue 2, rather than *the* eigenvector corresponding to that eigenvalue. (You might like to confirm for yourself that $[4 \quad -2]^T$ and $[-1 \quad \frac{1}{2}]^T$ are also eigenvectors that correspond to the eigenvalue 2, since they are each of the form $k\mathbf{z}$, with $k = -1$ and $k = \frac{1}{4}$, respectively.)

The vectors **w** and **z** together with their scaled variants comprise all the possible eigenvectors of **A**, and the eigenvalues 2 and 5 are the only eigenvalues of **A**. So the particular transformation that we have been examining has two distinct eigenvalues, both of which happen to be positive. It should be noted, however, that this is not always the case. Eigenvalues may be positive or negative or zero, and real, imaginary or complex. As you will see later, a matrix may even have repeated eigenvalues, so while each eigenvector corresponds to a single eigenvalue, there is no guarantee that each eigenvector corresponds to a *different* eigenvalue.

Exercise 10

In each of the following cases, verify that **v** is an eigenvector of **A**, and write down the corresponding eigenvalue.

(a) $\mathbf{A} = \begin{bmatrix} 2 & 3 \\ 2 & 1 \end{bmatrix}$, $\mathbf{v} = \begin{bmatrix} 3 \\ 2 \end{bmatrix}$.

(b) $\mathbf{A} = \begin{bmatrix} 2 & 3 \\ 2 & 1 \end{bmatrix}$, $\mathbf{v} = \begin{bmatrix} 1 \\ -1 \end{bmatrix}$.

(c) $\mathbf{A} = \begin{bmatrix} 2 & 0 \\ 1 & 2 \end{bmatrix}$, $\mathbf{v} = \begin{bmatrix} 0 \\ 6 \end{bmatrix}$.

(d) $\mathbf{A} = \begin{bmatrix} 2 & 1 \\ 4 & 2 \end{bmatrix}$, $\mathbf{v} = \begin{bmatrix} 1 \\ -2 \end{bmatrix}$.

Exercise 11

The term **real matrix** means that the matrix has real elements.

The real 2×2 matrix $\begin{bmatrix} 3 & -2 \\ 4 & -1 \end{bmatrix}$ has the complex eigenvectors

$$\mathbf{v}_1 = \begin{bmatrix} 1 \\ 1 - i \end{bmatrix} \quad \text{and} \quad \mathbf{v}_2 = \begin{bmatrix} 1 \\ 1 + i \end{bmatrix}.$$

Show that the eigenvalues of the matrix are $1 - 2i$ and $1 + 2i$, and determine which eigenvalue corresponds to which eigenvector.

Sometimes it is possible to deduce information about the eigenvectors and eigenvalues of a given matrix from its geometric effects. This is so for each of the three cases considered in Figure 12. In each case, the geometric action of the matrix is illustrated by its effect on a unit square with vertices $(0, 0)$, $(1, 0)$, $(1, 1)$ and $(0, 1)$. Also shown is the effect of the transformation on the perpendicular unit vectors drawn along two adjoining sides of the unit square.

Matrix	Comment	Transformation of the unit square	Eigenvectors	Eigenvalues
$\begin{bmatrix} 3 & 0 \\ 0 & 2 \end{bmatrix}$	A scaling by 3 in the x-direction and by 2 in the y-direction (i.e. a $(3,2)$ scaling)	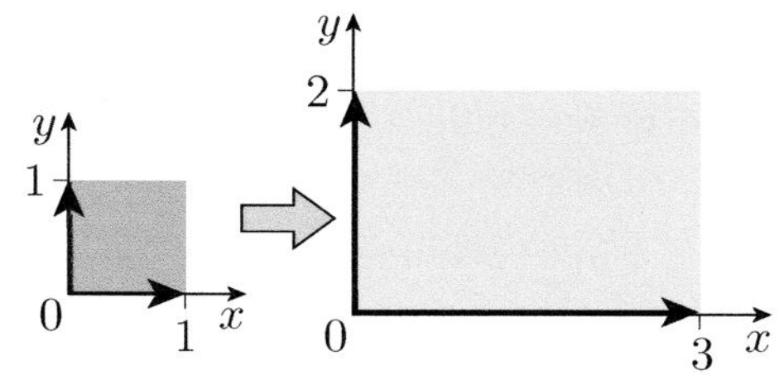	$[1 \quad 0]^T$ $[0 \quad 1]^T$	3 2
$\begin{bmatrix} 1 & 0 \\ 0 & -1 \end{bmatrix}$	A reflection in the x-axis	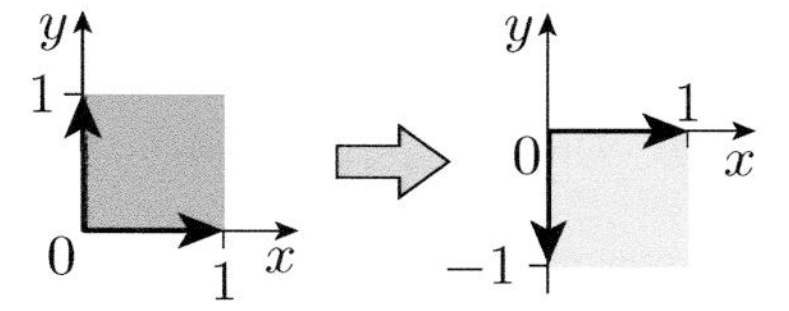	$[1 \quad 0]^T$ $[0 \quad 1]^T$	1 -1
$\begin{bmatrix} \frac{1}{\sqrt{2}} & -\frac{1}{\sqrt{2}} \\ \frac{1}{\sqrt{2}} & \frac{1}{\sqrt{2}} \end{bmatrix}$	A rotation through $\frac{\pi}{4}$ anticlockwise about the origin	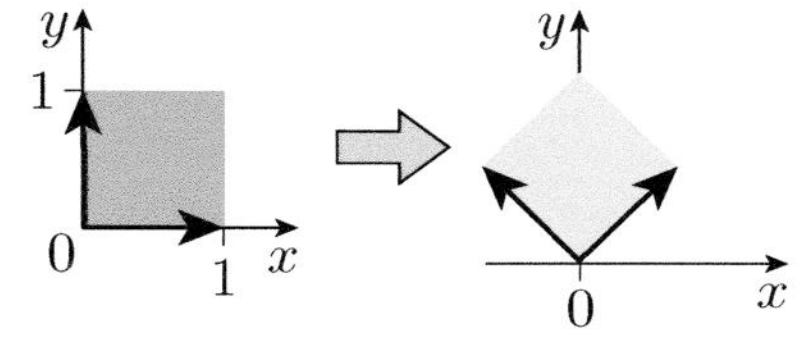	No real eigenvectors	No real eigenvalues

Figure 12 Three matrices representing transformations of the plane, together with their real eigenvectors and corresponding eigenvalues

In the case of the matrix $\begin{bmatrix} 3 & 0 \\ 0 & 2 \end{bmatrix}$, it is clear from the geometric properties of the linear transformation that vectors along the coordinate axes $\mathbf{i} = [1 \quad 0]^T$ and $\mathbf{j} = [0 \quad 1]^T$ are eigenvectors, as these are transformed to vectors in the same directions. Vector $\mathbf{i}$ (and its scalar multiples) has eigenvalue 3, and vector $\mathbf{j}$ (and its scalar multiples) has eigenvalue 2.

In the case of the matrix $\begin{bmatrix} 1 & 0 \\ 0 & -1 \end{bmatrix}$, we see that reflection in the x-axis leaves the vector represented by $\mathbf{i} = [1 \quad 0]^T$ unchanged, and reverses the direction of $\mathbf{j} = [0 \quad 1]^T$, so these must be eigenvectors corresponding to the eigenvalues 1 and -1, respectively.

In the third case of Figure 12, the matrix describes rotation through $\pi/4$ anticlockwise about the origin. In this case we would not expect to find any real eigenvectors because the direction of every vector is changed by the linear transformation. However, even this matrix does have eigenvectors and eigenvalues; they simply happen to involve complex quantities. This puts them beyond the kind of simple geometric interpretation that we are using here, though they can be studied using the algebraic methods that will be introduced in Section 3.

The matrix $\mathbf{A} = \begin{bmatrix} 0 & 1 \\ 1 & 0 \end{bmatrix}$ corresponds to reflection in a line through the origin at an angle $\pi/4$ to the x-axis. What are the eigenvectors of $\mathbf{A}$ and their corresponding eigenvalues?

(*Hint*: Find two lines through the origin that are transformed to themselves by the reflection, then consider what happens to a point on each line.)

2.3   The eigenvalue equation

Having seen several examples, we are now in a good position to write down some formal definitions and list some of the properties of eigenvectors and eigenvalues. We begin with the simple but very important relationship often referred to as the *eigenvalue equation*.

The restriction to non-zero column vectors means that we never have to deal with an eigenvector of the form $\mathbf{v} = [0 \quad \cdots \quad 0]^T$.

> **Eigenvalue equation**
>
> Let $\mathbf{A}$ be any square matrix. A non-zero column vector $\mathbf{v}$ is an **eigenvector** of $\mathbf{A}$ if it satisfies the **eigenvalue equation** for $\mathbf{A}$:
>
> $$\mathbf{A}\mathbf{v} = \lambda \mathbf{v} \quad \text{for some scalar } \lambda. \tag{3}$$
>
> The scalar λ is said to be the **eigenvalue** of $\mathbf{A}$ that corresponds to the eigenvector $\mathbf{v}$.

Confirm that the transition matrix (considered in Subsection 2.1)

$$\mathbf{T} = \begin{bmatrix} 0.9 & 0.2 \\ 0.1 & 0.8 \end{bmatrix}$$

has eigenvectors $[2 \quad 1]^T$ and $[1 \quad -1]^T$, and find the corresponding eigenvalues.

If we count all the scaled versions of an eigenvector as equivalent, it can be shown that no $n \times n$ matrix may have more than n eigenvectors and n eigenvalues. Thus the two eigenvalues of $\mathbf{T}$ quoted in Exercise 13 are the *only* eigenvalues of $\mathbf{T}$, and the two given eigenvectors are its only eigenvectors (apart from their scalar multiples).

When dealing with a general $n \times n$ matrix, there are several complications that can arise when counting the number of eigenvalues and eigenvectors. We will say something about those complications in Section 3. For the present, however, we avoid them by considering only the simplest and most common case, in which an $n \times n$ matrix has n distinct eigenvalues and n distinct eigenvectors. This is what many would regard as the 'normal' case, so it is natural to give it particular attention. Even so, we need to be clear about what we mean by 'distinct' eigenvalues and 'distinct' eigenvectors.

As far as eigenvalues are concerned, the notion of 'distinct' is simple: it just means different, i.e. unequal. The situation regarding eigenvectors is not so straightforward. We have already indicated that to be regarded as distinct, an eigenvector must not be a scalar multiple of any other eigenvector. However, with future developments in mind, we really need to go beyond this to define what we mean by distinct eigenvectors. In fact, we require a new concept called *linear independence*, which is the topic of the next subsection.

2.4 Linear independence

For the moment, let us forget about eigenvectors and just think about vectors in general. Linear independence is a property of sets of vectors. We begin with a simple geometric approach, first for two vectors, then for three vectors.

Two (non-zero) vectors $\mathbf{v}_1$ and $\mathbf{v}_2$ are said to be *linearly dependent* if they are collinear, i.e. one is parallel or antiparallel to the other. Conversely, $\mathbf{v}_1$ and $\mathbf{v}_2$ are said to be *linearly independent* if they are not collinear (see Figure 13).

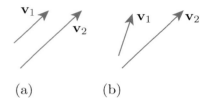

(a)   (b)

Figure 13 (a) Two linearly dependent vectors. (b) Two linearly independent vectors.

Now consider the case of three vectors. Three (non-zero) vectors $\mathbf{v}_1$, $\mathbf{v}_2$ and $\mathbf{v}_3$ are said to be *linearly dependent* if they are coplanar, i.e. they all lie in the same plane. Conversely, $\mathbf{v}_1$, $\mathbf{v}_2$ and $\mathbf{v}_3$ are said to be *linearly independent* if they are not coplanar (see Figure 14).

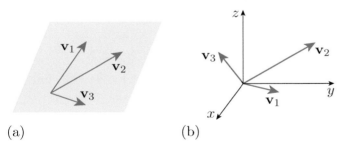

(a)   (b)

Figure 14 (a) A plane (in blue), containing three linearly dependent vectors. (b) Three linearly independent vectors in three-dimensional space.

Considering pairs and triples of vectors is as far as we can go using the geometric approach. So let us introduce an algebraic approach that will allow us to generalise to any number of vectors.

As stated, two vectors $\mathbf{v}_1$ and $\mathbf{v}_2$ are *linearly dependent* if they are collinear, which is equivalent to $\mathbf{v}_1 = k\mathbf{v}_2$ for some number k. So they are *linearly independent* if $\mathbf{v}_1 \neq k\mathbf{v}_2$ for any k. Another way of saying this is: $\mathbf{v}_1$ and $\mathbf{v}_2$ are linearly independent if the only solution of the equation

$$\alpha_1 \mathbf{v}_1 + \alpha_2 \mathbf{v}_2 = \mathbf{0} \quad \text{(where } \alpha_1 \text{ and } \alpha_2 \text{ are numbers)} \tag{4}$$

is $\alpha_1 = \alpha_2 = 0$.

This is equivalent to the previous statement because if we could find a solution of (4) with, say, $\alpha_1 \neq 0$, then $\mathbf{v}_1 = k\mathbf{v}_2$ with $k = -\alpha_2/\alpha_1$.

Now, three vectors $\mathbf{v}_1$, $\mathbf{v}_2$ and $\mathbf{v}_3$ are *linearly dependent* if they are coplanar. This is equivalent to saying that one vector can be expressed as a linear combination of the other two, say $\mathbf{v}_1 = k_2\mathbf{v}_2 + k_3\mathbf{v}_3$ for some numbers k_2 and k_3 (for example, in Figure 14(a), the vectors satisfy $\mathbf{v}_2 = \mathbf{v}_1 + \mathbf{v}_3$). The vectors are *linearly independent* if this is *not* possible. Mathematically we state this as follows: $\mathbf{v}_1$, $\mathbf{v}_2$ and $\mathbf{v}_3$ are linearly independent if the only solution of the equation

If we could find a solution of equation (5) with, say, $\alpha_1 \neq 0$, then we would have

$$\mathbf{v}_1 = -\frac{\alpha_2}{\alpha_1}\mathbf{v}_2 - \frac{\alpha_3}{\alpha_1}\mathbf{v}_3.$$

$$\alpha_1\mathbf{v}_1 + \alpha_2\mathbf{v}_2 + \alpha_2\mathbf{v}_3 = \mathbf{0} \quad \text{(where the } \alpha_i \text{ are numbers)} \tag{5}$$

is $\alpha_1 = \alpha_2 = \alpha_3 = 0$.

You should by now be noticing a pattern emerging, so we move to the general case. n vectors $\mathbf{v}_i$ $(i = 1, \ldots, n)$ are said to be linearly dependent if one of the vectors can be expressed as a linear combination of the others, e.g. $\mathbf{v}_1 = k_2\mathbf{v}_2 + k_3\mathbf{v}_3 + \cdots + k_n\mathbf{v}_n$ for some numbers k_i. If it is not possible to do this, then we say that the vectors are linearly independent. This is equivalent to the following definition.

> ### Linear independence
>
> n vectors $\mathbf{v}_1, \mathbf{v}_2, \ldots, \mathbf{v}_n$ are **linearly independent** if the only solution of the equation
>
> $$\alpha_1\mathbf{v}_1 + \alpha_2\mathbf{v}_2 + \cdots + \alpha_n\mathbf{v}_n = \mathbf{0} \quad \text{(where the } \alpha_i \text{ are numbers)} \tag{6}$$
>
> is $\alpha_1 = \alpha_2 = \alpha_3 = \ldots = \alpha_n = 0$.
>
> If the vectors are not linearly independent, then they are said to be **linearly dependent**, and one of the vectors can be expressed as a linear combination of the others.

Example 6

In two dimensions, are the unit vectors $\mathbf{i} = \begin{bmatrix} 1 & 0 \end{bmatrix}^T$ and $\mathbf{j} = \begin{bmatrix} 0 & 1 \end{bmatrix}^T$ linearly dependent or linearly independent?

Solution

Clearly, $\alpha_1\mathbf{i} + \alpha_2\mathbf{j}$ never gives the zero vector unless $\alpha_1 = \alpha_2 = 0$. Hence the vectors are linearly independent.

This is also clear geometrically, since the vectors are neither parallel nor antiparallel.

Example 7

Show that the vectors $\mathbf{i} = \begin{bmatrix} 1 & 0 & 0 \end{bmatrix}^T$, $\mathbf{j} = \begin{bmatrix} 0 & 1 & 0 \end{bmatrix}^T$ and $\mathbf{v} = \begin{bmatrix} 3 & 2 & 0 \end{bmatrix}^T$ are linearly dependent.

Solution

Since $\mathbf{v} = 3\mathbf{i} + 2\mathbf{j}$, we can write $\mathbf{v} - 3\mathbf{i} - 2\mathbf{j} = \mathbf{0}$. This is equivalent to equation (6), with $n = 3$, $\mathbf{v}_1 = \mathbf{v}$, $\mathbf{v}_2 = \mathbf{i}$, $\mathbf{v}_3 = \mathbf{j}$, $\alpha_1 = 1$, $\alpha_2 = -3$ and $\alpha_3 = -2$. So the vectors are linearly dependent.

This is also clear geometrically, since all three vectors lie in the xy-plane.

Exercise 14

Show that if there is a solution of equation (6) with $\alpha_1 \neq 0$, then one of the vectors can be written as a linear combination of the others.

Exercise 15

Are the following sets of three-dimensional column vectors linearly independent or linearly dependent? Justify your answers.

(a) $\mathbf{i} = [1 \quad 0 \quad 0]^T$, $\mathbf{j} = [0 \quad 1 \quad 0]^T$, $\mathbf{k} = [0 \quad 0 \quad 1]^T$.

(b) $\mathbf{v}_1 = [1 \quad -1 \quad 0]^T$, $\mathbf{v}_2 = [-1 \quad 1 \quad 0]^T$, $\mathbf{v}_3 = [0 \quad 0 \quad 1]^T$.

It is the concept of linear independence that really captures what we mean by 'distinct' eigenvectors: the eigenvectors of a matrix are said to be distinct if they are linearly independent. We return to this in the next subsection, but for now, let us continue our exploration of linear independence.

Linear independence and dimension

Linear independence of vectors is intimately connected with the dimension of the space in which they live. In fact, we often use the definition of linear independence to define what is meant by the *dimension* of a **vector space**. (The term *vector space* is often used to describe spaces of vectors in higher dimensions.) It should be fairly obvious that in two dimensions, we can have no more than two linearly independent vectors, because if we had three, they would all lie in the same plane and hence be linearly dependent. So in two dimensions, if we have two linearly independent vectors $\mathbf{v}_1$ and $\mathbf{v}_2$, then we can express any other vector as a linear combination of them: $\mathbf{v} = \alpha\mathbf{v}_1 + \beta\mathbf{v}_2$ (because $\mathbf{v}_1$, $\mathbf{v}_2$ and $\mathbf{v}$ are linearly dependent); see Figure 15.

Likewise, in three dimensions we can have no more than three linearly independent vectors. And if we have three linearly independent vectors $\mathbf{v}_1$, $\mathbf{v}_2$ and $\mathbf{v}_3$, then we can express any other vector as a linear combination of them: $\mathbf{v} = \alpha\mathbf{v}_1 + \beta\mathbf{v}_2 + \gamma\mathbf{v}_3$ (because $\mathbf{v}_1$, $\mathbf{v}_2$, $\mathbf{v}_3$ and $\mathbf{v}$ are linearly dependent).

We use these observations to provide a definition of the dimension of a vector space.

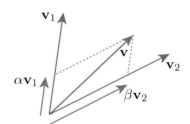

Figure 15   In two dimensions, any vector $\mathbf{v}$ may be written as a linear combination of any two linearly independent vectors $\mathbf{v}_1$ and $\mathbf{v}_2$

Dimension and basis

The **dimension** of a vector space is equal to the maximum number of linearly independent vectors that it allows.

In an n-dimensional vector space, if we have n linearly independent vectors $\mathbf{v}_1, \mathbf{v}_2, \ldots, \mathbf{v}_n$, then we can express any other vector as a linear combination of them:

$$\mathbf{v} = c_1\mathbf{v}_1 + c_2\mathbf{v}_2 + \cdots + c_n\mathbf{v}_n. \tag{7}$$

The set of linearly independent vectors $\{\mathbf{v}_1, \mathbf{v}_2, \ldots, \mathbf{v}_n\}$ is called a **basis** for the n-dimensional vector space.

This follows because in n dimensions, if $\mathbf{v}_1, \mathbf{v}_2, \ldots, \mathbf{v}_n$ are linearly independent and we add another vector $\mathbf{v}$, then $\mathbf{v}, \mathbf{v}_1, \mathbf{v}_2, \ldots, \mathbf{v}_n$ are linearly dependent, hence $\mathbf{v}$ can be expressed as a linear combination of the others.

Example 8

The vectors $\mathbf{v}_1 = \begin{bmatrix} 1 & 3 \end{bmatrix}$ and $\mathbf{v}_2 = \begin{bmatrix} 2 & -1 \end{bmatrix}$ are linearly independent. Express the vector $\mathbf{v} = \begin{bmatrix} 1 & 1 \end{bmatrix}^T$ as a linear combination of them.

Solution

Setting $\mathbf{v} = \alpha\mathbf{v}_1 + \beta\mathbf{v}_2$, we have

$$\begin{bmatrix} 1 \\ 1 \end{bmatrix} = \alpha \begin{bmatrix} 1 \\ 3 \end{bmatrix} + \beta \begin{bmatrix} 2 \\ -1 \end{bmatrix},$$

from which we get the simultaneous linear equations

$$1 = \alpha + 2\beta,$$
$$1 = 3\alpha - \beta.$$

Solving these, we obtain $\alpha = 3/7$ and $\beta = 2/7$.

Exercise 16

Are the following three-dimensional column vectors linearly independent or linearly dependent?

$$\mathbf{v}_1 = \begin{bmatrix} 1 & 0 & 2 \end{bmatrix}^T, \quad \mathbf{v}_2 = \begin{bmatrix} 1 & -\frac{1}{2} & 0 \end{bmatrix}^T,$$
$$\mathbf{v}_3 = \begin{bmatrix} 0 & \frac{1}{2} & -1 \end{bmatrix}^T, \quad \mathbf{v}_4 = \begin{bmatrix} 0 & 0 & -2 \end{bmatrix}^T.$$

Exercise 17

The vectors $\mathbf{v}_1 = \begin{bmatrix} 1 & 1 \end{bmatrix}^T$ and $\mathbf{v}_2 = \begin{bmatrix} -2 & 1 \end{bmatrix}^T$ are linearly independent. Express the vector $\mathbf{v} = \begin{bmatrix} 1 & 3 \end{bmatrix}^T$ as a linear combination of them.

Until now, in two dimensions we have taken the (linearly independent) unit Cartesian vectors $\mathbf{i}$ and $\mathbf{j}$ as the basis, and expressed every other vector as a linear combination of them: $\mathbf{v} = v_x\mathbf{i} + v_y\mathbf{j}$. Similarly, in three dimensions we have taken $\mathbf{i}$, $\mathbf{j}$ and $\mathbf{k}$ as the basis, and expressed every other vector as a linear combination of them: $\mathbf{v} = v_x\mathbf{i} + v_y\mathbf{j} + v_z\mathbf{k}$.

However, what we now know is that it is not necessary to use orthogonal unit vectors as a basis. In n dimensions, *any* set of n vectors will suffice as a basis, provided that they are all linearly independent.

Having explored the notion of linear independence, we now return to our main topic and apply these ideas (which apply to vectors in general) to the eigenvectors of a matrix.

2.5 Application of linear independence to eigenvector expansions

Recall that given an $n \times n$ matrix $\mathbf{A}$, there are a set of numbers λ (the eigenvalues) and a set of vectors $\mathbf{v}$ (the eigenvectors) that satisfy the eigenvalue equation

$$\mathbf{A}\mathbf{v} = \lambda\mathbf{v}.$$

Furthermore, if $\mathbf{v}$ is an eigenvector (with eigenvalue λ), then so is the scalar multiple $k\mathbf{v}$ (for any number k), so $\mathbf{v}$ and $k\mathbf{v}$ are not regarded as distinct eigenvectors.

In the 'usual' case there are n distinct eigenvalues with n distinct eigenvectors. 'Distinct eigenvalues' means that they are not equal. We are now in a position to say what we mean by the term 'distinct eigenvectors'.

> A matrix has n distinct eigenvectors $\mathbf{v}_1, \mathbf{v}_2, \ldots, \mathbf{v}_n$ if they are linearly independent.

Let us check that the 2×2 matrix discussed in Subsection 2.2 does indeed have only two linearly independent eigenvectors.

Example 9

In Subsection 2.2 we showed that the matrix $\mathbf{A} = \begin{bmatrix} 3 & 2 \\ 1 & 4 \end{bmatrix}$ has eigenvectors of the form $[k \quad k]^T$, corresponding to the eigenvalue 5, and eigenvectors of the form $[-2k \quad k]^T$, corresponding to the eigenvalue 2. Answer the following questions regarding these eigenvectors, justifying each of your answers.

(a) Are the eigenvectors $[1 \quad 1]^T$ and $[2 \quad 2]^T$ linearly dependent?

 (These correspond to the first eigenvector, with $k = 1$ and $k = 2$, respectively.)

(b) Are the eigenvectors $[-2 \quad 1]^T$ and $[2 \quad -1]^T$ linearly dependent?

 (These correspond to the second eigenvector, with $k = 1$ and $k = -1$, respectively.)

(c) Are the eigenvectors $[1 \quad 1]^T$ and $[-2 \quad 1]^T$ linearly dependent?

 (These correspond to the first and second eigenvectors, both with $k = 1$.)

Solution

(a) Yes, since

$$2[1 \quad 1]^T - [2 \quad 2]^T = [0 \quad 0]^T,$$

so the eigenvectors fail the test for linear independence, and are therefore linearly dependent. This is also clear geometrically, since the vectors are collinear.

(b) Yes, since

$$[-2 \quad 1]^T - [2 \quad -1]^T = [0 \quad 0]^T,$$

so the eigenvectors fail the test for linear independence, and are therefore linearly dependent. This is also clear geometrically, since the vectors are collinear.

(c) No. For the vectors to be linearly dependent, we would need to be able to find non-zero scalars α_1 and α_2 such that

$$\alpha_1 \begin{bmatrix} 1 \\ 1 \end{bmatrix} + \alpha_2 \begin{bmatrix} -2 \\ 1 \end{bmatrix} = \begin{bmatrix} 0 \\ 0 \end{bmatrix}.$$

For this to be possible, we require

$$\alpha_1 - 2\alpha_2 = 0,$$
$$\alpha_1 + \ \alpha_2 = 0.$$

However, the only solution of this pair of equations is $\alpha_1 = 0$ and $\alpha_2 = 0$, so the two eigenvectors corresponding to different eigenvalues are linearly independent (and therefore distinct).

This example demonstrates that although $\mathbf{A} = \begin{bmatrix} 3 & 2 \\ 1 & 4 \end{bmatrix}$ has an infinity of eigenvectors of the forms $[k \quad k]^T$ and $[-2k \quad k]^T$, there are only two linearly independent eigenvectors. We are free to choose any value of k. Choosing $k = 1$, we say that $\mathbf{A}$ has two linearly independent eigenvectors $\mathbf{v}_1 = [1 \quad 1]^T$ and $\mathbf{v}_2 = [-2 \quad 1]^T$. In fact, since one only ever talks about *linearly independent* eigenvectors, a statement such as this is often abbreviated to '$\mathbf{A}$ has two eigenvectors, $\mathbf{v}_1 = [1 \quad 1]^T$ and $\mathbf{v}_2 = [-2 \quad 1]^T$'.

The obvious question is: when does an $n \times n$ matrix have n linearly independent eigenvectors? It turns out that *if the eigenvalues are distinct, then so are their corresponding eigenvectors*.

This is a powerful statement, but its proof, although not difficult, is beyond the scope of this module.

> If an $n \times n$ matrix has n distinct eigenvalues, then it has n linearly independent eigenvectors.

In fact, in many (but not all) cases, even if the eigenvalues are not all distinct, we can still have n linearly independent eigenvectors.

Exercise 18

The matrix

$$\mathbf{A} = \begin{bmatrix} 1 & -2 & 4 \\ -2 & 7 & -10 \\ -1 & 4 & -6 \end{bmatrix}$$

has distinct eigenvalues $\lambda_1 = -1$, $\lambda_2 = 1$, $\lambda_3 = 2$, and corresponding eigenvectors $\mathbf{v}_1 = [-1 \quad 1 \quad 1]^T$, $\mathbf{v}_2 = [1 \quad 2 \quad 1]^T$ and $\mathbf{v}_1 = [0 \quad 2 \quad 1]^T$ (up to a multiplicative constant). Show that the eigenvectors are linearly independent.

Eigenvector expansions

We have already seen that in an n-dimensional vector space, any set of n linearly independent vectors $\mathbf{v}_1, \mathbf{v}_2, \ldots, \mathbf{v}_n$ can be used as a basis, i.e. any vector can be expressed as a linear combination of the $\mathbf{v}_i$ as in equation (7).

This means that in the 'normal' case that we are considering, when an $n \times n$ matrix $\mathbf{A}$ has n linearly independent eigenvectors, we can use these as the basis vectors. This is called an *eigenvector expansion*.

> ### Eigenvector expansion
>
> If $\mathbf{A}$ is an $n \times n$ matrix with n linearly independent eigenvectors $\mathbf{v}_1, \mathbf{v}_2, \ldots, \mathbf{v}_n$, and $\mathbf{v}$ is any n-dimensional vector, then there exist scalars $c_1, c_2, \ldots, c_n$ such that
>
> $$\mathbf{v} = c_1 \mathbf{v}_1 + c_2 \mathbf{v}_2 + \cdots + c_n \mathbf{v}_n. \tag{8}$$
>
> This is called the **eigenvector expansion** of $\mathbf{v}$.

Example 10

We saw in Exercise 13 that in the population model of Subsection 2.1, the transition matrix

$$\mathbf{T} = \begin{bmatrix} 0.9 & 0.2 \\ 0.1 & 0.8 \end{bmatrix}$$

has eigenvectors $[2 \quad 1]^T$ and $[1 \quad -1]^T$ that correspond to the distinct eigenvalues 1 and 0.7. Use this information to determine an eigenvector expansion of the two-dimensional column vector $\mathbf{x}_0 = [10\,000 \quad 8000]^T$ that represents the initial populations of Exton and Wyeville.

Solution

The eigenvectors correspond to different eigenvalues, so are linearly independent. This is also obvious because they are not collinear.

They therefore form a basis for two-dimensional vectors, so we can write

$$\mathbf{x}_0 = \begin{bmatrix} 10\,000 \\ 8000 \end{bmatrix} = c_1 \begin{bmatrix} 2 \\ 1 \end{bmatrix} + c_2 \begin{bmatrix} 1 \\ -1 \end{bmatrix} = \begin{bmatrix} 2c_1 + c_2 \\ c_1 - c_2 \end{bmatrix}.$$

Equating corresponding elements of the column vectors on the right and the left shows that

$$2c_1 + c_2 = 10\,000 \quad \text{and} \quad c_1 - c_2 = 8000.$$

Solving this simple system of linear equations, we see that $c_1 = 6000$ and $c_2 = -2000$. Thus

$$\mathbf{x}_0 = 6000 \begin{bmatrix} 2 \\ 1 \end{bmatrix} - 2000 \begin{bmatrix} 1 \\ -1 \end{bmatrix}.$$

Why is an eigenvector expansion of this kind particularly useful? The answer lies in the very simple effect that a matrix has on its own eigenvectors. To take a two-dimensional example, let λ_1 and λ_2 be the eigenvalues corresponding to the linearly independent eigenvectors $\mathbf{v}_1$ and $\mathbf{v}_2$, so $\mathbf{A}\mathbf{v}_i = \lambda_i \mathbf{v}_i$ for $i = 1, 2$. It then follows from the eigenvector expansion of any vector $\mathbf{v}$ that

$$\mathbf{A}\mathbf{v} = \mathbf{A}(c_1\mathbf{v}_1 + c_2\mathbf{v}_2) = c_1\lambda_1\mathbf{v}_1 + c_2\lambda_2\mathbf{v}_2.$$

The value of this kind of simplification will be made clear in the next subsection. However, before that you can apply it for yourself in the following exercise.

Exercise 19

We saw in Subsection 2.2 that the transformation of the plane represented by the matrix

$$\mathbf{A} = \begin{bmatrix} 3 & 2 \\ 1 & 4 \end{bmatrix}$$

has eigenvectors $[1 \quad 1]^T$ and $[-2 \quad 1]^T$ that correspond to the distinct eigenvalues 5 and 2.

(a) Use this information to determine an eigenvector expansion of the position column vector $\mathbf{r}_0 = [-2 \quad 4]^T$.

(b) Use the eigenvector expansion to calculate $\mathbf{A}\mathbf{r}_0$ without using matrix multiplication.

2.6 Convergence towards an eigenvector

We can use what we have just learned about eigenvector expansions to provide insight into the behaviour of the population model of Subsection 2.1.

You will recall that the annual changes in population of Exton and Wyeville were represented by the action of a transition matrix $\mathbf{T}$ that transformed the populations at the beginning of year n into those at the beginning of year $n+1$. We already know, from Example 10, that the initial populations of Exton and Wyeville can be written as

$$\mathbf{x}_0 = \begin{bmatrix} 10\,000 \\ 8000 \end{bmatrix} = 6000\mathbf{v}_1 - 2000\mathbf{v}_2,$$

where $\mathbf{v}_1 = [2 \quad 1]^T$ and $\mathbf{v}_2 = [1 \quad -1]^T$ are the eigenvectors corresponding to the eigenvalues $\lambda_1 = 1$ and $\lambda_2 = 0.7$ of the matrix $\mathbf{T}$.

Now consider the effect of repeatedly applying the transition matrix $\mathbf{T}$ to the initial population vector $\mathbf{x}_0 = 6000\mathbf{v}_1 - 2000\mathbf{v}_2$. Remembering that $\mathbf{T}\mathbf{v}_1 = \lambda_1\mathbf{v}_1$ and $\mathbf{T}\mathbf{v}_2 = \lambda_2\mathbf{v}_2$, a single application of $\mathbf{T}$ to $\mathbf{x}_0$ gives

$$\begin{aligned} \mathbf{x}_1 = \mathbf{T}\mathbf{x}_0 &= \mathbf{T}(6000\mathbf{v}_1 - 2000\mathbf{v}_2) \\ &= 6000\mathbf{T}\mathbf{v}_1 - 2000\mathbf{T}\mathbf{v}_2 \\ &= 6000\lambda_1\mathbf{v}_1 - 2000\lambda_2\mathbf{v}_2. \end{aligned}$$

A second application of $\mathbf{T}$ gives

$$\mathbf{x}_2 = \mathbf{T}\mathbf{x}_1 = \mathbf{T}(6000\lambda_1\mathbf{v}_1 - 2000\lambda_2\mathbf{v}_2) = 6000\lambda_1^2\mathbf{v}_1 - 2000\lambda_2^2\mathbf{v}_2.$$

A third application of $\mathbf{T}$ gives

$$\mathbf{x}_3 = \mathbf{T}\mathbf{x}_2 = \mathbf{T}(6000\lambda_1^2\mathbf{v}_1 - 2000\lambda_2^2\mathbf{v}_2) = 6000\lambda_1^3\mathbf{v}_1 - 2000\lambda_2^3\mathbf{v}_2,$$

and after k applications,

$$\mathbf{x}_k = \mathbf{T}\mathbf{x}_{k-1} = 6000\lambda_1^k\mathbf{v}_1 - 2000\lambda_2^k\mathbf{v}_2.$$

Now, $\lambda_1 = 1$, so λ_1^k is also equal to 1. However, $\lambda_2 = 0.7$, so $\lambda_2^2 = 0.49$, $\lambda_2^3 = 0.343$ and $\lambda_2^{30} = 0.000\,022\,5$ (to three significant figures). As we repeatedly apply $\mathbf{T}$ to $\mathbf{x}_0$, we will find that the contribution of $\mathbf{v}_2$ will become smaller and smaller as k increases, so we have

$$\mathbf{x}_k \simeq 6000\mathbf{v}_1 = \begin{bmatrix} 12\,000 \\ 6000 \end{bmatrix} \quad \text{for large } k.$$

This is exactly what happened in the population model, where we found that the populations approached 12 000 in Exton and 6000 in Wyeville.

Suppose that we start with some other initial population $\mathbf{x}_0$. Because we can always write $\mathbf{x}_0 = c_1\mathbf{v}_1 + c_2\mathbf{v}_2$, repeated application of $\mathbf{T}$ will give

$$\begin{aligned} \mathbf{x}_k = \mathbf{T}^k(c_1\mathbf{v}_1 + c_2\mathbf{v}_2) \\ = c_1\mathbf{T}^k\mathbf{v}_1 + c_2\mathbf{T}^k\mathbf{v}_2 \\ = c_1\lambda_1^k\mathbf{v}_1 + c_2\lambda_2^k\mathbf{v}_2 \\ \simeq c_1\mathbf{v}_1 \quad \text{for large } k. \end{aligned}$$

More generally, suppose that we have an arbitrary $n \times n$ matrix $\mathbf{A}$ and a vector $\mathbf{x}$. What will be the result of repeated application of $\mathbf{A}$ to $\mathbf{x}$, i.e. what is $\mathbf{A}^k\mathbf{x}$? If $\mathbf{A}$ has n linearly independent eigenvectors $\mathbf{v}_i$, then we can always write $\mathbf{x}$ as an eigenvector expansion

$$\mathbf{x} = c_1\mathbf{v}_1 + c_2\mathbf{v}_2 + \cdots + c_n\mathbf{v}_n.$$

Let us assume that we have chosen our initial vector $\mathbf{x}$ so that no c_i is zero. Then since $\mathbf{A}\mathbf{v}_i = \lambda_i \mathbf{v}_i$, where λ_i is the eigenvalue corresponding to eigenvector $\mathbf{v}_i$, we have

$$\mathbf{A}^k \mathbf{v}_i = \lambda_i^k \mathbf{v}_i.$$

Hence

$$\begin{aligned}
\mathbf{A}^k \mathbf{x} &= \mathbf{A}^k (c_1 \mathbf{v}_1 + c_2 \mathbf{v}_2 + \cdots + c_n \mathbf{v}_n) \\
&= c_1 \mathbf{A}^k \mathbf{v}_1 + c_2 \mathbf{A}^k \mathbf{v}_2 + \cdots + c_n \mathbf{A}^k \mathbf{v}_n \\
&= c_1 \lambda_1^k \mathbf{v}_1 + c_2 \lambda_2^k \mathbf{v}_2 + \cdots + c_n \lambda_n^k \mathbf{v}_n.
\end{aligned}$$

As k gets larger and larger, the eigenvalue with largest modulus will dominate. So if λ_p is the eigenvalue with largest modulus, we have

$$\mathbf{A}^k \mathbf{x} \simeq c_p \lambda_p^k \mathbf{v}_p \quad \text{for large } k.$$

So we see that for (almost) any initial vector $\mathbf{x}$, for large k, $\mathbf{A}^k \mathbf{x}$ is proportional to the eigenvector with largest modulus eigenvalue. And since we ignore any scaling of eigenvectors, we can say that $\mathbf{A}^k \mathbf{x}$ is equal to the eigenvector with largest modulus eigenvalue. This observation is the basis for many numerical algorithms for finding eigenvectors of very large matrices.

Exercise 20

Use $\mathbf{A}$, $\mathbf{r}_0$ and the eigenvector expansion of Exercise 19 to determine (to two significant figures) $\mathbf{r}_8 = \mathbf{A}^8 \mathbf{r}_0$, $\mathbf{r}_9 = \mathbf{A}^9 \mathbf{r}_0$ and $\mathbf{r}_{10} = \mathbf{A}^{10} \mathbf{r}_0$. Comment on your results.

Google's PageRank algorithm: the world's largest eigenvector problem

Before Google, web search engines were a hit and miss affair, often returning masses of irrelevant links. The advent of Google, in the late 1990s, changed all that. Apart from its phenomenal speed, it seemed to deliver 'the best' pages available to a given search. The principal reason for this is its PageRank algorithm (see Figure 16), named after its co-inventor Larry Page (Figure 17), who also co-founded Google.

Figure 16   An illustration of how the PageRank algorithm works: the size of each face is proportional to the total size of the other faces that are pointing to it

Figure 17   Larry Page, co-inventor of the PageRank algorithm

The PageRank algorithm quantitatively assesses the 'importance' of each page on the web by the number of other 'important' web pages that link to it. One way to get a feel for how it works is to imagine playing a (rather dull) game. Start on any web page and click on any link at random. From the new web page, again click on any link at random. Keep doing this, very many times, randomly going from web page to web page via the links. The PageRank of a particular web page is the proportion of time spent visiting that web page.

Mathematically, this is modelled as follows. First label every page on the web by an integer i (the order is not important). Then construct a huge matrix $\mathbf{A}$, where every row and column represents a page on the web. ($\mathbf{A}$ is currently approximately of order $10^{10} \times 10^{10}$, corresponding to the $\simeq 10^{10}$ current web pages.) Roughly speaking, each element A_{ij} is set equal to the probability of going from web page i to web page j by randomly clicking on a link; e.g. $A_{5,23}$ is the probability of visiting web page 23 by randomly clicking on a link on web page 5. Now consider a vector, each element of which represents the probability of being on a web page. Starting the game on web page i is represented by the vector $\mathbf{x}_0$, all of whose elements are zero except for the ith element, which is unity. The vector $\mathbf{x}_1 = \mathbf{A}\mathbf{x}_0$ gives the probability of being on any web page after one click. The vector $\mathbf{x}_n = \mathbf{A}^n\mathbf{x}_0$ gives the probability of being on any web page after n clicks. The situation is very similar to the Exton–Wyeville population model, and the final PageRank is given by the eigenvector of $\mathbf{A}$ with largest eigenvalue, i.e. $\mathbf{x}_n$ for very large n. The web page with largest PageRank corresponds to the largest element of $\mathbf{x}_n$.

3 Finding eigenvalues and eigenvectors

You have now seen several examples of eigenvectors and eigenvalues, and some of their uses. You have also been told a little about finding eigenvectors and eigenvalues through iteration. The time has now come for a more detailed investigation of the determination of eigenvalues and eigenvectors. In the next subsection we introduce the important notion of the *characteristic equation* of a matrix. This is a polynomial equation, the roots of which are the eigenvalues of the matrix. Once the eigenvalues have been found, methods based on row operations can be used to construct the related eigenvectors. We will examine some examples based on 2×2 and 3×3 matrices, but you should be aware that many of the ideas are very general, and that modern applied mathematics makes extensive use of computer packages to find the eigenvectors and eigenvalues of matrices, often based on the row operations and iterative methods that have already been mentioned.

3.1 The characteristic equation

An eigenvector $\mathbf{v}$ of an $n \times n$ matrix $\mathbf{A}$ satisfies $\mathbf{Av} = \lambda\mathbf{v}$. By introducing an $n \times n$ identity matrix $\mathbf{I}$, this can be written as $\mathbf{Av} = \lambda\mathbf{Iv}$, i.e.

$$(\mathbf{A} - \lambda\mathbf{I})\mathbf{v} = \mathbf{0}. \tag{9}$$

Clearly $\mathbf{v} = \mathbf{0}$ is a solution of this equation – called the **trivial solution**. We are not interested in this because, by definition, $\mathbf{v} = \mathbf{0}$ is not an eigenvector. For there to be non-trivial solutions $\mathbf{v}$, the $n \times n$ square matrix on the left, $(\mathbf{A} - \lambda\mathbf{I})$, known as the **characteristic matrix** of $\mathbf{A}$, must be non-invertible. (If it were invertible, the unique solution would be $\mathbf{v} = (\mathbf{A} - \lambda\mathbf{I})^{-1}\mathbf{0} = \mathbf{0}$, which is trivial.) For the characteristic matrix to be non-invertible, it must be singular, i.e. its determinant must be zero: $\det(\mathbf{A} - \lambda\mathbf{I}) = 0$. Expanding the determinant gives a polynomial equation of degree n satisfied by every eigenvalue of $\mathbf{A}$.

For example, in the case of a 2×2 matrix $\mathbf{A} = [a_{ij}]$ and an eigenvector $\mathbf{v} = [v_1 \quad v_2]^T$, equation (9) is

$$\left(\begin{bmatrix} a_{11} & a_{12} \\ a_{21} & a_{22} \end{bmatrix} - \lambda \begin{bmatrix} 1 & 0 \\ 0 & 1 \end{bmatrix} \right) \begin{bmatrix} v_1 \\ v_2 \end{bmatrix} = \begin{bmatrix} 0 \\ 0 \end{bmatrix},$$

which can also be written as

$$\begin{bmatrix} a_{11} - \lambda & a_{12} \\ a_{21} & a_{22} - \lambda \end{bmatrix} \begin{bmatrix} v_1 \\ v_2 \end{bmatrix} = \begin{bmatrix} 0 \\ 0 \end{bmatrix}.$$

So for a non-trivial solution, we require

$$\begin{vmatrix} a_{11} - \lambda & a_{12} \\ a_{21} & a_{22} - \lambda \end{vmatrix} = 0.$$

The determinant here gives a quadratic equation for λ, whose two solutions are the eigenvalues of $\mathbf{A}$.

Characteristic equation

Let $\mathbf{A}$ be any square matrix. The equation

$$\det(\mathbf{A} - \lambda\mathbf{I}) = 0 \tag{10}$$

is called the **characteristic equation** of $\mathbf{A}$. Its roots, i.e. the values of λ that satisfy the characteristic equation, are the eigenvalues of $\mathbf{A}$.

Example 11

Write out the characteristic equation of the transition matrix introduced in the Exton–Wyeville population model,

$$\mathbf{T} = \begin{bmatrix} 0.9 & 0.2 \\ 0.1 & 0.8 \end{bmatrix},$$

and use it to determine the two eigenvalues that arise in that model.

Solution

In this case, the characteristic equation is given by

$$\begin{vmatrix} 0.9 - \lambda & 0.2 \\ 0.1 & 0.8 - \lambda \end{vmatrix} = 0.$$

Expanding the determinant gives

$$(0.9 - \lambda)(0.8 - \lambda) - 0.1 \times 0.2 = 0,$$

which can be rewritten as

$$\lambda^2 - 1.7\lambda + 0.7 = 0.$$

This is a quadratic equation in λ that may be either solved by the standard formula or factorised to give

$$(\lambda - 1.0)(\lambda - 0.7) = 0.$$

By either approach, it is clear that there are only two roots, $\lambda_1 = 1.0$ and $\lambda_2 = 0.7$. You learned earlier that these are the two eigenvalues of $\mathbf{T}$.

Exercise 21

Write out the characteristic equation of the matrix

$$\mathbf{A} = \begin{bmatrix} 3 & 2 \\ 1 & 4 \end{bmatrix},$$

and hence find the eigenvalues of $\mathbf{A}$.

3.2 Eigenvalues of 2×2 matrices

The following procedure, based on the characteristic equation, can be used to find the two eigenvalues of any 2×2 matrix.

Procedure 2   Finding eigenvalues of a 2×2 matrix

Let $\mathbf{A} = \begin{bmatrix} a & b \\ c & d \end{bmatrix}$. To find the eigenvalues of $\mathbf{A}$, do the following.

1. Write down the characteristic equation $\det(\mathbf{A} - \lambda\mathbf{I}) = 0$.

2. Expand this as

$$\begin{vmatrix} a - \lambda & b \\ c & d - \lambda \end{vmatrix} = \lambda^2 - (a + d)\lambda + (ad - bc) = 0. \qquad (11)$$

3. Solve this quadratic equation to find the two values of λ, which are the required eigenvalues.

Exercise 22

Calculate the eigenvalues of the following matrices.

(a) $\mathbf{G} = \begin{bmatrix} 3 & 2 \\ 1 & 2 \end{bmatrix}$ (b) $\mathbf{H} = \begin{bmatrix} 2 & 2 \\ -1 & 2 \end{bmatrix}$

Exercise 23

Calculate the eigenvalues of the following two-dimensional rotation and scaling matrices.

(a) $\mathbf{R} = \begin{bmatrix} \cos\theta & -\sin\theta \\ \sin\theta & \cos\theta \end{bmatrix}$ (b) $\mathbf{M} = \begin{bmatrix} l & 0 \\ 0 & k \end{bmatrix}$

For a 2×2 matrix we can always solve the quadratic equation that results from the characteristic equation and hence determine the two eigenvalues. Nonetheless, it is worth investigating the 2×2 case a little further because of the light that it can shed on a number of problems.

As a first step we introduce the quantity known as the *trace* of a matrix.

> **Trace of a matrix**
>
> Given any $n \times n$ matrix $\mathbf{A} = [a_{ij}]$, the **trace** of that matrix is denoted $\operatorname{tr}\mathbf{A}$ and is the sum of the elements on its leading diagonal:
>
> $$\operatorname{tr}\mathbf{A} = a_{11} + a_{22} + \cdots + a_{nn}. \tag{12}$$

It follows from this definition that in the case of a general 2×2 matrix $\mathbf{A} = \begin{bmatrix} a & b \\ c & d \end{bmatrix}$, its trace is given by $\operatorname{tr}\mathbf{A} = a + d$. However, for such a matrix the determinant is $\det\mathbf{A} = ad - bc$. It therefore follows from equation (11) that the expanded form of the characteristic equation of a 2×2 matrix can be written as follows.

> **Characteristic equation of a 2×2 matrix**
>
> $$\lambda^2 - \operatorname{tr}\mathbf{A}\,\lambda + \det\mathbf{A} = 0. \tag{13}$$

Note that this formula is valid *only* for 2×2 matrices.

Applying the generic formula for finding the roots of a quadratic equation, we see that the two eigenvalues are given by

$$\lambda = \tfrac{1}{2}\left(\operatorname{tr}\mathbf{A} \pm \sqrt{D}\right), \quad \text{where } D = (\operatorname{tr}\mathbf{A})^2 - 4\det\mathbf{A}. \tag{14}$$

The quantity D is known as the **discriminant**. For a 2×2 matrix $\mathbf{A} = \begin{bmatrix} a & b \\ c & d \end{bmatrix}$, the discriminant is

$$D = (a + d)^2 - 4(ad - bc) = (a - d)^2 + 4bc.$$

Hence the two eigenvalues can be expressed as follows.

> **Eigenvalues of a 2×2 matrix**
>
> $$\lambda = \tfrac{1}{2}\left(a + d \pm \sqrt{(a-d)^2 + 4bc}\right). \tag{15}$$

For a real 2×2 matrix we thus have three cases:

- a pair of distinct real eigenvalues if $D > 0$
- repeated real eigenvalues if $D = 0$
- a pair of complex eigenvalues if $D < 0$.

The first and third of these cases correspond to the normal situation with two distinct eigenvalues. Note, however, that when $D < 0$, we have $\lambda = \tfrac{1}{2}\left(\operatorname{tr}\mathbf{A} \pm \sqrt{-|D|}\right) = \tfrac{1}{2}\left(\operatorname{tr}\mathbf{A} \pm i\sqrt{|D|}\right)$, so the eigenvalues are complex, with one eigenvalue being the complex conjugate of the other. (You saw instances of this in Exercises 22 and 23.) The second case, when $D = 0$, means that the characteristic equation has a repeated root.

Exercise 24

Show that the characteristic equation of the matrix $\mathbf{S} = \begin{bmatrix} 1 & s \\ 0 & 1 \end{bmatrix}$, where s is a number, has a repeated root, and determine what it is.

There are two useful results that follow directly from equation (14). First, note that adding the two eigenvalues gives

$$\lambda_1 + \lambda_2 = \operatorname{tr}\mathbf{A}.$$

Second, note that multiplying the eigenvalues gives

$$\begin{aligned} \lambda_1\lambda_2 &= \tfrac{1}{2}\left(\operatorname{tr}\mathbf{A} + \sqrt{D}\right)\tfrac{1}{2}\left(\operatorname{tr}\mathbf{A} - \sqrt{D}\right) \\ &= \tfrac{1}{4}\left((\operatorname{tr}\mathbf{A})^2 - D\right) \\ &= \det\mathbf{A}. \end{aligned}$$

Although we have derived these results for a 2×2 matrix, they both turn out to be generally true for square matrices of any order. The two general results are as follows.

> **Trace and determinant rules for eigenvalues**
>
> For any $n \times n$ matrix:
> - the trace is equal to the sum of all its eigenvalues
> - the determinant is equal to the product of all its eigenvalues.

These results are frequently used to assist and check matrix calculations.

Exercise 25

Given that $\lambda_1 = 26.115$ and $\lambda_2 = -0.115$ are the eigenvalues of the matrix

$$\mathbf{A} = \begin{bmatrix} 11 & 12 \\ 14 & 15 \end{bmatrix},$$

confirm that they pass the trace and determinant checks (working to two decimal places).

3.3 Eigenvalues of larger matrices

Formulating and solving the characteristic equation of some 3×3 matrices is not too daunting, but beyond that the task becomes manually challenging. With the wide availability of computer packages, there is a tendency to turn rapidly to a machine that will either perform the necessary algebra or provide numerical estimates of the eigenvalues.

Example 12

Write down the characteristic equation of the matrix

$$\mathbf{A} = \begin{bmatrix} 3 & -1 & -1 \\ -1 & 3 & 1 \\ -1 & 1 & 5 \end{bmatrix},$$

and given that one of its roots is 6, find the other two roots. Confirm that the sum of the roots gives the trace of $\mathbf{A}$, and the product of the roots is the determinant of $\mathbf{A}$.

Solution

In this case the characteristic equation of $\mathbf{A}$ (equation (10)) is given by

$$\det(\mathbf{A} - \lambda\mathbf{I}) = \begin{vmatrix} 3-\lambda & -1 & -1 \\ -1 & 3-\lambda & 1 \\ -1 & 1 & 5-\lambda \end{vmatrix} = 0.$$

Using Laplace's rule (see Unit 4) to expand the determinant in terms of the elements of the top row gives

$$(3-\lambda)[(3-\lambda)(5-\lambda) - 1] - (-1)[-(5-\lambda) + 1] - 1[-1 + (3-\lambda)] = 0,$$

which may be rewritten as

$$\lambda^3 - 11\lambda^2 + 36\lambda - 36 = 0. \tag{16}$$

Knowing that one of the roots of this equation is $\lambda = 6$, we can extract a factor $(\lambda - 6)$ to obtain

$$(\lambda - 6)(\lambda^2 - 5\lambda + 6) = 0.$$

(Factorising an equation like this is best done in bits. First, knowing that $\lambda = 6$ is a root, we write $(\lambda - 6)(a\lambda^2 + b\lambda + c)$ for some constants a, b, c. Then comparing with equation (16) immediately gives $a = 1$ and $c = 6$. Finally, expanding $(\lambda - 6)(\lambda^2 + b\lambda + 6)$ and comparing with equation (16) gives $b = -5$.)

Then, either by using the usual formula to factorise the quadratic function, or factorising by inspection, we can write

$$(\lambda - 2)(\lambda - 3)(\lambda - 6) = 0.$$

This shows that the three eigenvalues are 2, 3 and 6.

Adding the three eigenvalues gives $2 + 3 + 6 = 11$, which is also the sum of the leading diagonal elements, $\operatorname{tr} \mathbf{A} = 3 + 3 + 5$. This confirms that the trace of $\mathbf{A}$ is equal to the sum of its eigenvalues.

Similarly, the product of the eigenvalues is $2 \times 3 \times 6 = 36$, while using Laplace's rule to expand $\det \mathbf{A}$ gives

$$\det \mathbf{A} = 3(15 - 1) - (-1)(-5 + 1) - 1(-1 + 3) = 42 - 4 - 2 = 36.$$

This confirms that the determinant of $\mathbf{A}$ is equal to the product of its eigenvalues.

Exercise 26

Find the eigenvalues of the following matrices, given that in each case one of the eigenvalues is 2.

(a) $\mathbf{A} = \begin{bmatrix} 1 & -2 & 4 \\ -2 & 7 & -10 \\ -1 & 4 & -6 \end{bmatrix}$ (b) $\mathbf{A} = \begin{bmatrix} 4 & 7 & 6 \\ 6 & 5 & 6 \\ -8 & -10 & -10 \end{bmatrix}$

Exercise 27

Check that your answers to Exercise 26 satisfy the trace and determinant rules for eigenvalues.

3.4   General results on eigenvalues

In this subsection we list some general results regarding the eigenvalues of certain types of $n \times n$ matrices. We mainly prove the results for 2×2 matrices, but you should note that they are valid in general.

We already know the trace and determinant rules, which are valid for any square matrix. Now let us consider some rules that apply to special types of matrices.

Real matrices

Recall that a **real matrix** is one whose elements are all real. In Subsection 3.2, we proved that for a real 2×2 matrix, if the eigenvalues are complex, then they occur in complex conjugate pairs; i.e. for a real matrix, if λ is an eigenvalue, then so is $\overline{\lambda}$.

It is trivial to prove this for any real $n \times n$ matrix. If $\mathbf{A}$ is a real matrix and λ is a complex eigenvalue with corresponding eigenvector $\mathbf{v}$, then $\mathbf{A}\mathbf{v} = \lambda\mathbf{v}$. So taking the complex conjugate of both sides, we get $\overline{\mathbf{A}\mathbf{v}} = \overline{\lambda}\overline{\mathbf{v}}$, which is equivalent to

$$\overline{\mathbf{A}}\overline{\mathbf{v}} = \overline{\lambda}\overline{\mathbf{v}}.$$

But $\mathbf{A}$ is real, so $\overline{\mathbf{A}} = \mathbf{A}$, and we have

$$\mathbf{A}\overline{\mathbf{v}} = \overline{\lambda}\overline{\mathbf{v}}.$$

Hence $\overline{\lambda}$ is also an eigenvalue of $\mathbf{A}$, with corresponding eigenvector $\overline{\mathbf{v}}$.

Exercise 28

The matrix

$$\mathbf{A} = \begin{bmatrix} 1 & 0 & 1 \\ 0 & 1 & 0 \\ -1 & 0 & 1 \end{bmatrix}$$

has one eigenvalue $\lambda_1 = 1 + i$. Determine the other two eigenvalues without solving the characteristic equation.

Triangular matrices

A matrix is **triangular** if all the entries above (or below) the leading diagonal are 0, e.g.

A **diagonal** matrix is a special type of triangular matrix.

$$\begin{bmatrix} a & b \\ 0 & d \end{bmatrix}, \begin{bmatrix} a & b & c \\ 0 & d & e \\ 0 & 0 & f \end{bmatrix}, \quad \begin{bmatrix} a & 0 \\ c & d \end{bmatrix}, \begin{bmatrix} a & 0 & 0 \\ b & c & 0 \\ d & e & f \end{bmatrix}, \quad \begin{bmatrix} a & 0 & 0 \\ 0 & b & 0 \\ 0 & 0 & c \end{bmatrix}.$$

(upper triangular)   (lower triangular)   (diagonal)

For a 2×2 triangular matrix $\begin{bmatrix} a & b \\ 0 & d \end{bmatrix}$ or $\begin{bmatrix} a & 0 \\ c & d \end{bmatrix}$, the characteristic equation is

$$(a - \lambda)(d - \lambda) = 0,$$

hence the eigenvalues are $\lambda = a$ and $\lambda = d$. Thus the eigenvalues of a triangular matrix are the diagonal entries. This is true for any $n \times n$ triangular matrix, and the proof is very similar to that given above.

Exercise 29

What are the eigenvalues of the matrix $\begin{bmatrix} 1 & 3 \\ 0 & 2 \end{bmatrix}$?

Real symmetric matrices

A matrix is **symmetric** if it is equal to its transpose, i.e. $\mathbf{A} = \mathbf{A}^T$ – that is, the entries are symmetric about the leading diagonal, e.g.

$$\begin{bmatrix} a & b \\ b & c \end{bmatrix}, \quad \begin{bmatrix} a & d & e \\ d & b & f \\ e & f & c \end{bmatrix}.$$

For a *real* 2×2 symmetric matrix $\mathbf{A} = \begin{bmatrix} a & b \\ b & d \end{bmatrix}$, the characteristic equation is (see equation (11))

$$\lambda^2 - (a + d)\lambda + (ad - b^2) = 0,$$

hence the eigenvalues are

$$\lambda = \tfrac{1}{2}\left(a + d \pm \sqrt{(a+d)^2 - 4(ad - b^2)}\right).$$

The term under the square root (i.e. the discriminant) is

$$(a + d)^2 - 4(ad - b^2) = (a^2 + 2ad + d^2) - 4ad + 4b^2 = (a - d)^2 + 4b^2,$$

which is the sum of two squares and therefore cannot be negative. It follows that the eigenvalues of a real symmetric matrix are real.

There is a well-known proof of this result for $n \times n$ real symmetric matrices, which we include in Subsection 4.2, but you are not required to know it.

Note that if a matrix has real eigenvalues, it is not necessarily true that it is a real symmetric matrix.

Exercise 30

Under what circumstances can a symmetric matrix $\begin{bmatrix} a & b \\ b & d \end{bmatrix}$ have a repeated eigenvalue?

Non-invertible matrices

A *non-invertible* matrix has determinant equal to 0 (see Unit 4). However, from the determinant rule, if $\lambda_1, \lambda_2, \ldots, \lambda_n$ are the eigenvalues of an $n \times n$ *non-invertible* matrix $\mathbf{A}$, then

$$\lambda_1 \lambda_2 \ldots \lambda_n = \det \mathbf{A} = 0.$$

It follows that a matrix is non-invertible if and only if at least one of its eigenvalues is 0. Also, a matrix is invertible if and only if all its eigenvalues are non-zero.

We summarise what we have learned.

Properties of eigenvalues – summary

- The product of the eigenvalues of $\mathbf{A}$ is $\det \mathbf{A}$.
- The sum of the eigenvalues of $\mathbf{A}$ is $\operatorname{tr} \mathbf{A}$.
- The complex eigenvalues and corresponding eigenvectors of a real matrix occur in complex conjugate pairs.
- The eigenvalues of a triangular matrix are the diagonal entries.
- The eigenvalues of a real symmetric matrix are real.
- A matrix is non-invertible if and only if at least one of its eigenvalues is 0.

Exercise 31

Without solving the characteristic equation, what can you say about the eigenvalues of each of the following matrices?

(a) $\mathbf{A} = \begin{bmatrix} 67 & 72 \\ 72 & -17 \end{bmatrix}$ (b) $\mathbf{A} = \begin{bmatrix} 67 & 72 \\ 0 & -17 \end{bmatrix}$ (c) $\mathbf{A} = \begin{bmatrix} 288 & 72 \\ 72 & 18 \end{bmatrix}$

We now turn to eigenvectors.

3.5 The eigenvector equation

An eigenvector $\mathbf{v}$ of a general $n \times n$ real matrix $\mathbf{A}$ satisfies $\mathbf{Av} = \lambda\mathbf{v}$. As you saw in Subsection 3.1 (equation (9)), by introducing an $n \times n$ identity matrix $\mathbf{I}$, this condition can be written as the following **eigenvector equation**.

> **Eigenvector equation**
> $$(\mathbf{A} - \lambda\mathbf{I})\mathbf{v} = \mathbf{0}. \tag{17}$$

Earlier we were interested in the determinant of the left-hand side that led to the characteristic equation and the eigenvalues. Now we need to find the non-zero solutions of the linear equations themselves. This is most easily described in the context of 2×2 matrices, as in the next subsection.

3.6 Eigenvectors of 2×2 matrices

Consider a 2×2 matrix
$$\mathbf{A} = \begin{bmatrix} a & b \\ c & d \end{bmatrix}.$$

Suppose that we have solved the characteristic equation $\det(\mathbf{A} - \lambda\mathbf{I}) = 0$ to find the eigenvalues of this matrix. Now let us try to find the eigenvectors. Suppose that the unknown eigenvector $\mathbf{v} = [x \quad y]^T$ has a known eigenvalue λ. Then the eigenvector equation
$$(\mathbf{A} - \lambda\mathbf{I})\mathbf{v} = \mathbf{0}$$
gives
$$\begin{bmatrix} a - \lambda & b \\ c & d - \lambda \end{bmatrix} \begin{bmatrix} x \\ y \end{bmatrix} = \begin{bmatrix} 0 \\ 0 \end{bmatrix},$$
which is equivalent to the equations
$$(a - \lambda)x + by = 0, \tag{18}$$
$$cx + (d - \lambda)y = 0. \tag{19}$$

Since we know a, b, c, d and λ, this is a pair of simultaneous linear equations that can be solved for x and y. We did this in Section 1. However, there is a subtlety: because $\det(\mathbf{A} - \lambda\mathbf{I}) = 0$, the system of equations is singular. Such systems of linear equations were discussed in

Subsection 1.4, where we discovered that they can have either no solution or an infinity of solutions. In fact, it turns out that the two equations (18) and (19) are really the same equation written in two different-looking ways. So we need to solve only one of them, as the other gives no information, thus we obtain an infinity of solutions (see Example 5(c) for a similar case).

To prove that the two equations are the same, use the fact that $\det(\mathbf{A} - \lambda\mathbf{I})$ $= (a - \lambda)(d - \lambda) - bc = 0.$

We should not be surprised by this, because the eigenvector equation determines the eigenvectors only up to an arbitrary scalar multiple. So when we solve equation (18) or (19) for x and y, we obtain a solution of the form $\mathbf{v} = k[x \quad y]^T$, for an arbitrary (non-zero) scalar k.

If we want, we can assign an arbitrary value to k, such as $k = 1$. It should then be understood that any (non-zero) scalar multiple is also an eigenvector. However we choose to handle it, having found the eigenvector corresponding to λ, our next step should be to use the other eigenvalue of $\mathbf{A}$ to find a second eigenvector.

Here is a numerical example of what we have just been describing.

Example 13

Find the eigenvalues and corresponding eigenvectors of

$$\mathbf{A} = \begin{bmatrix} 1 & 4 \\ 1 & -2 \end{bmatrix}.$$

Solution

The characteristic equation is

$$\begin{vmatrix} 1 - \lambda & 4 \\ 1 & -2 - \lambda \end{vmatrix} = 0.$$

Expanding gives $(1 - \lambda)(-2 - \lambda) - 4 = 0$, which simplifies to $\lambda^2 + \lambda - 6 = 0$. So the eigenvalues are $\lambda = 2$ and $\lambda = -3$.

Let $\mathbf{v} = [x \quad y]^T$ be an eigenvector. Then the eigenvector equation $(\mathbf{A} - \lambda\mathbf{I})\mathbf{v} = \mathbf{0}$ is

$$\begin{bmatrix} 1 - \lambda & 4 \\ 1 & -2 - \lambda \end{bmatrix} \begin{bmatrix} x \\ y \end{bmatrix} = \begin{bmatrix} 0 \\ 0 \end{bmatrix},$$

which is equivalent to the system

$$\begin{aligned} (1 - \lambda)x + \qquad 4y &= 0, \\ x + (-2 - \lambda)y &= 0. \end{aligned}$$

Now consider these for each of the eigenvalues in turn.

- For $\lambda = 2$, the eigenvector equations become

$$-x + 4y = 0 \quad \text{and} \quad x - 4y = 0.$$

Clearly these equations are the same, so we have the single equation $4y = x$. This single equation shows that if $x = k$, then $y = k/4$. So the eigenvector corresponding to $\lambda = 2$ has the general form $[k \quad k/4]^T$. Choosing $k = 4$ for convenience gives $[4 \quad 1]^T$ as an eigenvector corresponding to eigenvalue $\lambda = 2$. As usual, any non-zero scalar multiple is also an eigenvector.

Note that even though the two equations provide the same information, both are examined since this is a useful check.

- For $\lambda = -3$, the eigenvector equations become

$$4x + 4y = 0 \quad \text{and} \quad x + y = 0,$$

which are equivalent to the single equation $y = -x$. This single equation tells us that if $x = k$, then $y = -k$. So the eigenvector corresponding to $\lambda = -3$ has the general form $[k \quad -k]^T$; choosing $k = 1$ gives $[1 \quad -1]^T$.

Of course, it is always good practice to check that we have correctly determined our eigenvalues and eigenvectors by checking that they satisfy $\mathbf{A}\mathbf{v} = \lambda\mathbf{v}$ explicitly.

Here, as a summary, is the general procedure.

Procedure 3   Finding the eigenvectors of a 2×2 matrix

Let $\mathbf{A} = \begin{bmatrix} a & b \\ c & d \end{bmatrix}$. To find an eigenvector corresponding to the eigenvalue λ, do the following.

1. Write down the eigenvector equations

$$\begin{align} (a - \lambda)x + \quad\quad by &= 0, \tag{20} \\ cx + (d - \lambda)y &= 0. \tag{21} \end{align}$$

2. These equations reduce to a single equation that is readily solved for x and y. The eigenvector is given by $\mathbf{v} = [x \quad y]^T$, with x and y replaced by their solved values. Any non-zero scalar multiple is also an eigenvector.

3. Repeat for the second eigenvalue to find the second eigenvector.

Exercise 32

Find the eigenvalues and eigenvectors of the following matrices.

(a) $\mathbf{A} = \begin{bmatrix} 8 & -5 \\ 10 & -7 \end{bmatrix}$ (b) $\mathbf{A} = \begin{bmatrix} 2 & 1 \\ 1 & 2 \end{bmatrix}$

Exercise 33

Find the eigenvectors of

$$\mathbf{A} = \begin{bmatrix} \cos\theta & -\sin\theta \\ \sin\theta & \cos\theta \end{bmatrix}$$

when θ is not an integer multiple of π.

(*Hint*: The eigenvalues $\cos\theta \pm i\sin\theta = e^{\pm i\theta}$ were found in Exercise 23.)

3.7 Eigenvectors of larger matrices

In the general case, if $\mathbf{A}$ is an $n \times n$ matrix, there will be n eigenvalues. For each eigenvalue λ, the eigenvector equation $(\mathbf{A} - \lambda\mathbf{I})\mathbf{v} = \mathbf{0}$ will provide n simultaneous equations, and we must solve these to determine the n components of the corresponding eigenvector. As before, because $\det(\mathbf{A} - \lambda\mathbf{I}) = 0$, the system of n equations is singular with an infinity of solutions, corresponding to the fact that any (non-zero) scalar multiple of an eigenvector is also an eigenvector. That means that in at least one case (and perhaps more), we will not be able to determine a unique value for a component of $\mathbf{v}$, and we will have to represent that component by an arbitrary non-zero scalar k. The other components can then be expressed in terms of that value k.

Often, the best way of solving the system of eigenvector equations is to use Gaussian elimination, as described in Section 1. The procedure is to express the eigenvector equations in terms of an augmented matrix, then use row operations to reduce the coefficient matrix to upper triangular form. The fact that the system is singular will result in at least one row of zeros in the augmented matrix, indicating that the corresponding unknown can be assigned the arbitrary value k. This row can be made the bottom row of the augmented matrix. All the other components can then be expressed in terms of k, using back substitution.

Here is a numerical example.

Example 14

Find the three eigenvectors of

$$\mathbf{A} = \begin{bmatrix} 1 & -2 & 4 \\ -2 & 7 & -10 \\ -1 & 4 & -6 \end{bmatrix},$$

given that the eigenvalues are -1, 1 and 2.

Solution

The eigenvector equation for the given matrix, for $\mathbf{v} = [x_1 \quad x_2 \quad x_3]^T$, may be written

$$\begin{bmatrix} 1-\lambda & -2 & 4 \\ -2 & 7-\lambda & -10 \\ -1 & 4 & -6-\lambda \end{bmatrix} \begin{bmatrix} x_1 \\ x_2 \\ x_3 \end{bmatrix} = \begin{bmatrix} 0 \\ 0 \\ 0 \end{bmatrix}.$$

This is equivalent to the system

$$\begin{aligned}
(1-\lambda)x_1 - \quad 2x_2 + \quad 4x_3 &= 0, \\
-2x_1 + (7-\lambda)x_2 - \quad 10x_3 &= 0, \\
-x_1 + \quad 4x_2 + (-6-\lambda)x_3 &= 0.
\end{aligned}$$

- For $\lambda = -1$, the augmented matrix is

$$\left[\begin{array}{ccc|c} 2 & -2 & 4 & 0 \\ -2 & 8 & -10 & 0 \\ -1 & 4 & -5 & 0 \end{array}\right] \begin{array}{c} \mathbf{R}_1 \\ \mathbf{R}_2 \\ \mathbf{R}_3 \end{array}.$$

Reducing the elements below the leading diagonal in column 1 to zero:

$$\begin{array}{c} \\ \mathbf{R}_2 + \mathbf{R}_1 \\ \mathbf{R}_3 + \tfrac{1}{2}\mathbf{R}_1 \end{array} \left[\begin{array}{ccc|c} 2 & -2 & 4 & 0 \\ 0 & 6 & -6 & 0 \\ 0 & 3 & -3 & 0 \end{array}\right] \begin{array}{c} \mathbf{R}_1 \\ \mathbf{R}_{2a} \\ \mathbf{R}_{3a} \end{array}.$$

Reducing the element below the leading diagonal in column 2 to zero:

$$\begin{array}{c} \\ \\ \mathbf{R}_{3a} - \tfrac{1}{2}\mathbf{R}_{2a} \end{array} \left[\begin{array}{ccc|c} 2 & -2 & 4 & 0 \\ 0 & 6 & -6 & 0 \\ 0 & 0 & 0 & 0 \end{array}\right].$$

The final row of zeros (a result of the expected singular system) allows us to assign x_3 the value k, which is arbitrary apart from the requirement that the resulting eigenvector should be non-zero. Back substitution then tells us that $6x_2 = 6k$, so $x_2 = k$, and back substituting again gives $2x_1 - 2k + 4k = 0$, so $x_1 = -k$. Thus the general form of the eigenvector is $\mathbf{v} = k[-1 \quad 1 \quad 1]^T$, where k is an arbitrary non-zero value.

- For $\lambda = 1$, the augmented matrix is

$$\left[\begin{array}{ccc|c} 0 & -2 & 4 & 0 \\ -2 & 6 & -10 & 0 \\ -1 & 4 & -7 & 0 \end{array}\right].$$

In this case it will be helpful to interchange rows before doing anything else, so the starting arrangement will be

$$\left[\begin{array}{ccc|c} -1 & 4 & -7 & 0 \\ 0 & -2 & 4 & 0 \\ -2 & 6 & -10 & 0 \end{array}\right] \begin{array}{c} \mathbf{R}_1 \\ \mathbf{R}_2 \\ \mathbf{R}_3 \end{array}.$$

Completing the reduction of the elements below the leading diagonal in column 1 to zero:

$$\begin{array}{c} \\ \\ \mathbf{R}_3 - 2\mathbf{R}_1 \end{array} \left[\begin{array}{ccc|c} -1 & 4 & -7 & 0 \\ 0 & -2 & 4 & 0 \\ 0 & -2 & 4 & 0 \end{array}\right] \begin{array}{c} \mathbf{R}_1 \\ \mathbf{R}_2 \\ \mathbf{R}_{3a} \end{array}.$$

Reducing the element below the leading diagonal in column 2 to zero:

$$\begin{array}{c} \\ \\ \mathbf{R}_{3a} - \mathbf{R}_2 \end{array} \left[\begin{array}{ccc|c} -1 & 4 & -7 & 0 \\ 0 & -2 & 4 & 0 \\ 0 & 0 & 0 & 0 \end{array}\right].$$

The final row of zeros allows us to assign x_3 the arbitrary non-zero value k. Back substitution then tells us that $x_2 = 2k$, and back substituting again gives $x_1 = k$. Thus the general form of the eigenvector is $\mathbf{v} = k[1 \quad 2 \quad 1]^T$, where k is an arbitrary non-zero value.

- For $\lambda = 2$, the augmented matrix is

$$
\begin{bmatrix}
-1 & -2 & 4 & | & 0 \\
-2 & 5 & -10 & | & 0 \\
-1 & 4 & -8 & | & 0
\end{bmatrix}
\begin{matrix}
\mathbf{R}_1 \\
\mathbf{R}_2 \\
\mathbf{R}_3
\end{matrix} .
$$

Reducing the elements below the leading diagonal in column 1 to zero:

$$
\begin{matrix}
 \\
\mathbf{R}_2 - 2\mathbf{R}_1 \\
\mathbf{R}_3 - \mathbf{R}_1
\end{matrix}
\begin{bmatrix}
-1 & -2 & 4 & | & 0 \\
0 & 9 & -18 & | & 0 \\
0 & 6 & -12 & | & 0
\end{bmatrix}
\begin{matrix}
\mathbf{R}_1 \\
\mathbf{R}_{2a} \\
\mathbf{R}_{3a}
\end{matrix} .
$$

Reducing the element below the leading diagonal in column 2 to zero:

$$
\begin{matrix}
 \\
 \\
\mathbf{R}_{3a} - \tfrac{2}{3}\mathbf{R}_{2a}
\end{matrix}
\begin{bmatrix}
-1 & -2 & 4 & | & 0 \\
0 & 9 & -18 & | & 0 \\
0 & 0 & 0 & | & 0
\end{bmatrix} .
$$

The final row of zeros allows us to assign x_3 the arbitrary non-zero value k. Back substitution then tells us that $x_2 = 2k$, and back substituting again gives $x_1 = 0$. Thus the general form of the eigenvector is $\mathbf{v} = k[0 \quad 2 \quad 1]^T$, where k is an arbitrary non-zero value.

Here, as a summary, is the general procedure for finding eigenvectors.

Procedure 4   Finding eigenvectors in general

Let $\mathbf{A}$ be an $n \times n$ matrix. To find the eigenvectors of $\mathbf{A}$, first solve its characteristic equation, to find the eigenvalues. Then for each eigenvalue λ, solve the eigenvector equation $(\mathbf{A} - \lambda\mathbf{I})\mathbf{v} = \mathbf{0}$ to find $\mathbf{v}$.

If λ is not a repeated eigenvalue, this will determine an eigenvector up to an arbitrary scalar multiple.

When eigenvalues are repeated, there can be a number of subtleties, which we do not cover in this module.

Exercise 34

Find the eigenvalues and corresponding eigenvectors of the following matrices.

(a) $\begin{bmatrix} 2 & 1 & -1 \\ 0 & -3 & 2 \\ 0 & 0 & 4 \end{bmatrix}$ (b) $\begin{bmatrix} 0 & 2 & 0 \\ -2 & 0 & 0 \\ 0 & 0 & 1 \end{bmatrix}$

Exercise 35

Find the three eigenvectors of

$$
\mathbf{A} = \begin{bmatrix}
4 & 7 & 6 \\
6 & 5 & 6 \\
-8 & -10 & -10
\end{bmatrix},
$$

given that the eigenvalues are -2, -1 and 2.

3.8 Eigenvectors of real symmetric matrices

In Subsection 3.4 we defined a symmetric matrix as one that is equal to its own transpose. There we showed that *the eigenvalues of a real symmetric matrix are real.* Real symmetric matrices have several practical applications. For example, the matrix that describes the system of pipes and taps given in the Introduction is a real symmetric matrix. In this subsection we investigate the eigenvectors of real symmetric matrices.

Given that the eigenvalues of a real symmetric matrix are necessarily real, it follows that the eigenvectors of such a matrix can always be chosen to be real. This is because the eigenvector equation that can be used to determine the eigenvectors contains only real elements, and the process of solving that equation will not introduce any imaginary quantities. However, reality is not the only interesting issue concerning the eigenvectors of real symmetric matrices.

We say that the eigenvectors can be *chosen* to be real because having found an eigenvector, we can always choose to multiply it by an imaginary or complex number if we wish, and it will still be an eigenvector.

In Exercise 32(b) we showed that the real symmetric matrix $\mathbf{A} = \begin{bmatrix} 2 & 1 \\ 1 & 2 \end{bmatrix}$ has the (real) eigenvalues $\lambda_1 = 1$ and $\lambda_2 = 3$, and corresponding eigenvectors $\mathbf{v}_1 = \begin{bmatrix} 1 & -1 \end{bmatrix}^T$ and $\mathbf{v}_2 = \begin{bmatrix} 1 & 1 \end{bmatrix}^T$.

These eigenvectors are represented graphically in Figure 18 by the conventional (geometric) vectors $\mathbf{v}_1 = \mathbf{i} - \mathbf{j}$ and $\mathbf{v}_2 = \mathbf{i} + \mathbf{j}$.

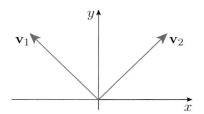

Figure 18 Eigenvectors of a real symmetric matrix corresponding to distinct (real) eigenvalues

As you can see, these two vectors are at right angles. Thus their scalar product is zero: $\mathbf{v}_1 \cdot \mathbf{v}_2 = \mathbf{i} \cdot \mathbf{i} - \mathbf{j} \cdot \mathbf{j} = 0$.

In fact, we do not have to write the eigenvectors in terms of $\mathbf{i}$ and $\mathbf{j}$ to see this, since we can use matrix algebra to define the scalar product. Recall that (in two dimensions) the scalar product of two vectors $\mathbf{v} = \begin{bmatrix} v_1 & v_1 \end{bmatrix}^T$ and $\mathbf{w} = \begin{bmatrix} w_1 & w_2 \end{bmatrix}^T$ in component form is $\mathbf{v} \cdot \mathbf{w} = v_1 w_1 + v_2 w_2$. However, using matrix algebra we see that the scalar product is simply

$$\mathbf{v}^T \mathbf{w} = \begin{bmatrix} v_1 & v_2 \end{bmatrix} \begin{bmatrix} w_1 \\ w_2 \end{bmatrix} = v_1 w_1 + v_2 w_2,$$

and the vectors are perpendicular if $\mathbf{v}^T \mathbf{w} = 0$.

So for the two eigenvectors $\mathbf{v}_1 = \begin{bmatrix} 1 & -1 \end{bmatrix}^T$ and $\mathbf{v}_2 = \begin{bmatrix} 1 & 1 \end{bmatrix}^T$, the scalar product is

$$\mathbf{v}_1^T \mathbf{v}_2 = \begin{bmatrix} 1 & -1 \end{bmatrix} \begin{bmatrix} 1 \\ 1 \end{bmatrix} = (1)(1) + (-1)(1) = 0,$$

and they are indeed perpendicular.

Clearly, this definition of the scalar product works for row vectors of *any* dimension. But in dimensions higher than 3, we tend to call the scalar product the **inner product**, and if the inner product of two vectors vanishes, we tend to say that they are **orthogonal** rather than perpendicular. (This was mentioned in Subsection 2.1 of Unit 4.)

Inner products and orthogonality

Given any two column matrices $\mathbf{v}$ and $\mathbf{w}$, their inner product is given by $\mathbf{v}^T\mathbf{w}$.

If $\mathbf{v}^T\mathbf{w} = 0$, then we say that $\mathbf{v}$ and $\mathbf{w}$ are orthogonal.

Returning to the case of the real symmetric matrix $\mathbf{A} = \begin{bmatrix} 2 & 1 \\ 1 & 2 \end{bmatrix}$, the orthogonality of the eigenvectors $\mathbf{v}_1$ and $\mathbf{v}_2$ is not a coincidence. It turns out that *for any real symmetric matrix, eigenvectors that correspond to distinct eigenvalues are always orthogonal*. A proof of this is given in Subsection 4.2, but you are not required to know it.

When eigenvalues are not distinct, it turns out that there are extra parameters in the eigenvectors, other than the scalar multiple, and we can always choose values for these parameters to make the eigenvectors orthogonal. This gives us the following powerful statement about eigenvectors of symmetric matrices.

For example, the 2×2 real symmetric matrix $\mathbf{A} = \mathbf{I}$ has two unit eigenvalues, and the eigenvectors are of the form $[x \quad y]^T$ for any x and any y. So we simply choose $x = 1$, $y = 0$ for $\mathbf{v}_1$ and $x = 0$, $y = 1$ for $\mathbf{v}_2$, giving $\mathbf{v}_1 = [1 \quad 0]^T$ and $\mathbf{v}_2 = [0 \quad 1]^T$.

For *any* real symmetric $n \times n$ matrix $\mathbf{A}$, it is always possible to find a set of n real orthogonal eigenvectors of $\mathbf{A}$.

We will use this result in Unit 7 to help us to classify the stationary points of a function of two variables.

Exercise 36

Find the inner product of each of the following pairs of column vectors, and hence determine which, if any, are orthogonal.

(a) $\mathbf{s}_1 = [2 \quad 1]^T$ and $\mathbf{s}_2 = [3 \quad -6]^T$

(b) $\mathbf{t}_1 = [2 \quad 2 \quad 1]^T$ and $\mathbf{t}_2 = [-2 \quad -2 \quad 0]^T$

Exercise 37

Calculate the eigenvectors of $\mathbf{A} = \begin{bmatrix} 5 & 2 \\ 2 & 2 \end{bmatrix}$, and show that they are orthogonal.

Let us summarise our results for real symmetric matrices.

Eigenvalues and eigenvectors of a real symmetric matrix

For a real symmetric matrix:

- the eigenvalues are real
- the eigenvectors may be chosen to be real and orthogonal.

Figure 19 Paul Dirac (1902–1984), one of the founders of quantum mechanics

Symmetric matrices – a complex perspective

Complex matrices are used in many applications, and are particularly important in quantum physics, which was developed in the 1920s by many people, including Paul Dirac (Figure 19). There, the closest analogue to a real symmetric matrix is known as a *Hermitian matrix*, which is defined by the requirement that the matrix should equal the complex conjugate of its own transpose (i.e. $(\mathbf{A}^T)^* = \mathbf{A}$, where the star indicates complex conjugation of all the elements). Clearly, if a Hermitian matrix has only real elements, then it is a symmetric matrix. Hermitian matrices also have real eigenvalues. Indeed, the proof (given in Subsection 4.2) that the eigenvalues of a real symmetric matrix are real is directly applicable to the case of Hermitian matrices. Nor does the similarity end there. An $n \times n$ Hermitian matrix also possesses n orthogonal eigenvectors, though they will generally be complex. Hermitian matrices, together with their eigenvalues and eigenvectors, are of fundamental importance in quantum physics, where they describe the dynamics of matter at the atomic and subatomic scale.

4 Further results and proofs regarding real symmetric matrices

The material in this section is optional, and will not be assessed.

Subsection 4.1 extends our analysis of symmetric matrices, showing how one can use the orthogonality of eigenvectors to construct a simple formula for the eigenvector expansion. Subsection 4.2 contains the proofs that the eigenvalues of a real symmetric matrix are real and the eigenvectors are orthogonal.

4.1 Real orthonormal bases

In Subsection 2.4 we introduced the *basis* of a vector space as a generalisation of the idea of Cartesian unit vectors. However, Cartesian unit vectors are especially easy to work with because they are *mutually orthogonal* (implying $\mathbf{i} \cdot \mathbf{j} = \mathbf{j} \cdot \mathbf{k} = \mathbf{i} \cdot \mathbf{k} = 0$), and *normalised* (implying $\mathbf{i} \cdot \mathbf{i} = \mathbf{j} \cdot \mathbf{j} = \mathbf{k} \cdot \mathbf{k} = 1$). These properties are not shared by the basis of a general vector space.

However, we have now seen that an $n \times n$ real symmetric matrix has n real eigenvectors $\mathbf{v}_1, \mathbf{v}_2, \ldots, \mathbf{v}_n$ that may be chosen to be mutually orthogonal in the sense that $\mathbf{v}_i^T \mathbf{v}_j = 0$. Moreover, each of those eigenvectors can be normalised in a way that is directly analogous to the way in which we form normalised Cartesian unit vectors (by dividing each vector by its own magnitude). In the case of a real eigenvector represented by a column vector $\mathbf{v}_i$, we define normalisation as follows.

Normalisation

Given a real eigenvector $\mathbf{v}_i$, the corresponding **normalised eigenvector** $\widehat{\mathbf{v}}_i$ is given by (see Subsection 1.4 of Unit 4)

$$\widehat{\mathbf{v}}_i = \frac{\mathbf{v}_i}{|\mathbf{v}_i|} = \frac{\mathbf{v}_i}{\sqrt{\mathbf{v}_i^T \mathbf{v}_i}}, \tag{22}$$

and it satisfies the **normalisation condition** $\widehat{\mathbf{v}}_i^T \widehat{\mathbf{v}}_i = 1$.

Here, the magnitude of $\mathbf{v}$ has been defined as $|\mathbf{v}| = \sqrt{\mathbf{v}_i^T \mathbf{v}_i}$.

Exercise 38

In Exercise 37 you showed that the matrix $\mathbf{A} = \begin{bmatrix} 5 & 2 \\ 2 & 2 \end{bmatrix}$ has orthogonal eigenvectors $\mathbf{v}_1 = [2 \quad 1]^T$ and $\mathbf{v}_2 = [1 \quad -2]^T$. Write down the corresponding normalised eigenvectors.

A set of vectors in which each element is normalised as well as being orthogonal to all the other vectors belonging to the set, is said to be **orthonormal**; e.g. $\mathbf{i}$, $\mathbf{j}$ and $\mathbf{k}$ are orthonormal. We therefore arrive at the following important conclusion regarding the eigenvectors of a real symmetric matrix.

Given any $n \times n$ real symmetric matrix, it is always possible to find a set of n real orthonormal eigenvectors $\widehat{\mathbf{v}}_1, \widehat{\mathbf{v}}_2, \ldots, \widehat{\mathbf{v}}_n$ for which

$$\widehat{\mathbf{v}}_i^T \widehat{\mathbf{v}}_j = 1 \quad \text{if } i = j \qquad \text{and} \qquad \widehat{\mathbf{v}}_i^T \widehat{\mathbf{v}}_j = 0 \quad \text{if } i \neq j.$$

Such a set is linearly independent, and therefore forms an **orthonormal basis** for the n-dimensional vector space.

It follows from this that for any n-dimensional column vector $\mathbf{v}$, we have the eigenvector expansion

$$\mathbf{v} = \alpha_1 \widehat{\mathbf{v}}_1 + \alpha_2 \widehat{\mathbf{v}}_2 + \cdots + \alpha_n \widehat{\mathbf{v}}_n. \tag{23}$$

We have seen eigenvector expansions before, but in those earlier cases the eigenvectors concerned were just linearly independent, not orthonormal. So working out the scalars $\alpha_1, \alpha_2, \ldots, \alpha_n$ was not easy and was largely avoided except for $n = 2$. However, orthonormality makes things much simpler. If we matrix multiply each side of equation (23) on the left by $\widehat{\mathbf{v}}_i^T$, we get

$$\widehat{\mathbf{v}}_i^T \mathbf{v} = \alpha_1 \widehat{\mathbf{v}}_i^T \widehat{\mathbf{v}}_1 + \alpha_2 \widehat{\mathbf{v}}_i^T \widehat{\mathbf{v}}_2 + \cdots + \alpha_n \widehat{\mathbf{v}}_i^T \widehat{\mathbf{v}}_n.$$

Then, using the orthogonality of the normalised eigenvectors, all of the inner products on the right-hand side (i.e. all the matrix products of the form $\widehat{\mathbf{v}}_i^T \widehat{\mathbf{v}}_j$) must vanish, apart from the one for which $j = i$. Thus

$$\widehat{\mathbf{v}}_i^T \mathbf{v} = \alpha_i \widehat{\mathbf{v}}_i^T \widehat{\mathbf{v}}_i.$$

We can now use the fact that each of the orthonormal eigenvectors has magnitude 1 (i.e. $\widehat{\mathbf{v}}_i^T \widehat{\mathbf{v}}_i = 1$) to write

$$\widehat{\mathbf{v}}_i^T \mathbf{v} = \alpha_i.$$

This equation gives all the coefficients α_i for $i = 1, 2, \ldots, n$. Hence equation (23) can be rewritten as follows.

> ### Real orthonormal eigenvector expansion
>
> $$\mathbf{v} = (\widehat{\mathbf{v}}_1^T \mathbf{v})\widehat{\mathbf{v}}_1 + (\widehat{\mathbf{v}}_2^T \mathbf{v})\widehat{\mathbf{v}}_2 + \cdots + (\widehat{\mathbf{v}}_n^T \mathbf{v})\widehat{\mathbf{v}}_n. \qquad (24)$$

This is a very useful expression that enables us to represent a vector as an eigenvector expansion of a real symmetric matrix.

Of course, all of this is expressed in the rather general language of linear algebra, but it should be clear that the real orthonormal eigenvectors $\widehat{\mathbf{v}}_i$ are nothing more than generalisations of the familiar Cartesian unit vectors $\mathbf{i}$, $\mathbf{j}$ and $\mathbf{k}$, which are also orthonormal. And equation (24) is simply a generalisation of $\mathbf{v} = v_x \mathbf{i} + v_y \mathbf{j} + v_z \mathbf{k}$, where $v_x = \mathbf{i} \cdot \mathbf{v}$, $v_y = \mathbf{j} \cdot \mathbf{v}$ and $v_z = \mathbf{k} \cdot \mathbf{v}$.

Here is a numerical application of equation (24).

Example 15

The real symmetric matrix $\mathbf{A} = \begin{bmatrix} 2 & 1 \\ 1 & 2 \end{bmatrix}$ has eigenvectors $\mathbf{v}_1 = \begin{bmatrix} 1 & -1 \end{bmatrix}^T$ and $\mathbf{v}_2 = \begin{bmatrix} 1 & 1 \end{bmatrix}^T$, corresponding to the eigenvalues $\lambda_1 = 1$ and $\lambda_2 = 3$.

(a) Find the normalised orthogonal eigenvectors $\widehat{\mathbf{v}}_1$ and $\widehat{\mathbf{v}}_2$.

(b) Express the vector $\mathbf{v} = \begin{bmatrix} 3 & -2 \end{bmatrix}^T$ as an eigenvector expansion using the orthonormal basis consisting of $\widehat{\mathbf{v}}_1$ and $\widehat{\mathbf{v}}_2$.

Solution

(a) Since $\mathbf{v}_1 = \begin{bmatrix} 1 & -1 \end{bmatrix}^T$ and $\mathbf{v}_2 = \begin{bmatrix} 1 & 1 \end{bmatrix}^T$ are already orthogonal, we only need to normalise them:

$$\widehat{\mathbf{v}}_1 = \frac{\mathbf{v}_1}{\sqrt{\mathbf{v}_1^T \mathbf{v}_1}} = \frac{1}{\sqrt{2}} \begin{bmatrix} 1 \\ -1 \end{bmatrix}, \quad \widehat{\mathbf{v}}_2 = \frac{\mathbf{v}_2}{\sqrt{\mathbf{v}_2^T \mathbf{v}_2}} = \frac{1}{\sqrt{2}} \begin{bmatrix} 1 \\ 1 \end{bmatrix}.$$

(b) From equation (24), $\mathbf{v} = (\widehat{\mathbf{v}}_1^T \mathbf{v})\widehat{\mathbf{v}}_1 + (\widehat{\mathbf{v}}_2^T \mathbf{v})\widehat{\mathbf{v}}_2$. Calculating the coefficients, we have

$$\widehat{\mathbf{v}}_1^T \mathbf{v} = \frac{1}{\sqrt{2}}\begin{bmatrix} 1 & -1 \end{bmatrix}\begin{bmatrix} 3 \\ -2 \end{bmatrix} = \frac{5}{\sqrt{2}} \quad \text{and} \quad \widehat{\mathbf{v}}_2^T \mathbf{v} = \frac{1}{\sqrt{2}}\begin{bmatrix} 1 & 1 \end{bmatrix}\begin{bmatrix} 3 \\ -2 \end{bmatrix} = \frac{1}{\sqrt{2}}.$$

Hence the eigenvector expansion is

$$\mathbf{v} = \frac{5}{\sqrt{2}}\widehat{\mathbf{v}}_1 + \frac{1}{\sqrt{2}}\widehat{\mathbf{v}}_2.$$

We can easily check this by substituting the values for $\mathbf{v}_1$ and $\mathbf{v}_2$:

$$\mathbf{v} = \frac{5}{2}\begin{bmatrix} 1 \\ -1 \end{bmatrix} + \frac{1}{2}\begin{bmatrix} 1 \\ 1 \end{bmatrix} = \frac{1}{2}\begin{bmatrix} 6 \\ -4 \end{bmatrix} = \begin{bmatrix} 3 \\ -2 \end{bmatrix},$$

as required.

Exercise 39

In Exercise 38 you showed that $\widehat{\mathbf{v}}_1 = \frac{1}{\sqrt{5}}\begin{bmatrix} 2 & 1 \end{bmatrix}^T$ and $\widehat{\mathbf{v}}_2 = \frac{1}{\sqrt{5}}\begin{bmatrix} 1 & -2 \end{bmatrix}^T$ are orthonormal eigenvectors of the matrix $\mathbf{A} = \begin{bmatrix} 5 & 2 \\ 2 & 2 \end{bmatrix}$. Express the vector $\mathbf{v} = \begin{bmatrix} 1 & 1 \end{bmatrix}^T$ in terms of this basis.

4.2 Proofs concerning real symmetric matrices

Proof that for real symmetric matrices the eigenvalues are real

Throughout the proof, stars are used to indicate complex conjugation. So given a complex quantity $z = a + ib$, its complex conjugate is $z^* = (a + ib)^* = (a - ib)$. Note that $z^*z = a^2 + b^2 = |z|^2$. The use of a star to indicate complex conjugation is a very common alternative to the overline that is used elsewhere in the module.

Let $\mathbf{A}$ be a real symmetric matrix, and let λ be one of its eigenvalues that corresponds to an eigenvector $\mathbf{v}$. In such a situation,

$$\mathbf{A}\mathbf{v} = \lambda\mathbf{v}. \tag{25}$$

We know that the elements of $\mathbf{A}$ are real, but at this stage we cannot be sure that either λ or $\mathbf{v}$ is necessarily real. Taking the transpose of both sides of equation (25) gives

The rule for taking the transpose of a product of matrices was discussed in Unit 4.

$$\mathbf{v}^T \mathbf{A}^T = \lambda\mathbf{v}^T.$$

Taking the complex conjugate of both sides then gives

$$(\mathbf{v}^T)^*(\mathbf{A}^T)^* = \lambda^*(\mathbf{v}^T)^*.$$

But $\mathbf{A}$ is both real and symmetric, so $(\mathbf{A}^T)^* = \mathbf{A}$, giving

$$(\mathbf{v}^T)^*\mathbf{A} = \lambda^*(\mathbf{v}^T)^*.$$

Matrix multiplying each side of this equation on the right by $\mathbf{v}$ then gives

$$(\mathbf{v}^T)^*\mathbf{A}\mathbf{v} = \lambda^*(\mathbf{v}^T)^*\mathbf{v}.$$

On the other hand, matrix multiplying each side of equation (25) on the left by $(\mathbf{v}^T)^*$ gives

$$(\mathbf{v}^T)^*\mathbf{A}\mathbf{v} = \lambda(\mathbf{v}^T)^*\mathbf{v}.$$

Subtracting these last two equations gives

$$0 = (\lambda - \lambda^*)(\mathbf{v}^T)^*\mathbf{v}. \tag{26}$$

However, if $\mathbf{v} = [v_1 \quad v_2 \quad \ldots \quad v_n]^T$, then

$$(\mathbf{v}^T)^*\mathbf{v} = v_1^*v_1 + v_2^*v_2 + \cdots + v_n^*v_n = |v_1|^2 + |v_2|^2 + \cdots + |v_n|^2,$$

which must be a positive quantity and non-zero because eigenvectors are always non-zero. Since $(\mathbf{v}^T)^*\mathbf{v}$ is positive, it follows from equation (26) that

$$0 = \lambda - \lambda^*,$$

from which we see that $\lambda = \lambda^*$, so λ must be real.

Proof that for real symmetric matrices the eigenvectors corresponding to distinct eigenvalues are orthogonal

Given that $\mathbf{A}\mathbf{v}_i = \lambda_i\mathbf{v}_i$ and $\mathbf{A}\mathbf{v}_j = \lambda_j\mathbf{v}_j$, taking the transpose of the equation involving $\mathbf{v}_i$ gives

$$\mathbf{v}_i^T\mathbf{A}^T = \lambda_i\mathbf{v}_i^T,$$

and matrix multiplying each side of this on the right by $\mathbf{v}_j$ gives

$$\mathbf{v}_i^T\mathbf{A}^T\mathbf{v}_j = \lambda_i\mathbf{v}_i^T\mathbf{v}_j.$$

Since $\mathbf{A}$ is symmetric, so that $\mathbf{A}^T = \mathbf{A}$, this may be rewritten as

$$\mathbf{v}_i^T\mathbf{A}\mathbf{v}_j = \lambda_i\mathbf{v}_i^T\mathbf{v}_j.$$

On the other hand, starting from the equation $\mathbf{A}\mathbf{v}_j = \lambda_j\mathbf{v}_j$, and matrix multiplying each side on the left by $\mathbf{v}_i^T$, we see that

$$\mathbf{v}_i^T\mathbf{A}\mathbf{v}_j = \lambda_j\mathbf{v}_i^T\mathbf{v}_j.$$

Subtracting the last two equations, we find

$$0 = (\lambda_i - \lambda_j)\mathbf{v}_i^T\mathbf{v}_j. \tag{27}$$

However, λ_i and λ_j are distinct, so $\lambda_i - \lambda_j \neq 0$. It therefore follows from equation (27) that $\mathbf{v}_i^T\mathbf{v}_j = 0$, which is just the condition for the real eigenvectors $\mathbf{v}_i$ and $\mathbf{v}_j$ to be orthogonal.

Learning outcomes

After studying this unit, you should be able to do the following.

- Solve 2×2 and 3×3 systems of linear equations by the Gaussian elimination method, using row interchanges where necessary.

- Determine whether such a system of equations has no solution, a unique solution, or an infinity of solutions.

- Explain the meaning of the terms eigenvector, eigenvalue, linearly independent and basis.

- Understand how repeated application of a matrix to a vector becomes proportional to the eigenvector with largest modulus eigenvalue.

- Use the characteristic equation and eigenvector equation to calculate the eigenvalues and eigenvectors of a 2×2 matrix.

- Calculate the eigenvalues and eigenvectors of a 3×3 matrix, where one of the eigenvalues is obvious or given.

- Appreciate that an $n \times n$ matrix with n distinct eigenvalues gives rise to n linearly independent eigenvectors that can be used as a basis.

- Know how to calculate an eigenvector expansion of a given vector.

- Appreciate that the eigenvalues of a matrix may be real or complex, and may be distinct or repeated.

- Appreciate that the complex eigenvalues and corresponding eigenvectors of real matrices occur in complex conjugate pairs.

- Write down the eigenvalues of a triangular matrix.

- Recall that the sum of the eigenvalues of a matrix $\mathbf{A}$ is $\operatorname{tr} \mathbf{A}$, and that the product is $\det \mathbf{A}$, and use these properties to help to check and determine eigenvalues.

- Know that a real symmetric matrix has real eigenvalues and that the eigenvectors can be chosen to be real and orthogonal.

Solutions to exercises

Solution to Exercise 1

Yes, the Cartesian equation of a plane is linear in x, y and z. This can be seen by comparing the Cartesian equation with the general linear equation for $n = 3$ and making the identifications $a_1 = a$, $x_1 = x$, $a_2 = b$, $x_2 = y$, $a_3 = c$, $x_3 = z$ and $d = 0$.

Solution to Exercise 2

(a) The required matrix form is
$$\begin{bmatrix} 1 & 1 & -1 \\ 5 & 2 & 2 \\ 4 & -2 & -3 \end{bmatrix} \begin{bmatrix} x_1 \\ x_2 \\ x_3 \end{bmatrix} = \begin{bmatrix} 2 \\ 20 \\ 15 \end{bmatrix}.$$

(b) The equations are just a messy rearrangement of those in part (a), so after further rearrangement to return them to the form given in part (a), we get the same answer as before.

(c) Remembering to insert zero coefficients in place of missing terms, the required matrix form is
$$\begin{bmatrix} 2 & 3 & -4 \\ 2 & 0 & 3 \\ 0 & 6 & -2 \end{bmatrix} \begin{bmatrix} x \\ y \\ z \end{bmatrix} = \begin{bmatrix} 0 \\ 3 \\ 0 \end{bmatrix}.$$

Solution to Exercise 3

The augmented matrix is
$$\left[\begin{array}{ccc|c} 1 & 1 & -1 & 2 \\ 5 & 2 & 2 & 20 \\ 4 & -2 & -3 & 15 \end{array} \right] \begin{array}{l} \mathbf{R}_1 \\ \mathbf{R}_2 \\ \mathbf{R}_3 \end{array}.$$

First, we reduce the elements below the leading diagonal in column 1 to zero:
$$\begin{array}{l} \\ \mathbf{R}_2 - 5\mathbf{R}_1 \\ \mathbf{R}_3 - 4\mathbf{R}_1 \end{array} \left[\begin{array}{ccc|c} 1 & 1 & -1 & 2 \\ 0 & -3 & 7 & 10 \\ 0 & -6 & 1 & 7 \end{array} \right] \begin{array}{l} \mathbf{R}_1 \\ \mathbf{R}_{2a} \\ \mathbf{R}_{3a} \end{array}.$$

Then we reduce the element below the leading diagonal in column 2 to zero:
$$\begin{array}{l} \\ \\ \mathbf{R}_{3a} - 2\mathbf{R}_{2a} \end{array} \left[\begin{array}{ccc|c} 1 & 1 & -1 & 2 \\ 0 & -3 & 7 & 10 \\ 0 & 0 & -13 & -13 \end{array} \right].$$

The equations represented by the new matrix are
$$\begin{aligned} x_1 + x_2 - x_3 &= 2, \\ -3x_2 + 7x_3 &= 10, \\ -13x_3 &= -13, \end{aligned}$$

which give $x_3 = 1$, $x_2 = \frac{1}{3}(7x_3 - 10) = -1$ and $x_1 = 2 - x_2 + x_3 = 4$.

We verify the solution as follows:

$$\begin{bmatrix} 1 & 1 & -1 \\ 5 & 2 & 2 \\ 4 & -2 & -3 \end{bmatrix} \begin{bmatrix} 4 \\ -1 \\ 1 \end{bmatrix} = \begin{bmatrix} 4-1-1 \\ 20-2+2 \\ 16+2-3 \end{bmatrix} = \begin{bmatrix} 2 \\ 20 \\ 15 \end{bmatrix}.$$

Solution to Exercise 4

Let the salaries (in thousands of rurs) of managers, software engineers and clerks at a bank be x_i, where $i = 1, 2, 3$, respectively. The problem is then specified by the simultaneous equations

$$3x_1 + 2x_2 + 24x_3 = 137,$$
$$x_1 + x_2 + 26x_3 = 137,$$
$$3x_2 + 25x_3 = 137.$$

This problem is unaffected by exchanging the order of the first two equations, to obtain the augmented matrix

$$\left[\begin{array}{ccc|c} 1 & 1 & 26 & 137 \\ 3 & 2 & 24 & 137 \\ 0 & 3 & 25 & 137 \end{array}\right] \begin{array}{c} \mathbf{R}_1 \\ \mathbf{R}_2 \\ \mathbf{R}_3 \end{array},$$

from which we obtain

$$\begin{array}{c} \\ \mathbf{R}_2 - 3\mathbf{R}_1 \\ {} \end{array} \left[\begin{array}{ccc|c} 1 & 1 & 26 & 137 \\ 0 & -1 & -54 & -274 \\ 0 & 3 & 25 & 137 \end{array}\right] \begin{array}{c} \mathbf{R}_1 \\ \mathbf{R}_{2\mathrm{a}} \\ \mathbf{R}_{3\mathrm{a}} \end{array}$$

without introducing fractional elements. We complete the elimination stage as follows:

$$\begin{array}{c} \\ \\ \mathbf{R}_{3\mathrm{a}} + 3\mathbf{R}_{2\mathrm{a}} \end{array} \left[\begin{array}{ccc|c} 1 & 1 & 26 & 137 \\ 0 & -1 & -54 & -274 \\ 0 & 0 & -137 & -685 \end{array}\right].$$

From this we see that $x_3 = 5$ for clerks, and back substitution gives $x_2 = 274 - 54x_3 = 4$ for software engineers, and $x_1 = 137 - x_2 - 26x_3 = 3$ for managers. Thus the numbers required are given by the vector $\mathbf{x} = [3 \quad 4 \quad 5]^T$, which can be confirmed as a solution of the original matrix equation.

So in Ruritania, clerks receive 5000 rurs per month, software engineers receive 4000 rurs per month, and managers receive 3000 rurs per month.

Solution to Exercise 5

Starting with

$$\left[\begin{array}{ccc|c} 0 & 0 & 1 & 2 \\ 2 & 1 & 0 & 5 \\ 1 & 2 & 0 & 7 \end{array}\right] \begin{array}{l} \mathbf{R}_1 \\ \mathbf{R}_2 \\ \mathbf{R}_3 \end{array},$$

we eliminate x_1 from the second row, to obtain

$$\begin{array}{l} \\ \mathbf{R}_2 - 2\mathbf{R}_3 \end{array} \left[\begin{array}{ccc|c} 0 & 0 & 1 & 2 \\ 0 & -3 & 0 & -9 \\ 1 & 2 & 0 & 7 \end{array}\right] \begin{array}{l} \mathbf{R}_1 \\ \mathbf{R}_{2a} \\ \mathbf{R}_3 \end{array}.$$

Then $\mathbf{R}_1$ gives $x_3 = 2$, $\mathbf{R}_{2a}$ gives $x_2 = 3$, and $\mathbf{R}_3$ gives $x_1 = 7 - 2x_2 = 1$. Hence the solution is $\mathbf{x} = [1 \quad 3 \quad 2]^T$. (As usual, it should be confirmed that the original matrix equation is satisfied by this solution.)

Solution to Exercise 6

Starting with

$$\left[\begin{array}{cccc|c} 1 & 1 & 1 & 1 & 10 \\ 1 & 1 & 2 & 1 & 12 \\ 1 & 3 & 1 & 1 & 16 \\ 4 & 1 & 1 & 1 & 22 \end{array}\right] \begin{array}{l} \mathbf{R}_1 \\ \mathbf{R}_2 \\ \mathbf{R}_3 \\ \mathbf{R}_4 \end{array},$$

we eliminate x_1 from the last three rows, to obtain

$$\begin{array}{l} \\ \mathbf{R}_2 - \mathbf{R}_1 \\ \mathbf{R}_3 - \mathbf{R}_1 \\ \mathbf{R}_4 - 4\mathbf{R}_1 \end{array} \left[\begin{array}{cccc|c} 1 & 1 & 1 & 1 & 10 \\ 0 & 0 & 1 & 0 & 2 \\ 0 & 2 & 0 & 0 & 6 \\ 0 & -3 & -3 & -3 & -18 \end{array}\right] \begin{array}{l} \mathbf{R}_1 \\ \mathbf{R}_{2a} \\ \mathbf{R}_{3a} \\ \mathbf{R}_{4a} \end{array}.$$

We could interchange rows to obtain an upper triangular augmented matrix, but it should also be clear that $\mathbf{R}_{2a}$ gives $x_3 = 2$, $\mathbf{R}_{3a}$ gives $x_2 = 3$, $\mathbf{R}_{4a}$ gives $x_4 = 6 - x_2 - x_3 = 1$, and $\mathbf{R}_1$ gives $x_1 = 10 - x_2 - x_3 - x_4 = 4$. (As usual, it should be confirmed that the original matrix equation is satisfied by the solution $\mathbf{x} = [4 \quad 3 \quad 2 \quad 1]^T$.)

Solution to Exercise 7

(a) From the augmented matrix

$$\left[\begin{array}{ccc|c} 1 & -2 & 5 & 7 \\ 1 & 3 & -4 & 20 \\ 1 & 18 & -31 & 40 \end{array}\right] \begin{array}{l} \mathbf{R}_1 \\ \mathbf{R}_2 \\ \mathbf{R}_3 \end{array},$$

we obtain

$$\begin{array}{l} \\ \mathbf{R}_2 - \mathbf{R}_1 \\ \mathbf{R}_3 - \mathbf{R}_1 \end{array} \left[\begin{array}{ccc|c} 1 & -2 & 5 & 7 \\ 0 & 5 & -9 & 13 \\ 0 & 20 & -36 & 33 \end{array}\right] \begin{array}{l} \mathbf{R}_1 \\ \mathbf{R}_{2a} \\ \mathbf{R}_{3a} \end{array}$$

and

$$\begin{array}{l} \\ \\ \mathbf{R}_{3a} - 4\mathbf{R}_{2a} \end{array} \left[\begin{array}{ccc|c} 1 & -2 & 5 & 7 \\ 0 & 5 & -9 & 13 \\ 0 & 0 & 0 & -19 \end{array}\right].$$

The third equation reads $0 = -19$, which is impossible. So the equations are inconsistent and there is no solution.

(b) From the augmented matrix

$$\left[\begin{array}{ccc|c} 1 & -2 & 5 & 6 \\ 1 & 3 & -4 & 7 \\ 2 & 6 & -12 & 12 \end{array}\right] \begin{array}{l} \mathbf{R}_1 \\ \mathbf{R}_2 \\ \mathbf{R}_3 \end{array},$$

we obtain

$$\begin{array}{l} \\ \mathbf{R}_2 - \mathbf{R}_1 \\ \mathbf{R}_3 - 2\mathbf{R}_1 \end{array} \left[\begin{array}{ccc|c} 1 & -2 & 5 & 6 \\ 0 & 5 & -9 & 1 \\ 0 & 10 & -22 & 0 \end{array}\right] \begin{array}{l} \mathbf{R}_1 \\ \mathbf{R}_{2a} \\ \mathbf{R}_{3a} \end{array}$$

and

$$\begin{array}{l} \\ \\ \mathbf{R}_{3a} - 2\mathbf{R}_{2a} \end{array} \left[\begin{array}{ccc|c} 1 & -2 & 5 & 6 \\ 0 & 5 & -9 & 1 \\ 0 & 0 & -4 & -2 \end{array}\right],$$

then back substitution gives a unique solution.

(c) From the augmented matrix

$$\left[\begin{array}{ccc|c} 1 & -4 & 1 & 14 \\ 5 & -1 & -1 & 2 \\ 6 & 14 & -6 & -52 \end{array}\right] \begin{array}{l} \mathbf{R}_1 \\ \mathbf{R}_2 \\ \mathbf{R}_3 \end{array},$$

we obtain

$$\begin{array}{l} \\ \mathbf{R}_2 - 5\mathbf{R}_1 \\ \mathbf{R}_3 - 6\mathbf{R}_1 \end{array} \left[\begin{array}{ccc|c} 1 & -4 & 1 & 14 \\ 0 & 19 & -6 & -68 \\ 0 & 38 & -12 & -136 \end{array}\right] \begin{array}{l} \mathbf{R}_1 \\ \mathbf{R}_{2a} \\ \mathbf{R}_{3a} \end{array}$$

and

$$\begin{array}{l} \\ \\ \mathbf{R}_{3a} - 2\mathbf{R}_{2a} \end{array} \left[\begin{array}{ccc|c} 1 & -4 & 1 & 14 \\ 0 & 19 & -6 & -68 \\ 0 & 0 & 0 & 0 \end{array}\right].$$

The third equation reads $0 = 0$, which is true but does not provide any limitation on the possible value of x_3. So there is an infinity of solutions. In this case we may assign x_3 any real non-zero value that we choose, say $x_3 = p$. Then from the second equation we get $x_2 = \frac{1}{19}(-68 + 6p)$, and from the first equation we get $x_1 = 14 + 4x_2 - x_3 = \frac{1}{19}(-6 + 5p)$.

The existence of an infinity of solutions is indicated by the infinity of possible choices for p.

Solution to Exercise 8

Matrix multiplication shows that the column vectors given in (b) and (d) are both eigenvectors (corresponding to the eigenvalue 1), but those given in (a) and (c) are not. The results of the matrix multiplications in the four cases are as follows.

(a) $\begin{bmatrix} 0.9 & 0.2 \\ 0.1 & 0.8 \end{bmatrix} \begin{bmatrix} 1000 \\ 1000 \end{bmatrix} = \begin{bmatrix} 1000 \\ 900 \end{bmatrix}$

(b) $\begin{bmatrix} 0.9 & 0.2 \\ 0.1 & 0.8 \end{bmatrix} \begin{bmatrix} 120 \\ 60 \end{bmatrix} = \begin{bmatrix} 120 \\ 60 \end{bmatrix}$

(c) $\begin{bmatrix} 0.9 & 0.2 \\ 0.1 & 0.8 \end{bmatrix} \begin{bmatrix} 500 \\ 300 \end{bmatrix} = \begin{bmatrix} 510 \\ 290 \end{bmatrix}$

(d) $\begin{bmatrix} 0.9 & 0.2 \\ 0.1 & 0.8 \end{bmatrix} \begin{bmatrix} 20 \\ 10 \end{bmatrix} = \begin{bmatrix} 20 \\ 10 \end{bmatrix}$

Solution to Exercise 9

The scaled vector $k\mathbf{w}$ is represented by the column vector $\mathbf{v} = k\mathbf{w} = [k \quad k]^T$, so

$$\mathbf{Av} = \begin{bmatrix} 3 & 2 \\ 1 & 4 \end{bmatrix} \begin{bmatrix} k \\ k \end{bmatrix} = \begin{bmatrix} 5k \\ 5k \end{bmatrix} = 5\mathbf{v}.$$

So $\mathbf{A}$ does indeed map $k\mathbf{w}$ to $5k\mathbf{w}$. This shows that any scaled vector $\mathbf{v} = k\mathbf{w}$ is an eigenvector of $\mathbf{A}$ corresponding to the eigenvalue 5.

Solution to Exercise 10

(a) $\begin{bmatrix} 2 & 3 \\ 2 & 1 \end{bmatrix} \begin{bmatrix} 3 \\ 2 \end{bmatrix} = \begin{bmatrix} 12 \\ 8 \end{bmatrix} = 4 \begin{bmatrix} 3 \\ 2 \end{bmatrix}$,

so $[3 \quad 2]^T$ is an eigenvector with eigenvalue 4.

(b) $\begin{bmatrix} 2 & 3 \\ 2 & 1 \end{bmatrix} \begin{bmatrix} 1 \\ -1 \end{bmatrix} = \begin{bmatrix} -1 \\ 1 \end{bmatrix} = (-1) \begin{bmatrix} 1 \\ -1 \end{bmatrix}$,

so $[1 \quad -1]^T$ is an eigenvector with eigenvalue -1.

(c) $\begin{bmatrix} 2 & 0 \\ 1 & 2 \end{bmatrix} \begin{bmatrix} 0 \\ 6 \end{bmatrix} = \begin{bmatrix} 0 \\ 12 \end{bmatrix} = 2 \begin{bmatrix} 0 \\ 6 \end{bmatrix}$,

so $[0 \quad 6]^T$ is an eigenvector with eigenvalue 2.

(d) $\begin{bmatrix} 2 & 1 \\ 4 & 2 \end{bmatrix} \begin{bmatrix} 1 \\ -2 \end{bmatrix} = \begin{bmatrix} 0 \\ 0 \end{bmatrix} = 0 \begin{bmatrix} 1 \\ -2 \end{bmatrix}$,

so $[1 \quad -2]^T$ is an eigenvector with eigenvalue 0.

Solution to Exercise 11

$$\begin{bmatrix} 3 & -2 \\ 4 & -1 \end{bmatrix} \begin{bmatrix} 1 \\ 1-i \end{bmatrix} = \begin{bmatrix} 1+2i \\ 3+i \end{bmatrix} = (1+2i) \begin{bmatrix} 1 \\ 1-i \end{bmatrix}.$$

So $1+2i$ is an eigenvalue and corresponds to eigenvector $\mathbf{v}_1$.

$$\begin{bmatrix} 3 & -2 \\ 4 & -1 \end{bmatrix} \begin{bmatrix} 1 \\ 1+i \end{bmatrix} = \begin{bmatrix} 1-2i \\ 3-i \end{bmatrix} = (1-2i) \begin{bmatrix} 1 \\ 1+i \end{bmatrix}.$$

So $1-2i$ is an eigenvalue and corresponds to eigenvector $\mathbf{v}_2$.

Solution to Exercise 12

The eigenvectors act along the line of reflection $y = x$ and perpendicular to it, so they are the scalar multiples of $[1 \quad 1]^T$ and $[1 \quad -1]^T$. The vector $[1 \quad 1]^T$ is scaled by a factor of 1 by the transformation, while for $[1 \quad -1]^T$ the scale factor is -1; these scale factors are the corresponding eigenvalues.

We may check our conclusion by evaluating

$$\begin{bmatrix} 0 & 1 \\ 1 & 0 \end{bmatrix} \begin{bmatrix} 1 \\ 1 \end{bmatrix} = \begin{bmatrix} 1 \\ 1 \end{bmatrix},$$

so $[1 \quad 1]^T$ corresponds to the eigenvalue 1, and

$$\begin{bmatrix} 0 & 1 \\ 1 & 0 \end{bmatrix} \begin{bmatrix} 1 \\ -1 \end{bmatrix} = \begin{bmatrix} -1 \\ 1 \end{bmatrix} = -1 \begin{bmatrix} 1 \\ -1 \end{bmatrix},$$

so $[1 \quad -1]^T$ corresponds to the eigenvalue -1.

Solution to Exercise 13

Explicit matrix multiplication shows that

$$\begin{bmatrix} 0.9 & 0.2 \\ 0.1 & 0.8 \end{bmatrix} \begin{bmatrix} 2 \\ 1 \end{bmatrix} = \begin{bmatrix} 2 \\ 1 \end{bmatrix},$$

so $[2 \quad 1]^T$ is an eigenvector with eigenvalue 1.

Similarly,

$$\begin{bmatrix} 0.9 & 0.2 \\ 0.1 & 0.8 \end{bmatrix} \begin{bmatrix} 1 \\ -1 \end{bmatrix} = 0.7 \begin{bmatrix} 1 \\ -1 \end{bmatrix},$$

so $[1 \quad -1]^T$ is an eigenvector with eigenvalue 0.7.

Solution to Exercise 14

If $\alpha_1 \neq 0$, then rearranging equation (6) gives

$$\mathbf{v}_1 = -\frac{\alpha_2}{\alpha_1}\mathbf{v}_2 - \frac{\alpha_3}{\alpha_1}\mathbf{v}_3 - \cdots - \frac{\alpha_n}{\alpha_1}\mathbf{v}_n.$$

Solution to Exercise 15

(a) $\mathbf{i}$, $\mathbf{j}$ and $\mathbf{k}$ are certainly linear independent, since they are not coplanar.

(b) These vectors are linearly dependent. The first vector is -1 times the second vector, so those two vectors are antiparallel, and the three vectors are coplanar. Also, the system fails the test for linear independence since

$$\alpha_1 \mathbf{v}_1 + \alpha_2 \mathbf{v}_2 + \alpha_3 \mathbf{v}_3 = \mathbf{0}$$

is satisfied, for example, by the values $\alpha_1 = 1$, $\alpha_2 = -1$, $\alpha_3 = 0$, which are not all zero.

Solution to Exercise 16

These vectors are linearly dependent, as there cannot be more than three linearly independent vectors in a three-dimensional space.

In fact, the vectors are related as follows: $\mathbf{v}_4 = -\frac{2}{3}\mathbf{v}_1 + \frac{2}{3}\mathbf{v}_2 + \frac{2}{3}\mathbf{v}_3$.

Solution to Exercise 17

Setting $\mathbf{v} = \alpha \mathbf{v}_1 + \beta \mathbf{v}_2$, we have

$$\begin{bmatrix} 1 \\ 3 \end{bmatrix} = \alpha \begin{bmatrix} 1 \\ 1 \end{bmatrix} + \beta \begin{bmatrix} -2 \\ 1 \end{bmatrix},$$

from which we get the simultaneous linear equations

$$1 = \alpha - 2\beta,$$
$$3 = \alpha + \beta.$$

Solving these, we obtain $\alpha = 7/3$ and $\beta = 2/3$.

Solution to Exercise 18

From the definition of linear independence (see equation (6)), we need to show that the only solution of $\alpha_1 \mathbf{v}_1 + \alpha_2 \mathbf{v}_2 + \alpha_3 \mathbf{v}_3 = \mathbf{0}$ is $\alpha_1 = \alpha_2 = \alpha_3 = 0$.

We have

$$\alpha_1 \begin{bmatrix} -1 \\ 1 \\ 1 \end{bmatrix} + \alpha_2 \begin{bmatrix} 1 \\ 2 \\ 1 \end{bmatrix} + \alpha_3 \begin{bmatrix} 0 \\ 2 \\ 1 \end{bmatrix} = \begin{bmatrix} 0 \\ 0 \\ 0 \end{bmatrix}.$$

This gives a system of three equations for $\alpha_1, \alpha_2, \alpha_3$, which we put in augmented matrix form:

$$\left[\begin{array}{ccc|c} -1 & 1 & 0 & 0 \\ 1 & 2 & 2 & 0 \\ 1 & 1 & 1 & 0 \end{array} \right] \begin{array}{c} \mathbf{R}_1 \\ \mathbf{R}_2 \\ \mathbf{R}_3 \end{array} .$$

We now solve these equations by Gaussian elimination:

$$\begin{array}{c} \\ \mathbf{R}_2 + \mathbf{R}_1 \\ \mathbf{R}_3 + \mathbf{R}_1 \end{array} \left[\begin{array}{ccc|c} -1 & 1 & 0 & 0 \\ 0 & 3 & 2 & 0 \\ 0 & 2 & 1 & 0 \end{array} \right] \begin{array}{c} \mathbf{R}_1 \\ \mathbf{R}_{2a} \\ \mathbf{R}_{3a} \end{array} ,$$

$$\mathbf{R}_{3a} - \tfrac{2}{3}\mathbf{R}_{2a} \left[\begin{array}{ccc|c} -1 & 1 & 0 & 0 \\ 0 & 3 & 2 & 0 \\ 0 & 0 & -\tfrac{1}{3} & 0 \end{array} \right].$$

Back substitution gives $\alpha_1 = \alpha_2 = \alpha_3 = 0$, hence the eigenvectors are linearly independent.

Solution to Exercise 19

(a) The eigenvectors correspond to different eigenvalues, so are distinct. This is also obvious because they are not collinear. They therefore form a basis for two-dimensional vectors, so we can write

$$\mathbf{r}_0 = \begin{bmatrix} -2 \\ 4 \end{bmatrix} = c_1 \begin{bmatrix} 1 \\ 1 \end{bmatrix} + c_2 \begin{bmatrix} -2 \\ 1 \end{bmatrix} = \begin{bmatrix} c_1 - 2c_2 \\ c_1 + c_2 \end{bmatrix}.$$

Equating corresponding elements of the column vectors on the right and the left shows that

$$c_1 - 2c_2 = -2 \quad \text{and} \quad c_1 + c_2 = 4.$$

Solving this simple system of linear equations, we see that $c_1 = 2$ and $c_2 = 2$. Thus

$$\mathbf{r}_0 = 2 \begin{bmatrix} 1 \\ 1 \end{bmatrix} + 2 \begin{bmatrix} -2 \\ 1 \end{bmatrix}.$$

(b) Using the eigenvector expansion gives

$$\mathbf{A} \begin{bmatrix} -2 \\ 4 \end{bmatrix} = \mathbf{A} \left(2 \begin{bmatrix} 1 \\ 1 \end{bmatrix} + 2 \begin{bmatrix} -2 \\ 1 \end{bmatrix} \right) = 10 \begin{bmatrix} 1 \\ 1 \end{bmatrix} + 4 \begin{bmatrix} -2 \\ 1 \end{bmatrix} = \begin{bmatrix} 2 \\ 14 \end{bmatrix}.$$

Solution to Exercise 20

From the solution to Exercise 19, we have

$$\mathbf{r}_0 = \begin{bmatrix} -2 \\ 4 \end{bmatrix} = 2\mathbf{v}_1 + 2\mathbf{v}_2,$$

where $\mathbf{v}_1 = [1 \ \ 1]^T$ and $\mathbf{v}_2 = [-2 \ \ 1]^T$ are the eigenvectors of $\mathbf{A}$ that correspond to the real eigenvalues $\lambda_1 = 5$ and $\lambda_2 = 2$. Hence

$$\begin{aligned} \mathbf{r}_8 = \mathbf{A}^8 \mathbf{r}_0 &= 2\mathbf{A}^8 \mathbf{v}_1 + 2\mathbf{A}^8 \mathbf{v}_2 \\ &= 2\lambda_1^8 \mathbf{v}_1 + 2\lambda_2^8 \mathbf{v}_2 \\ &= 2(5^8) \begin{bmatrix} 1 \\ 1 \end{bmatrix} + 2(2^8) \begin{bmatrix} -2 \\ 1 \end{bmatrix} = \begin{bmatrix} 780\,226 \\ 781\,762 \end{bmatrix}. \end{aligned}$$

Thus to two significant figures,

$$\mathbf{r}_8 = \begin{bmatrix} 78 \times 10^4 \\ 78 \times 10^4 \end{bmatrix} \simeq 2(5^8) \begin{bmatrix} 1 \\ 1 \end{bmatrix}.$$

Similarly,

$$\mathbf{r}_9 = \begin{bmatrix} 39 \times 10^5 \\ 39 \times 10^5 \end{bmatrix} \simeq 2(5^9) \begin{bmatrix} 1 \\ 1 \end{bmatrix} \quad \text{and} \quad \mathbf{r}_{10} = \begin{bmatrix} 20 \times 10^6 \\ 20 \times 10^6 \end{bmatrix} \simeq 2(5^{10}) \begin{bmatrix} 1 \\ 1 \end{bmatrix}.$$

The significance of these results is that, working to two significant figures, the contribution of the eigenvector corresponding to the smaller of the two eigenvalues is negligible in the eighth, ninth and tenth iterations. So to two significant figures, $\mathbf{A}^k\mathbf{x} \simeq 2\lambda_1^k\mathbf{v}_1$ for $k \geq 8$.

Solution to Exercise 21

With $\mathbf{A} = \begin{bmatrix} 3 & 2 \\ 1 & 4 \end{bmatrix}$ we obtain

$$\det(\mathbf{A} - \lambda\mathbf{I}) = \begin{vmatrix} 3 - \lambda & 2 \\ 1 & 4 - \lambda \end{vmatrix} = (3 - \lambda)(4 - \lambda) - 2,$$

so the characteristic equation may be written as $\lambda^2 - 7\lambda + 10 = 0$, the roots of which, i.e. the eigenvalues $\lambda_1 = 2$ and $\lambda_2 = 5$, may be found using the formula or factorising.

Solution to Exercise 22

(a) The characteristic equation of $\mathbf{G}$ gives

$$\begin{vmatrix} 3 - \lambda & 2 \\ 1 & 2 - \lambda \end{vmatrix} = (3 - \lambda)(2 - \lambda) - 2 = 0.$$

This becomes $\lambda^2 - 5\lambda + 4 = 0$. Solving this using the standard formula, we get

$$\lambda = \frac{5 \pm \sqrt{25 - 16}}{2}.$$

So the eigenvalues of $\mathbf{G}$ are 1 and 4.

(b) The characteristic equation of $\mathbf{H}$ gives

$$\begin{vmatrix} 2 - \lambda & 2 \\ -1 & 2 - \lambda \end{vmatrix} = (2 - \lambda)(2 - \lambda) + 2 = 0.$$

This becomes $\lambda^2 - 4\lambda + 6 = 0$. Solving this using the standard formula, we get

$$\lambda = \frac{4 \pm \sqrt{16 - 24}}{2} = \frac{4 \pm \sqrt{-8}}{2}.$$

So the eigenvalues of $\mathbf{H}$ are $2 + i\sqrt{2}$ and $2 - i\sqrt{2}$.

Solution to Exercise 23

(a) The characteristic equation of $\mathbf{R}$ gives
$$\lambda^2 - (\cos\theta + \cos\theta)\lambda + (\cos^2\theta + \sin^2\theta) = 0.$$

Using the fact that $\cos^2\theta + \sin^2\theta = 1$, we get
$$\lambda^2 - 2\lambda\cos\theta + 1 = 0.$$

Solving this using the standard formula, we get
$$\begin{aligned}
\lambda &= \frac{2\cos\theta \pm \sqrt{4\cos^2\theta - 4}}{2} \\
&= \cos\theta \pm \sqrt{\cos^2\theta - 1} \\
&= \cos\theta \pm \sqrt{-\sin^2\theta} = \cos\theta \pm i\sin\theta = e^{\pm i\theta}.
\end{aligned}$$

Note that we could have obtained this solution much more quickly by working directly from the characteristic equation:
$$\begin{vmatrix} \cos\theta - \lambda & -\sin\theta \\ \sin\theta & \cos\theta - \lambda \end{vmatrix} = (\cos\theta - \lambda)^2 + \sin^2\theta = 0.$$

This gives $(\cos\theta - \lambda)^2 = -\sin^2\theta$, so taking the square root of both sides gives $(\cos\theta - \lambda) = \pm i\sin\theta$, hence $\lambda = \cos\theta \pm i\sin\theta$. Using Euler's theorem, this can also be expressed as $\lambda = e^{\pm i\theta}$.

(b) The characteristic equation of $\mathbf{M}$ is $(l - \lambda)(k - \lambda) = 0$, hence the eigenvalues are l and k.

Solution to Exercise 24

The characteristic equation of $\mathbf{S}$ is
$$\begin{vmatrix} 1 - \lambda & s \\ 0 & 1 - \lambda \end{vmatrix} = (1 - \lambda)^2 = 0,$$

hence we have a pair of repeated eigenvalues $\lambda = 1$.

Solution to Exercise 25

$$\operatorname{tr}\mathbf{A} = 11 + 15 = 26 \quad \text{and} \quad \det\mathbf{A} = 11 \times 15 - 14 \times 12 = -3.$$

To the required level of accuracy,
$$\lambda_1 + \lambda_2 = 26.00 = \operatorname{tr}\mathbf{A} \quad \text{and} \quad \lambda_1\lambda_2 = -3.00 = \det\mathbf{A}.$$

The given values therefore satisfy the trace and determinant checks for eigenvalues of $\mathbf{A}$.

Solution to Exercise 26

(a) In this case the characteristic equation of $\mathbf{A}$ is given by

$$\det(\mathbf{A} - \lambda\mathbf{I}) = \begin{vmatrix} 1 - \lambda & -2 & 4 \\ -2 & 7 - \lambda & -10 \\ -1 & 4 & -6 - \lambda \end{vmatrix} = 0.$$

Using Laplace's rule to expand the determinant in terms of the elements of the top row gives

$$(1 - \lambda)[(7 - \lambda)(-6 - \lambda) + 40] - (-2)[-2(-6 - \lambda) - 10] + 4[-8 + (7 - \lambda)] = 0.$$

This gives

$$\lambda^3 - 2\lambda^2 - \lambda + 2 = 0. \tag{28}$$

Given that one of the factors is 2, we factorise this by writing

$$(\lambda - 2)(a\lambda^2 + b\lambda + c) = 0,$$

for some constants a, b, c. Expanding this, we get

$$a\lambda^3 + (b - 2)\lambda^2 + (c - 2b)\lambda - 2c = 0.$$

Comparing with equation (28), we see that $a = 1$, $b = 0$ and $c = -1$. So equation (28) can be factorised to give

$$(\lambda - 2)(\lambda^2 - 1) = (\lambda - 2)(\lambda - 1)(\lambda + 1) = 0,$$

hence the eigenvalues are -1, 1 and 2.

(b) In this case the characteristic equation of $\mathbf{A}$ is given by

$$\det(\mathbf{A} - \lambda\mathbf{I}) = \begin{vmatrix} 4 - \lambda & 7 & 6 \\ 6 & 5 - \lambda & 6 \\ -8 & -10 & -10 - \lambda \end{vmatrix} = 0.$$

Using Laplace's rule to expand the determinant in terms of the elements of the top row gives

$$(4 - \lambda)[(5 - \lambda)(-10 - \lambda) + 60] - 7[6(-10 - \lambda) + 48] + 6[-60 + 8(5 - \lambda)] = 0,$$

which becomes

$$\lambda^3 + \lambda^2 - 4\lambda - 4 = 0. \tag{29}$$

Given that one of the roots is 2, we factorise this to give

$$(\lambda - 2)(\lambda^2 + 3\lambda + 2) = 0$$

or

$$(\lambda - 2)(\lambda + 2)(\lambda + 1) = 0,$$

hence the eigenvalues are -2, -1 and 2.

Solution to Exercise 27

(a) For the matrix in Exercise 26(a), $\operatorname{tr}\mathbf{A} = 1 + 7 - 6 = 2$. Comparing this with the sum of the eigenvalues $\lambda_1 + \lambda_2 + \lambda_3 = -1 + 1 + 2 = 2$, we see that they are equal.

We could calculate $\det\mathbf{A}$ by hand. But instead let us note that from the equations leading up to equation (28), we have

$$\det(\mathbf{A} - \lambda\mathbf{I}) = -(\lambda^3 - 2\lambda^2 - \lambda + 2).$$

Setting $\lambda = 0$ then gives $\det\mathbf{A} = -2$. Comparing this with the product of the eigenvalues $\lambda_1 \times \lambda_2 \times \lambda_3 = -1 \times 1 \times 2 = -2$, we see that they are equal.

(b) For the matrix in Exercise 26(b), comparing $\operatorname{tr}\mathbf{A} = 4 + 5 - 10 = -1$ with $\lambda_1 + \lambda_2 + \lambda_3 = -2 - 1 + 2 = -1$, we see that they are equal.

Also, from equation (29) and the equations leading up to it, $\det(\mathbf{A} - \lambda\mathbf{I}) = -(\lambda^3 + \lambda^2 - 4\lambda - 4)$, so setting $\lambda = 0$ we get $\det\mathbf{A} = 4$. Comparing this with $\lambda_1 \times \lambda_2 \times \lambda_3 = -2 \times -1 \times 2 = 4$, we see that they are equal.

Solution to Exercise 28

Since $\mathbf{A}$ is a real matrix, another eigenvalue must be the complex conjugate of λ_1, i.e. $\lambda_2 = \overline{\lambda_1} = 1 - i$.

Further, the trace rule $\lambda_1 + \lambda_2 + \lambda_3 = \operatorname{tr}\mathbf{A}$ gives

$$(1 + i) + (1 - i) + \lambda_3 = 3,$$

hence $\lambda_3 = 1$.

Solution to Exercise 29

Because the matrix is triangular, the eigenvalues are 1 and 2.

Solution to Exercise 30

For the eigenvalue to be repeated, we require $\sqrt{(a + d)^2 - 4(ad - b^2)} = 0$, i.e. $(a - d)^2 + 4b^2 = 0$. This is true only if $a = d$ and $b = 0$, so the only symmetric 2×2 matrices with a repeated eigenvalue are of the form $\begin{bmatrix} a & 0 \\ 0 & a \end{bmatrix}$.

Solution to Exercise 31

(a) The eigenvalues are real, since $\mathbf{A}$ is real and symmetric. One is positive and the other negative, since $\lambda_1\lambda_2 = \det\mathbf{A} < 0$. Also, $\lambda_1 + \lambda_2 = \operatorname{tr}\mathbf{A} = 50$.

(b) The eigenvalues are the diagonal entries 67 and -17, since $\mathbf{A}$ is triangular.

(c) The eigenvalues are real, since $\mathbf{A}$ is real and symmetric. In fact, $\mathbf{A}$ is non-invertible, since $\det\mathbf{A} = 0$. Thus one eigenvalue is 0. Hence the other is 306, since $0 + \lambda_2 = \operatorname{tr}\mathbf{A} = 306$.

Solution to Exercise 32

(a) The characteristic equation is

$$\begin{vmatrix} 8 - \lambda & -5 \\ 10 & -7 - \lambda \end{vmatrix} = 0.$$

Expanding this gives $(8 - \lambda)(-7 - \lambda) + 50 = 0$, which simplifies to $\lambda^2 - \lambda - 6 = 0$. So the eigenvalues are $\lambda = 3$ and $\lambda = -2$.

Let $\mathbf{v} = [x \quad y]^T$ be an eigenvector.

- For $\lambda = 3$, the eigenvector equations (20) and (21) become

  $$5x - 5y = 0 \quad \text{and} \quad 10x - 10y = 0,$$

  which reduce to the single equation $y = x$. So (setting $x = 1$) an eigenvector corresponding to $\lambda = 3$ is $[1 \quad 1]^T$.

- For $\lambda = -2$, the eigenvector equations become

  $$10x - 5y = 0 \quad \text{and} \quad 10x - 5y = 0,$$

  which reduce to the single equation $y = 2x$. So (setting $x = 1$) an eigenvector corresponding to $\lambda = -2$ is $[1 \quad 2]^T$.

(b) The characteristic equation is

$$\begin{vmatrix} 2 - \lambda & 1 \\ 1 & 2 - \lambda \end{vmatrix} = 0.$$

Expanding this gives $(2 - \lambda)^2 - 1 = 0$, which simplifies to $\lambda^2 - 4\lambda + 3 = 0$. So the eigenvalues are $\lambda = 3$ and $\lambda = 1$.

Let $\mathbf{v} = [x \quad y]^T$ be an eigenvector.

- For $\lambda = 3$, the eigenvector equations (20) and (21) become

  $$-x + y = 0 \quad \text{and} \quad x - y = 0,$$

  which reduce to the single equation $y = x$. So (setting $x = 1$) an eigenvector corresponding to $\lambda = 3$ is $[1 \quad 1]^T$.

- For $\lambda = 1$, the eigenvector equations become

  $$x + y = 0 \quad \text{and} \quad x + y = 0,$$

  which reduce to the single equation $y = -x$. So (setting $x = 1$) an eigenvector corresponding to $\lambda = -1$ is $[1 \quad -1]^T$.

Solution to Exercise 33

The eigenvector equations are

$$(\cos\theta - \lambda)x - (\sin\theta)y = 0,$$
$$(\sin\theta)x + (\cos\theta - \lambda)y = 0.$$

- For $\lambda = \cos\theta + i\sin\theta$, the eigenvector equations become

  $$-(i\sin\theta)x - (\sin\theta)y = 0 \quad \text{and} \quad (\sin\theta)x - (i\sin\theta)y = 0,$$

  which reduce to the single equation $iy = x$ (since $\sin\theta \neq 0$ as θ is not an integer multiple of π). So setting $x = i$, a corresponding eigenvector is $[i \quad 1]^T$.

(Had we set $x = 1$, the eigenvector would be $[1 \quad -i]^T$, which is equally valid as it is just the first eigenvector multiplied by $-i$.)

- For $\lambda = \cos\theta - i\sin\theta$, the eigenvector equations become

$$(i\sin\theta)x - (\sin\theta)y = 0 \quad \text{and} \quad (\sin\theta)x + (i\sin\theta)y = 0,$$

which reduce to the single equation $-iy = x$ (since $\sin\theta \neq 0$), so a corresponding eigenvector is $[-i \quad 1]^T$ or any scalar multiple.

Solution to Exercise 34

(a) The matrix is upper triangular, so the eigenvalues are 2, -3 and 4.

The eigenvector equations for $\mathbf{v} = [x_1 \quad x_2 \quad x_3]^T$ are

$$
\begin{aligned}
(2-\lambda)x_1 + \quad x_2 - \quad x_3 &= 0, \\
(-3-\lambda)x_2 + \quad 2x_3 &= 0, \\
(4-\lambda)x_3 &= 0.
\end{aligned}
$$

- For $\lambda = 2$, the eigenvector equations become

$$x_2 - x_3 = 0, \quad -5x_2 + 2x_3 = 0, \quad 2x_3 = 0,$$

which reduce to $x_2 = x_3 = 0$. If we assign $x_1 = k$, for arbitrary non-zero k, then a corresponding eigenvector is $k[1 \quad 0 \quad 0]^T$. Choosing $k = 1$ gives $\mathbf{v} = [1 \quad 0 \quad 0]^T$.

- For $\lambda = -3$, the eigenvector equations become

$$5x_1 + x_2 - x_3 = 0, \quad 2x_3 = 0, \quad 7x_3 = 0,$$

which reduce to $5x_1 + x_2 = 0$ and $x_3 = 0$. So assigning $x_1 = k$, for arbitrary non-zero k, we get a corresponding eigenvector $k[1 \quad -5 \quad 0]^T$. Choosing $k = 1$ gives $\mathbf{v} = [1 \quad -5 \quad 0]^T$.

- For $\lambda = 4$, the eigenvector equations become

$$-2x_1 + x_2 - x_3 = 0, \quad -7x_2 + 2x_3 = 0, \quad 0 = 0.$$

Choosing $x_3 = 14$ keeps the numbers simple, and a corresponding eigenvector is $\mathbf{v} = [-5 \quad 4 \quad 14]^T$.

(b) The characteristic equation is

$$
\begin{vmatrix}
-\lambda & 2 & 0 \\
-2 & -\lambda & 0 \\
0 & 0 & 1-\lambda
\end{vmatrix} = 0.
$$

To simplify the evaluation of the determinant, we interchange the first and third rows (remember that this just changes the sign of the determinant). This gives the characteristic equation as $(1-\lambda)(\lambda^2 + 4) = 0$, so the eigenvalues are 1, $2i$ and $-2i$.

The eigenvector equations for $\mathbf{v} = [x_1 \quad x_2 \quad x_3]^T$ are

$$
\begin{aligned}
-\lambda x_1 + 2x_2 \quad &= 0, \\
-2x_1 - \lambda x_2 \quad &= 0, \\
(1-\lambda)x_3 &= 0.
\end{aligned}
$$

- For $\lambda = 1$, the eigenvector equations become
$$-x_1 + 2x_2 = 0, \quad -2x_1 - x_2 = 0, \quad 0 = 0.$$
These give $x_1 = x_2 = 0$. So choosing $x_3 = 1$, a corresponding eigenvector is $[0 \quad 0 \quad 1]^T$.

- For $\lambda = 2i$, the eigenvector equations become
$$-2ix_1 + 2x_2 = 0, \quad -2x_1 - 2ix_2 = 0, \quad (1 - 2i)x_3 = 0,$$
which reduce to $x_2 = ix_1$ and $x_3 = 0$. So choosing $x_1 = 1$, a corresponding eigenvector is $[1 \quad i \quad 0]^T$.

- Similarly, an eigenvector corresponding to $\lambda = -2i$ is $[1 \quad -i \quad 0]^T$.

Solution to Exercise 35

The eigenvector equations for $\mathbf{v} = [x_1 \quad x_2 \quad x_3]^T$ are
$$\begin{aligned}
(4 - \lambda)x_1 + \quad\quad 7x_2 + \quad\quad\quad 6x_3 &= 0, \\
6x_1 + (5 - \lambda)x_2 + \quad\quad\quad 6x_3 &= 0, \\
-8x_1 - \quad\quad 10x_2 + (-10 - \lambda)x_3 &= 0.
\end{aligned}$$

- For $\lambda = -2$, the augmented matrix is
$$\left[\begin{array}{ccc|c}
6 & 7 & 6 & 0 \\
6 & 7 & 6 & 0 \\
-8 & -10 & -8 & 0
\end{array} \right].$$

In this case it is helpful to interchange rows before doing anything else, so the starting arrangement will be
$$\left[\begin{array}{ccc|c}
-8 & -10 & -8 & 0 \\
6 & 7 & 6 & 0 \\
6 & 7 & 6 & 0
\end{array} \right] \begin{array}{l} \mathbf{R}_1 \\ \mathbf{R}_2 \\ \mathbf{R}_3 \end{array}.$$

Reducing the elements below the leading diagonal in column 1 to zero (and shortcutting the usual procedure by subtracting the two identical rows at this early stage):
$$\begin{array}{l} \\ \mathbf{R}_2 + \frac{3}{4}\mathbf{R}_1 \\ \mathbf{R}_3 - \mathbf{R}_2 \end{array} \left[\begin{array}{ccc|c}
-8 & -10 & -8 & 0 \\
0 & -\frac{1}{2} & 0 & 0 \\
0 & 0 & 0 & 0
\end{array} \right] \begin{array}{l} \mathbf{R}_1 \\ \mathbf{R}_{2a} \\ \mathbf{R}_{3a} \end{array}.$$

The final row of zeros allows us to assign x_3 the arbitrary non-zero value k. The second row tells us that $x_2 = 0$, and back substituting gives $x_1 = -k$. Thus the general form of the eigenvector is $\mathbf{v} = k[1 \quad 0 \quad -1]^T$, where k is an arbitrary non-zero value.

- For $\lambda = -1$, the augmented matrix is
$$\left[\begin{array}{ccc|c}
5 & 7 & 6 & 0 \\
6 & 6 & 6 & 0 \\
-8 & -10 & -9 & 0
\end{array} \right] \begin{array}{l} \mathbf{R}_1 \\ \mathbf{R}_2 \\ \mathbf{R}_3 \end{array}.$$

Reducing the elements below the leading diagonal in column 1 to zero:

$$\begin{array}{c} \\ 5\mathbf{R}_2 - 6\mathbf{R}_1 \\ 5\mathbf{R}_3 + 8\mathbf{R}_1 \end{array} \left[\begin{array}{ccc|c} 5 & 7 & 6 & 0 \\ 0 & -12 & -6 & 0 \\ 0 & 6 & 3 & 0 \end{array} \right] \begin{array}{c} \mathbf{R}_1 \\ \mathbf{R}_{2a} \\ \mathbf{R}_{3a} \end{array}.$$

Reducing the element below the leading diagonal in column 2 to zero:

$$\begin{array}{c} \\ \\ 2\mathbf{R}_{3a} + \mathbf{R}_{2a} \end{array} \left[\begin{array}{ccc|c} 5 & 7 & 6 & 0 \\ 0 & -12 & -6 & 0 \\ 0 & 0 & 0 & 0 \end{array} \right].$$

The final row of zeros allows us to assign x_3 the arbitrary non-zero value k. Back substitution then tells us that $x_2 = -\frac{1}{2}k$, and back substituting again gives $x_1 = -\frac{1}{2}k$. Thus the general form of the eigenvector is $\mathbf{v} = k[-\frac{1}{2} \quad -\frac{1}{2} \quad 1]^T$, where k is an arbitrary non-zero value. Choosing $k = 2$ gives $\mathbf{v} = [-1 \quad -1 \quad 2]^T$.

- For $\lambda = 2$, the augmented matrix is

$$\left[\begin{array}{ccc|c} 2 & 7 & 6 & 0 \\ 6 & 3 & 6 & 0 \\ -8 & -10 & -12 & 0 \end{array} \right] \begin{array}{c} \mathbf{R}_1 \\ \mathbf{R}_2 \\ \mathbf{R}_3 \end{array}.$$

Reducing the elements below the leading diagonal in column 1 to zero:

$$\begin{array}{c} \\ \mathbf{R}_2 - 3\mathbf{R}_1 \\ \mathbf{R}_3 + 4\mathbf{R}_1 \end{array} \left[\begin{array}{ccc|c} 2 & 7 & 6 & 0 \\ 0 & -18 & -12 & 0 \\ 0 & 18 & 12 & 0 \end{array} \right] \begin{array}{c} \mathbf{R}_1 \\ \mathbf{R}_{2a} \\ \mathbf{R}_{3a} \end{array}.$$

Reducing the element below the leading diagonal in column 2 to zero:

$$\begin{array}{c} \\ \\ \mathbf{R}_{3a} + \mathbf{R}_{2a} \end{array} \left[\begin{array}{ccc|c} 2 & 7 & 6 & 0 \\ 0 & -18 & -12 & 0 \\ 0 & 0 & 0 & 0 \end{array} \right].$$

The final row of zeros allows us to assign x_3 the arbitrary non-zero value k. Back substitution then tells us that $x_2 = -\frac{2}{3}k$, and back substituting again gives $x_1 = -\frac{2}{3}k$. Thus the general form of the eigenvector is $\mathbf{v} = k[-\frac{2}{3} \quad -\frac{2}{3} \quad 1]^T$, where k is an arbitrary non-zero value. Choosing $k = 3$ gives $\mathbf{v} = [-2 \quad -2 \quad 3]^T$.

Solution to Exercise 36

(a) $\mathbf{s}_1^T \mathbf{s}_2 = (2)(3) + (1)(-6) = 0$, so the column vectors are orthogonal.

(b) $\mathbf{t}_1^T \mathbf{t}_2 = (2)(-2) + (2)(-2) + (1)(0) = -8$, so the column vectors are not orthogonal.

Solution to Exercise 37

The characteristic equation is

$$\begin{vmatrix} 5-\lambda & 2 \\ 2 & 2-\lambda \end{vmatrix} = 0.$$

Expanding the determinant gives $(5-\lambda)(2-\lambda) - 4 = 0$, hence the characteristic equation may be written as $\lambda^2 - 7\lambda + 6 = 0$, the roots of which are the eigenvalues $\lambda_1 = 6$ and $\lambda_2 = 1$. Clearly both eigenvalues are real, as they should be for a real symmetric matrix.

The eigenvector equation is

$$\begin{bmatrix} 5-\lambda & 2 \\ 2 & 2-\lambda \end{bmatrix} \begin{bmatrix} x \\ y \end{bmatrix} = \begin{bmatrix} 0 \\ 0 \end{bmatrix}.$$

- $\lambda_1 = 6$ gives the pair of equations

  $$-x + 2y = 0 \quad \text{and} \quad 2x - 4y = 0,$$

  which are equivalent to $x = 2y$. Choosing $y = 1$, we get $\mathbf{v}_1 = [2 \quad 1]^T$.

- $\lambda_2 = 1$ gives the pair of equations

  $$4x + 2y = 0 \quad \text{and} \quad 2x + y = 0,$$

  which are equivalent to $y = -2x$. Choosing $x = 1$, we get $\mathbf{v}_2 = [1 \quad -2]^T$.

The inner product is $\mathbf{v}_1^T \mathbf{v}_2 = 2(1) + (-2)1 = 0$, so the eigenvectors are orthogonal.

Solution to Exercise 38

Since $\mathbf{v}_1^T \mathbf{v}_1 = 4 + 1 = 5$ and $\mathbf{v}_2^T \mathbf{v}_2 = 1 + 4 = 5$, we have

$$\widehat{\mathbf{v}}_1 = \frac{1}{\sqrt{5}} \begin{bmatrix} 2 \\ 1 \end{bmatrix}, \quad \widehat{\mathbf{v}}_2 = \frac{1}{\sqrt{5}} \begin{bmatrix} 1 \\ -2 \end{bmatrix}.$$

Solution to Exercise 39

From equation (24), $\mathbf{v} = (\widehat{\mathbf{v}}_1^T \mathbf{v})\widehat{\mathbf{v}}_1 + (\widehat{\mathbf{v}}_2^T \mathbf{v})\widehat{\mathbf{v}}_2$. Calculating the coefficients, we have

$$\widehat{\mathbf{v}}_1^T \mathbf{v} = \frac{1}{\sqrt{5}} [2 \quad 1] \begin{bmatrix} 1 \\ 1 \end{bmatrix} = \frac{3}{\sqrt{5}} \quad \text{and} \quad \widehat{\mathbf{v}}_2^T \mathbf{v} = \frac{1}{\sqrt{5}} [1 \quad -2] \begin{bmatrix} 1 \\ 1 \end{bmatrix} = -\frac{1}{\sqrt{5}}.$$

Hence

$$\mathbf{v} = \frac{3}{\sqrt{5}} \widehat{\mathbf{v}}_1 - \frac{1}{\sqrt{5}} \widehat{\mathbf{v}}_2.$$

We can easily check this by substituting the values for $\mathbf{v}_1$ and $\mathbf{v}_2$:

$$\mathbf{v} = \frac{3}{5} \begin{bmatrix} 2 \\ 1 \end{bmatrix} - \frac{1}{5} \begin{bmatrix} 1 \\ -2 \end{bmatrix} = \frac{1}{5} \begin{bmatrix} 5 \\ 5 \end{bmatrix} = \begin{bmatrix} 1 \\ 1 \end{bmatrix}.$$

Acknowledgements

Grateful acknowledgement is made to the following sources:

Figure 16: This file is licensed under the Creative Commons Attribution-Share Alike Licence http://creativecommons.org/licenses/by-sa/3.0.

Figure 17: Larry Page / This file is licensed under the Creative Commons Attribution-Share Alike Licence http://creativecommons.org/licenses/by-sa/3.0.

Every effort has been made to contact copyright holders. If any have been inadvertently overlooked, the publishers will be pleased to make the necessary arrangements at the first opportunity.

Systems of linear differential equations

Introduction

In Unit 2 you saw that the solution of the differential equation

$$\frac{dx}{dt} = Ax \tag{1}$$

(where A is a constant) is

$$x(t) = x_0 e^{At}. \tag{2}$$

Here x_0 is an arbitrary constant. This unit generalises this differential equation and solution to the case of a system of several differential equations with more than one dependent variable. An example is the pair of differential equations

$$\frac{dx}{dt} = ax + by, \tag{3}$$

$$\frac{dy}{dt} = cx + dy, \tag{4}$$

where a, b, c and d are real constants. Here $x(t)$ and $y(t)$ are the dependent variables for which we want to find solutions. Such systems of differential equations arise frequently across all the mathematical sciences – in fact, whenever a system has constituent parts that interact with each other.

Because both of the unknown functions, $x(t)$ and $y(t)$, occur in both of the differential equations, they must be solved 'simultaneously'. At first sight this appears to be a difficult task. However, by using matrices it turns out that equations (3) and (4) can be cast in a form that is very similar to equation (1):

$$\begin{bmatrix} \dot{x} \\ \dot{y} \end{bmatrix} = \begin{bmatrix} a & b \\ c & d \end{bmatrix} \begin{bmatrix} x \\ y \end{bmatrix},$$

which can then be written as

$$\dot{\mathbf{x}} = \mathbf{A}\mathbf{x}, \quad \text{where } \mathbf{x} = \begin{bmatrix} x \\ y \end{bmatrix} \text{ and } \mathbf{A} = \begin{bmatrix} a & b \\ c & d \end{bmatrix}. \tag{5}$$

Don't worry if you can't follow all the details here. This introduction is meant to be a sketch of what is to come. We cover the same material at a slower pace and in more depth in Section 1.

This looks just like equation (1), and it would be satisfying to find a solution inspired by equation (2). An obvious extension to try is a solution of the form

$$\mathbf{x}(t) = \mathbf{v}e^{\lambda t}, \tag{6}$$

where λ is some constant scalar and $\mathbf{v}$ is a constant vector. Substituting this into the left-hand side of equation (5), we get

$$\dot{\mathbf{x}} = \frac{d}{dt}\left(\mathbf{v}e^{\lambda t}\right) = \mathbf{v}\frac{d}{dt}e^{\lambda t} = \lambda\mathbf{v}e^{\lambda t}.$$

Substituting from equation (6) into the right-hand side of equation (5), $\dot{\mathbf{x}} = \mathbf{A}\mathbf{x}$, gives

$$\mathbf{A}\mathbf{x} = \mathbf{A}\mathbf{v}e^{\lambda t}.$$

Equating both sides of equation (5), we get

$$\mathbf{A}\mathbf{v} = \lambda\mathbf{v}.$$

But this is the eigenvalue equation that we studied in Unit 5. So we see that equation (6) is a solution of equation (5) when λ and $\mathbf{v}$ are an eigenvalue and an eigenvector of the matrix $\mathbf{A}$. In fact, this observation is the central message of this unit, and we highlight it because of its importance.

> Putting systems of differential equations into matrix form and finding the eigenvalues and eigenvectors of the matrix of coefficients, is the key to solving systems of any number of linear differential equations of any order.

Before developing the mathematics further, let us first look at a example of how equations like (5) arise in a simple model. We will not give full details of the modelling process, since the aim is to provide motivation and to give a fairly rapid impression of where and how systems of differential equations might occur in practice. You should not spend too much time dwelling on the details, as we will never ask you to derive the differential equations for a system in any assessment.

Fluid in tanks and pipes

Many engineering processes involve fluids being transferred in pipes from one tank to another. An example is shown in Figure 1. This could describe an industrial process where a liquid is pumped into a tank A, where it is treated in some way, before being transferred through a pipe to tank B, where it is stored before being supplied to run a machine.

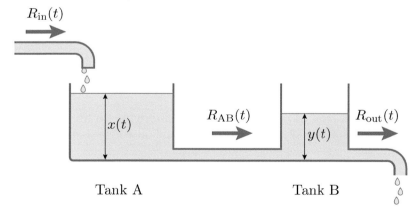

Figure 1   The depths of liquid in two tanks are $x(t)$ and $y(t)$

To describe the behaviour of this system we need two variables, namely the depth of the liquid in each tank. The depths of liquid at time t in tank A and tank B are $x(t)$ and $y(t)$, respectively (measured in metres). We assume that liquid is poured into tank A at a rate of $R_{\mathrm{in}}(t)$ (measured in cubic metres per second). There is a flow of liquid from tank A to tank B at a rate $R_{\mathrm{AB}}(t)$, and fluid is pumped out of tank B at a rate $R_{\mathrm{out}}(t)$.

The rate of change of the depths is proportional to the rate at which fluid is added:

$$\dot{x} = k_A \left[R_{\text{in}}(t) - R_{\text{AB}}(t) \right], \tag{7}$$

$$\dot{y} = k_B \left[R_{\text{AB}}(t) - R_{\text{out}}(t) \right], \tag{8}$$

where k_A and k_B are two constants. We assume that the rate at which liquid flows through the pipe connecting tank A and tank B is proportional to the difference in height of the fluid in the two tanks, i.e. there is no pumping of fluid from tank A to tank B.

Thus we write

$$R_{\text{AB}} = K_{\text{AB}}(x - y), \tag{9}$$

where K_{AB} is a constant.

Substituting equation (9) into equations (7) and (8) gives the equations of motion for the heights of the fluid:

$$\dot{x} = -k_A K_{\text{AB}}\, x + k_A K_{\text{AB}}\, y + k_A\, R_{\text{in}}(t),$$

$$\dot{y} = k_B K_{\text{AB}}\, x - k_B K_{\text{AB}}\, y - k_B\, R_{\text{out}}(t).$$

These equations have the form

$$\dot{x} = ax + by + f(t), \tag{10}$$

$$\dot{y} = cx + dy + g(t). \tag{11}$$

Here a, b, c and d are constants, and $f(t)$ and $g(t)$ are functions of time describing the rate at which fluid is poured into the first tank and pumped out of the second tank, respectively: $f(t) = k_A R_{\text{in}}(t)$, $g(t) = -k_B R_{\text{out}}(t)$.

The values of the constants are $a = -k_A K_{\text{AB}}$, $b = -a$, $c = k_B K_{\text{AB}}$, $d = -c$.

If we set $f(t) = 0$ and $g(t) = 0$, so that no fluid is entering the first tank or being pumped from the second tank, then equations (10) and (11) are exactly the same as equations (3) and (4), with solution given by equation (6) in terms of the eigenvalues and eigenvectors of the matrix of coefficients $\mathbf{A} = \begin{bmatrix} a & b \\ c & d \end{bmatrix}$. For $f \neq 0$ and $g \neq 0$, a solution in terms of eigenvalues and eigenvectors can still be found, as we will see in the next section. In fact, the main job of Section 1 will be to find the general solution of systems of differential equations that have the same form as equations (10) and (11).

This application to the flow of fluid in tanks may seem somewhat specialised. However, all fluid flows obey the same physical laws, and systems of coupled linear differential equations find applications in many contexts involving fluid flow, such as understanding the drainage of rainwater by river systems.

The mathematical equations that describe the flow of fluids also apply to other physical phenomena such as the flow of current in electrical circuits, and non-physical phenomena such as models of the flow of money in the economy. The box below tells the story of an ingenious economist who exploited this duality to build an analogue computer to model the British economy.

163

Figure 2 Bill Phillips with his MONIAC

The MONIAC (Monetary National Income Analogue Computer) was created in 1949 by electrical engineer turned economist Bill Phillips to model the economy of the United Kingdom (UK) – see Figure 2. Phillips was still a student at the London School of Economics when he created his first MONIAC in his landlady's garage in Croydon at a cost of £400.

The MONIAC was an analogue computer that used the flow of water to model the workings of an economy. It consisted of a series of transparent tanks and pipes. Each tank represented some aspect of the UK national economy, and the flow of money around the economy was illustrated by coloured water. At the top was a large tank called the treasury. Water (representing money) flowed from the treasury to other tanks representing the various ways in which the country could spend its money – for example, there were tanks for health and education. To increase spending on health, a tap could be opened to drain water from the treasury to the tank that represented health spending. Water then ran further down the model to other tanks, representing other interactions in the economy. Water could be pumped back to the treasury from some of the tanks to represent taxation. Changes in tax rates were modelled by increasing or decreasing pumping speeds. Import and export were represented by water draining from the model and additional water being poured into the model.

Phillips had realised that the set of differential equations that described the flow of money around the economy was the same as the set that described the flow of fluids between tanks. So by building the MONIAC, he was building a model of the economy.

The MONIAC had primarily been designed as a teaching aid, but was soon discovered also to be an effective economic simulator (accurate to $\pm 2\%$), at a time when electronic digital computers that could run complex economic simulations were unavailable. A number of MONIAC machines were eventually built, ending up in companies, banks and universities around the world. One of the few remaining working machines is now on permanent display at the British Science Museum.

Systems of coupled linear equations in a broader context

Equations like (3) and (4) are described as linear because the right-hand side involves only linear functions of x and y. However, most dynamical systems are described by *non-linear* equations of the form

$$\dot{x} = f(x, y),$$
$$\dot{y} = g(x, y),$$

where $f(x, y)$ and $g(x, y)$ are *any* functions of x and y. Although in general it is not possible to solve such equations analytically, it is possible to get a lot of information about how the solutions behave using analytical methods. In particular, the behaviour of the solution near *equilibrium points*, where $\dot{x} = \dot{y} = 0$, is studied using the techniques of this section. We will return to the discussion of non-linear dynamics in Unit 13.

There is another reason for studying systems of coupled linear equations. Quantum mechanics, which is our most fundamental theory of physical processes, can be expressed in terms of an equation of motion, similar to equation (5), for vectors in an abstract space of physical states.

From coupled differential equations to images of brains

Particles like electrons and protons have a property called spin, which allows them to behave like tiny magnets when placed in a strong magnetic field. Hospitals use an invaluable imaging technique called magnetic resonance imaging (MRI) that is based on this idea.

Your body contains many hydrogen atoms distributed unevenly across your various tissues. At the heart of each hydrogen atom is a spinning proton that can be thought of as a tiny magnet. According to the general principles of quantum physics, the spin of such a proton is represented by a two-component column vector $\mathbf{v}$, called the *spin state vector*. The components of this vector are complex numbers, and they tell us about the orientation of the proton's spin at any given instant. The spin state vector may vary with time, satisfying an equation known as the *Schrödinger equation*, which takes the form

$$\frac{d\mathbf{v}}{dt} = \frac{1}{i\hbar}\mathbf{H}\mathbf{v}. \tag{12}$$

Here, $\mathbf{H}$ is a 2×2 matrix called the *Hamiltonian*, $\mathbf{v}$ is a 2×1 column vector (the spin state vector) and $\hbar$ is a physical constant that appears throughout quantum physics. The only unusual feature of equation (12) is that it involves complex numbers: in general, $\mathbf{H}$ and $\mathbf{v}$ both have complex elements. Otherwise, equation (12) is of exactly the form that you have met before.

A concerted oscillation, in the directions of proton spins, is set off by the MRI scanner somewhere inside your body. This produces a tiny electromagnetic signal that can be detected outside. So understanding how to solve equation (12), and hence the motion of proton spins, provides the key to creating MRI images such as that shown in Figure 3.

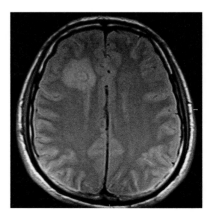

Figure 3 MRI image of the brain

Study guide

In this unit we show you how to find the solution of certain systems of differential equations. We begin in the next section with systems where the derivatives are of first order, like those in equations (3) and (4), and equations (10) and (11). In Section 2 we consider the most commonly occurring systems where the derivatives are of second order. In the physical or engineering sciences, these systems describe the motion of objects that are coupled together in such a way that they have a vibrating or oscillating motion. In Section 3 we consider a special type of vibration, called 'normal modes', where the components of the system all vibrate with the same frequency.

This unit assumes a knowledge of first- and second-order differential equations, as covered in Units 2 and 3, and of eigenvalues and eigenvectors, as covered in Unit 5.

1   First-order systems

In this section we describe the techniques that you need in order to solve systems of first-order differential equations. Most of the examples and exercises concentrate on systems with only two (occasionally three) dependent variables, because the algebra is easier to understand. Once you have learned how to solve these, the extension of the technique to higher numbers of dependent variables is straightforward.

Subsection 1.1 describes how to write systems of differential equations in matrix form, and defines two types: homogeneous and inhomogeneous. Subsections 1.2 and 1.3 show you how to solve the homogeneous type. Subsections 1.4 and 1.5 show you how to solve the inhomogeneous type. The method parallels the methods that you saw in Unit 3 for solving second-order homogeneous and inhomogeneous differential equations of a single dependant variable.

1.1   Matrix notation

In Unit 5 you saw that any system of linear equations can be written in matrix form. For example, the equations

$$\begin{cases} 3x + 2y = 5, \\ x + 4y = 5, \end{cases}$$

Note that sometimes we group a system of equations using a brace ({), as here, but often we do not.

can be written in matrix form as

$$\begin{bmatrix} 3 & 2 \\ 1 & 4 \end{bmatrix} \begin{bmatrix} x \\ y \end{bmatrix} = \begin{bmatrix} 5 \\ 5 \end{bmatrix},$$

that is, as

$$\mathbf{A}\mathbf{x} = \mathbf{b}, \quad \text{where } \mathbf{A} = \begin{bmatrix} 3 & 2 \\ 1 & 4 \end{bmatrix}, \ \mathbf{x} = \begin{bmatrix} x \\ y \end{bmatrix} \text{ and } \mathbf{b} = \begin{bmatrix} 5 \\ 5 \end{bmatrix}.$$

In a similar way, we can write systems of linear differential equations in matrix form. To see what is involved, consider the system

$$\begin{cases} \dot{x} = 3x + 2y + 5t, \\ \dot{y} = x + 4y + 5, \end{cases} \tag{13}$$

where x and y are functions of t. This has the same form as equations (10) and (11) derived in the Introduction. It can be written in matrix form as

$$\begin{bmatrix} \dot{x} \\ \dot{y} \end{bmatrix} = \begin{bmatrix} 3 & 2 \\ 1 & 4 \end{bmatrix} \begin{bmatrix} x \\ y \end{bmatrix} + \begin{bmatrix} 5t \\ 5 \end{bmatrix},$$

that is, as

$$\dot{\mathbf{x}} = \mathbf{A}\mathbf{x} + \mathbf{h}, \quad \text{where } \mathbf{A} = \begin{bmatrix} 3 & 2 \\ 1 & 4 \end{bmatrix}, \; \mathbf{x} = \begin{bmatrix} x \\ y \end{bmatrix} \text{ and } \mathbf{h} = \begin{bmatrix} 5t \\ 5 \end{bmatrix}.$$

So we have converted a system of differential equations into a single matrix differential equation. Note that the components of $\mathbf{x}$ are functions of t, and so generally are the components of $\mathbf{h}$. The matrix $\mathbf{A}$ is independent of t and is called the **matrix of coefficients**.

We can similarly represent systems of three, or more, linear differential equations in matrix form. For example, the system

$$\begin{cases} \dot{x} = 3x + 2y + 2z + e^t, \\ \dot{y} = 2x + 2y + 2e^t, \\ \dot{z} = 2x + 4z, \end{cases}$$

Notice that we write the derivatives on the left-hand side. On the right-hand side we vertically align all the terms in x, y and z separately, leaving a space where a term is zero.

can be written in matrix form as $\dot{\mathbf{x}} = \mathbf{A}\mathbf{x} + \mathbf{h}$, where

$$\mathbf{A} = \begin{bmatrix} 3 & 2 & 2 \\ 2 & 2 & 0 \\ 2 & 0 & 4 \end{bmatrix}, \quad \mathbf{x} = \begin{bmatrix} x \\ y \\ z \end{bmatrix} \quad \text{and} \quad \mathbf{h} = \begin{bmatrix} e^t \\ 2e^t \\ 0 \end{bmatrix} = \begin{bmatrix} 1 \\ 2 \\ 0 \end{bmatrix} e^t. \tag{14}$$

There are two types of matrix differential equation that you must be able to recognise. These are defined as follows.

> **Definition**
>
> A matrix differential equation of the form $\dot{\mathbf{x}} = \mathbf{A}\mathbf{x} + \mathbf{h}$ is said to be **homogeneous** if $\mathbf{h} = \mathbf{0}$, and **inhomogeneous** otherwise.

Note that in an inhomogeneous system, some, *but not all*, of the components of $\mathbf{h}$ may be 0.

For example, the system

$$\begin{cases} \dot{x} = 2x + 3y, \\ \dot{y} = 2x + y, \end{cases} \tag{15}$$

Here x and y are functions of t.

has matrix form

$$\begin{bmatrix} \dot{x} \\ \dot{y} \end{bmatrix} = \begin{bmatrix} 2 & 3 \\ 2 & 1 \end{bmatrix} \begin{bmatrix} x \\ y \end{bmatrix} \tag{16}$$

and so is homogeneous, whereas systems (13) and (14) are inhomogeneous.

Exercise 1

Write each of the following systems in matrix form, and classify it as homogeneous or inhomogeneous.

(a) $\begin{cases} \dot{x} = 2x + y + 1 \\ \dot{y} = x - 2 \end{cases}$

(b) $\begin{cases} \dot{x} = y \\ \dot{y} = t \end{cases}$

(c) $\begin{cases} \dot{x} = 5x \\ \dot{y} = x + 2y + z \\ \dot{z} = x + y + 2z \end{cases}$

1.2   Homogeneous systems: the eigenvalue method

General solution

We now show how to solve the first-order homogeneous case, $\dot{\mathbf{x}} = \mathbf{A}\mathbf{x}$. This was partially discussed in the Introduction, where we discovered that the method involves calculating eigenvalues and eigenvectors of matrices, which was covered in the previous unit.

Suppose that we are given a set of coupled, first-order, homogeneous, linear differential equations, like those in system (15). Then we put them in matrix form

$$\dot{\mathbf{x}} = \mathbf{A}\mathbf{x}, \qquad (17)$$

as in equation (16). We assume that the matrix $\mathbf{A}$ has coefficients that are constants, i.e. do not depend on the independent variable t. Then $\mathbf{A}$ has eigenvectors $\mathbf{v}$ and eigenvalues λ that are also independent of t and satisfy the eigenvalue equation

$$\mathbf{A}\mathbf{v} = \lambda\mathbf{v}. \qquad (18)$$

In guessing this form for the solution, we are assuming that all components have the same exponential dependence on time.

Then it is easy to show that $\mathbf{x}(t) = \mathbf{v}e^{\lambda t}$ is a solution of the differential equation. Substituting $\mathbf{x}(t) = \mathbf{v}e^{\lambda t}$ into the left-hand side of equation (17), we get

$$\dot{\mathbf{x}} = \frac{d}{dt}\left(\mathbf{v}e^{\lambda t}\right) = \mathbf{v}\frac{d}{dt}e^{\lambda t} = \lambda\mathbf{v}e^{\lambda t}.$$

Substituting into the right-hand side of equation (17) and using equation (18), we get

$$\mathbf{A}\mathbf{x} = \mathbf{A}\mathbf{v}e^{\lambda t} = \lambda\mathbf{v}e^{\lambda t}.$$

So the left- and right-hand sides are equal, and we have the following result.

A system of differential equations

$$\dot{\mathbf{x}} = \mathbf{A}\mathbf{x}$$

has a solution given by

$$\mathbf{x} = \mathbf{v}e^{\lambda t},$$

where λ is an eigenvalue of the matrix $\mathbf{A}$ corresponding to an eigenvector $\mathbf{v}$.

The question now arises as to how we find the *general solution*. The following example illustrates the idea for a pair of simultaneous differential equations.

Example 1

(a) Find two independent solutions of the simultaneous differential equations

$$\begin{cases} \dot{x} = x + 4y, \\ \dot{y} = x - 2y. \end{cases}$$

(*Hint*: The matrix $\begin{bmatrix} 1 & 4 \\ 1 & -2 \end{bmatrix}$ has eigenvectors $\begin{bmatrix} 4 \\ 1 \end{bmatrix}$ and $\begin{bmatrix} 1 \\ -1 \end{bmatrix}$, with corresponding eigenvalues 2 and -3.)

(b) Find the general solution.

Solution

(a) The differential equations can be written in the matrix form

$$\begin{bmatrix} \dot{x} \\ \dot{y} \end{bmatrix} = \begin{bmatrix} 1 & 4 \\ 1 & -2 \end{bmatrix} \begin{bmatrix} x \\ y \end{bmatrix}.$$

So the matrix of coefficients is

$$\mathbf{A} = \begin{bmatrix} 1 & 4 \\ 1 & -2 \end{bmatrix}.$$

Therefore using values for the eigenvalues and eigenvectors given in the hint, we can construct two independent solutions $\mathbf{v}e^{\lambda t}$:

$$\mathbf{x}_1 = \begin{bmatrix} 4 \\ 1 \end{bmatrix} e^{2t} \quad \text{and} \quad \mathbf{x}_2 = \begin{bmatrix} 1 \\ -1 \end{bmatrix} e^{-3t}.$$

(b) So there are two independent solutions, $\mathbf{x}_1(t)$ and $\mathbf{x}_2(t)$. It turns out, for reasons discussed below, that the general solution is a general linear combination of these, i.e. $\alpha\mathbf{x}_1 + \beta\mathbf{x}_2$. Hence the general solution is

$$\begin{bmatrix} x \\ y \end{bmatrix} = \alpha \begin{bmatrix} 4 \\ 1 \end{bmatrix} e^{2t} + \beta \begin{bmatrix} 1 \\ -1 \end{bmatrix} e^{-3t},$$

where α and β are arbitrary constants. So the general solution in component form is

$$x = 4\alpha e^{2t} + \beta e^{-3t} \quad \text{and} \quad y = \alpha e^{2t} - \beta e^{-3t}.$$

Important note Note that we *cannot* change the equation for x to $x = \alpha e^{2t} + \beta e^{-3t}$ (i.e. absorb the constant 4 into α) and leave the equation for y unchanged, since α occurs in both the equation for x and the equation for y. This is an important difference between differential equations of a single variable and coupled differential equations.

Exercise 2

(a) Find two independent solutions of

$$\begin{cases} \dot{x} = 3x + 2y, \\ \dot{y} = x + 4y. \end{cases}$$

(*Hint*: The eigenvectors of $\begin{bmatrix} 3 & 2 \\ 1 & 4 \end{bmatrix}$ are $\begin{bmatrix} 1 \\ 1 \end{bmatrix}$ and $\begin{bmatrix} -2 \\ 1 \end{bmatrix}$, with corresponding eigenvalues 5 and 2.)

(b) Find the general solution.

The reason why the linear combination of solutions is the general solution can be seen as follows. First, since $\dot{\mathbf{x}}_1 = \mathbf{A}\mathbf{x}_1$ and $\dot{\mathbf{x}}_2 = \mathbf{A}\mathbf{x}_2$, the linear combination $\mathbf{x} = \alpha \mathbf{x}_1 + \beta \mathbf{x}_2$ satisfies

$$\dot{\mathbf{x}} = \alpha \dot{\mathbf{x}}_1 + \beta \dot{\mathbf{x}}_2 = \alpha \mathbf{A}\mathbf{x}_1 + \beta \mathbf{A}\mathbf{x}_2 = \mathbf{A}(\alpha \mathbf{x}_1 + \beta \mathbf{x}_2) = \mathbf{A}\mathbf{x}.$$

This is a simple extension of the principle of superposition discussed in Unit 3.

So $\mathbf{x} = \alpha \mathbf{x}_1 + \beta \mathbf{x}_2$ is a solution of the system of differential equations if $\mathbf{x}_1$ and $\mathbf{x}_2$ are. The fact that it is the *general solution* follows because $\mathbf{x}$ contains two arbitrary constants (α and β), and this is sufficient for a system of two first-order differential equations.

In Example 1 we saw that a system of two differential equations has a 2×2 matrix of coefficients, which gives rise to two independent solutions. The general solution is a general linear combination of these and so has two arbitrary constants (α and β). In the general case, a system of n differential equations has an $n \times n$ matrix of coefficients, which gives rise to n independent solutions of the form $\mathbf{v}e^{\lambda t}$. The general solution is a general linear combination of these and contains n arbitrary constants.

You should note that the method outlined above works only when the $n \times n$ matrix of coefficients has n (linearly independent) eigenvectors. The method fails if it has fewer. However, we do not consider such anomalous cases in this module.

Although this method works for both real and complex eigenvalues, in the next subsection we will find that it is convenient to modify it slightly in the complex case. So we use it in this form only for the real case. We summarise our method for real eigenvalues as follows.

The case of complex eigenvalues will be covered in Subsection 1.3. The case where **A** does not have n eigenvectors is beyond the scope of this module.

> ## Procedure 1   Solution of a homogeneous system with real eigenvalues
>
> To solve a system of linear constant-coefficient first-order differential equations $\dot{\mathbf{x}} = \mathbf{A}\mathbf{x}$, where $\mathbf{A}$ is an $n \times n$ matrix, do the following.
>
> 1. Find the eigenvalues $\lambda_1, \lambda_2, \ldots, \lambda_n$ and a corresponding set of eigenvectors $\mathbf{v}_1, \mathbf{v}_2, \ldots, \mathbf{v}_n$.
>
> 2. Write down the general solution in the form
> $$\mathbf{x} = C_1\mathbf{v}_1 e^{\lambda_1 t} + C_2\mathbf{v}_2 e^{\lambda_2 t} + \cdots + C_n\mathbf{v}_n e^{\lambda_n t}, \tag{19}$$
> where $C_1, C_2, \ldots, C_n$ are arbitrary constants.

The next example applies this procedure to find the general solution of a system of three differential equations.

Example 2

Find the general solution of the system of differential equations
$$\begin{cases} \dot{x} = 3x + 2y + 2z, \\ \dot{y} = 2x + 2y, \\ \dot{z} = 2x \qquad + 4z. \end{cases}$$

(*Hint*: The matrix $\begin{bmatrix} 3 & 2 & 2 \\ 2 & 2 & 0 \\ 2 & 0 & 4 \end{bmatrix}$ has eigenvectors $\begin{bmatrix} 2 \\ 1 \\ 2 \end{bmatrix}$, $\begin{bmatrix} 1 \\ 2 \\ -2 \end{bmatrix}$ and $\begin{bmatrix} -2 \\ 2 \\ 1 \end{bmatrix}$, with corresponding eigenvalues $\lambda_1 = 6$, $\lambda_2 = 3$ and $\lambda_3 = 0$.)

Solution

The matrix of coefficients is
$$\mathbf{A} = \begin{bmatrix} 3 & 2 & 2 \\ 2 & 2 & 0 \\ 2 & 0 & 4 \end{bmatrix}.$$

Using the values for the eigenvalues and eigenvectors in the hint, the general solution is therefore
$$\begin{bmatrix} x \\ y \\ z \end{bmatrix} = \alpha \begin{bmatrix} 2 \\ 1 \\ 2 \end{bmatrix} e^{6t} + \beta \begin{bmatrix} 1 \\ 2 \\ -2 \end{bmatrix} e^{3t} + \gamma \begin{bmatrix} -2 \\ 2 \\ 1 \end{bmatrix},$$

where α, β and γ are arbitrary constants. So in component form this becomes
$$x = 2\alpha e^{6t} + \beta e^{3t} - 2\gamma,$$
$$y = \alpha e^{6t} + 2\beta e^{3t} + 2\gamma,$$
$$z = 2\alpha e^{6t} - 2\beta e^{3t} + \gamma.$$

Note that the last term on the right-hand side corresponds to the term in $e^{\lambda_3 t} = e^{0t} = 1$.

Exercise 3

Find the general solution of

$$\begin{cases} \dot{x} = 5x + 2y, \\ \dot{y} = 2x + 5y. \end{cases}$$

(*Hint:* The eigenvectors of $\begin{bmatrix} 5 & 2 \\ 2 & 5 \end{bmatrix}$ are $\begin{bmatrix} 1 \\ 1 \end{bmatrix}$ and $\begin{bmatrix} 1 \\ -1 \end{bmatrix}$, with corresponding eigenvalues 7 and 3.)

Initial conditions

Now that we know how to find the general solution of a system of differential equations, let us use this to find solutions that satisfy specific initial conditions. The basic procedure is the same as used in Units 2 and 3, i.e. use the initial conditions to find particular values of the arbitrary constants. The following example illustrates the idea.

Example 3

A particle moves in the xy-plane in such a way that its position (x, y) at any time t satisfies the simultaneous differential equations

$$\begin{cases} \dot{x} = x + 4y, \\ \dot{y} = x - 2y. \end{cases}$$

Find the position (x, y) at time t if $x(0) = 2$ and $y(0) = 3$.

Solution

This system of differential equations was solved in Example 1. The general solution was found to be

$$\begin{bmatrix} x \\ y \end{bmatrix} = \alpha \begin{bmatrix} 4 \\ 1 \end{bmatrix} e^{2t} + \beta \begin{bmatrix} 1 \\ -1 \end{bmatrix} e^{-3t},$$

where α and β are arbitrary constants.

Since $x(0) = 2$ and $y(0) = 3$, we have, on putting $t = 0$,

$$\begin{cases} 2 = 4\alpha + \beta, \\ 3 = \alpha - \beta. \end{cases}$$

Solving these equations gives $\alpha = 1$, $\beta = -2$, so the required particular solution is

$$\begin{bmatrix} x \\ y \end{bmatrix} = \begin{bmatrix} 4 \\ 1 \end{bmatrix} e^{2t} + \begin{bmatrix} -2 \\ 2 \end{bmatrix} e^{-3t}.$$

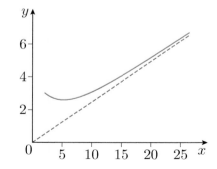

Figure 4 Behaviour of the solution to Example 3. For $t = 0$ the solution (orange line) starts at the point $(2, 3)$, but as t increases it approaches $y = \frac{1}{4}x$ (green dashed line).

In the above example the particle starts at the point $(2, 3)$ when $t = 0$, and follows a certain path as t increases. The ultimate direction of this path is easy to determine, because e^{-3t} is much smaller than e^{2t} when t is large, so we have $[x \quad y]^T \simeq [4 \quad 1]^T e^{2t}$, that is, $x \simeq 4e^{2t}$ and $y \simeq e^{2t}$, so $y \simeq \frac{1}{4}x$. Thus the solution approaches the line $y = \frac{1}{4}x$ as t increases. This behaviour is illustrated in Figure 4.

Exercise 4

(a) Use the above method to solve the system of differential equations

$$\begin{cases} \dot{x} = 5x + 2y, \\ \dot{y} = 2x + 5y, \end{cases}$$

given that $x = 4$ and $y = 0$ when $t = 0$.

(*Hint*: The result of Exercise 3 will be useful.)

(b) How does the solution behave for large t?

Exercise 5

A particle moves in three-dimensional space in such a way that its position (x, y, z) at any time t satisfies the simultaneous differential equations

$$\begin{cases} \dot{x} = 5x, \\ \dot{y} = x + 2y + z, \\ \dot{z} = x + y + 2z. \end{cases}$$

Find the position (x, y, z) at time t if $x(0) = 4$, $y(0) = 6$ and $z(0) = 0$.

(*Hint*: The eigenvectors of $\begin{bmatrix} 5 & 0 & 0 \\ 1 & 2 & 1 \\ 1 & 1 & 2 \end{bmatrix}$ are $\begin{bmatrix} 2 \\ 1 \\ 1 \end{bmatrix}$, $\begin{bmatrix} 0 \\ 1 \\ 1 \end{bmatrix}$ and $\begin{bmatrix} 0 \\ 1 \\ -1 \end{bmatrix}$,

corresponding to eigenvalues 5, 3 and 1.)

In the next subsection we investigate what happens when the eigenvalues of the matrix $\mathbf{A}$ are complex numbers.

An alternative method

There is an alternative method for solving systems of differential equations, which is occasionally used when the system is particularly simple. The idea is to eliminate all but one dependent variable. The technique can be illustrated with a pair of first-order equations such as

$$\dot{x} = -2y,$$
$$\dot{y} = 2x.$$

Differentiating the first equation gives $\ddot{x} = -2\dot{y}$, so that $\dot{y} = -\frac{1}{2}\ddot{x}$. Then substituting this into the second equation gives

$$\ddot{x} = -4x.$$

So we have eliminated one of the variables, but obtained a differential equation of higher order, in this case a second-order differential equation that can be solved for x using the methods of Unit 3. However, using this technique on larger systems of differential equations is not practical, so we do not use it in this module.

> **Solving systems of differential equations on a computer**
>
> In fact, the method described above is the opposite of what is commonly done when solving a higher-order differential equation on a computer. Given a second-order differential equation such as $\ddot{y} + \dot{y} - 6y = 0$, we would first define a new variable $x = \dot{y}$, then write the second-order equation as a pair of first-order equations:
>
> $$\dot{x} = -x + 6y,$$
> $$\dot{y} = x.$$
>
> Likewise, given a third-order differential equation such as $\dddot{y} + 2\ddot{y} - 3\dot{y} + y = 0$, we would define two new variables $x = \dot{y}$ and $z = \ddot{y} = \dot{x}$, then write this as a system of three first-order equations:
>
> $$\dot{x} = z,$$
> $$\dot{y} = x,$$
> $$\dot{z} = 3x - y - 2z.$$
>
> These are then solved with one of the numerous computer packages that are designed specifically for solving systems of first-order differential equations.

1.3 Complex eigenvalues

This subsection deals with complex quantities. Before you begin, try the following warm-up exercise.

Exercise 6

If $z = 4 + 3i$, show the following.

(a) $\overline{\overline{z}} = z$ (b) $\operatorname{Re} z = \frac{1}{2}(z + \overline{z})$ (c) $\operatorname{Im} z = \frac{1}{2i}(z - \overline{z})$

So far, all our examples and exercises have involved only *real* eigenvalues. We now investigate what happens when we have *complex* eigenvalues. In fact, because the arguments leading to Procedure 1 do not rely on the eigenvalues being real, they can also be used for the complex case. However, using equation (19) with complex eigenvalues λ_i means that the arbitrary constants $C_1, C_2, \ldots$ must also be complex for the solution $\mathbf{x}$ to be real. It would be much more convenient if a real solution $\mathbf{x}$ were expressed in terms of real quantities only. In this subsection we see how to modify equation (19) to a more useful form.

We begin with a simple example that leads to complex eigenvalues and illustrates the problem. Suppose that we want to solve the system of differential equations

$$\begin{cases} \dot{x} = y, \\ \dot{y} = -x. \end{cases} \tag{20}$$

We find the solution using Procedure 1. The matrix of coefficients is

$$\mathbf{A} = \begin{bmatrix} 0 & 1 \\ -1 & 0 \end{bmatrix},$$

and the eigenvalues of $\mathbf{A}$ are easily shown to be

$\lambda = i$ with eigenvector $[1 \quad i]^T$,

$\lambda = -i$ with eigenvector $[1 \quad -i]^T$.

Notice that one eigenvalue is the complex conjugate of the other, and similarly for the eigenvectors.

Now since Procedure 1 works for complex as well as real eigenvalues, the general solution of the given system of differential equations can be written as

$$\begin{bmatrix} x \\ y \end{bmatrix} = C \begin{bmatrix} 1 \\ i \end{bmatrix} e^{it} + D \begin{bmatrix} 1 \\ -i \end{bmatrix} e^{-it}, \tag{21}$$

where C and D are arbitrary *complex* constants.

Since x and y are real, we would very much like the right-hand side of equation (21) to be written in terms of real quantities. In order to see how to do this, notice that the eigenvalues and eigenvectors λ and $\mathbf{v}$ occur in complex conjugate pairs. (The complex conjugate of a vector $\mathbf{v}$ is the vector $\overline{\mathbf{v}}$ whose elements are the complex conjugates of the respective elements of $\mathbf{v}$. For example, if $\mathbf{v} = [1 + 2i \quad -3i]^T$, then $\overline{\mathbf{v}} = [1 - 2i \quad 3i]^T$.) This is always true for a matrix with real elements. So the solution will always be of the form

The problem is analogous to the one in Unit 3 when we had complex roots of the auxiliary equation.

$$\mathbf{x} = C\mathbf{v}e^{\lambda t} + D\overline{\mathbf{v}}e^{\overline{\lambda} t}, \tag{22}$$

where C and D are arbitrary complex constants. This is the form of equation (21). Now, since $\mathbf{x}$ is real, when we take the complex conjugate of both sides, we get

$$\mathbf{x} = \overline{\mathbf{x}} = \overline{C}\overline{\mathbf{v}}e^{\overline{\lambda} t} + \overline{D}\mathbf{v}e^{\lambda t}. \tag{23}$$

Here we have used the fact that $\mathbf{x}$ and t are real, and $z = \overline{\overline{z}}$ for any z. Comparing equations (22) and (23), we see that $D = \overline{C}$ and hence

$$\mathbf{x} = C\mathbf{v}e^{\lambda t} + \overline{C}\overline{\mathbf{v}}e^{\overline{\lambda} t}. \tag{24}$$

This equation for $\mathbf{x}$ is now manifestly real. To see this, simply take the complex conjugate of both sides and check that $\mathbf{x} = \overline{\mathbf{x}}$. Now let us set $C = \alpha + i\beta$, where α and β are real. Then

$$\mathbf{x} = (\alpha + i\beta)\mathbf{v}e^{\lambda t} + (\alpha - i\beta)\overline{\mathbf{v}}e^{\overline{\lambda} t}$$
$$= \alpha(\mathbf{v}e^{\lambda t} + \overline{\mathbf{v}}e^{\overline{\lambda} t}) + i\beta(\mathbf{v}e^{\lambda t} - \overline{\mathbf{v}}e^{\overline{\lambda} t}).$$

But for any complex number z, $\operatorname{Re} z = \frac{1}{2}(z + \overline{z})$ and $\operatorname{Im} z = \frac{1}{2i}(z - \overline{z})$, hence

$$\mathbf{x} = 2\alpha \operatorname{Re}(\mathbf{v}e^{\lambda t}) - 2\beta \operatorname{Im}(\mathbf{v}e^{\lambda t}).$$

Since C was an arbitrary complex constant, α and β are arbitrary real constants, so we can absorb the factors of 2 and -2 into them, giving

$$\mathbf{x} = \alpha \operatorname{Re}(\mathbf{v}e^{\lambda t}) + \beta \operatorname{Im}(\mathbf{v}e^{\lambda t}). \tag{25}$$

This is a simple form for $\mathbf{x}$ that is obviously real and as such is sometimes called a **real-valued solution**. Let us apply it to the preceding example.

Example 4

For the system in equation (20), find a form of the solution $\mathbf{x}$ that is clearly real.

Solution

The eigenvalues of the matrix of coefficients are

$$\lambda = i \text{ with eigenvector } \mathbf{v} = [1 \quad i]^T$$

and their complex conjugates

$$\overline{\lambda} = -i \text{ with eigenvector } \overline{\mathbf{v}} = [1 \quad -i]^T.$$

We are aiming to use equation (25), so let us choose

$$\mathbf{v}e^{\lambda t} = \begin{bmatrix} 1 \\ i \end{bmatrix} e^{it}.$$

Euler's formula was used in a similar way in Unit 3, where it gave trigonometric solutions of second-order differential equations.

We use Euler's formula, $e^{it} = \cos t + i \sin t$, to find the real and imaginary parts of $\mathbf{v}e^{\lambda t}$:

$$\mathbf{v}e^{\lambda t} = \begin{bmatrix} 1 \\ i \end{bmatrix} (\cos t + i \sin t)$$

$$= \underbrace{\begin{bmatrix} \cos t \\ -\sin t \end{bmatrix}}_{\text{real part}} + \quad i \quad \underbrace{\begin{bmatrix} \sin t \\ \cos t \end{bmatrix}}_{\text{imaginary part}}.$$

We can now apply equation (25), to obtain

$$\mathbf{x} = \alpha \begin{bmatrix} \cos t \\ -\sin t \end{bmatrix} + \beta \begin{bmatrix} \sin t \\ \cos t \end{bmatrix},$$

where α and β are arbitrary real constants.

For the case of a system of more than two differential equations, complex eigenvalues and eigenvectors also come in complex conjugate pairs – i.e. if $\lambda, \mathbf{v}$ are eigenvalue and eigenvector, then so are $\overline{\lambda}, \overline{\mathbf{v}}$. So we generalise Procedure 1, incorporating equation (25), in the following way.

Procedure 2   Solution of a homogeneous system with complex eigenvalues

To obtain a real-valued solution of a system of linear constant-coefficient first-order differential equations $\dot{\mathbf{x}} = \mathbf{A}\mathbf{x}$, where $\mathbf{A}$ is an $n \times n$ matrix with distinct eigenvalues, some of which are complex (occurring in complex conjugate pairs λ and $\overline{\lambda}$, with corresponding complex conjugate eigenvectors $\mathbf{v}$ and $\overline{\mathbf{v}}$), do the following.

1. Find the eigenvalues $\lambda_1, \lambda_2, \ldots, \lambda_n$ and a corresponding set of eigenvectors $\mathbf{v}_1, \mathbf{v}_2, \ldots, \mathbf{v}_n$.

2. Write down the general solution in the form
    $$\mathbf{x} = C_1\mathbf{v}_1 e^{\lambda_1 t} + C_2\mathbf{v}_2 e^{\lambda_2 t} + \cdots + C_n\mathbf{v}_n e^{\lambda_n t}.$$

3. Replace the complex terms $\mathbf{v}e^{\lambda t}$ and $\overline{\mathbf{v}}e^{\overline{\lambda} t}$ appearing in the general solution with $\mathrm{Re}(\mathbf{v}e^{\lambda t})$ and $\mathrm{Im}(\mathbf{v}e^{\lambda t})$.

    The general solution will then be real-valued for real $C_1, C_2, \ldots, C_n$.

Example 5

(a) Find the general solution of the system of differential equations
$$\begin{cases} \dot{x} = 3x - y, \\ \dot{y} = 2x + y, \end{cases}$$

(*Hint*: The eigenvectors of $\begin{bmatrix} 3 & -1 \\ 2 & 1 \end{bmatrix}$ are $\mathbf{v} = \begin{bmatrix} 1 \\ 1 - i \end{bmatrix}$ and $\overline{\mathbf{v}} = \begin{bmatrix} 1 \\ 1 + i \end{bmatrix}$, with corresponding eigenvalues $\lambda = 2 + i$ and $\overline{\lambda} = 2 - i$.)

(b) Find the particular solution satisfying $x = 3$ and $y = 1$ when $t = 0$.

Solution

(a) The matrix of coefficients is
$$\mathbf{A} = \begin{bmatrix} 3 & -1 \\ 2 & 1 \end{bmatrix},$$

so using the hint, the general solution can be written as
$$\mathbf{x} = C\mathbf{v}e^{\lambda t} + D\overline{\mathbf{v}}e^{\overline{\lambda} t} = C\begin{bmatrix} 1 \\ 1 - i \end{bmatrix} e^{(2+i)t} + D\begin{bmatrix} 1 \\ 1 + i \end{bmatrix} e^{(2-i)t},$$

where C and D are arbitrary complex constants.

To obtain a real-valued solution, we follow Procedure 2 and write
$$
\begin{aligned}
\mathbf{v}e^{\lambda t} &= \begin{bmatrix} 1 \\ 1 - i \end{bmatrix} e^{(2+i)t} \\
&= e^{2t} \begin{bmatrix} 1 \\ 1 - i \end{bmatrix} e^{it} \\
&= e^{2t} \begin{bmatrix} 1 \\ 1 - i \end{bmatrix} (\cos t + i\sin t) \\
&= e^{2t} \begin{bmatrix} \cos t + i\sin t \\ (1 - i)(\cos t + i\sin t) \end{bmatrix} \\
&= e^{2t} \begin{bmatrix} \cos t + i\sin t \\ (\cos t + \sin t) + i(\sin t - \cos t) \end{bmatrix} \\
&= \underbrace{e^{2t} \begin{bmatrix} \cos t \\ \cos t + \sin t \end{bmatrix}}_{\text{real part}} + \underbrace{i\, e^{2t} \begin{bmatrix} \sin t \\ \sin t - \cos t \end{bmatrix}}_{\text{imaginary part}}.
\end{aligned}
$$

The real-valued general solution of the given system of equations is therefore

$$\begin{bmatrix} x \\ y \end{bmatrix} = \alpha\, e^{2t} \begin{bmatrix} \cos t \\ \cos t + \sin t \end{bmatrix} + \beta\, e^{2t} \begin{bmatrix} \sin t \\ \sin t - \cos t \end{bmatrix}, \tag{26}$$

where α and β are arbitrary real constants.

(b) In order to find the required particular solution, we substitute $x = 3$, $y = 1$ and $t = 0$ into equation (26), to obtain

$$\begin{bmatrix} 3 \\ 1 \end{bmatrix} = \alpha \begin{bmatrix} 1 \\ 1 \end{bmatrix} + \beta \begin{bmatrix} 0 \\ -1 \end{bmatrix},$$

so $3 = \alpha$ and $1 = \alpha - \beta$, giving $\beta = 2$, and the solution is therefore

$$\begin{bmatrix} x \\ y \end{bmatrix} = \begin{bmatrix} (3\cos t + 2\sin t) \\ (\cos t + 5\sin t) \end{bmatrix} e^{2t}.$$

Exercise 7

(a) Find the general solution of the system of differential equations

$$\begin{cases} \dot{x} = -3x - 2y, \\ \dot{y} = 4x + y. \end{cases}$$

(*Hint:* The eigenvectors of $\begin{bmatrix} -3 & -2 \\ 4 & 1 \end{bmatrix}$ are $\begin{bmatrix} 1 \\ -1-i \end{bmatrix}$ and $\begin{bmatrix} 1 \\ -1+i \end{bmatrix}$, with corresponding eigenvalues $-1+2i$ and $-1-2i$.)

(b) Find the particular solution satisfying $x = y = 1$ when $t = 0$.

Exercise 8

(a) Find the general real-valued solution of the system of equations

$$\begin{cases} \dot{x} = x + z, \\ \dot{y} = x + 2y + z, \\ \dot{z} = -x + z. \end{cases}$$

(*Hint:* The eigenvectors of $\begin{bmatrix} 1 & 0 & 1 \\ 1 & 2 & 1 \\ -1 & 0 & 1 \end{bmatrix}$ are $\begin{bmatrix} 0 \\ 1 \\ 0 \end{bmatrix}$, $\begin{bmatrix} 1 \\ -i \\ i \end{bmatrix}$ and $\begin{bmatrix} 1 \\ i \\ -i \end{bmatrix}$, with corresponding eigenvalues 2, $\lambda = 1 + i$ and $\bar{\lambda} = 1 - i$.)

(b) Find the solution for which $x = y = 1$ and $z = 2$ when $t = 0$.

Anomalous cases

The method outlined in the last two subsections works only when the $n \times n$ matrix of coefficients has n (linearly independent) eigenvectors. As was mentioned in Unit 5, it can happen that an $n \times n$ matrix has fewer than n eigenvectors. In this case, when we construct the solution for $\mathbf{x}$ given in Step 2 of Procedure 1, we find that it contains fewer than n arbitrary constants, so although it is a solution, it is not the *general* solution.

There are techniques for dealing with such anomalous cases, but they are not discussed in this module because they are not often employed in science. The reason for this is that in science, the systems of differential equations that we solve normally contain physical parameters – for example, the matrix of coefficients in the fluid example of the Introduction was formed from physical parameters like $k_A K_{AB}$. And for almost all values of these parameters, the $n \times n$ matrix of coefficients will have n linearly independent eigenvectors. If there are particular values of the parameters where the matrix has fewer than n eigenvectors, then we can usually just alter them slightly to make the matrix well behaved again.

1.4   First-order inhomogeneous systems

In the previous subsections you saw how to solve a system of differential equations of the form $\dot{\mathbf{x}} = \mathbf{A}\mathbf{x}$, where $\mathbf{A}$ is a given constant-coefficient matrix. We now extend our discussion to systems of the form

$$\dot{\mathbf{x}} = \mathbf{A}\mathbf{x} + \mathbf{h}(t),$$

where $\mathbf{h}(t)$ is a given function of t. Our method involves finding a 'particular integral' for the system, and mirrors the approach that we took for inhomogeneous second-order differential equations in Unit 3.

Here we write $\mathbf{h}(t)$ to emphasise that $\mathbf{h}$ is a function of t. Henceforth we will abbreviate this to $\mathbf{h}$.

In Unit 3 we discussed inhomogeneous differential equations such as

$$\frac{d^2y}{dx^2} + 9y = 2e^{3x}. \tag{27}$$

See Unit 3, Example 9.

To solve such an equation, we proceed as follows.

1. We first find the *complementary function* of the corresponding homogeneous equation

    $$\frac{d^2y}{dx^2} + 9y = 0,$$

    which is, in this case,

    $$y_c = C_1 \cos 3x + C_2 \sin 3x,$$

    where C_1 and C_2 are arbitrary constants.

2. We then find a *particular integral* of the inhomogeneous equation (27). It is easy to check that

    $$y_p = \tfrac{1}{9}e^{3x}$$

    is such a particular integral.

The general solution y of the original equation is then obtained by adding these two functions to give

$$y = y_c + y_p = C_1 \cos 3x + C_2 \sin 3x + \tfrac{1}{9}e^{3x}.$$

A similar situation holds for systems of linear first-order differential equations. For example, in order to find the general solution of the inhomogeneous system

$$\begin{cases} \dot{x} = 3x + 2y + 4e^{3t}, \\ \dot{y} = \ \ x + 4y - e^{3t}, \end{cases} \tag{28}$$

which in matrix form becomes

$$\begin{bmatrix} \dot{x} \\ \dot{y} \end{bmatrix} = \begin{bmatrix} 3 & 2 \\ 1 & 4 \end{bmatrix} \begin{bmatrix} x \\ y \end{bmatrix} + \begin{bmatrix} 4e^{3t} \\ -e^{3t} \end{bmatrix},$$

This is $\dot{\mathbf{x}} = \mathbf{A}\mathbf{x} + \mathbf{h}$, where $\mathbf{h} = [4e^{3t} \quad -e^{3t}]^T$.

we first find the general solution of the corresponding homogeneous system

$$\begin{cases} \dot{x} = 3x + 2y, \\ \dot{y} = \ \ x + 4y, \end{cases}$$

which is the **complementary function**

$$\mathbf{x}_c = \begin{bmatrix} x_c \\ y_c \end{bmatrix} = \alpha \begin{bmatrix} 1 \\ 1 \end{bmatrix} e^{5t} + \beta \begin{bmatrix} -2 \\ 1 \end{bmatrix} e^{2t}, \tag{29}$$

where α and β are arbitrary constants (see the solution to Exercise 2(b)).

We use the term *particular integral* rather than particular solution. The latter is more appropriately used for the solution of system (28) that satisfies given initial or boundary conditions.

We next find a particular solution, or **particular integral**, of the original inhomogeneous system (28). In Subsection 1.5 we will show that

$$\mathbf{x}_p = \begin{bmatrix} x_p \\ y_p \end{bmatrix} = \begin{bmatrix} 3 \\ -2 \end{bmatrix} e^{3t}, \tag{30}$$

is such a particular integral. The general solution of the original system (28) is then obtained by adding equations (29) and (30):

$$\begin{aligned} \begin{bmatrix} x \\ y \end{bmatrix} &= \begin{bmatrix} x_c \\ y_c \end{bmatrix} + \begin{bmatrix} x_p \\ y_p \end{bmatrix} \\ &= \alpha \begin{bmatrix} 1 \\ 1 \end{bmatrix} e^{5t} + \beta \begin{bmatrix} -2 \\ 1 \end{bmatrix} e^{2t} + \begin{bmatrix} 3 \\ -2 \end{bmatrix} e^{3t}. \end{aligned}$$

That this is the *general solution* can be seen as follows. Since $\mathbf{x}_c$ is the general solution of the homogeneous equation $\dot{\mathbf{x}}_c = \mathbf{A}\mathbf{x}_c$, and $\mathbf{x}_p$ is a particular integral of the inhomogeneous equation $\dot{\mathbf{x}}_p = \mathbf{A}\mathbf{x}_p + \mathbf{h}$, setting $\mathbf{x} = \mathbf{x}_c + \mathbf{x}_p$ gives

$$\begin{aligned} \dot{\mathbf{x}} = \dot{\mathbf{x}}_c + \dot{\mathbf{x}}_p &= \mathbf{A}\mathbf{x}_c + \mathbf{A}\mathbf{x}_p + \mathbf{h} \\ &= \mathbf{A}(\mathbf{x}_c + \mathbf{x}_p) + \mathbf{h} \\ &= \mathbf{A}\mathbf{x} + \mathbf{h}. \end{aligned}$$

Therefore $\mathbf{x}$ is a solution of the inhomogeneous equation and contains two arbitrary constants (from $\mathbf{x}_c$). This is sufficient to guarantee that $\mathbf{x}$ must be the general solution of the inhomogeneous equation. This argument is of course true for a system of any number of differential equations, so we have the following result.

General solution of an inhomogeneous system

If $\mathbf{x}_c$ is the complementary function of the homogeneous system $\dot{\mathbf{x}} = \mathbf{A}\mathbf{x}$, and $\mathbf{x}_p$ is a particular integral of the system $\dot{\mathbf{x}} = \mathbf{A}\mathbf{x} + \mathbf{h}$, then $\mathbf{x}_c + \mathbf{x}_p$ is the **general solution** of the system $\dot{\mathbf{x}} = \mathbf{A}\mathbf{x} + \mathbf{h}$.

Exercise 9

Write down the general solution of the system

$$\begin{cases} \dot{x} = 3x + 2y + t, \\ \dot{y} = x + 4y + 7t, \end{cases}$$

given that a particular integral is

$$x_p = t + \tfrac{4}{5}, \quad y_p = -2t - \tfrac{7}{10}.$$

(*Hint*: The eigenvectors of $\begin{bmatrix} 3 & 2 \\ 1 & 4 \end{bmatrix}$ are $\begin{bmatrix} 1 \\ 1 \end{bmatrix}$ and $\begin{bmatrix} -2 \\ 1 \end{bmatrix}$, with corresponding eigenvalues 5 and 2.)

Although it is easy to verify that equation (30) is a solution of the given system, by direct substitution, we now show you how to *determine* it.

1.5 Finding particular integrals

We now show you how to find a particular integral $\mathbf{x}_p$ in some special cases. We consider the system $\dot{\mathbf{x}} = \mathbf{A}\mathbf{x} + \mathbf{h}$ in the situations where $\mathbf{h}$ is a vector whose components are:

- polynomial functions
- exponential functions.

Our treatment will be similar to that in Unit 3, where we found particular integrals for linear second-order differential equations using the method of undetermined coefficients. To illustrate the ideas involved, we consider the system

$$\dot{\mathbf{x}} = \mathbf{A}\mathbf{x} + \mathbf{h}, \quad \text{where } \mathbf{A} = \begin{bmatrix} 3 & 2 \\ 1 & 4 \end{bmatrix}.$$

The first stage in solving any inhomogeneous system is to find the complementary function, that is, the solution of the system $\dot{\mathbf{x}} = \mathbf{A}\mathbf{x}$. The complementary function for this system was found in the solution to Exercise 2(b):

$$\begin{bmatrix} x_c \\ y_c \end{bmatrix} = \alpha \begin{bmatrix} 1 \\ 1 \end{bmatrix} e^{5t} + \beta \begin{bmatrix} -2 \\ 1 \end{bmatrix} e^{2t}. \tag{31}$$

To this complementary function we add a particular integral that depends on the form of $\mathbf{h}$. We now look at examples of the above two forms for $\mathbf{h}$, and derive a particular integral in each case.

Example 6

Find the general solution of the system

$$\begin{cases} \dot{x} = 3x + 2y + t, \\ \dot{y} = x + 4y + 7t. \end{cases}$$

Solution

The complementary function is given in equation (31).

Here $\mathbf{h} = [t \quad 7t]^T$, so $\mathbf{h}$ is linear in t.

We note that $\mathbf{h}$ consists entirely of linear functions, so it seems natural to seek a particular integral of the form

$$\begin{bmatrix} x \\ y \end{bmatrix} = \begin{bmatrix} at + b \\ ct + d \end{bmatrix},$$

where a, b, c and d are constants that we need to determine. So $x = at + b$, $y = ct + d$, and differentiating these we get $\dot{x} = a$, $\dot{y} = c$. Substituting these values into the simultaneous equations gives

You may have been tempted to use a simpler trial solution, of the form

$$\begin{bmatrix} x \\ y \end{bmatrix} = \begin{bmatrix} at \\ ct \end{bmatrix}.$$

Unfortunately, this does not work – try it and see! You may recall something similar in Unit 3.

$$\begin{cases} a = 3(at + b) + 2(ct + d) + t, \\ c = (at + b) + 4(ct + d) + 7t. \end{cases}$$

We now rearrange these equations, separating constant terms from the terms linear in t:

$$\begin{cases} (3a + 2c + 1)t + (3b + 2d - a) = 0, \\ (a + 4c + 7)t + (b + 4d - c) = 0. \end{cases} \tag{32}$$

These equations hold for *all* values of t, which means that each of the bracketed terms must be zero.

Equating the coefficients of t to zero in equations (32) gives

$$\begin{cases} 3a + 2c + 1 = 0, \\ a + 4c + 7 = 0, \end{cases}$$

which have the solution

$$a = 1, \quad c = -2.$$

Equating the constant terms to zero in equations (32), and putting $a = 1$, $c = -2$, gives the equations

$$\begin{cases} 3b + 2d - 1 = 0, \\ b + 4d + 2 = 0, \end{cases}$$

which have the solution

$$b = \tfrac{4}{5}, \quad d = -\tfrac{7}{10}.$$

Thus the required particular integral is

$$\begin{bmatrix} x_{\mathrm{p}} \\ y_{\mathrm{p}} \end{bmatrix} = \begin{bmatrix} t + \tfrac{4}{5} \\ -2t - \tfrac{7}{10} \end{bmatrix},$$

and the general solution is

$$\begin{bmatrix} x \\ y \end{bmatrix} = \begin{bmatrix} x_{\mathrm{c}} \\ y_{\mathrm{c}} \end{bmatrix} + \begin{bmatrix} x_{\mathrm{p}} \\ y_{\mathrm{p}} \end{bmatrix} = \alpha \begin{bmatrix} 1 \\ 1 \end{bmatrix} e^{5t} + \beta \begin{bmatrix} -2 \\ 1 \end{bmatrix} e^{2t} + \begin{bmatrix} t + \tfrac{4}{5} \\ -2t - \tfrac{7}{10} \end{bmatrix}.$$

Exercise 10

Find the general solution of the system

$$\begin{cases} \dot{x} = x + 4y - t + 2, \\ \dot{y} = x - 2y + 5t. \end{cases}$$

(*Hint*: For the complementary function, see Example 1.)

Example 7

Find the general solution of the system

$$\begin{cases} \dot{x} = 3x + 2y + 4e^{3t}, \\ \dot{y} = \ x + 4y - e^{3t}. \end{cases}$$

Here $\mathbf{h} = [4e^{3t} \quad -e^{3t}]^T$, so $\mathbf{h}$ is exponential.

Solution

The complementary function is given in equation (31). We note that both components of $\mathbf{h}$ include the same exponential function e^{3t}, so it seems natural to seek a particular integral of the form

$$\begin{bmatrix} x \\ y \end{bmatrix} = \begin{bmatrix} ae^{3t} \\ be^{3t} \end{bmatrix} = \begin{bmatrix} a \\ b \end{bmatrix} e^{3t},$$

where a and b are constants that we need to determine. So $x = ae^{3t}$, $y = be^{3t}$, and differentiating these gives $\dot{x} = 3ae^{3t}$, $\dot{y} = 3be^{3t}$. Substituting these values into the simultaneous equations gives

$$\begin{cases} 3ae^{3t} = 3ae^{3t} + 2be^{3t} + 4e^{3t}, \\ 3be^{3t} = ae^{3t} + 4be^{3t} - e^{3t}, \end{cases}$$

or, on dividing by e^{3t},

$$\begin{cases} 3a = 3a + 2b + 4, \\ 3b = \ a + 4b - 1. \end{cases}$$

Rearranging these equations gives

$$\begin{cases} \quad\ \ 2b = -4, \\ a + \ b = \quad 1, \end{cases}$$

which have the solution

$$a = 3, \quad b = -2.$$

Thus the required particular integral is

$$\begin{bmatrix} x_{\mathrm{p}} \\ y_{\mathrm{p}} \end{bmatrix} = \begin{bmatrix} 3e^{3t} \\ -2e^{3t} \end{bmatrix} = \begin{bmatrix} 3 \\ -2 \end{bmatrix} e^{3t},$$

and the general solution is

$$\begin{bmatrix} x \\ y \end{bmatrix} = \begin{bmatrix} x_{\mathrm{c}} \\ y_{\mathrm{c}} \end{bmatrix} + \begin{bmatrix} x_{\mathrm{p}} \\ y_{\mathrm{p}} \end{bmatrix}$$

$$= \alpha \begin{bmatrix} 1 \\ 1 \end{bmatrix} e^{5t} + \beta \begin{bmatrix} -2 \\ 1 \end{bmatrix} e^{2t} + \begin{bmatrix} 3 \\ -2 \end{bmatrix} e^{3t}.$$

Exercise 11

Find the general solution of the system

$$\begin{cases} \dot{x} = x + 4y + 4e^{-t}, \\ \dot{y} = x - 2y + 5e^{-t}. \end{cases}$$

(*Hint*: The complementary function is the same as that of Exercise 10.)

We summarise our results in the following procedure.

> **Procedure 3   Finding particular integrals**
>
> To find a particular integral $\mathbf{x}_p = [x_p \quad y_p]^T$ for the system $\dot{\mathbf{x}} = \mathbf{Ax} + \mathbf{h}$, do the following.
>
> 1. When the elements of $\mathbf{h}$ are polynomials of degree k or less, choose x_p and y_p to be polynomials of degree k.
>
> 2. When the elements of $\mathbf{h}$ are multiples of the same exponential function, choose x_p and y_p to be multiples of this exponential function.
>
> To determine the coefficients in x_p and y_p, substitute into the system of differential equations and equate coefficients if necessary.

Exercise 12

Consider the system of differential equations

$$\begin{cases} \dot{x} = 2x + 3y + e^{2t}, \\ \dot{y} = 2x + y + 4e^{2t}. \end{cases}$$

(a) Evaluate the eigenvalues and eigenvectors of the matrix of coefficients.

(b) Find the solution of this system subject to the initial conditions $x(0) = \frac{5}{6}$, $y(0) = \frac{2}{3}$.

(c) How does the solution found in part (b) behave for large t?

Other cases

> This short subsection is included for completeness, but **the material in it will not be assessed**.

Combinations of cases

Procedure 3 allows you to determine the particular integral when the inhomogeneous term $\mathbf{h}$ has components that are simple functions like polynomials or exponentials. When $\mathbf{h}$ is a linear combination of these simple functions, for example

$$\mathbf{h}(t) = \mathbf{h}_1(t) + \mathbf{h}_2(t), \quad \text{where } \mathbf{h}_1 = \begin{bmatrix} 4 \\ -1 \end{bmatrix} e^{3t} \text{ and } \mathbf{h}_2 = \begin{bmatrix} 1 \\ 7 \end{bmatrix} t,$$

we find a particular integral for each of $\mathbf{h}_1$ and $\mathbf{h}_2$ separately, using the above method (see Examples 6 and 7), then add the two particular integrals together. We would use a similar trick if $\mathbf{h}_1$ and $\mathbf{h}_2$ were two exponential terms with different exponents.

Exceptional cases

Occasionally Procedure 3 will fail to find a particular integral of an inhomogeneous system $\dot{\mathbf{x}} = \mathbf{A}\mathbf{x} + \mathbf{h}$. This usually occurs when the inhomogeneous part $\mathbf{h}$ is related to the complementary function $\mathbf{x}_c$. For example,

$$\begin{cases} \dot{x} = 3x + 2y + 6e^{2t}, \\ \dot{y} = x + 4y + 3e^{2t}, \end{cases}$$

has a complementary function given by equation (31):

$$\begin{bmatrix} x_c \\ y_c \end{bmatrix} = \alpha \begin{bmatrix} 1 \\ 1 \end{bmatrix} e^{5t} + \beta \begin{bmatrix} -2 \\ 1 \end{bmatrix} e^{2t}.$$

We see that the term e^{2t} occurs in both the complementary function and the inhomogeneous part $\mathbf{h}$. If we follow Procedure 3 and try to find a particular integral of the form $\mathbf{x}_p = [a_1 \quad a_2]^T e^{2t}$, then we will find that the system of equations for a_1 and a_2 has no solution and so the method fails.

The resolution is identical to that discussed in Unit 3 when the method of undetermined coefficients failed for the same reason: we simply try a more general form for the particular integral. In this case we would try a solution of the form

$$\mathbf{x}_p = \begin{bmatrix} a_1 + b_1 t \\ a_2 + b_2 t \end{bmatrix} e^{2t}.$$

This is analogous to what was done in Unit 3 for second-order differential equations.

2 Second-order systems

In this section we show how the methods already introduced to solve systems of first-order differential equations can be adapted to systems of second-order differential equations. We restrict ourselves to considering homogeneous second-order systems, as the inhomogeneous case can be handled using the same technique as in the previous section. We begin with a short motivational section describing how the motion of bodies coupled by springs leads naturally to such equations. Don't worry too much about the details, as you will not be assessed on deriving equations of motion.

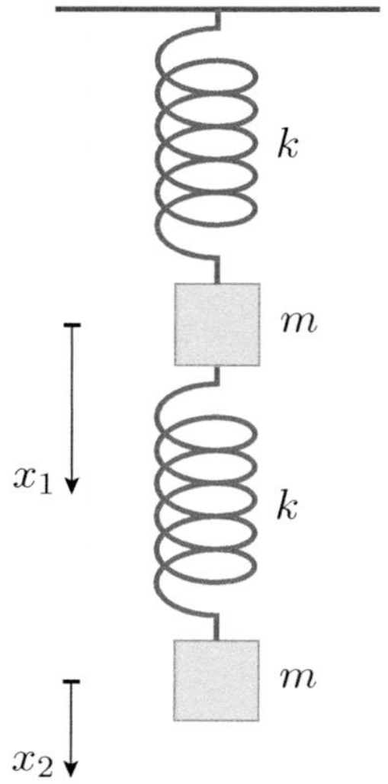

2.1 Mechanical oscillations and normal modes

In Unit 3 we discussed the motion of a mass suspended on a spring. We showed that this system exhibits a sinusoidal motion called simple harmonic motion. Here we consider a generalisation of this mass and spring system, illustrated in Figure 5. The system consists of two particles, each of mass m, suspended by springs with spring constant k, with one mass suspended below the other.

Figure 5   A compound harmonic oscillator; we analyse the vertical motion of these two masses, connected by springs

This system can rest in equilibrium with both masses stationary. In order to describe the motion of this system, we need to describe the displacement of the masses from this equilibrium position. Let the downward displacement of the upper mass from its equilibrium point be x_1, and let the downward displacement of the lower mass from its equilibrium point be x_2. We need to find equations of motion for $x_1(t)$ and $x_2(t)$. These are obtained from Newton's second law:

$$m\frac{d^2x_1}{dt^2} = F_1, \quad m\frac{d^2x_2}{dt^2} = F_2, \tag{33}$$

where F_1 is the force on the upper mass due to its displacement from its equilibrium position, and F_2 is the force on the lower mass. These forces are linear in x_1 and x_2, and can be shown to satisfy

$$F_1 = k(x_2 - x_1) - kx_1 = k(x_2 - 2x_1),$$
$$F_2 = k(x_1 - x_2).$$

We do not expect you to be able to derive such equations. However, the following is an argument that makes them plausible.

Forces and accelerations are normally written as vectors. However, when we have motion in only one direction, we just consider the vertical component as we have done here.

Don't worry if you can't follow this argument; it is not important for what follows.

Look at Figure 5. Suppose that we move the upper mass down by a positive amount Δ and hold the lower mass still, so that $x_1 = \Delta > 0$ and $x_2 = 0$. Then we expect an upwards restoring force from both springs on the upper mass, and a downwards restoring force from just the lower spring on the lower mass.

The equations for the forces give $F_1 = k(x_2 - 2x_1) = -2k\Delta$ and $F_2 = k(x_1 - x_2) = k\Delta$. So F_1 is upwards, F_2 is downwards, and $|F_1|$ is twice $|F_2|$, which is what we expect by intuition.

Now suppose that we move the lower mass down by a positive amount Δ and hold the upper mass still, so that $x_1 = 0$ and $x_2 = \Delta > 0$. Then we expect a downwards restoring force on the upper mass, and an equal and opposite upwards restoring force on the lower mass.

The equations for the forces give $F_1 = k(x_2 - 2x_1) = k\Delta$ and $F_2 = k(x_1 - x_2) = -k\Delta$, which is what we expect by intuition.

Substituting these equations for the forces into equations (33), we obtain equations of motion for the pair of masses:

$$m\ddot{x}_1 = k(x_2 - 2x_1),$$
$$m\ddot{x}_2 = k(x_1 - x_2).$$

This can be written in matrix form as

$$\begin{bmatrix} \ddot{x}_1 \\ \ddot{x}_2 \end{bmatrix} = \frac{k}{m} \begin{bmatrix} -2 & 1 \\ 1 & -1 \end{bmatrix} \begin{bmatrix} x_1 \\ x_2 \end{bmatrix}, \tag{34}$$

or as

$$\ddot{\mathbf{x}} = \mathbf{A}\mathbf{x}, \quad \text{where } \mathbf{x} = \begin{bmatrix} x_1 \\ x_2 \end{bmatrix} \text{ and } \mathbf{A} = \frac{k}{m} \begin{bmatrix} -2 & 1 \\ 1 & -1 \end{bmatrix}. \tag{35}$$

This is similar in form to equation (5) of the Introduction, except that it involves second derivatives. In this section and the next we will see that there are solutions, derived from the eigenvalues and eigenvectors of $\mathbf{A}$ and analogous to equation (6), in the form of a constant vector multiplying a function of time.

Among all the possible motions of this system there is a special motion, where the two masses oscillate with the same angular frequency ω, but with possibly different amplitudes a_1 and a_2. In this case the function of time is a sinusoidal function, and the solution typically has the form

$$\begin{bmatrix} x_1(t) \\ x_2(t) \end{bmatrix} = \sin(\omega t + \phi) \begin{bmatrix} a_1 \\ a_2 \end{bmatrix},$$

where ϕ is a constant. These special solutions are called the *normal modes* of oscillation of the system and will be discussed in Section 3.

Dynamics of other physical systems near equilibrium

Second-order equations of the form $\ddot{\mathbf{x}} = \mathbf{A}\mathbf{x}$ find applications in many other physical situations. When we make a small displacement x of any system from equilibrium, the restoring forces can be expanded as a Taylor series in x:

$$F(x) = Cx + Dx^2 + \cdots,$$

where C and D are constants.

Note that the constant term in the series is equal to zero because the force is zero at the equilibrium: $F(0) = 0$.

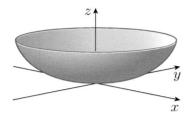

Figure 6 A bowl

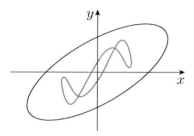

Figure 7 Typical path of a ball in an elliptical bowl, looked at from above

When the displacement x is small, the quadratic and higher-order terms can be neglected, so that $F \simeq Cx$ and hence using Newton's second law we get

$$\ddot{x} = Ax,$$

where $A = C/m$, and m represents the mass of the system. If two or more coordinates $(x_1, x_2, \ldots)$ are required to describe the displacement from equilibrium, then the equation of motion for the small displacements takes a form similar to equation (35):

$$\ddot{\mathbf{x}} = \mathbf{A}\mathbf{x}, \tag{36}$$

where $\mathbf{A}$ is a matrix and $\mathbf{x} = [x_1 \quad x_2 \quad \ldots]^T$ is a vector formed by the displacements. This equation describes the dynamics of most physical systems near equilibrium.

A simple example of this is when a ball bearing (a small metal ball) is placed in a bowl, like that in Figure 6, and set in motion. In that case, $\mathbf{x}$ represents the vector displacement of the ball from the lowest part of the bowl, when looked at from above. And when $|\mathbf{x}|$ is not too large, the motion of the ball can be described by equation (36), where the coefficients of the matrix $\mathbf{A}$ are determined from the shape of the bottom of the bowl. Figure 7 illustrates a typical path that you might see if you looked down onto the surface of the bowl from above.

Let us now move on to the topic of how to solve systems of second-order differential equations.

2.2 Solving second-order systems

We will consider systems of linear constant-coefficient second-order differential equations of the form

$$\ddot{\mathbf{x}} = \mathbf{A}\mathbf{x}. \tag{37}$$

We will try to solve this equation in a similar manner to the way in which we solved the first-order case $\dot{\mathbf{x}} = \mathbf{A}\mathbf{x}$ in the previous section.

Let $\mathbf{v}$ be an eigenvector of the matrix $\mathbf{A}$ with eigenvalue λ, so $\mathbf{A}\mathbf{v} = \lambda\mathbf{v}$. For the moment we will assume $\lambda \neq 0$ (the case $\lambda = 0$ will be covered shortly). Let us try a solution of the form $\mathbf{x}(t) = \mathbf{v}e^{\mu t}$ for some number μ. Substituting into the left- and right-hand sides of equation (37), we get

$$\frac{d^2}{dt^2}\mathbf{v}e^{\mu t} = \mathbf{A}\mathbf{v}e^{\mu t},$$

so

$$\mu^2 \mathbf{v}e^{\mu t} = \lambda\mathbf{v}e^{\mu t}.$$

Thus $\mu^2 = \lambda$, hence $\mathbf{x}(t) = \mathbf{v}e^{\sqrt{\lambda}t}$ and $\mathbf{x}(t) = \mathbf{v}e^{-\sqrt{\lambda}t}$ are both solutions. So we have the following result.

For a system of differential equations

$$\ddot{\mathbf{x}} = \mathbf{A}\mathbf{x},$$

solutions are given by

$$\mathbf{x} = \mathbf{v}e^{\pm\sqrt{\lambda}t},$$

where λ is an eigenvalue of the matrix $\mathbf{A}$ corresponding to an eigenvector $\mathbf{v}$.

The *general solution* is, as you may already have guessed, a linear combination of the solutions $\mathbf{v}e^{+\sqrt{\lambda}t}$ and $\mathbf{v}e^{-\sqrt{\lambda}t}$ for all eigenvalues λ. We must consider two cases: $\lambda > 0$ and $\lambda < 0$. Let us consider the positive case first; the following example illustrates how to construct the general solution for a pair of simultaneous differential equations.

Example 8

Find the general solution of the system of differential equations

$$\begin{cases} \ddot{x} = 3x + 2y, \\ \ddot{y} = x + 4y. \end{cases}$$

(*Hint*: The eigenvectors of $\begin{bmatrix} 3 & 2 \\ 1 & 4 \end{bmatrix}$ are $\mathbf{v}_1 = \begin{bmatrix} 1 \\ 1 \end{bmatrix}$ and $\mathbf{v}_2 = \begin{bmatrix} -2 \\ 1 \end{bmatrix}$, with corresponding eigenvalues $\lambda_1 = 5$ and $\lambda_2 = 2$.)

Solution

The matrix of coefficients is

$$\mathbf{A} = \begin{bmatrix} 3 & 2 \\ 1 & 4 \end{bmatrix}.$$

Using the hint, it follows that $\mathbf{v}_1 e^{\pm\sqrt{\lambda_1}t} = \begin{bmatrix} 1 & 1 \end{bmatrix}^T e^{\pm\sqrt{5}t}$ and $\mathbf{v}_2 e^{\pm\sqrt{\lambda_2}t} = \begin{bmatrix} -2 & 1 \end{bmatrix}^T e^{\pm\sqrt{2}t}$ are solutions. Hence the general solution is a linear combination of these:

$$\begin{bmatrix} x \\ y \end{bmatrix} = \begin{bmatrix} 1 \\ 1 \end{bmatrix}\left(C_1 e^{\sqrt{5}t} + C_2 e^{-\sqrt{5}t}\right) + \begin{bmatrix} -2 \\ 1 \end{bmatrix}\left(C_3 e^{\sqrt{2}t} + C_4 e^{-\sqrt{2}t}\right),$$

where C_1, C_2, C_3 and C_4 are arbitrary constants.

In this example, we see that two second-order differential equations give rise to a general solution with four arbitrary constants – four terms arise from the positive and negative square roots of each eigenvalue. Not surprisingly, a system of n second-order differential equations gives rise to a general solution with $2n$ arbitrary constants.

Exercise 13

Find the general solution of the system of differential equations

$$\begin{cases} \ddot{x} = 5x + 2y, \\ \ddot{y} = 2x + 5y. \end{cases}$$

(*Hint*: The eigenvectors of $\begin{bmatrix} 5 & 2 \\ 2 & 5 \end{bmatrix}$ are $\begin{bmatrix} 1 \\ 1 \end{bmatrix}$ and $\begin{bmatrix} 1 \\ -1 \end{bmatrix}$, with corresponding eigenvalues 7 and 3.)

All this is fine when the eigenvalues are positive. However, if an eigenvalue λ is negative, then $\sqrt{\lambda} = i\sqrt{-\lambda}$ is pure imaginary, and we have solutions of the form

$$\mathbf{x} = C_1 \mathbf{v} e^{i\sqrt{-\lambda}t} + C_2 \mathbf{v} e^{-i\sqrt{-\lambda}t} + \text{other eigenvalue terms.}$$

Hence the constants C_1 and C_2 must be complex for $\mathbf{x}$ to be real. A similar problem occurred in Subsection 1.3, and as there, we use Euler's formula to manipulate our solution into one involving sines and cosines. So (ignoring the other eigenvalue terms) we have

$$\begin{aligned} \mathbf{x} &= C_1 \mathbf{v} \big(\cos(\sqrt{-\lambda}t) + i\sin(\sqrt{-\lambda}t) \big) + C_2 \mathbf{v} \big(\cos(\sqrt{-\lambda}t) - i\sin(\sqrt{-\lambda}t) \big) \\ &= (C_1 + C_2)\mathbf{v}\cos(\sqrt{-\lambda}t) + i(C_1 - C_2)\mathbf{v}\sin(\sqrt{-\lambda}t) \\ &= \alpha\mathbf{v}\cos(\sqrt{-\lambda}t) + \beta\mathbf{v}\sin(\sqrt{-\lambda}t), \end{aligned}$$

where $\alpha = C_1 + C_2$ and $\beta = i(C_1 - C_2)$. Since C_1 and C_2 are arbitrary, so are α and β. Furthermore, if $\mathbf{x}$ is real, then clearly α and β must be real too. We summarise this as follows.

> If λ is a *negative* eigenvalue of the matrix $\mathbf{A}$ corresponding to an eigenvector $\mathbf{v}$, then
>
> $$\mathbf{x} = \mathbf{v}\cos(\sqrt{-\lambda}t) \quad \text{and} \quad \mathbf{x} = \mathbf{v}\sin(\sqrt{-\lambda}t)$$
>
> are solutions of the system of differential equations $\ddot{\mathbf{x}} = \mathbf{A}\mathbf{x}$.

Example 9

Find the general solution of the system of differential equations

$$\begin{cases} \ddot{x} = x + 4y, \\ \ddot{y} = x - 2y. \end{cases}$$

Solution

The matrix of coefficients is

$$\mathbf{A} = \begin{bmatrix} 1 & 4 \\ 1 & -2 \end{bmatrix}.$$

The eigenvectors of $\mathbf{A}$ can be shown to be

$$\mathbf{v}_1 = \begin{bmatrix} 4 & 1 \end{bmatrix}^T \text{ with eigenvalue } \lambda_1 = 2,$$
$$\mathbf{v}_2 = \begin{bmatrix} 1 & -1 \end{bmatrix}^T \text{ with eigenvalue } \lambda_2 = -3.$$

So we have one positive and one negative eigenvalue. For the positive eigenvalue we get the solution

$$\mathbf{x}_1 = C_1 \begin{bmatrix} 4 \\ 1 \end{bmatrix} e^{\sqrt{2}t} + C_2 \begin{bmatrix} 4 \\ 1 \end{bmatrix} e^{-\sqrt{2}t}.$$

We could write the solution for the negative eigenvalue as

$$\mathbf{x}_2 = C_3 \begin{bmatrix} 1 \\ -1 \end{bmatrix} e^{i\sqrt{3}t} + C_4 \begin{bmatrix} 1 \\ -1 \end{bmatrix} e^{-i\sqrt{3}t},$$

but as discussed above, this is not so convenient because then C_3 and C_4 have to be complex. So instead we use the above result and write the solution in terms of sines and cosines:

$$\mathbf{x}_2 = C_3 \begin{bmatrix} 1 \\ -1 \end{bmatrix} \cos(\sqrt{3}t) + C_4 \begin{bmatrix} 1 \\ -1 \end{bmatrix} \sin(\sqrt{3}t).$$

Adding all the solutions ($\mathbf{x}_1 + \mathbf{x}_2$), we get the general solution:

$$\begin{bmatrix} x \\ y \end{bmatrix} = \begin{bmatrix} 4 \\ 1 \end{bmatrix} \left(C_1 e^{\sqrt{2}t} + C_2 e^{-\sqrt{2}t} \right) + \begin{bmatrix} 1 \\ -1 \end{bmatrix} \left(C_3 \cos(\sqrt{3}t) + C_4 \sin(\sqrt{3}t) \right),$$

where C_1, C_2, C_3 and C_4 are *real* constants.

The above ideas can be formalised in the following procedure, which also tells you what to do when an eigenvalue of the matrix of coefficients is zero.

Procedure 4   Solving a second-order homogeneous linear system

To solve a system $\ddot{\mathbf{x}} = \mathbf{A}\mathbf{x}$, where $\mathbf{A}$ is an $n \times n$ matrix with n distinct real eigenvalues, do the following.

1.   Find the eigenvalues $\lambda_1, \lambda_2, \ldots, \lambda_n$ of $\mathbf{A}$, and a corresponding set of eigenvectors $\mathbf{v}_1, \mathbf{v}_2, \ldots, \mathbf{v}_n$.

2.   Each *positive* eigenvalue λ, corresponding to an eigenvector $\mathbf{v}$, gives rise to two linearly independent solutions

$$\mathbf{v}e^{\sqrt{\lambda}t} \quad \text{and} \quad \mathbf{v}e^{-\sqrt{\lambda}t}.$$

Each *negative* eigenvalue λ, corresponding to an eigenvector $\mathbf{v}$, gives rise to two linearly independent solutions

$$\mathbf{v}\cos(\sqrt{-\lambda}t) \quad \text{and} \quad \mathbf{v}\sin(\sqrt{-\lambda}t).$$

A *zero* eigenvalue corresponding to an eigenvector $\mathbf{v}$ gives rise to two linearly independent solutions

$$\mathbf{v} \quad \text{and} \quad \mathbf{v}t.$$

3.   The general solution is then an arbitrary linear combination of the $2n$ linearly independent solutions found in Step 2, involving $2n$ arbitrary real constants.

Complex eigenvalues and repeated real eigenvalues are not discussed here, but they can be dealt with by generalising what we have discussed.

We do not prove this here, but you can verify it in any particular case (see Example 10 below).

We illustrate this procedure in the following example.

Example 10

Find the general solution of the system of differential equations

$$\begin{cases} \ddot{x} = 3x + 2y + 2z, \\ \ddot{y} = 2x + 2y, \\ \ddot{z} = 2x + 4z. \end{cases}$$

Solution

The matrix of coefficients is

$$\mathbf{A} = \begin{bmatrix} 3 & 2 & 2 \\ 2 & 2 & 0 \\ 2 & 0 & 4 \end{bmatrix}.$$

The eigenvectors of $\mathbf{A}$ can be shown to be

$$[2 \quad 1 \quad 2]^T \text{ with eigenvalue } \lambda = 6,$$
$$[1 \quad 2 \quad -2]^T \text{ with eigenvalue } \lambda = 3,$$
$$[-2 \quad 2 \quad 1]^T \text{ with eigenvalue } \lambda = 0.$$

It follows from Procedure 4 that the general solution of the system is

$$\begin{bmatrix} x \\ y \\ z \end{bmatrix} = \begin{bmatrix} 2 \\ 1 \\ 2 \end{bmatrix} \left(C_1 e^{\sqrt{6}t} + C_2 e^{-\sqrt{6}t} \right) + \begin{bmatrix} 1 \\ 2 \\ -2 \end{bmatrix} \left(C_3 e^{\sqrt{3}t} + C_4 e^{-\sqrt{3}t} \right)$$
$$+ \begin{bmatrix} -2 \\ 2 \\ 1 \end{bmatrix} (C_5 + C_6 t).$$

You may like to verify that $[-2 \quad 2 \quad 1]^T$ and $[-2 \quad 2 \quad 1]^T t$ are both solutions of the system.

Exercise 14

Find the general solution of the system of differential equations

$$\begin{cases} \ddot{x} = 2x + y - z, \\ \ddot{y} = -3y + 2z, \\ \ddot{z} = 4z. \end{cases}$$

(*Hint*: The eigenvectors of $\begin{bmatrix} 2 & 1 & -1 \\ 0 & -3 & 2 \\ 0 & 0 & 4 \end{bmatrix}$ are $\begin{bmatrix} 1 \\ 0 \\ 0 \end{bmatrix}$, $\begin{bmatrix} 1 \\ -5 \\ 0 \end{bmatrix}$ and $\begin{bmatrix} -5 \\ 4 \\ 14 \end{bmatrix}$, with corresponding eigenvalues 2, -3 and 4.)

In the next example and exercise, we first find the general solution of a system of second-order differential equations, then find a particular solution for given initial conditions. This will be relevant for Section 3 on normal modes.

Example 11

(a) Find the general solution of the system of differential equations

$$\begin{cases} \ddot{x} = -3x + y, \\ \ddot{y} = x - 3y. \end{cases}$$

(*Hint*: Eigenvectors of $\begin{bmatrix} -3 & 1 \\ 1 & -3 \end{bmatrix}$ can be shown to be

$$\mathbf{v}_1 = \begin{bmatrix} 1 & 1 \end{bmatrix}^T \text{ with eigenvalue } \lambda_2 = -2,$$
$$\mathbf{v}_2 = \begin{bmatrix} 1 & -1 \end{bmatrix}^T \text{ with eigenvalue } \lambda_1 = -4.)$$

(b) Find the particular solution that satisfies the initial conditions
$\mathbf{x}(0) = \mathbf{v}_1$, $\dot{\mathbf{x}}(0) = \mathbf{0}$, where $\mathbf{v}_1$ is the eigenvector given in the hint.

Solution

(a) Using the hint, we see that there are two negative eigenvalues. The first eigenvalue gives the term

$$\mathbf{x}_1 = C_1 \begin{bmatrix} 1 \\ 1 \end{bmatrix} \cos(\sqrt{2}t) + C_2 \begin{bmatrix} 1 \\ 1 \end{bmatrix} \sin(\sqrt{2}t).$$

The second eigenvalue gives the term

$$\mathbf{x}_2 = C_3 \begin{bmatrix} 1 \\ -1 \end{bmatrix} \cos(2t) + C_4 \begin{bmatrix} 1 \\ -1 \end{bmatrix} \sin(2t).$$

Adding the solutions $(\mathbf{x}_1 + \mathbf{x}_2)$, we get the general solution:

$$\mathbf{x}(t) = \begin{bmatrix} 1 \\ 1 \end{bmatrix} \left(C_1 \cos(\sqrt{2}t) + C_2 \sin(\sqrt{2}t) \right)$$
$$+ \begin{bmatrix} 1 \\ -1 \end{bmatrix} \left(C_3 \cos(2t) + C_4 \sin(2t) \right).$$

(b) Setting $t = 0$ in the general solution gives

$$\mathbf{x}(0) = C_1 \begin{bmatrix} 1 \\ 1 \end{bmatrix} + C_3 \begin{bmatrix} 1 \\ -1 \end{bmatrix} = \begin{bmatrix} C_1 + C_3 \\ C_1 - C_3 \end{bmatrix}.$$

Using the initial condition $\mathbf{x}(0) = \mathbf{v}_1$ then gives

$$\begin{bmatrix} 1 \\ 1 \end{bmatrix} = \begin{bmatrix} C_1 + C_3 \\ C_1 - C_3 \end{bmatrix}.$$

Hence $C_1 + C_3 = 1$ and $C_1 - C_3 = 1$, which have solution $C_3 = 0$, $C_1 = 1$.

Now, differentiating the general solution with respect to t, we get

$$\dot{\mathbf{x}}(t) = \sqrt{2} \begin{bmatrix} 1 \\ 1 \end{bmatrix} \left(-C_1 \sin(\sqrt{2}t) + C_2 \cos(\sqrt{2}t) \right)$$
$$+ 2 \begin{bmatrix} 1 \\ -1 \end{bmatrix} \left(-C_3 \sin(2t) + C_4 \cos(2t) \right),$$

and then setting $t = 0$ and using the initial condition $\dot{\mathbf{x}}(0) = \mathbf{0}$ gives

$$\dot{\mathbf{x}}(0) = \mathbf{0} = \sqrt{2}C_2 \begin{bmatrix} 1 \\ 1 \end{bmatrix} + 2C_4 \begin{bmatrix} 1 \\ -1 \end{bmatrix}.$$

This gives $\sqrt{2}C_2 + 2C_4 = 0$ and $\sqrt{2}C_2 - 2C_4 = 0$, which have solution $C_2 = C_4 = 0$.

So we have $C_2 = C_3 = C_4 = 0$ and $C_1 = 1$. Substituting into the general solution gives

$$\mathbf{x}(t) = \begin{bmatrix} 1 \\ 1 \end{bmatrix} \cos(\sqrt{2}t).$$

Clearly this satisfies the initial conditions.

Exercise 15

For the system in Example 11, find the particular solution that satisfies the initial conditions $\mathbf{x}(0) = \mathbf{v}_2$, $\dot{\mathbf{x}}(0) = \mathbf{0}$, where $\mathbf{v}_2$ is the eigenvector given in the hint.

The particular solutions found in Example 11(b) and Exercise 15 are called *normal mode* solutions and are the topic of the next section.

3   Normal modes

In Subsection 2.1 we described a compound harmonic oscillator consisting of two masses and two springs (see Figure 5). We mentioned that the equations of motion for this system have special solutions, called normal modes, in which the two masses oscillate at the same frequency. Here we show (in Subsection 3.1) how these normal mode solutions are obtained in a simple system, and how they are combined to describe the general solution of the equations of motion.

In Subsection 3.2 we consider an important scientific application of these ideas, by applying normal modes to describe the oscillations of certain types of simple molecule. These oscillations help scientists to explain how the Earth's atmosphere traps so much of the heat from the Sun, due to the *greenhouse effect*.

3.1   Motion of a simple two-mass system

An oscillating system and its equations of motion

We begin by describing the equations of motion for a rather special oscillating system.

Consider a system of two particles with equal masses m moving without friction on a rail, connected to three springs as illustrated in Figure 8. The two outer springs have spring stiffness K and are connected to rigid supports at either end. The middle spring has stiffness k. The displacements of the masses to the right of their equilibrium positions are x_1 and x_2 (for the left and right masses, respectively).

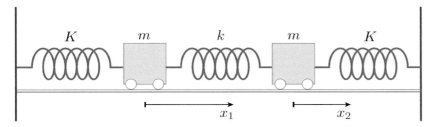

Figure 8 Two masses slide without friction on a rail; the force on each mass is provided by two springs

The equations of motion for this system are derived from Newton's second law and can be shown to be

$$m \begin{bmatrix} \ddot{x}_1 \\ \ddot{x}_2 \end{bmatrix} = \begin{bmatrix} -(k + K) & k \\ k & -(k + K) \end{bmatrix} \begin{bmatrix} x_1 \\ x_2 \end{bmatrix}. \tag{38}$$

We do not expect you to be able to derive such equations – they will be given to you if needed in assessment questions. However, the following is an argument that makes them plausible. (Don't worry if you can't follow this argument; it is not important for what follows).

From Newton's second law and equation (38), the force on the left-hand mass is seen to be

$$F_1 = -(k + K)x_1 + kx_2.$$

This makes sense because if we displace the left-hand mass to the right by a distance x_1 and leave the right-hand mass fixed so $x_2 = 0$, then $F_1 = -(k + K)x_1$, so the right-hand mass is pushed in the opposite direction by both springs attached to it. Further, if we hold the left-hand mass fixed ($x_1 = 0$) and displace the right-hand mass to the right by x_2, then $F_1 = kx_2$, so the left-hand mass is pulled to the right by the middle spring.

A similar line of reasoning can be used to show that it is plausible that the force on the right-hand mass is $F_2 = kx_1 - (k + K)x_2$.

Forces and displacements are normally written as vectors. But as the motion is in one direction here, we simply consider the components of the forces and displacements in that direction.

We now move on to solving these equations of motion.

Solving the equations of motion

Equation (38) is a system of equations of the form $\ddot{\mathbf{x}} = \mathbf{A}\mathbf{x}$, where the matrix of coefficients is

$$\mathbf{A} = \frac{1}{m} \begin{bmatrix} -(k + K) & k \\ k & -(k + K) \end{bmatrix}.$$

From Section 2 we know that solutions are constructed using the eigenvalues and eigenvectors of $\mathbf{A}$.

You studied how to calculate eigenvectors and eigenvalues in Unit 5. The method is straightforward but a little tedious, so we will simply tell you what they are, and let you verify for yourself that they satisfy $\mathbf{A}\mathbf{v} = \lambda\mathbf{v}$.

The eigenvectors are

$$\mathbf{v}_1 = \begin{bmatrix} 1 \\ 1 \end{bmatrix}, \quad \mathbf{v}_2 = \begin{bmatrix} 1 \\ -1 \end{bmatrix}, \tag{39}$$

and the corresponding eigenvalues are

$$\lambda_1 = -\frac{K}{m}, \quad \lambda_2 = -\frac{K+2k}{m}. \tag{40}$$

Note that the components of both eigenvectors $\mathbf{v} = \begin{bmatrix} v_1 & v_2 \end{bmatrix}$ satisfy $|v_1| = |v_2|$. This is because the system in Figure 8 has a reflection symmetry about its midpoint, i.e. the symmetry of the system is linked to the solution to the eigenvalue problem.

We note that because K, k and m are all positive, both of the eigenvalues are negative. Hence from Procedure 4, the solutions of $\ddot{\mathbf{x}} = \mathbf{A}\mathbf{x}$ are of the form

$$\mathbf{x}(t) = \cos(\omega_i t)\,\mathbf{v}_i, \quad \mathbf{x}(t) = \sin(\omega_i t)\,\mathbf{v}_i,$$

where

$$\omega_i = \sqrt{-\lambda_i}. \tag{41}$$

The general solution is a linear combination of all of these solutions. We have four solutions, two for each eigenvalue:

$$\begin{aligned} \mathbf{x}(t) = {}& \big(C_1 \sin(\omega_1 t) + D_1 \cos(\omega_1 t)\big)\mathbf{v}_1 \\ & + \big(C_2 \sin(\omega_2 t) + D_2 \cos(\omega_2 t)\big)\mathbf{v}_2, \end{aligned} \tag{42}$$

where C_1, D_1, C_2 and D_2 are arbitrary real constants.

Normal modes of vibration

We note that the general solution, equation (42), can be written as the sum of two terms

$$\mathbf{x}(t) = \mathbf{x}_{\omega_1}(t) + \mathbf{x}_{\omega_2}(t),$$

where

$$\begin{aligned} \mathbf{x}_{\omega_1}(t) &= \big(C_1 \sin(\omega_1 t) + D_1 \cos(\omega_1 t)\big)\mathbf{v}_1, \\ \mathbf{x}_{\omega_2}(t) &= \big(C_2 \sin(\omega_2 t) + D_2 \cos(\omega_2 t)\big)\mathbf{v}_2. \end{aligned}$$

$\mathbf{x}_{\omega_1}(t)$ is the part of the solution that oscillates with angular frequency ω_1, and $\mathbf{x}_{\omega_2}(t)$ is the part of the solution that oscillates with angular frequency ω_2. These are called the **normal modes** of oscillation of the system.

If we were to set $C_2 = D_2 = 0$ in the general solution, then $\mathbf{x}(t) = \mathbf{x}_{\omega_1}(t)$, and we would have a solution where both of the masses oscillated with the same angular frequency ω_1. Likewise, if we set $C_1 = D_1 = 0$, then both masses would oscillate with angular frequency ω_2. In fact, this defines what we mean by a normal mode for a system with any number of dependent variables.

Normal mode

A *normal mode of oscillation* is one in which all of the coordinates of the system oscillate sinusoidally with the same angular frequency.

Suppose that we were to choose initial conditions so that $\mathbf{x}(t) = \mathbf{x}_{\omega_1}(t)$. Then since $\mathbf{v}_1 = [1 \quad 1]^T$, we have

$$\begin{bmatrix} x_1(t) \\ x_2(t) \end{bmatrix} = \mathbf{x}_{\omega_1}(t) = \big(C_1 \sin(\omega_1 t) + D_1 \cos(\omega_1 t)\big) \begin{bmatrix} 1 \\ 1 \end{bmatrix},$$

hence the displacement of the masses would obey the equations

$$x_1(t) = x_2(t) = \big(C_1 \sin(\omega_1 t) + D_1 \cos(\omega_1 t)\big) \quad \text{for } \mathbf{x}(t) = \mathbf{x}_{\omega_1}(t). \qquad (43)$$

There are two coefficients, C_1 and D_1, that are determined by the initial conditions. We solved a system just like this, for the special case of $m = 1$, $k = 1$, $K = 2$, in Example 11. In part (b) we found that the initial conditions $\mathbf{x}(0) = \mathbf{v}_1$ and $\dot{\mathbf{x}}(0) = \mathbf{0}$ lead to the normal mode solution $\mathbf{x}(t) = \cos(\omega_1 t)\,\mathbf{v}_1$. In fact, these initial conditions give this normal mode solution for any values of m, k and K.

In fact, C_1 and D_1 determine the amplitude and phase of the oscillation.

Likewise, if we chose initial conditions so that $\mathbf{x}(t) = \mathbf{x}_{\omega_2}(t)$, then since $\mathbf{v}_2 = [1 \quad -1]^T$, the displacements of the masses would obey the equations

$$x_1(t) = -x_2(t) = \big(C_2 \sin(\omega_2 t) + D_2 \cos(\omega_2 t)\big) \quad \text{for } \mathbf{x}(t) = \mathbf{x}_{\omega_2}(t). \qquad (44)$$

Again, the two coefficients, C_2 and D_2 are determined by the initial conditions. For example, the initial conditions $\mathbf{x}(0) = \mathbf{v}_2$ and $\dot{\mathbf{x}}(0) = \mathbf{0}$ lead to the normal mode solution $\mathbf{x}(t) = \cos(\omega_2 t)\,\mathbf{v}_2$: see Exercise 15 for the special case of $m = 1$, $k = 1$, $K = 2$.

The normal mode with frequency ω_1 (equations (43)) is called the **symmetric** or **in-phase mode** of oscillation, because the masses always move in the same direction together. In this case $x_1(t) = x_2(t)$, hence the displacements of the masses are always equal. The normal mode with frequency ω_2 (equations (44)) is called the **antisymmetric** or **out-of-phase mode**, because the masses are always moving in opposite directions. In this case $x_1(t) = -x_2(t)$, hence the displacements are always of equal magnitude but opposite sign. The motion of the masses in the two normal modes is illustrated in Figure 9.

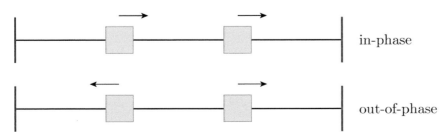

in-phase

out-of-phase

Figure 9   Normal modes for the symmetric two-mass system

From equations (40) and (41), the angular frequencies of the normal modes are given by

$$\omega_1 = \sqrt{\frac{K}{m}} \;\; \text{(in-phase)} \quad \text{and} \quad \omega_2 = \sqrt{\frac{K + 2k}{m}} \;\; \text{(out-of-phase)}. \qquad (45)$$

Note that for the in-phase normal mode solution we have $x_1(t) = x_2(t)$, hence $x_1(t) - x_2(t) = 0$, so the length of the middle spring never changes. That is why the frequency of the in-phase normal mode, ω_2, is the same as that for a simple harmonic oscillator with a spring stiffness equal to K. Also note that since K, k and m are all positive, $\omega_2 > \omega_1$, so the out-of-phase mode oscillates with a higher frequency than the in-phase mode. This is because each mass is being pulled by two springs instead of one as in the in-phase case.

The motion of each normal mode is a simple sinusoidal oscillation with a single angular frequency. Only special initial conditions like the ones given in Example 11 and Exercise 15 give rise to such normal mode motions. For arbitrary initial conditions (e.g. $\mathbf{x}(0) = [1 \quad 2]^T$, $\dot{\mathbf{x}}(0) = [0 \quad 1]^T$) the solution is a combination of sinusoidal oscillations with two different frequencies. In other words it is a linear combination of normal mode solutions, where the displacements of the two masses move in a seemingly complicated manner and are not proportional to each other.

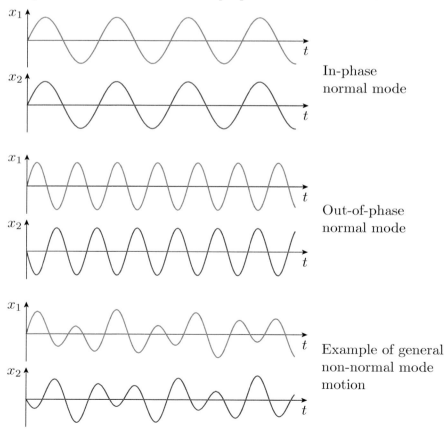

In-phase normal mode

Out-of-phase normal mode

Example of general non-normal mode motion

Figure 10   General non-normal mode motions are a combination of oscillations at the frequencies of the normal modes

Typical motions for these cases are illustrated in Figure 10. Note that these normal modes are rather special, since the in-phase mode has $x_1(t) = x_2(t)$ and the out-of-phase mode has $x_1(t) = -x_2(t)$. This special motion arises because of the reflection symmetry of the system – the masses and spring constants on either side are equal. For $m_1 \neq m_2$ or different springs on either side, there are still two normal modes, where both masses oscillate with the same frequency and $x_1(t) = \alpha \, x_2(t)$, for some number α. The in-phase mode is characterised by α being positive, and the out-of-phase mode is characterised by α being negative. The angular frequency of the out-of-phase normal mode is always greater than that of the in-phase normal mode.

Example 12

A system of two masses has its motion given by the system

$$\begin{bmatrix} \ddot{x}_1 \\ \ddot{x}_2 \end{bmatrix} = \begin{bmatrix} -2 & 2 \\ \frac{5}{2} & -6 \end{bmatrix} \begin{bmatrix} x_1 \\ x_2 \end{bmatrix}.$$

Note that this does not correspond to a *symmetric* two-mass system connected by springs.

(a) Write down the normal mode solutions and identify them as in-phase or out-of-phase.

(*Hint*: $\mathbf{A} = \begin{bmatrix} -2 & 2 \\ \frac{5}{2} & -6 \end{bmatrix}$ has eigenvectors $\mathbf{v}_1 = [2 \quad 1]^T$ and $\mathbf{v}_2 = [-\frac{2}{5} \quad 1]^T$, with corresponding eigenvalues $\lambda_1 = -1$ and $\lambda_2 = -7$.)

(b) Which motion will initial conditions $\mathbf{x}(0) = \mathbf{v}_1$, $\dot{\mathbf{x}}(0) = \mathbf{0}$ give rise to?

Solution

(a) The matrix of coefficients has negative eigenvalues. The first eigenvalue gives the term

$$\mathbf{x}_1 = \begin{bmatrix} 2 \\ 1 \end{bmatrix} \left(C_1 \cos(t) + C_2 \sin(t) \right),$$

where C_1 and C_2 are arbitrary real constants. This is the in-phase normal mode solution, because the components of $\mathbf{v}_1$ have the same sign. The second eigenvalue gives the term

$$\mathbf{x}_2 = \begin{bmatrix} -\frac{2}{5} \\ 1 \end{bmatrix} \left(C_3 \cos(\sqrt{7}t) + C_4 \sin(\sqrt{7}t) \right),$$

where C_3 and C_4 are arbitrary real constants. This is the out-of-phase normal mode solution, because the components of $\mathbf{v}_2$ have opposite signs.

We note that the angular frequency of the out-of-phase normal mode ($\omega_{\text{out}} = \sqrt{7}$) is greater than the in-phase normal mode ($\omega_{\text{in}} = 1$), as expected.

(b) Following the same reasoning as in Example 11 and Exercise 15, these initial conditions give rise to the normal mode solution

$$\mathbf{x}(t) = \mathbf{v}_1 \cos(t) = \begin{bmatrix} 2 \\ 1 \end{bmatrix} \cos(t).$$

It is obvious that this solution satisfies the given initial conditions.

Exercise 16

A system of two masses connected by springs has two normal mode angular frequencies: $\omega_1 = 2$ and $\omega_2 = 4$. Which is the in-phase frequency?

Exercise 17

A system of two masses connected by springs has a characteristic matrix with eigenvectors $\mathbf{v}_1 = [1 \quad -2]^T$ and $\mathbf{v}_2 = [1 \quad 4]^T$. Which gives rise to the in-phase mode?

Exercise 18

Two masses connected by springs have their motion given by the system
$$\begin{bmatrix} \ddot{x}_1 \\ \ddot{x}_2 \end{bmatrix} = \begin{bmatrix} -4 & 1 \\ 1 & -4 \end{bmatrix} \begin{bmatrix} x_1 \\ x_2 \end{bmatrix}.$$

(a) Write down the normal mode solutions and identify them as in-phase or out-of-phase.

(*Hint:* $\mathbf{A} = \begin{bmatrix} -4 & 1 \\ 1 & -4 \end{bmatrix}$ has eigenvectors $\mathbf{v}_1 = [1 \quad 1]^T$ and $\mathbf{v}_2 = [1 \quad -1]^T$, with corresponding eigenvalues $\lambda_1 = -3$ and $\lambda_2 = -5$.)

(b) Which motion will the initial conditions $\mathbf{x}(0) = \mathbf{v}_1$, $\dot{\mathbf{x}}(0) = \mathbf{0}$ give rise to?

Normal modes in engineering

You may have seen footage of a wine glass breaking when someone sings or plays a loud (usually amplified) note at exactly the right pitch. This occurs because the frequency of the note matches a 'natural frequency' of the wine glass, causing it to vibrate. Other objects – from molecules to buildings – have 'natural frequencies' at which they prefer to vibrate. These 'natural frequencies' are in fact the normal mode frequencies of the objects.

The vibration of many objects can be modelled by systems of differential equations that are generalisations of the type that we have considered here. The general solution is a linear combination of normal mode solutions, each of which is a sinusoidal motion with a single frequency – the normal mode frequency.

It is very important for engineers to be able to predict the normal modes of vibration of the objects that they build, because the normal mode frequencies of a structure are those frequencies at which the structure will tend to resonate (i.e. vibrate with large amplitude).

In structural engineering, it is imperative that a building's normal mode frequencies do not match the frequencies of expected earthquakes, otherwise an earthquake may make the structure vibrate, causing damage. The periodic variation of wind gusts can be another cause of resonant vibration in structures like bridges or very tall buildings, and measures have to be taken to avoid the vibrations becoming too large. For example, the 509 m tall Taipei 101 building in Taiwan (the tallest in the world until 2010), shown in Figure 11, has a 660 tonne steel pendulum suspended from its 92nd floor to dampen resonant vibrations caused by wind gusts.

Figure 11   The Taipei 101 building

3.2   An application: vibrations of simple molecules

This optional subsection discusses one of the most important physical applications of normal modes. **You will not be assessed on any of the material in this subsection.**

Simple molecules consist of a small number of atoms held together by 'chemical bonds'. Figure 12 illustrates some simple molecules. You can think of the atoms as behaving like point masses. The chemical bonds are not entirely rigid: they can behave like springs, so that the molecule can oscillate. We end this unit by considering a model for the frequency of oscillation of some simple molecules.

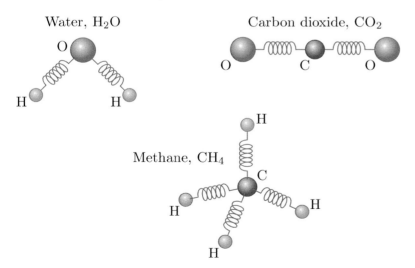

Figure 12   Some simple molecules, modelled as masses connected by springs

Molecular vibrations and the greenhouse effect

Oscillations of molecules occur at very high frequencies, typically of the order of 10^{13} oscillations per second. Such rapid oscillations cannot be recorded by any mechanical instrument, but they do correspond to the frequency at which electric fields oscillate in infrared light (a type of light that is not visible to the human eye). In fact, molecules absorb infrared light by a resonance effect.

This absorption in the infrared is important for determining the climate of the Earth. Light from the Sun passes through the atmosphere and warms the surface of the Earth. The warm surface of the Earth radiates infrared light, which cannot escape into space because it is absorbed by molecules in the atmosphere (especially water and carbon dioxide). If it were not for this absorption, the Earth would be considerably colder. This is called the greenhouse effect. It is topical because of concerns that too much carbon dioxide in the atmosphere may cause a dangerous increase in the greenhouse effect.

The frequencies of oscillation of molecules depend on their geometry and on the masses of the atoms and the 'spring stiffnesses' of the chemical bonds. For most molecules, the normal modes of vibration form a complicated three-dimensional motion. In this subsection we consider only the vibrations of a simple type of molecule, called a *linear triatomic molecule*. Carbon dioxide is an example of such a molecule. Its small oscillations can be of two types. There are bending vibrations, and there are motions that involve stretching of the chemical bonds while the atoms move along the same line (see Figure 13). In this subsection we confine our attention to the stretching motion, and we do not consider the bending modes of vibration.

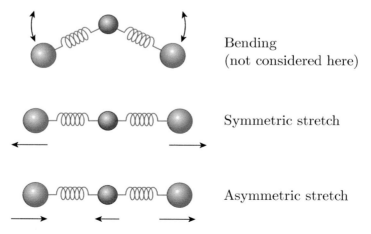

Figure 13   Modes of vibration of carbon dioxide

Our model for the carbon dioxide molecule consists of three atoms in a row, with masses m, M and m. Each of the outer masses is connected to the central mass by a 'spring' with stiffness constant k. The displacements of the three masses from their equilibrium positions are x_1, x_2 and x_3, respectively, as shown in Figure 14. The forces due to the 'springs' can be shown to be $F_1 = k(x_2 - x_1)$, $F_2 = k(x_1 - x_2) + k(x_3 - x_2)$ and $F_3 = k(x_2 - x_3)$, so that the equations of motion are

$$m\ddot{x}_1 = k(x_2 - x_1),$$
$$M\ddot{x}_2 = k(x_1 - 2x_2 + x_3),$$
$$m\ddot{x}_3 = k(x_2 - x_3).$$

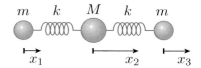

Figure 14   Displacement of atoms from their equilibrium positions

As in earlier models, these equations are actually the components of the vector equations for forces and displacements, in the direction of motion.

This system is equivalent to the matrix equation

$$\ddot{\mathbf{x}} = \mathbf{A}\mathbf{x}, \quad \text{where } \mathbf{A} = \begin{bmatrix} -\frac{k}{m} & \frac{k}{m} & 0 \\ \frac{k}{M} & -\frac{2k}{M} & \frac{k}{M} \\ 0 & \frac{k}{m} & -\frac{k}{m} \end{bmatrix}.$$

Once again the general solution and normal modes are determined from the eigenvalues and eigenvectors of the coefficient matrix $\mathbf{A}$. It is not difficult to show that the characteristic equation is

$$\det(\mathbf{A} - \lambda\mathbf{I}) = \lambda\left(\lambda + \frac{k}{m}\right)\left(\lambda + \frac{k}{m} + 2\frac{k}{M}\right) = 0.$$

From this we deduce that the eigenvalues are

$$\lambda_1 = -\frac{k}{m}, \quad \lambda_2 = -\frac{k}{m}\left(1 + \frac{2m}{M}\right), \quad \lambda_3 = 0.$$

λ_1 and λ_2 are both negative, so they correspond to oscillations or vibrations of the molecule with frequencies

$$\omega_1 = \sqrt{\frac{k}{m}} \quad \text{and} \quad \omega_2 = \sqrt{\frac{k}{m}}\sqrt{\frac{M + 2m}{M}}.$$

You are no doubt wondering what sort of motion the zero eigenvalue λ_3 corresponds to. It turns out that its eigenvector is $\mathbf{v}_3 = [1 \quad 1 \quad 1]^T$. This has a simple physical interpretation: it corresponds to a motion where all of the atoms move together in the same direction by the same amount, so the motion does not stretch either of the springs.

We now return to consider the modes of vibration. The vibration at frequency ω_1 corresponds to the eigenvector $[1 \quad 0 \quad -1]^T$, for which the motion is a *symmetric stretch*. The frequency ω_2 has eigenvector $[1 \quad -2m/M \quad 1]^T$, and corresponds to an *asymmetric stretch* normal mode (see Figure 13).

Consider how this works for carbon dioxide. The masses of atoms are measured in units of the mass of a hydrogen atom, m_H. Carbon dioxide (chemical symbol CO_2) is a symmetric linear triatomic molecule, with two oxygen atoms, each of mass $m = 16m_H$, and a carbon atom, of mass $M = 12m_H$.

The ratio of the two stretching vibrational frequencies is therefore expected to be

$$\frac{\omega_2}{\omega_1} = \sqrt{\frac{M + 2m}{M}} = \sqrt{\frac{44}{12}} \simeq 1.9.$$

To convert units of cm^{-1} to Hertz, multiply by the speed of light, $c \simeq 3 \times 10^{10}\, cm\, s^{-1}$.

The frequencies can be investigated by looking for resonances in the absorption of carbon dioxide as the frequency of a light source is varied. In a unit favoured by spectroscopists (cm^{-1}), the frequencies of vibration of carbon dioxide molecules are found to be 667, 1388 and 2349. The smallest of these is the frequency of bending vibrations, and the other two correspond to the two stretching vibrations. The ratios of the observed stretching vibration frequencies is $2349/1388 \simeq 1.7$. This is quite close to 1.9, indicating that the simple mass and spring model is a reasonable model for the vibrations of the CO_2 molecule.

For a better model we need to turn to quantum mechanics and solve the Schrödinger equation for carbon dioxide.

Learning outcomes

After studying this unit, you should be able to do the following.

- Understand and use the terminology associated with systems of linear constant-coefficient differential equations.

- Obtain the general solution of a homogeneous system of two or three first-order differential equations, by applying knowledge of the eigenvalues and eigenvectors of the coefficient matrix.

- Obtain a particular integral of an inhomogeneous system of two first-order differential equations in certain simple cases, by using a trial solution.

- Obtain the general solution of an inhomogeneous system of two or three first-order differential equations, by combining its complementary function and a particular integral.

- Apply given initial conditions to obtain the solution of an initial-value problem that features a system of two or three first-order differential equations.

- Obtain the general solution of a homogeneous system of two or three second-order equations, by applying knowledge of the eigenvalues and eigenvectors of the coefficient matrix.

- Obtain a particular solution of a pair of second-order homogeneous equations, by applying initial conditions.

- Identify normal mode solutions for systems of two masses.

Solutions to exercises

Solution to Exercise 1

(a) $\begin{bmatrix} \dot{x} \\ \dot{y} \end{bmatrix} = \begin{bmatrix} 2 & 1 \\ 1 & 0 \end{bmatrix} \begin{bmatrix} x \\ y \end{bmatrix} + \begin{bmatrix} 1 \\ -2 \end{bmatrix}$; inhomogeneous.

(b) $\begin{bmatrix} \dot{x} \\ \dot{y} \end{bmatrix} = \begin{bmatrix} 0 & 1 \\ 0 & 0 \end{bmatrix} \begin{bmatrix} x \\ y \end{bmatrix} + \begin{bmatrix} 0 \\ t \end{bmatrix}$; inhomogeneous.

(c) $\begin{bmatrix} \dot{x} \\ \dot{y} \\ \dot{z} \end{bmatrix} = \begin{bmatrix} 5 & 0 & 0 \\ 1 & 2 & 1 \\ 1 & 1 & 2 \end{bmatrix} \begin{bmatrix} x \\ y \\ z \end{bmatrix}$; homogeneous.

Solution to Exercise 2

(a) The matrix of coefficients is
$$\mathbf{A} = \begin{bmatrix} 3 & 2 \\ 1 & 4 \end{bmatrix}.$$

Using the given eigenvalues and eigenvectors, we can construct two independent solutions $\mathbf{v}e^{\lambda t}$:
$$\mathbf{x}_1 = \begin{bmatrix} 1 \\ 1 \end{bmatrix} e^{5t} \quad \text{and} \quad \mathbf{x}_2 = \begin{bmatrix} -2 \\ 1 \end{bmatrix} e^{2t}.$$

(b) The general solution is a general linear combination of the two independent solutions:
$$\begin{bmatrix} x \\ y \end{bmatrix} = \alpha \begin{bmatrix} 1 \\ 1 \end{bmatrix} e^{5t} + \beta \begin{bmatrix} -2 \\ 1 \end{bmatrix} e^{2t},$$

where α and β are arbitrary constants.

Solution to Exercise 3

The matrix of coefficients is
$$\mathbf{A} = \begin{bmatrix} 5 & 2 \\ 2 & 5 \end{bmatrix}.$$

We are given that the eigenvectors of $\mathbf{A}$ are $\begin{bmatrix} 1 & 1 \end{bmatrix}^T$ with corresponding eigenvalue $\lambda = 7$, and $\begin{bmatrix} 1 & -1 \end{bmatrix}^T$ with corresponding eigenvalue $\lambda = 3$. The general solution is therefore
$$\begin{bmatrix} x \\ y \end{bmatrix} = \alpha \begin{bmatrix} 1 \\ 1 \end{bmatrix} e^{7t} + \beta \begin{bmatrix} 1 \\ -1 \end{bmatrix} e^{3t},$$

where α and β are arbitrary constants.

Solution to Exercise 4

(a) In Exercise 3 we showed that the general solution of these differential equations is

$$\begin{bmatrix} x \\ y \end{bmatrix} = \alpha \begin{bmatrix} 1 \\ 1 \end{bmatrix} e^{7t} + \beta \begin{bmatrix} 1 \\ -1 \end{bmatrix} e^{3t}.$$

Since $x = 4$ and $y = 0$ when $t = 0$, we have

$$\begin{cases} 4 = \alpha + \beta, \\ 0 = \alpha - \beta. \end{cases}$$

Thus $\alpha = 2$ and $\beta = 2$, so

$$\begin{aligned} \begin{bmatrix} x \\ y \end{bmatrix} &= 2 \begin{bmatrix} 1 \\ 1 \end{bmatrix} e^{7t} + 2 \begin{bmatrix} 1 \\ -1 \end{bmatrix} e^{3t} \\ &= \begin{bmatrix} 2 \\ 2 \end{bmatrix} e^{7t} + \begin{bmatrix} 2 \\ -2 \end{bmatrix} e^{3t}. \end{aligned}$$

(b) For large t, e^{7t} is much greater than e^{3t}, hence $x \simeq 2e^{7t}$ and $y \simeq 2e^{7t}$. Hence the solution approaches the line $x = y$ for large t.

Solution to Exercise 5

The matrix of coefficients is

$$\mathbf{A} = \begin{bmatrix} 5 & 0 & 0 \\ 1 & 2 & 1 \\ 1 & 1 & 2 \end{bmatrix}.$$

We are given that the eigenvectors of $\mathbf{A}$ are $\begin{bmatrix} 2 & 1 & 1 \end{bmatrix}^T$, $\begin{bmatrix} 0 & 1 & 1 \end{bmatrix}^T$ and $\begin{bmatrix} 0 & 1 & -1 \end{bmatrix}^T$, corresponding to the eigenvalues 5, 3 and 1.

The general solution is therefore

$$\begin{bmatrix} x \\ y \\ z \end{bmatrix} = \alpha \begin{bmatrix} 2 \\ 1 \\ 1 \end{bmatrix} e^{5t} + \beta \begin{bmatrix} 0 \\ 1 \\ 1 \end{bmatrix} e^{3t} + \gamma \begin{bmatrix} 0 \\ 1 \\ -1 \end{bmatrix} e^{t}.$$

Since $x = 4$, $y = 6$ and $z = 0$ when $t = 0$, we have

$$\begin{cases} 4 = 2\alpha, \\ 6 = \alpha + \beta + \gamma, \\ 0 = \alpha + \beta - \gamma. \end{cases}$$

From this we can deduce that $\alpha = 2$, $\beta = 1$ and $\gamma = 3$, so

$$\begin{aligned} \begin{bmatrix} x \\ y \\ z \end{bmatrix} &= 2 \begin{bmatrix} 2 \\ 1 \\ 1 \end{bmatrix} e^{5t} + \begin{bmatrix} 0 \\ 1 \\ 1 \end{bmatrix} e^{3t} + 3 \begin{bmatrix} 0 \\ 1 \\ -1 \end{bmatrix} e^{t} \\ &= \begin{bmatrix} 4 \\ 2 \\ 2 \end{bmatrix} e^{5t} + \begin{bmatrix} 0 \\ 1 \\ 1 \end{bmatrix} e^{3t} + \begin{bmatrix} 0 \\ 3 \\ -3 \end{bmatrix} e^{t}. \end{aligned}$$

Solution to Exercise 6

(a) If $z = 4 + 3i$, then $\bar{z} = 4 - 3i$, which gives $\bar{\bar{z}} = 4 + 3i$.

Hence $\bar{\bar{z}} = z$.

(b) If $z = 4 + 3i$, then $\operatorname{Re} z = 4$. On the other hand, $\bar{z} = 4 - 3i$, which gives $\frac{1}{2}(z + \bar{z}) = \frac{1}{2}((4 + 3i) + (4 - 3i)) = 4$.

Hence $\operatorname{Re} z = \frac{1}{2}(z + \bar{z})$.

(c) If $z = 4 + 3i$, then $\operatorname{Im} z = 3$. On the other hand,
$\frac{1}{2i}(z - \bar{z}) = \frac{1}{2i}((4 + 3i) - (4 - 3i)) = \frac{6i}{2i} = 3$.

Hence $\operatorname{Im} z = \frac{1}{2i}(z - \bar{z})$.

Solution to Exercise 7

(a) The matrix of coefficients is
$$\mathbf{A} = \begin{bmatrix} -3 & -2 \\ 4 & 1 \end{bmatrix}.$$

Using the given eigenvalues and eigenvectors, we obtain the general solution
$$\begin{bmatrix} x \\ y \end{bmatrix} = C \begin{bmatrix} 1 \\ -1 - i \end{bmatrix} e^{(-1+2i)t} + D \begin{bmatrix} 1 \\ -1 + i \end{bmatrix} e^{(-1-2i)t}.$$

Now
$$\begin{bmatrix} 1 \\ -1 - i \end{bmatrix} e^{(-1+2i)t} = \begin{bmatrix} e^{-t}(\cos 2t + i \sin 2t) \\ (-1 - i)e^{-t}(\cos 2t + i \sin 2t) \end{bmatrix}$$
$$= \begin{bmatrix} e^{-t}\cos 2t + i e^{-t}\sin 2t \\ e^{-t}(\sin 2t - \cos 2t) - i e^{-t}(\sin 2t + \cos 2t) \end{bmatrix}.$$

So we have
$$\operatorname{Re}\left(\begin{bmatrix} 1 \\ -1 - i \end{bmatrix} e^{(-1+2i)t}\right) = \begin{bmatrix} \cos 2t \\ \sin 2t - \cos 2t \end{bmatrix} e^{-t},$$
$$\operatorname{Im}\left(\begin{bmatrix} 1 \\ -1 - i \end{bmatrix} e^{(-1+2i)t}\right) = \begin{bmatrix} \sin 2t \\ -\sin 2t - \cos 2t \end{bmatrix} e^{-t},$$

and the general real-valued solution can be written as
$$\begin{bmatrix} x \\ y \end{bmatrix} = \alpha \begin{bmatrix} \cos 2t \\ \sin 2t - \cos 2t \end{bmatrix} e^{-t} + \beta \begin{bmatrix} \sin 2t \\ -\sin 2t - \cos 2t \end{bmatrix} e^{-t}.$$

(b) Since $x = y = 1$ when $t = 0$, we have
$$1 = \alpha \quad \text{and} \quad 1 = -\alpha - \beta,$$

so $\alpha = 1$, $\beta = -2$, and the required particular solution is
$$\begin{bmatrix} x \\ y \end{bmatrix} = \begin{bmatrix} \cos 2t - 2 \sin 2t \\ 3 \sin 2t + \cos 2t \end{bmatrix} e^{-t}.$$

Solution to Exercise 8

(a) Using the given eigenvalues and eigenvectors in Procedure 2, we have

$$\mathbf{v}e^{\lambda t} = \begin{bmatrix} 1 \\ -i \\ i \end{bmatrix} e^{(1+i)t} = e^t \begin{bmatrix} 1 \\ -i \\ i \end{bmatrix} (\cos t + i \sin t)$$

$$= e^t \begin{bmatrix} \cos t + i \sin t \\ \sin t - i \cos t \\ -\sin t + i \cos t \end{bmatrix}$$

$$= e^t \underbrace{\begin{bmatrix} \cos t \\ \sin t \\ -\sin t \end{bmatrix}}_{\text{real part}} + i\, e^t \underbrace{\begin{bmatrix} \sin t \\ -\cos t \\ \cos t \end{bmatrix}}_{\text{imaginary part}}.$$

Thus the general real-valued solution is

$$\begin{bmatrix} x \\ y \\ z \end{bmatrix} = C_1 \begin{bmatrix} 0 \\ 1 \\ 0 \end{bmatrix} e^{2t} + C_2 e^t \begin{bmatrix} \cos t \\ \sin t \\ -\sin t \end{bmatrix} + C_3 e^t \begin{bmatrix} \sin t \\ -\cos t \\ \cos t \end{bmatrix},$$

where C_1, C_2 and C_3 are real constants.

(b) Putting $x = y = 1$ and $z = 2$ when $t = 0$, we have

$$\begin{bmatrix} 1 \\ 1 \\ 2 \end{bmatrix} = C_1 \begin{bmatrix} 0 \\ 1 \\ 0 \end{bmatrix} + C_2 \begin{bmatrix} 1 \\ 0 \\ 0 \end{bmatrix} + C_3 \begin{bmatrix} 0 \\ -1 \\ 1 \end{bmatrix},$$

so $C_2 = 1$, $C_3 = 2$ and $C_1 - C_3 = 1$, giving $C_1 = 3$. Thus the required solution is

$$\begin{bmatrix} x \\ y \\ z \end{bmatrix} = \begin{bmatrix} 0 \\ 3 \\ 0 \end{bmatrix} e^{2t} + \begin{bmatrix} \cos t + 2 \sin t \\ -2 \cos t + \sin t \\ 2 \cos t - \sin t \end{bmatrix} e^t.$$

Solution to Exercise 9

$$\begin{bmatrix} x \\ y \end{bmatrix} = \alpha \begin{bmatrix} 1 \\ 1 \end{bmatrix} e^{5t} + \beta \begin{bmatrix} -2 \\ 1 \end{bmatrix} e^{2t} + \begin{bmatrix} t + \frac{4}{5} \\ -2t - \frac{7}{10} \end{bmatrix}.$$

Solution to Exercise 10

From Example 1, the complementary function is

$$\begin{bmatrix} x_c \\ y_c \end{bmatrix} = \alpha \begin{bmatrix} 4 \\ 1 \end{bmatrix} e^{2t} + \beta \begin{bmatrix} 1 \\ -1 \end{bmatrix} e^{-3t}.$$

For a particular integral, we try

$$\begin{bmatrix} x \\ y \end{bmatrix} = \begin{bmatrix} at + b \\ ct + d \end{bmatrix},$$

where a, b, c, d are constants to be determined.

Substituting $x = at + b$, $y = ct + d$ into the differential equations gives

$$\begin{cases} a = (at + b) + 4(ct + d) - t + 2, \\ c = (at + b) - 2(ct + d) + 5t, \end{cases}$$

which become

$$\begin{cases} (a + 4c - 1)t + (b + 4d + 2 - a) = 0, \\ (a - 2c + 5)t + (b - 2d - c) = 0. \end{cases}$$

Equating the coefficients of t to zero gives

$$\begin{cases} a + 4c - 1 = 0, \\ a - 2c + 5 = 0, \end{cases}$$

which have the solution $a = -3$, $c = 1$.

Equating the constant terms to zero, and putting $a = -3$, $c = 1$, gives

$$\begin{cases} b + 4d + 5 = 0, \\ b - 2d - 1 = 0, \end{cases}$$

which have the solution $b = -1$, $d = -1$.

Thus the required particular integral is

$$\begin{bmatrix} x_{\mathrm{p}} \\ y_{\mathrm{p}} \end{bmatrix} = \begin{bmatrix} -3t - 1 \\ t - 1 \end{bmatrix},$$

and the general solution is

$$\begin{bmatrix} x \\ y \end{bmatrix} = \begin{bmatrix} x_{\mathrm{c}} \\ y_{\mathrm{c}} \end{bmatrix} + \begin{bmatrix} x_{\mathrm{p}} \\ y_{\mathrm{p}} \end{bmatrix}$$

$$= \alpha \begin{bmatrix} 4 \\ 1 \end{bmatrix} e^{2t} + \beta \begin{bmatrix} 1 \\ -1 \end{bmatrix} e^{-3t} + \begin{bmatrix} -3t - 1 \\ t - 1 \end{bmatrix}.$$

Solution to Exercise 11

The complementary function is

$$\begin{bmatrix} x_{\mathrm{c}} \\ y_{\mathrm{c}} \end{bmatrix} = \alpha \begin{bmatrix} 4 \\ 1 \end{bmatrix} e^{2t} + \beta \begin{bmatrix} 1 \\ -1 \end{bmatrix} e^{-3t}.$$

For a particular integral, we try

$$\begin{bmatrix} x \\ y \end{bmatrix} = \begin{bmatrix} a \\ b \end{bmatrix} e^{-t},$$

where a and b are constants to be determined.

Substituting $x = ae^{-t}$, $y = be^{-t}$ into the differential equations gives

$$\begin{cases} -ae^{-t} = ae^{-t} + 4be^{-t} + 4e^{-t}, \\ -be^{-t} = ae^{-t} - 2be^{-t} + 5e^{-t}, \end{cases}$$

which, on dividing by e^{-t} and rearranging, become

$$\begin{cases} 2a + 4b = -4, \\ a - b = -5. \end{cases}$$

These equations have the solution $a = -4$, $b = 1$.

Thus the required particular integral is

$$\begin{bmatrix} x_{\mathrm{p}} \\ y_{\mathrm{p}} \end{bmatrix} = \begin{bmatrix} -4 \\ 1 \end{bmatrix} e^{-t},$$

and the general solution is

$$\begin{bmatrix} x \\ y \end{bmatrix} = \begin{bmatrix} x_{\mathrm{c}} \\ y_{\mathrm{c}} \end{bmatrix} + \begin{bmatrix} x_{\mathrm{p}} \\ y_{\mathrm{p}} \end{bmatrix}$$

$$= \alpha \begin{bmatrix} 4 \\ 1 \end{bmatrix} e^{2t} + \beta \begin{bmatrix} 1 \\ -1 \end{bmatrix} e^{-3t} + \begin{bmatrix} -4 \\ 1 \end{bmatrix} e^{-t}.$$

Solution to Exercise 12

(a) The matrix of coefficients is

$$\mathbf{A} = \begin{bmatrix} 2 & 3 \\ 2 & 1 \end{bmatrix}.$$

First, we find its eigenvalues. The characteristic equation is

$$\det(\mathbf{A} - \lambda \mathbf{I}) = \begin{vmatrix} 2 - \lambda & 3 \\ 2 & 1 - \lambda \end{vmatrix} = 0.$$

Expanding this gives $(2 - \lambda)(1 - \lambda) - 6 = 0$, which simplifies to $\lambda^2 - 3\lambda - 4 = 0$. This factorises as $(\lambda - 4)(\lambda + 1) = 0$, so the eigenvalues are $\lambda = -1$ and $\lambda = 4$.

Now we find the eigenvectors.

- For $\lambda = -1$, let the eigenvector be $\mathbf{v} = [x \quad y]^T$. Then the eigenvector equations are

$$(\mathbf{A} - \lambda \mathbf{I})\mathbf{v} = (\mathbf{A} + \mathbf{I})\mathbf{v} = \begin{bmatrix} 3 & 3 \\ 2 & 2 \end{bmatrix} \begin{bmatrix} x \\ y \end{bmatrix} = \mathbf{0}.$$

These give the simultaneous equations

$$3x + 3y = 0 \quad \text{and} \quad 2x + 2y = 0,$$

which reduce to the single equation $y = -x$. So (setting $x = 1$), an eigenvector corresponding to $\lambda = -1$ is $[1 \quad -1]^T$.

- For $\lambda = 4$, the eigenvector equations are

$$(\mathbf{A} - \lambda \mathbf{I})\mathbf{v} = (\mathbf{A} - 4\mathbf{I})\mathbf{v} = \begin{bmatrix} -2 & 3 \\ 2 & -3 \end{bmatrix} \begin{bmatrix} x \\ y \end{bmatrix} = \mathbf{0},$$

which give

$$-2x + 3y = 0 \quad \text{and} \quad 2x - 3y = 0,$$

which reduce to the single equation $y = 2x/3$. So (setting $x = 3$) an eigenvector corresponding to $\lambda = 4$ is $[3 \quad 2]^T$.

(b) Using the calculated eigenvalues and eigenvectors, the complementary function is

$$\begin{bmatrix} x_c \\ y_c \end{bmatrix} = \alpha \begin{bmatrix} 1 \\ -1 \end{bmatrix} e^{-t} + \beta \begin{bmatrix} 3 \\ 2 \end{bmatrix} e^{4t}.$$

We try a particular integral

$$\begin{bmatrix} x \\ y \end{bmatrix} = \begin{bmatrix} a \\ b \end{bmatrix} e^{2t}.$$

Then

$$\begin{cases} 2ae^{2t} = 2ae^{2t} + 3be^{2t} + e^{2t}, \\ 2be^{2t} = 2ae^{2t} + be^{2t} + 4e^{2t}, \end{cases}$$

which give $3b + 1 = 0$ and $b - 2a = 4$, so $b = -\frac{1}{3}$ and $a = -\frac{13}{6}$. The general solution is therefore

$$\begin{bmatrix} x \\ y \end{bmatrix} = \alpha \begin{bmatrix} 1 \\ -1 \end{bmatrix} e^{-t} + \beta \begin{bmatrix} 3 \\ 2 \end{bmatrix} e^{4t} - \frac{1}{6} \begin{bmatrix} 13 \\ 2 \end{bmatrix} e^{2t}.$$

Putting $t = 0$, we obtain

$$\tfrac{5}{6} = \alpha + 3\beta - \tfrac{13}{6}, \qquad \tfrac{2}{3} = -\alpha + 2\beta - \tfrac{1}{3},$$

so $\alpha + 3\beta = 3$ and $-\alpha + 2\beta = 1$, which give $\alpha = \frac{3}{5}$ and $\beta = \frac{4}{5}$.

The required solution is therefore

$$\begin{bmatrix} x \\ y \end{bmatrix} = \tfrac{3}{5} \begin{bmatrix} 1 \\ -1 \end{bmatrix} e^{-t} + \tfrac{4}{5} \begin{bmatrix} 3 \\ 2 \end{bmatrix} e^{4t} - \tfrac{1}{6} \begin{bmatrix} 13 \\ 2 \end{bmatrix} e^{2t}.$$

(c) As t gets large, the e^{4t} term will become larger than any of the other terms. Hence

$$\begin{bmatrix} x \\ y \end{bmatrix} \simeq \tfrac{4}{5} \begin{bmatrix} 3 \\ 2 \end{bmatrix} e^{4t} \quad \text{for large } t.$$

So $x = \frac{12}{5} e^{4t}$ and $y = \frac{8}{5} e^{4t}$. Hence $x/y = \frac{12}{8} = \frac{3}{2}$, thus the solution will approach the line $x = 3y/2$ for large t.

Solution to Exercise 13

The matrix of coefficients is

$$\mathbf{A} = \begin{bmatrix} 5 & 2 \\ 2 & 5 \end{bmatrix},$$

and we are given that the eigenvectors are $[1 \quad 1]^T$ corresponding to the eigenvalue $\lambda = 7$, and $[1 \quad -1]^T$ corresponding to the eigenvalue $\lambda = 3$.

It follows that the general solution is

$$\begin{bmatrix} x \\ y \end{bmatrix} = \begin{bmatrix} 1 \\ 1 \end{bmatrix} \left(C_1 e^{\sqrt{7}t} + C_2 e^{-\sqrt{7}t} \right) + \begin{bmatrix} 1 \\ -1 \end{bmatrix} \left(C_3 e^{\sqrt{3}t} + C_4 e^{-\sqrt{3}t} \right).$$

Solution to Exercise 14

Using the given eigenvalues and eigenvectors, we obtain the general solution

$$\begin{bmatrix} x \\ y \\ z \end{bmatrix} = \begin{bmatrix} 1 \\ 0 \\ 0 \end{bmatrix} \left(C_1 e^{\sqrt{2}t} + C_2 e^{-\sqrt{2}t} \right) + \begin{bmatrix} 1 \\ -5 \\ 0 \end{bmatrix} \left(C_3 \cos(\sqrt{3}t) + C_4 \sin(\sqrt{3}t) \right)$$
$$+ \begin{bmatrix} -5 \\ 4 \\ 14 \end{bmatrix} \left(C_5 e^{2t} + C_6 e^{-2t} \right).$$

Solution to Exercise 15

In the solution to Example 11(b), we used a rather pedestrian approach to finding the particular solution. Let's do this a bit more smartly this time. First, write the general solution as

$$\mathbf{x}(t) = \mathbf{v}_1 \left(C_1 \cos(\sqrt{2}t) + C_2 \sin(\sqrt{2}t) \right) + \mathbf{v}_2 \left(C_3 \cos(2t) + C_4 \sin(2t) \right).$$

Setting $t = 0$ and using the initial condition $\mathbf{x}(0) = \mathbf{v}_2$ gives

$$\mathbf{x}(0) = \mathbf{v}_2 = C_1 \mathbf{v}_1 + C_3 \mathbf{v}_2.$$

Clearly this has solution $C_1 = 0$ and $C_3 = 1$.

Now, differentiating the general solution with respect to t gives

$$\dot{\mathbf{x}}(t) = \sqrt{2} \mathbf{v}_1 \left(-C_1 \sin(\sqrt{2}t) + C_2 \cos(\sqrt{2}t) \right)$$
$$+ 2\mathbf{v}_2 \left(-C_3 \sin(2t) + C_4 \cos(2t) \right),$$

and using the initial condition $\dot{\mathbf{x}}(0) = \mathbf{0}$ gives

$$\mathbf{0} = \sqrt{2} C_2 \mathbf{v}_1 + 2 C_4 \mathbf{v}_2.$$

This clearly has solution $C_2 = C_4 = 0$. Substituting these values in the general solution gives

$$\mathbf{x}(t) = \mathbf{v}_2 \cos(2t) = \begin{bmatrix} 1 \\ -1 \end{bmatrix} \cos(2t).$$

Clearly this satisfies the initial conditions.

Solution to Exercise 16

$\omega_2 > \omega_1$, so ω_2 is out-of-phase and ω_1 is in-phase.

Solution to Exercise 17

Since the components of $\mathbf{v}_2$ have the same sign, this must give rise to the in-phase mode.

Solution to Exercise 18

(a) The matrix of coefficients has negative eigenvalues. The first eigenvalue gives the term

$$\mathbf{x}_1 = \begin{bmatrix} 1 \\ 1 \end{bmatrix} \left(C_1 \cos(\sqrt{3}t) + C_2 \sin(\sqrt{3}t) \right),$$

where C_1 and C_2 are arbitrary real constants. This is the in-phase normal mode solution. The second eigenvalue gives the term

$$\mathbf{x}_2 = \begin{bmatrix} 1 \\ -1 \end{bmatrix} \left(C_3 \cos(\sqrt{5}t) + C_4 \sin(\sqrt{5}t) \right),$$

where C_3 and C_4 are arbitrary real constants. This is the out-of-phase normal mode solution.

(b) Following the same reasoning as in Example 11 and Exercise 15, these initial conditions give rise to the normal mode solution

$$\mathbf{x}(t) = \mathbf{v}_1 \cos(\sqrt{3}t) = \begin{bmatrix} 1 \\ 1 \end{bmatrix} \cos(\sqrt{3}t).$$

It is obvious that this solution satisfies the given initial conditions.

Acknowledgements

Grateful acknowledgement is made to the following sources:

Figure 2: Taken from:
http://en.wikipedia.org/wiki/File:Phillips_and_MONIAC_LSE.jpg.

Figure 3: Nevit Dilmen. This file is licensed under the Creative Commons Attribution-Share Alike Licence
http://creativecommons.org/licenses/by-sa/3.0.

Figure 11: Achim Raschka. This file is licensed under the Creative Commons Attribution-Share Alike Licence
http://creativecommons.org/licenses/by-sa/3.0.

Every effort has been made to contact copyright holders. If any have been inadvertently overlooked, the publishers will be pleased to make the necessary arrangements at the first opportunity.

Index